RESURRECTED

ALSO BY DR. DEBBIE RICH

Resurrected

Giving

Desperate Hunger Gets God's Attention

RESURRECTED

OVERCOMING DEATH, DESTRUCTION, AND DEFEAT

DR DEBBIE RICH

Without limiting the rights under copyright(s) reserved below, no part of this publication may be reproduced, stored in or introduced into a retrieval system, or transmitted, in any form, or by any means (electronic, mechanical, photocopying, recording, or otherwise) without the prior permission of the publisher and the copyright owner.

The content of this book is provided "AS IS." The Publisher and the Author make no guarantees or warranties as to the accuracy, adequacy or completeness of or results to be obtained from using the content of this book, including any information that can be accessed through hyperlinks or otherwise, and expressly disclaim any warranty expressed or implied, including but not limited to implied warranties of merchantability or fitness for a particular purpose. This limitation of liability shall apply to any claim or cause whatsoever whether such claim or cause arises in contract, tort, or otherwise. In short, you, the reader, are responsible for your choices and the results they bring.

The scanning, uploading, and distributing of this book via the internet or via any other means without the permission of the publisher and copyright owner is illegal and punishable by law. Please purchase only authorized copies, and do not participate in or encourage piracy of copyrighted materials. Your support of the author's rights is appreciated.

Unless otherwise noted, all scriptures are from the KING JAMES VERSION, public domain.

Scripture quotations marked (Amp) are taken from the AMPLIFIED® BIBLE, Copyright© 1954, 1958, 1962, 1964, 1965, 1987 by the Lockman Foundation Used by Permission. (www.Lockman.org)

Copyright © 2022, 2024 by Debra Kay Rich. All rights reserved.

SECOND EDITION
Released: September 2024
ISBN: 978-1-64457-741-7 (Paperback)
ISBN: 978-1-64457-742-4 (Hardcover)

Rise UP Publications
644 Shrewsbury Commons Ave
Ste 249
Shrewsbury PA 17361
United States of America

www.riseUPpublications.com
Phone: 866-846-5123

I give all the glory to the One who saved, healed, restored, called, and gave me favor. Jesus Christ is everything to me. Without Him, I have nothing, while with Him by my side, I can achieve anything and everything.

Pastor Robert Rester: the love of my life.

The next person is my loving husband, Robert Dellano Rester, who graduated to Heaven before I could finish the book on Nov. 3, 2020. God used him to love me as I have never been loved before. When he proposed, he said, "Debbie, I am older than you and have no idea how long we will have together. I may not be able to promise you a lot of years or riches, but I promise you that for the first time in your life, you will know what it is like to be loved as Christ loves the Church." He fulfilled his promise. I pray that every Godly woman will know that kind of love from a man of God.

Next, I dedicate this book to my three wonderful sons. All three of you walked this out with me and we have seen it to the other side. I love you so very much! You are part of the restoration that came from brokenness. Thank you for all you endured without complaint, allowing me to travel the world to plunder Hell and populate Heaven. My greatest desire is to be with all three of you in Heaven throughout eternity.

I had fainted, unless I had believed to see the goodness of the Lord in the land of the living.

PSALM 27:13 (KJV)

CONTENTS

Foreword   11
Acknowledgments   13
Introduction   15

Chapter 1   19
Coming Back from the Dead, Literally

Chapter 2   29
The Call of God

Chapter 3   45
The Marriage That Almost Killed Me

Chapter 4   63
A Divine Visitation

Chapter 5   67
A Fresh Start Leads to a Dead End

Chapter 6   89
The Ministry is Resurrected from the Dead

Chapter 7   115
Reawakening the Villages

Chapter 8   125
The Fire of God Comes to Nome, the Kenai Peninsula, and the Places in Between

Chapter 9   145
From the Villages to Madison Square Garden and the World

Chapter 10   161
The River at Tampa Bay

Chapter 11   187
The Devil Tried to Kill the Call Again

Chapter 12   203
The Glamorous Life of the Traveling Evangelist

Chapter 13   215
The Breaking of an Alabaster Box

Chapter 14   225
The Death of Another Marriage

Chapter 15   247
Restoration, at Last, My Knight in Shining Armor

Chapter 16   261
Proposal, Wedding & Honeymoons

Chapter 17   275
The End of A Ministry Chapter Brings Forth New Life

Chapter 18   285
Coming Back from the Dead After Terminal Illness

Chapter 19   303
The Resurrection of a Lost Dream, Word, and Spirit Institute NW

Chapter 20   325
Taking a Stand in Washington

Chapter 21   331
The Homeward Stretch

Chapter 22   349
Looking Back

Recommended Reading   363
Desperate Hunger Gets God's Attention   364
About Debbie Rich   366

FOREWORD

In her book, Resurrected, Overcoming Death, Destruction and Defeat, Dr. Debbie Rich shares her incredible journey of 'Survival to Revival'... from being a single mom struggling to survive in Alaska, to facing failed marriages and a death experience precipitated by a blood clot from a pulmonary embolism in both lungs. Debbie never lost her faith and determination to serve God and to see what she knew the Lord had promised her as a little girl.
Debbie has now traveled to nearly 50 nations of the world and crisscrossed the United States, preaching the gospel of Jesus Christ and sharing her powerful testimony of resilience and hope.
Through her frank and candid storytelling, Debbie reveals the transformative power of Jesus Christ in her life. She reveals how, despite hardships and setbacks, she was never abandoned by God and has always been given the strength and joy to persevere. She simply would not quit.
Debbie's story is a testament to the truth of 2 Corinthians 9:7b: "...for God loves (He takes pleasure in, prizes above other things, and is unwilling to abandon or do without) a cheerful (joyous, "prompt to do it") giver [whose heart is in his giving]." —AMPC.
This is why she is still alive—she is a giver, and God will not abandon her.
As you read *Resurrected,* you will be inspired and encouraged by Debbie's indomitable spirit and unwavering faith. Her story is a reminder that no matter

FOREWORD

how difficult or impossible our circumstances may seem, with God's help, we can overcome any obstacle and rise victorious.

We are proud of Debbie and grateful for the impact she has made in the world through her ministry and her testimony. May her story inspire you to trust in God's power and never give up on your own journey toward victory and resurrection.

Dr. Rodney Howard-Browne
President, Revival Ministries International
Senior Pastor and Founder, The River at Tampa Bay Church

ACKNOWLEDGMENTS

I want to acknowledge the efforts of Noel and Edna DeVries, who sacrificed so much for our family and my ministry. Thank you for your love and belief in the call upon my life. Thank you for never giving up on me, sharing your home with us, traveling with me, and loving me.

Several Alaskan friends have been an important part of this journey; Jean Thomas went with me to places no one desired. What a Holy Ghost adventure we experienced together! The anointing upon her life, powerful prayer life, sense of humor, and infectious laugh will never be forgotten. She went home to be with the Lord recently. Katie DeVries Holmes was not only my assistant for many years but my best friend. LaShawn Bedsole was the next assistant at my side and remains a dear friend; both were an important part of my ministry.

Last but not least, I acknowledge Drs. Rodney and Adonica Howard-Browne. You recognized the call upon my life at a time when it made all the difference. I often pinch myself to ensure that I am not dreaming about receiving such grace and favor. I honor our relationship. I recognized the anointing upon your lives from the first time I heard you at Rhema. I know God called you to spearhead revival and a great awakening in this nation and worldwide. I am so thankful for your ministry. It has impacted my life and ministry forever, and God used you to heal my broken heart. Thank you for standing by me, continuing to believe in the call upon my life, forgiving me when I made wrong decisions, advising me, and not letting me give up and quit. I don't have words to thank you.

I am so thankful to be pastored by you and be part of the greatest church on earth, The River at Tampa Bay. I love you both very much.

INTRODUCTION
WHY DO BAD THINGS HAPPEN TO GOOD PEOPLE?

Have you ever had a defining, soul-shattering moment when you knew that life would never be the same? Perhaps you received a fearful diagnosis from a doctor, or your spouse just walked out the door, leaving you devastated, torn, and alone. Maybe the career that you chose is no longer possible. Possibly your life savings was lost, either through someone's treachery or your own misguided decisions.

Was the love of your life snatched from this earth far too early, leaving you to grieve and cope alone? Have you lost a child you nursed, loved more than life, and never expected to bury? Has your body betrayed you and refused to function or allow you to do the everyday things you used to enjoy? Perhaps the company that you believed you would retire from abruptly shut the door on your future. Maybe a friend or loved one has betrayed you and shattered your trust and confidence. Have you found out that one of your children is in trouble and there is nothing you can do to rescue him? Have your life-long dreams been shattered, never to be realized?

If you ask the question, "Why do bad things happen to good people," you will find your answer here.

Perhaps you have found yourself looking at endless mounds of self-help books to realize that there is nothing anyone can tell you to ease the pain or bring hope. So, you walk away slowly, feeling dead inside. Everyone you observe seems to have it together, laughing, talking, sharing, and oblivious to your pain. It seems you are in a terrible movie, watching everything take place in slow

INTRODUCTION

motion, unable to change the outcome. You ask yourself about a hundred times a day, "Will I ever really live again?" If you still have breath and can read this, I tell you, most certainly, that you can and will live again. What my God has done for me, He will do for you. He is no respecter of persons.

Everyone goes through times of trial, pain, and suffering in their life. Yes, even Christians. We live on a planet that is dying. God meant for man to live in a paradise, subdue the earth, be fruitful, enjoy His presence, and live forever. However, man decided to do it his way. Adam's way has cost every one of us dearly. Ever since Eve was deceived and she and Adam sinned, humanity has had problems. They ate themselves out of house and home. When we don't do things God's way, we cannot expect His results.

The book is not an autobiography. Rather, it is an account of my spiritual journey and a record of how I learned to walk with Jesus and to move and cooperate with the Holy Spirit. As such, it will cover in detail some of my life's most challenging and painful episodes and the highest of highs. I will be honest with you about my mistakes—episodes on which I look back now and think, 'How could you be so stupid?' But it will also convey the mighty ways in which God rescued, forgave, restored, and used me to fulfill my calling to preach the Gospel.

As such, there are periods of my life that I do not go into in detail, for they are not pertinent to my spiritual journey.

Everything I am about to tell happened as accurately as a person can remember. Naturally, I've changed the names of some people in this book to protect their privacy. It is not my intention to smear the name of any person. I feel no need for revenge or to get my side of the story out. I have forgiven all involved, and God has restored me to a place where I can move on. I only tell some of the uglier stories because they are relevant to my spiritual journey. One cannot tell the story of how big our God is without knowing how big our mistakes were. I cannot convey to you how God restored me without telling you a good deal about what He restored me from.

As in all books, I struggled with how much to leave in and how much to leave out. I believe I have decided on the right balance—enough for you to see and fully appreciate the journey I have had with God. I hope that someone reading this book, who may be going through similarly difficult circumstances, will read things on these pages with which they can relate. And more importantly, I hope they will learn from these pages that they, too, should never give up on their calling and that we serve a God of second chances, a God who can undo any scheme or trap the devil has used to derail our lives. If nothing else rings forth from these pages, I will have accomplished my purpose if you walk away knowing that we serve a big God, a God who gives up on no one, a God who is working endlessly to bring every last human on earth into restoration with His plan for his or her life.

When I felt that I had made more mistakes than others, the Lord reminded me of the mistakes and sins of others He used greatly.

King David's book would look something like this:

Chapter 1 -Betrayal toward a man who served me well
Chapter 2 -Adultery and forcing a woman to sin against her will
Chapter 3 -I murdered a man.
Chapter 4 -My kids are a mess and murdering each other and trying to murder me.
Chapter 5 -I couldn't even see my sin until the prophet came.
Chapter 6 -God forgave me and called me a man after His own heart.

The Apostle Peter's book might have these chapter titles:

Chapter 1 -The Lord warned me that I would be tempted to deny Him but I laughed.
Chapter 2 -I followed afar. I back-slid and warmed myself at the fire of the world.
Chapter 3 -I not only denied Him but used filthy language while doing it.
Chapter 4 -While the Lord looked at me, I swore I never knew Him.
Chapter 5 -I ran away from the Lord and the cross.
Chapter 6 -It's all over for me. I have no hope.
Chapter 7 -He chose me to preach the birth of the church on Pentecost.

My book does not have adultery (on my part), swearing, denial, or murder. However, it includes many mistakes where I was unwise and undiscerning. It includes allowing emotions to dictate above the leading of the Holy Spirit. It contains health problems, setbacks, hard times, spiritual attacks, and heartbreaks. How does it all turn out? I'll give you a sneak preview. It ends with the blood of Jesus wiping these pages clean, as He has my heart. He wants to do the same for you and cause you to rise above every mistake, failure, and sin to become all He has called you to be.

ONE

COMING BACK FROM THE DEAD, LITERALLY

The evening seemed like any other evening in Tampa, Florida. It was warm and humid outside. I had returned to my home from a visit to the local Walmart for a few items. It wasn't easy to shop in those days. One month earlier, I underwent foot and ankle surgery. I was born with extremely flat feet. Podiatrists told me that my flat feet were the worst case they ever saw.

Prior to this, I ministered in Argentina, and my host asked me to climb a tower that overlooked the city. I knew that I shouldn't. My foot and ankle were swollen and more painful than ever. However, because I never wanted to disappoint anyone, I proceeded. I was halfway up the tower when I felt a snap in my foot. Excruciating pain followed. I didn't tell anyone. I endured the pain, kept a stiff upper lip, and finished climbing. The results were devastating. Over the next several months, my ankle swelled and became feverish every time I went for a walk. I saw great healings and miracles in the ministry while I suffered personally. After months of excruciating pain, I saw another podiatrist. He took X-rays and walked into the examination room with a strange look on his face. He told me that my tendon was completely severed from the bone. He believed it was impossible to walk with a torn tendon. He had never seen it before. I told him I knew it had happened months earlier while climbing the tower. I told him that I had traveled to many places since then. He was amazed and explained how he would fix the problem. There was a relatively new medical procedure where he would repair the torn tendon and fuse my ankle. That would give me an arch for the first time in my life. I would lose some mobility, but not much. The surgery would take three and a half hours. I agreed to have the minor surgery and then I could resume ministry.

Everything went as planned. I wore a boot for twelve weeks and taught at the River Bible Institute in Tampa. I recovered with no complications. The doctor was amazed at the speedy recovery. Three years later, the same pain and swelling in the other foot drove me back to the podiatrist.

Interestingly, I felt some uneasiness about the second surgery. A good friend encouraged me not to do it. I should have trusted God for my healing. I received several healings through the years and witnessed miracles in my ministry. However, I was so busy believing for the needs of others that I got lazy about having faith for my own needs. The previous surgery had gone so well that I wanted to get it over with. I was eager to travel in ministry, without pain or swelling.

There are many lessons to be learned from my experience, but one of the biggest is this: never override that small, inward voice of the Holy Spirit. Just because we have done something one way, one time, doesn't mean that we should do it the same way again. We must be careful to seek God and hear from Him every time. This is one of several reasons that bad things happen to good people: we ignore that small voice of the Holy Spirit.

At first, it seemed that the surgery went fine. I was recovering nicely. I even pushed the envelope a bit. I was determined to attend every meeting of my pastor's upcoming campmeeting. I preached in some of those meetings while on crutches. A few weeks later, I took a road trip to pray for someone who was in a coma in another state. My doctor advised me against traveling in a car after leg or foot surgery. Immobility on trips is a predetermining factor for blood clots in many situations. However, I was confident that nothing would happen to me. That was not faith; it was presumption.

After the road trip, I returned to Tampa. I went shopping on crutches and still wore a boot. I noticed earlier in the day that I had a cough. I thought it would pass. After I returned from the store, I knelt on my bed to fold some clothes. One moment, I was completely fine, and one moment later, I couldn't breathe.

We have no idea how fragile life is until we face death. No wonder the Bible says our life is like a vapor (James 4:14). It is here one moment and gone the next, sometimes without warning.

I felt like I was drowning. I gasped for air and tried to put my head up. It seemed that I would be able to breathe if I could get higher. That was the last thing I remember before I opened my eyes and found myself on my bedroom floor full of vomit and feces. I still couldn't breathe and did not remember the fall. I discovered later that I hit the bedposts and the decorative bench at my footboard before hitting the ground. I knew that I was dying, but I couldn't understand why. I tried to lift myself off the floor to sit up but could not move. The pain between my shoulder blades felt like someone drove a spear through me. I still couldn't get a breath.

I tried to call for help, but it came out like a whisper. Thank God that it was enough. Someone heard my call, ran into the bedroom, and saw me lying there. I passed out again. This time, I left my body and could see my body on the ground. I thought, 'Where am I?' I knew my spirit hovered at the top of the room, observing my natural body. From above, I knew that the devil was trying to take my life a few weeks before I turned fifty. I knew that it was not God's will for me to leave the earth before my time. Suddenly, I was struck with the thought that I could go back into my body and fight. I was also aware that the pain and suffocation had ceased. That was wonderful. I knew I could go to my eternal home without any more pain. I had no fear whatsoever but knew that I was needed on earth. I decided to fight to get back into my body.

This is an important lesson. You and I must have a fighting spirit when life knocks us down. We cannot be like Doris Day with a *que sera, sera* attitude.

I said within my spirit, 'In Jesus' name, get back in your body, Debbie.' I slipped back into my body at that moment. I opened my eyes and saw paramedics working on me. I heard one say, "You may have had a massive heart attack, honey, but we will take you to the hospital."

I could feel my heart beating at an unbelievable rate. It felt like it was exploding. The pain between my shoulders grew unbearable again. I wondered if I had made the right decision to return to my body.

Later, I was told that there was a moment when I was rolling on the floor with a death rattle in my throat, trying to pull some invisible thing off my neck as if a serpent was wrapped around it. The person who found me later told me it looked and sounded pitiful. I was trying to breathe.

I remember being inside the ambulance. There were several medics over me. They argued and shouted at each other, unsure of what to do. One asked, "What is her blood pressure?"

"Zero over zero."

"Don't just take it by machine. Take it manually."

"I did, and it's still zero over zero. We have to get a line in her so her blood pressure rises. I can't find a vein anywhere. She's never going to make it. Her only hope is a trauma hospital, but it will take too long to get there."

"Well, we've sat here long enough trying to get a line in her. Just step on it, and don't let the grass grow under your feet."

I was aware of lights, sirens, and high speed.

I left my body again and watched them working on me. I heard them talking about me as though I were already dead. It made me angry. I thought, 'They don't know anything about my God or His miraculous power. They know nothing of my relationship with Him or my will to fight.' I once again commanded my spirit to get back inside my body, even though I knew it would be painful. There was an oxygen mask on my face. I removed it and whispered, "Oh, I will live and not die. I have a big God!" Some trust in horses (or helicopters); some trust in men, but my trust was in the Lord, my God.

The eyes of the medic working on me became huge. He swallowed and said, "We're sorry. We didn't think you could hear us. I hope you will live, and I am glad you believe in a big God." Another one said that my only hope was a helicopter and called for one.

I remember the powerful blades of the helicopter as I passed under them. The night was hot and humid. I hoped the air from the helicopter blades would cool me off. I also tried to breathe in some of that moving air but could not. Oxygen flowed through my mask, but my lungs couldn't take it in. I gurgled and gasped but kept on fighting. I knew it would be easy to give in and go on to be with the Lord. However, I also knew I had work to do.

I was aware that a helicopter was transporting me to a hospital. First, the ambulance driver stopped at a fire station not very far from my house and waited for the helicopter to take me to Tampa General Hospital, where a cardiac critical care team had already been notified of my arrival. A team was waiting outside. While still in the helicopter, I again left my body and could see and hear them. The fight was getting to be too much for me. I felt complacency settling in. I could easily just go to heaven. I had to command myself with everything I could muster. I wanted to go on, but I knew that dying and going to heaven would be the easy thing to do.

I woke up to see a doctor standing beside my bed. He seemed quite serious; but then, they usually do. His voice was somber and ominous.

"You have the largest blood clot in your lungs we have ever seen. You threw a clot in the leg where you had surgery, and it broke loose and went to your lungs. It is not only larger than any clot we have ever seen; it is in a dangerous location. You have something called a "saddle embolism." That means that it came to rest between both of your lungs at the same time. It has fingers that reach into all five lobes of both lungs. The clot cuts off all oxygen supply to your lungs. Your heart can barely transport oxygen to any part of your body. The heart is beating fast because it is trying to get oxygen to the cells and organs. This resulted in your heart becoming enlarged. Your body has been without oxygen now for about an hour, and we have no idea how you are alive.

"We have had people on the operating table with saddle embolisms half this size and have not been able to resuscitate them. You weren't even in the hospital when it happened, yet you survived the last hour. It seems that you have already beaten many odds, but I must be honest: I believe there is very little chance that you will live through the night. We are taking you upstairs to administer clot-busting drugs. However, they take time to dissolve, and we don't think you have enough time. I believe in being honest with my patients." (Apparently, he believed in being brutally honest.)

Once again, I removed my oxygen mask. I was so weak that the slightest movement caused great distress, but the effort was worth it for me. I said in a hushed voice, "I will live and not die. I have a big God and a call upon my life."

He was shocked by what I had said and that I could say anything at all. He smiled and said, "You're going to need Him."

Next, I remember becoming conscious in a critical care unit with machines and buzzers going off all around me. Many people hovered around me, yet I felt extreme peace and knew everything would be all right. They told me they couldn't get my blood pressure above fifty over thirty, but I was engulfed in complete peace.

My sons were notified of my condition. My firstborn son, Joshua, is an officer in the United States Navy and was stationed in Norfolk, Virginia at the time. Josh was told that there was a good chance that I would die. He had medical training as an EMT and degrees in psychology, biology, and hospital administration. He knew my odds were not good. He and his wife, Stacie, drove to Florida to be with me. They wondered if they could get there in time to say their goodbyes.

I wanted to see my pastors, Rodney and Adonica Howard-Browne. They were away on a ministry trip to Oral Roberts' University in Tulsa, Oklahoma. Someone had called them and told them I was taken by helicopter to the hospital, but they didn't know why. Pastor Rodney walked to the pulpit when he received the note. He was surprised but checked in with the Holy Spirit on the inside of him. He heard the Holy Spirit say, "Debbie is going to be all right." He said he was so sure of it that he didn't even stop and pray.

As soon as the Friday night meeting was over, Pastors Rodney and Adonica flew back to Tampa and came to the hospital to be with me at 4 a.m. I managed to smile as I saw them come into that intensive care room. They told me what God had spoken to them. I was especially shocked when Pastor Adonica told me what the Holy Spirit spoke to her: "Debbie is going to be fine. I can't do without her. She is a giver." I was elated but had never heard anything like that before. The fact that my giving had gone up before God and had helped me receive my healing was quite a surprise. They reminded me of the story of Cornelius in the Bible. His praying and giving came up before God and caused God to move on his behalf (Acts 10:31).

It's not that we could ever buy healing. Jesus paid for that long ago when He bore those stripes on His back. It was already accomplished and is a gift, like salvation. It is received through faith. However, our obedience and worship get God's attention and prepare our hearts to receive from Him. You never know what your giving is preparing you for. It is too late in a time of emergency to become a big giver.

I joked and asked, "Didn't God say anything about my great preaching?"

They replied, "No."

We've since laughed about that. They took my hand and agreed in faith for my healing. One minute later, my blood pressure went up to ninety over sixty-five, which was my normal blood pressure reading. The nurses came running and were quite surprised. Everyone rejoiced.

I began to improve rapidly. Every day, I hosted several interns in my hospital room. Tampa General Hospital is a teaching hospital. Every time the group came into the room, the doctor in charge discussed my case, showed them my chart and test results, and asked them why I didn't die. No one could ever come up with an answer. Even the head doctor concluded by saying, "None of us can answer that. This woman should not be alive. It is impossible, but she is."

Then I smiled and told them why. "I have a big God, and He's not finished with me yet." What an opportunity to testify!

Cardiac surgeons, specialists of all kinds, and other doctors paraded through my room each day. Some said that they had nothing to do with my case but heard about it and wanted to come to see the "miracle woman." On the last day that I spent in the hospital (the eighth day), my doctor came to discharge me. He asked me if I knew what he was carrying in his hand. I replied that I did not. He told me that he had a picture of my blood clot in his hand and was taking it to a medical convention to speak about my case. He planned to speak on a different topic but changed his mind because this was such a rare case. Nobody would believe that I survived the saddle embolism. He even called it a miracle.

It is amazing how reluctant the medical community can be to accept God's healing power. After telling me that I couldn't be alive and that I had experienced a miracle, he went on to say that I would have to accept that I would never preach again, never fly, and would not be able to do simple household chores. I wouldn't have the energy. He said I would be on blood thinners and oxygen for the rest of my life. The prognosis sounded worse than death to me. I knew my God would not do this much and leave me in that condition. I chose to come back into my body so I could preach the Gospel and reap a harvest. If I could not do this, I would rather be in heaven. I told my physician that the healing would continue, and I would be whole and fly all over the world again. He smiled rather patronizingly as I left the hospital. I smiled for a different reason. I knew my big God!

Over the next few weeks, God continued to do great things for me. I fought discouragement at times. I was connected to oxygen tanks and tubes. I carried portable oxygen tanks when I left the house. I turned fifty years of age the following day after being discharged from the hospital. I had not planned to celebrate my fiftieth birthday hooked up to an oxygen tank. Doesn't life have a way of throwing unexpected curveballs our way? We can either lie down and die or get up and fight.

My friends threw a birthday party for me. Much to my surprise, my pastors and a large part of their staff came to my home to celebrate and make it a wonderful day. I was determined to blow out my candles. I unhooked the oxygen tubes, walked about five steps with the help of a walker, and attempted the feat. I had some help from others, and we collectively blew them out. Friends called from all over the world to encourage and pray for me.

When I came home from the hospital, I found myself going to doctors and clinics at least three times a week to have blood drawn. When a person is on the blood thinner Warfarin, blood must be drawn often to ensure that it is not too thin but thin enough. I also had another unique problem. My veins are extra small, well hidden, and difficult to find. In ordinary situations, nurses and lab technicians struggle to draw my blood. Usually, five or six people attempt it. Sometimes, they have to send me home without any results, just to try another day. When I was in the hospital, specialists had to be called from another hospital to draw blood. After the blood clot, it was even more difficult. I had to have it done more often. They told me to expect this for the rest of my life. I wondered how I would ever travel under those circumstances. Then, I reminded myself that these circumstances were only temporary. My God heals all the way, and this was not over yet.

I continued to confess the truth of God's Word concerning healing. I reminded God of the call upon my life. It is important to plead your case with God. I booked meetings and made plans to travel as always. I taught in Bible school for a few weeks while still in a boot for my ankle.

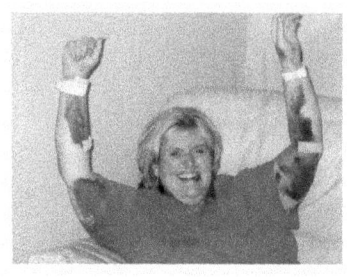

Blood Clot

This picture was taken the day I was waiting to be released from the hospital, eight days after collapsing off my bed and hitting the floor. You can imagine how bruised I was earlier. Every part of my body that knocked against the bed frame turned black and blue after the doctors injected blood thinners into my body. Half of my face, arms, and legs were bruised. I looked as though I had been through a war. I had!

After three weeks, I asked the doctor if I could be released from oxygen and blood thinners. He couldn't believe that I was asking such a thing. He thought it was impossible. He finally agreed to do a test. He asked me to walk around the perimeter of his office once and said that he would test my oxygen levels at the end of the walk. When he did, he couldn't believe the results. The measurements showed that I had one hundred percent oxygen saturation levels. He said that was almost unheard of, even with a normal, healthy person who has never had a blood clot. He said, "You're right, young lady. Anyone with one hundred percent saturation levels has no business being on oxygen." That day, I shed the oxygen tanks. Next would be the blood thinner challenge. Many experts told me that once someone is on blood thinner, they rarely come off. The risk of another clot is too big. I did some homework and found that a test can be taken to see if a person has genetic qualities that would predispose them to clots. There are five main factors that they test for. Most of my doctors believed that I probably had the tendency. I asked for the test, and it came back negative. They were surprised and concluded that the only reason that a clot had formed in my leg was that I had leg surgery, followed by a road trip.

The first night that I was admitted to the hospital, I was taken to another floor, where they opened the jugular vein in my neck and inserted a filter into my chest. The purpose of this filter was to keep any other clots from moving to my lungs or heart. After my release, I never thought about the filter until months later.

I didn't want any trace of that clot or its repercussions in my body. I went to the doctor and was told that a filter must be removed within a year of its insertion, or it cannot be removed. After a time, the blood vessels grow around the filter. That produces a dangerous situation when it is removed. A person could bleed to death. The doctor said that it should have been removed within three months or not at all. I never was told that, and now I had only one day left, according to the law. I decided to have the procedure. The doctor said that he would try only once to pull on the filter. If it didn't come out easily, he would leave it intact. I agreed and believed God would help me. He brought me this far. And He would finish what He began. When I woke up, the doctor told me that the filter came out easily, with the first tug. There was no longer anything artificial in my body to remind me that I ever had this saddle pulmonary embolism.

Five months later, I sold my home in Tampa, Florida. I packed up everything and loaded a truck for Tennessee. I had the job of buying a home in Tennessee, unpacking a truck, painting, cleaning, lifting heavy boxes up two stories, and remodeling some of the rooms. This was all done in between trips to other nations. I was gaining strength every day after being back from the dead. The life of Christ triumphed over the power of the enemy. And while this may have been the most dramatic time God turned my life around, it wasn't the first time, and it certainly wouldn't be the last.

TWO

THE CALL OF GOD

The Bible speaks about the people whom God loves to use. It tells us in 1 Corinthians 1:26-29, *"For ye see your calling, brethren, how that not many wise men after the flesh, not many mighty, not many noble, are called: But God hath chosen the foolish things of the world to confound the wise; and God hath chosen the weak things of the world to confound the things which are mighty; And base things of the world, and things which are despised, hath God chosen, yea, and things which are not, to bring to nought things that are: That no flesh should glory in his presence."*

My life is living proof of this scripture. I was born in Bossier City, Louisiana (a suburb of Shreveport), where my father was stationed at the Barksdale Air Force Base. While still very young, my parents took me to the place of my birth and explained to me their depth of poverty when I was born.

My mother entered labor at the Air Force hospital on April Fools' Day, 1956. However, I fooled her and refused to be born until the second day of April. I believe, since my birth, I was destined to fool the devil. Whenever he thought he had seen the last of me, God raised me again to plunder the devil's kingdom and populate heaven.

I have been called to the ministry for as long as I can remember. I always knew that a divine destiny awaited me, and I was chosen for a heavenly assignment. Like Jeremiah of old, I was called to preach from my mother's womb. I gave my life to Jesus when I was only three years old (after a life of riotous living). I recall sitting in the lap of Grandpa Bates (maternal grandfather) and telling him that I would preach to people of many colors all over the earth. God kept that dream before me.

Grandpa Bates & I when I was a little girl.

I practiced preaching as a child. Shortly after my birth, my family and I moved back to my hometown, Dakota City, Nebraska, which was far from a thriving metropolis. The population was only one thousand people at that time.

Our yard had several anthills with a huge ant population. I preached to the ants, stepped on them, killed them, and preached at their funerals. From dust to dust, and ashes to ashes. I also conducted their graveside service, where I set up official crosses. They were ant tombstones made out of toothpicks. I was an official minister of the Gospel, so I performed both crusades and funerals. Looking back, it would have been appropriate to call it the ministry of Filled or Killed.

Me, as a little girl already talking about the call of God on my life.

Our church in Nebraska used to host many guest evangelists. Listening to them was pure pleasure, as I loved revival meetings!

My maternal grandparents were old-time Pentecostals, and my mother was raised in a strict Pentecostal home. However, there was a lot of legalism in the church. She eventually turned away from her church upbringing. She then dated my father, who was raised as a Catholic but did not attend church. My Pentecostal grandparents would not allow her to date a Catholic, so my parents eloped. Grandpa and Grandma Bates were furious!

It was an uncomfortable beginning, but over the years, relationships mended. My parents had an unspoken compromise between them. My mother wanted to attend church, but my father didn't. Mom didn't want to go alone, so they both stayed home.

My grandparents were determined not to have heathen grandchildren and asked permission from my parents to take my brother and me to church even if my parents didn't attend. They allowed it, so Grandma and Grandpa Bates regularly picked us up for Sunday school, church, and mid-week services. The Lord and the church became my life.

I often spent the weekends at my grandparents' house, keeping them awake all night and asking questions about God, the Bible, and the miracles they had witnessed first-hand.

Grandpa & Grandma Bates
(Floyd & Esther)

Grandma and Grandpa had attended many old-time revival meetings; they had seen people healed of blindness, deafness, and cancer, and standing up from their wheelchairs. One of the evangelists that they followed the most was Oral Roberts. They also went to the meetings of A. A. Allen, Jack Coe, and William Branham. I loved to hear the details of those healings over and over again. After a few years, I memorized the details but pretended that I was hearing them for the first time. My grandmother often said, "Honey, it's time to sleep. No more stories."

My grandparents loved my hunger for God and helped to nourish it even further. I am thankful for the Gospel seeds they planted in my young heart. They made many sacrifices so I would know Jesus and have a personal relationship with Him. It wasn't until many years later that I realized how much those sacrifices cost them.

I had the privilege of being the Master of Ceremonies for their fiftieth wedding anniversary. As I gathered facts about them from relatives and neighbors, I found something that made me cry.

My grandfather always wanted to own a farm. In his young years, he was a tenant farmer. He eventually owned his own excavating business, driving big Allis Chalmers bulldozers for local farmers. He used to dig terraces to prevent erosion and was successful at it, but he desired to own a farm.

One day, he got a chance to buy a farm he could afford. The only problem was that its location was too out-of-the-way for him to drive my brother and me to church. He let go of the opportunity and never told me.

Even if you have children away from God, you can still make a big difference in your grandchildren's lives. It is so important to sow the Word of God into them. It will not return void and will accomplish its purpose. Pray for them, and tell them about Jesus. Share beautiful testimonies of the goodness of God with them.

My spiritual heritage runs deep. I had seven living grandmothers, including great-grandmothers and great-great grandmothers, and three grandfathers, including a great-grandfather. Most of them lived until I was about ten to twelve years old. All of them were Pentecostal, except for two Irish Catholics. They all prayed for their offspring.

Me, at 2 years, my mother (r), 2 grandmothers, 3 great-grandmothers, and 2 great-great-grandmothers

Having parents who were not serving God or attending church was difficult for me. They were morally good people. They loved one another and their children; they believed in discipline and were more strict than my church friends' parents. My parents didn't drink, smoke, swear, cheat, lie, or do anyone harm. My father wouldn't allow me to wear make-up or pierce my ears. He was a military man who had served in Vietnam. He had high standards about our dress. He wouldn't allow me to wear the latest fads. He considered most of them to be "hippie clothes." He said that we would be disowned if we ever slept with someone before we were married, drank alcohol, or tried drugs. My father's high moral values made him somewhat self-righteous. He believed that he didn't need God in his life. For him, religion was a crutch for people who couldn't live decent lives on their own. He reminded me that he lived a better life than most church people. Unfortunately, that was true in many cases.

I remember the night I was baptized in the Holy Spirit. I was twelve years old and came home from church with the presence of God still on my face. When I walked in the door, my father was reading a newspaper and looked up and asked, "What's wrong with you? A little religion may be all right, but you don't want to go off the deep end. Be careful that your grandparents don't turn you into some sort of a religious nut."

I was hurt and wondered why I couldn't have Christian parents who would encourage me in the things of God. I had to learn to develop my walk with God and could not ride on my parents' relationship with Him, as I saw many of the youth in our church do. Many years later, I led my father to the Lord, but for now, it was Jesus and me.

Mom and Dad

The characteristic that has defined my spiritual journey the most is hunger. Spiritual hunger was evident in my life as a little girl. I never understood a person who was not spiritually hungry. My Sunday school and children's church teachers loved me. I was well-behaved and never gave them a problem. Much of that was because of my upbringing and discipline.

Even though my parents did not attend church, I knew that if I ever got into trouble at church or school, there would be much more trouble at home. When the other kids were whispering, talking out of turn, throwing spit-wads, and playing pranks, I was hanging onto every word my teachers spoke. I asked questions and could recite the stories by heart. Discipline was only a part of it; the main reason was my spiritual hunger. I desired to know God more every day!

As much as I loved children's church, I couldn't wait until I was old enough to attend the adult services. I was eager to hear the Word of God expounded and wanted to worship in the main auditorium. When I turned twelve, I left the children's church behind and joined the choir, eventually becoming a pianist. I offered my services and talents to do whatever was needed; helping the youth group, painting the church, and contributing to many activities. I never wanted to miss one service. I remember being at the altar at 11:00 p.m. on Sunday nights. My grandparents said, "We have to take you home, honey. Your parents will never let you come with us again. You have school tomorrow."

As a teenager, I began to feel a pull. Like so many other young people, I wanted to be accepted. I experienced peer pressure. I was popular in my public school. I joined the drill team, became a cheerleader, participated in speech and drama, joined the choir, and became an honor student.

As a cheerleader, I received invitations to parties and dates from football players. I refused because I knew they weren't serving God. I knew what the Bible had to say about being unequally yoked together with unbelievers (2 Cor. 6:14). I was determined to wait for God's man of faith and power and wanted to marry a preacher someday.

I had a little girl crush on every preacher who came to our church. I wanted to hang out with the preachers. We had a water fountain at the back of the church. When one of the preachers stood in line for a drink of water, guess what little girl was also thirsty, standing in line behind him? I wasn't as thirsty for natural water as for the anointing of the Holy Spirit. I always recognized the tangible, transmittable presence of God.

My church was called Gospel Lighthouse Revival Center in South Sioux City, Nebraska. The town is located in the upper northeast part of Nebraska. It was a small church of about fifty people. Initially, it was a Foursquare church. My pastor went to Aimee Semple McPherson's Bible College in Los Angeles, California. Eventually, he brought the church out of the Foursquare denomination and became independent.

There were many times that our church went to a restaurant after service. That seems to be a habit of Pentecostals. The fellowship was great but wasn't so good for our health or waistlines. I loved those times of fellowship and often asked my grandparents if we could go out with others after church. I would frequently be stuck at a table with kids similar in age and listen with one ear to the adults' table where the preachers sat. That was where my interest and focus were.

My great-uncle was our youth leader. His daughter was my cousin and a close friend. I often asked for permission to spend the night with her. I spent most of the evenings talking to her father about the things of God. He introduced me to the ministry of T. L. Osborn, which fascinated me because of their "foreign crusades."

One night my cousin said, "I don't think you come to be with me. You just like talking to my dad." That was partially true. I could stay up all night talking to the adults about the things of God. Most of the youth group was no more interested in those stories. I wondered what made me so different.

The majority of the youth group members strayed away from the teachings that were taught to them by the time they were fifteen. They drank, smoked, dated unsaved people, slept with people before marriage, swore, and acted no different from the world. Yet, they cried at the altar every Sunday night. Usually, there was no heart change. Those things affected me.

I did not want to live one way during the week and another way on Sunday. I would either completely commit myself to God or the world. The idea forced me to isolate myself from the rest of the youth group. It seemed that almost no one was hungry for God like I was. Consequently, I spent more time with the adults, for which I received continuous flak from my youth group. They poked fun at my name and called me "Reverend Rich" in derision. They also started resenting me for encouraging them to live right.

I began preaching on youth nights. Pastor Graydon Graham encouraged me from an early age. When I was about ten years old, I gave a one or two-minute testimony on a Sunday morning. When I sat down, he looked at me and said, "Little girl, you are a real soldier for the Lord, and He is going to use you mightily." The words of my pastor greatly encouraged me. We must remember that edifying words greatly affect a child's life. My pastor invited me to preach on a Sunday night when I was only twelve years old. I remember my first sermon. It was called, "Let Your Light Shine Before Men," and was ten minutes long. That's the first and last time I ever preached that short of a message. I knew that this was what I was born for.

My father sang country-western music as a hobby. He was offered a music contract in Shreveport, Louisiana, while in the Air Force. He refused it, knowing that in the nightclubs, there would be alcohol, something he couldn't tolerate.

Years later, he recorded two albums for friends and family and was elected to the Iowa Hall of Fame of Amateur Country Music. Music has been my father's life for as long as I can remember. We had music get-togethers in our home about once or twice a week and used to attend monthly country music shows in Sioux City, Iowa.

I took piano lessons as a little girl and eventually began to play reasonably well. I could also play it by ear. My father played the guitar, sang, and wrote music. I grew up harmonizing with him and sang on my own. I entered two county talent contests at the ages of nine and ten and won both. My family and friends encouraged me to "go all the way" with country music.

However, around age fourteen, I felt convicted about singing songs involving drinking, divorce, and cheating and told my father that I could no longer sing those songs with him. He explained that they were just songs for entertainment and that he didn't live that kind of life. However, he respected my feelings and only called me up at the end of the evening to sing a hymn with him. (All good country-western singers close with a hymn.) I passed one temptation to do something other than the call of God, but more would come.

There was a constant struggle between my parents and me. They could not understand my relationship with the Lord or the call of God upon my life. My mom told me that she hated that she wasn't allowed to be "normal" in high school. My grandmother's legalistic ideas prohibited her from wearing in-style clothing. She was not allowed to be a cheerleader, bowl, or roller skate.

I agree that the legalism of her day took things too far. However, a Biblical standard cannot be taken for granted. The problem is that the devil takes a mile when given an inch. Small compromises, in the beginning, end with total backsliding. On the other side of the coin, religion and self-righteousness are wicked twins. The Bible is the final authority on every question. Where specific things are not found in the Bible, a person must be led by the Holy Spirit. Hence, a personal relationship with the Person of the Holy Spirit is vital. We must be sensitive to His voice inside our spirits and be careful not to grieve Him.

My parents took us to my first drive-in movie when I was very young. It was Disney's *The Incredible Journey*, a sweet family story of two dogs and a cat. I was taught that movies were wrong, so I sat in the backseat crying with my hands over my eyes. I was afraid that if Jesus came at that moment, I would not be taken up.

Today, we can find humor in the story, but my parents didn't find any then. I wanted to do what was right but did not know how to discern the difference between man's rules and God's.

However, God continued to honor my heart attitude as I grew in understanding. Shortly after that incident, my parents, younger brother, and I went to California for vacation. En route, we went through Las Vegas. My father tried to give us a memorable vacation. He was anxious for us to see the glittering lights of the casinos.

My dad, Don Rich, with his guitar.

We walked the streets of Sin City. We were told to stay on the sidewalk (within sight of my parents) while Mom and Dad tried a slot machine. It was a hot, humid night, and I was miserable. I was sick from the sin-filled atmosphere. I could not believe that my parents were gambling for about ten minutes, even though it was only once. Disillusioned, I began to cry on the sidewalk. They saw me and came out asking what was wrong. I told them that gambling was a sin and that I was disappointed in them. They shook their heads at me. It would not be the last time they thought I was going off the deep end of religion, which they called a relationship with God.

The day came in a few years when I found myself praying and weeping because they threatened to keep me home from revival and youth group meetings. They said that I was using too much gasoline to go to church. They also thought I was crazy for choosing not to go to my prom. I didn't believe in dancing or rock-and-roll music. Being dedicated to the purpose of God, I just wanted to please God.

Newspaper article about me winning the talent show.

We were taught a very important attribute that I must have heard a million times, "What will people think?" My mother grew up being embarrassed for most of her life. I have already mentioned the extreme legalist mindset of my grandma. My mother was elected to be the homecoming queen of her class and was not allowed to receive the honor or become a cheerleader because the dresses were too short. She felt that she could never lead a normal teenage life.

Moreover, my grandma was somewhat of a hoarder. The Great Depression affected her greatly; hence, she didn't want to be without any essential items again. Consequently, she would buy fifty items of the same thing if on sale. Her house was filled with too many boxes of plastic-wrapped, rainbow-colored notebooks, toilet paper, etc.

My mother felt she couldn't ask friends to come because there was no room to sit on the furniture. Grandma stacked items all over the furniture. Thus, she made a vow to herself never to be embarrassed again. Consequently, almost everything she did throughout her life returned to the question, "What would people think?"

Also, Mom and Dad grew up in poverty. My dad wrote a sad song that used to make me cry when he sang it. The title was "Don't a Poor Boy Like Me Supposed to Fall in Love." It was essential for my parents to dress, talk, and be above reproach in every area. The house had to be perfect at all times. As a result, we never had one thing out of place and were known as the perfect family. As kids, we were supposed to have the best grades, be the best-behaved children, never rock the boat, never question authority, be polite, and say the right things.

When I was a little girl and had a doctor's appointment to get a vaccination, I was always told, "Don't cry or even wince. We want the doctor to know we have a good little girl. If you cry, we'll give you something to cry about." I never cried when I had a tooth pulled at the dentist or was in pain. It was important for me to be a model child to earn my parents' approval, though that approval always seemed hard to come by.

Mom and Dad had grown up in a time when they were indoctrinated not to spoil the children. "Do not brag on them too much, or it will get to their head." My father felt that a part of discipline should be public humiliation when you miss the mark. I remember being ridiculed when I spilled a glass of milk on the table. My straight A's were never commented on. However, I was always questioned whenever an A slipped to a B+. "What happened here?"

My friends' parents bribed their children with hundred-dollar bills if they brought up their D grade to a C. My youth group friends were drinking and sleeping with boyfriends, yet they received continual praise from their parents. If they didn't do well in school, the teacher would be in trouble. On the other hand, I was always told that if I ever got into trouble in school, I would be in greater trouble at home.

One of my most painful childhood memories was about how I kept the drawers in my dresser and how I made the bed. My mother came into my room for an inspection. I had to fold the bedspread back neatly and never use it. My friends did not enjoy coming over because we could never sit on the bed or use the room. I never had clothing anywhere except on hangers in the closet. My room was the neatest one of all of my friends. However, it was not neat enough for my mother. On one occasion, she found a wrinkle in the bed. She pulled back the spread, told me that I couldn't do anything right, and said she would have to make the bed herself. She opened the drawers of my dresser. My sock pile fell onto the underwear pile, making her very unhappy.

However, the last straw on the camel's back for me was an incident involving my clothes closet. Two hangers were facing the wrong direction. I rarely did that, but I was in a big hurry that day. That was the last straw on the camel's back for her, too. She cried. I had never seen her cry before. She said, "I give up. I've tried to raise you right, but you don't seem to care. I can't do anything with you. You're grounded."

I knew I was about to say something that would cost me considerably. I decided that it would be worth it. I said, "I have friends drinking, on drugs, flunking school, and getting pregnant. I am a straight-A student, serving God, and you are grounding me because I have two hangers backwards?"

Her reply was two-folded. First, she slapped me on the face and then said, "I don't care what others are doing. You are my daughter, and you will do what we say." Such incidents caused a greater longing in me for love, approval, and acceptance.

I have by now come to realize that my primary love language (for those who have read the book "The Five Love Languages") is words of affirmation. My secondary one is physical affection, such as hugs. Both of my parents had the same love language, which is acts of service. Mom showed me that she loved me by creating a beautiful, spotless home. She poured love into doing our laundry, cooking and baking delicious food, and being the best housewife she could be. It was not registering with me then because I needed to be hugged and told that I was loved. We spoke different languages; how I longed to hear that I was doing all right and that they loved me! This would be significant later, as the enemy sought a way to destroy me.

Myself, brother Randy, & sister Donaline.

It is essential in relationships to learn one another's love language. The point is not to express love in the way that comes naturally to us but to discover what the other person needs to hear. Otherwise, we speak two different languages, and sometimes the other person never understands how much we love them. I have realized that my children, like my parents and siblings, speak different love languages. Children need to be held accountable for inappropriate behavior and yet need to experience unconditional love. It is a delicate balance that only God can help us maintain.

My grandparents told me that out of their thirteen grandchildren, I was the one who was most eager to please. When I was only two years old, I did not require spanking. After touching something I shouldn't, I would be found in a corner crying two hours later. My grandma would ask what was wrong, and I replied with a question, "Are you still mad at me?"

She answered, "No, of course not. We were never mad at you, honey. You just can't touch that."

I recall a time when a great-aunt babysat me. She was known to be a grouchy person who was widowed years earlier. I accidentally let a broken screen door slam behind me, and she yelled at me. I sat crying for hours until my parents got home, afraid I had disappointed my aunt. That eagerness to please was a flaw that would cost me considerably in my life. I suspect that some of you can relate. The devil used my people-pleasing nature to his advantage several times. Thank God for the blood of Jesus and the ability to rise again and change.

When I was ten, my mother left my younger brother and me with a great-uncle. Mom and my great-aunt went to the laundromat for a couple of hours. I prided myself on being completely obedient. We all knew that my great-uncle was an arrogant, brutal man. He mistreated his wife with verbal abuse. He enjoyed shooting the neighbor's pet dogs with a pellet gun when they got close to the perimeter of his property. He laughed and bragged about the days of his youth when he got drunk and threw Native Americans through the glass storefronts. However, my mother believed it would be safe to leave us with him for a few short hours. She was wrong!

When he began to fondle me, I ran from him and was hysterical. He called me a brat, told me that I was not behaving, and threatened that I would be in a lot of trouble. I only remember running from him. To this day, I can't recall everything that took place. When my mother returned, she could not understand why I wouldn't quit crying and begged her not to leave me with him again. It took days for me to get up the courage to tell her. When I did, she said she would never leave me alone with him again but that we could never tell anyone. It would bring too much hurt to the family. My parents went to their house for dinner about once a week for the rest of my time at home, and I had to go with them. My uncle looked at me with a torturous smile as if to say, "I won, kid, and there is nothing you can do about it." I learned never to rock the boat and always to keep the peace.

Looking back, I see many times the devil tried to destroy my life, even physically. He doesn't know everything. He is not omniscient like God, but he can sense some things. He hears prophecies and what we say to ourselves. The enemy knew that I had a call from God upon my life and was out to destroy that in any way he could. I was at a crossroads.

When I was about fourteen, our youth group joined others at a youth camp. After services, everyone went back to their respective tents to sleep. However, many youths thought that was a perfect time to get into mischief after the counselors and youth leaders slept. They snuck alcohol into the tents and visited the opposite sex's tents. I walked down that country road alone and knelt to pray in the wooded surroundings. I still remember the wonderful smells of the warm summer night. I poured my heart out to my heavenly Father about my relationship with Him, the call of God upon my life, and asked for grace to not give in to peer pressure.

Before that night was over, I dedicated myself afresh to the plans and purposes of God. I wrote my first song, "What Side of the Road Will You Take?" The battle was won, at least for a long time to come. I knew I was different in my calling and desires. I would never "fit in". I was His, and He was mine. I was bought with the precious price of the blood of Jesus Christ. There was a call on my life with divine destiny written all over it. I would not blow that call or taint the precious anointing. I would not presume upon the blood of Jesus Christ. Nothing could come close to that anointing, and nothing would be worth selling out to. I knew that could not be explained to my parents, friends, or the youth group.

This episode in my life brings up a concept that many people struggle with. There is an age-old argument about the security of our salvation. People debate the "once saved, always saved," eternal security doctrine against extreme Arminianism. The in-depth theological explanation of the difference between salvation and rededication is for another book. Suffice it to say that upon committing a sin or even finding ourselves lukewarm and apathetic, we must run back to God and not away from Him. 1 John 1:9 says, *"If we confess our sins, he is faithful and just to forgive us our sins, and to cleanse us from all unrighteousness."*

We cannot have faith if our conscience condemns us. When you are sensitive to the Holy Spirit, you tend to get a realization upon crossing the lines. We do not live in fear of losing our salvation as long as our hearts are soft. However, if we continue to override the voice of the Holy Spirit, we can become calloused and eventually stray too far. I don't know if any of us know where all of those lines are, but I have no desire to push the limit. God is holy, and we are to be holy and live consecrated lives that show the fruit of our salvation.

When I was in a public high school, at the age of fifteen, I had an English teacher who was born-again and Spirit-filled. I sensed that, and she knew the same about me. She was a member of an Episcopal church and loved Jesus. I became her aide and was invited to stay after class and help her correct papers. We had wonderful conversations about the Lord. She invited me to come to speak at her church. It was my first invitation outside of my church. When I arrived, this Pentecostal girl received quite a surprise.

The service was held in the church's fellowship hall instead of the main auditorium. The priest was smoking a cigarette which was a big shock for me. I sensed the anointing equipping me for the purpose at hand. At the end of the service, many were born again, including the priest. This was only the beginning of many invitations that would follow from other churches. My evangelistic ministry began at the age of fifteen.

I began writing for the school newspaper and became bolder with my testimony. Several students inquired about my relationship with the Lord. Even though I refused invitations to parties and received a lot of sarcastic jokes about my beliefs, students respected me for the things I stood for. They knew that they could come to me for prayer. In a high school of six hundred students, pupils and teachers voted for me to read the Scripture at our graduation vesper service. You never know who is watching your walk, not just listening to your talk.

My high school graduation picture.

However, the enemy continues to prod and look for the blind spot, the weak area. He will try to wear us down through loneliness, symptoms in our bodies, disappointments, hurts, and betrayals. Thank God the Bible says in Romans 11:29 that *"the gifts and callings of God are without repentance."* At the same time, we must be aware that it is possible to shipwreck the call of God. We must always be on our toes.

Little did I know at this time, that a day would come when I would rise again, more than once, from the ashes of my mistakes and misjudgments. I had to learn how to get up again and exercise faith that God would resurrect my life and ministry. Thank God that my God is the God of the second and third chance, and more, if we genuinely repent. We have to put it all under the blood of Jesus. The Apostle Peter found out God is a God of the second chance after denying the Lord. King David discovered the mercy of God after he committed adultery and murder.

As you continue to read this book, you will learn how to rise again after divorce, after losing everything financially, after betrayals, losing your identity and your friends, losing your reputation, being misunderstood, and more. The past can cripple, stop, and defeat us, but only if we allow it to. It is the past. What we do with today is what counts. Everyone has a degree of dysfunction in their family and their past. Will we rise from it? Will we repent for our part? Will we forgive others? Will we get stronger? Will we trust God? Will we use it to help others?

THREE

THE MARRIAGE THAT ALMOST KILLED ME

Most girls dream of a fairy-tale wedding, but I dreamed of it more than most. I am romantic at heart. After taking several different personality tests, the tests revealed a common theme. I am peace-loving, agreeable, adaptable, spontaneous, and very trusting. Also, they reveal that I am, by nature, extremely romantic.

I have found that romantic part very frustrating regarding the call of God. As a young girl, I used to think about women who gave their lives to the mission without the fulfillment of marriage. When I was young, I thought I was supposed to live that way. I laid my life down on the altar of consecration again and again. That level of consecration involved asking the Lord to burn away my romantic notions. Since then, I have learned that He doesn't want to change our personalities but would rather temper those traits with His guidance and the Spirit of God inside us. The Bible says in 2 Corinthians 3:18, *"But we all, with open face beholding as in a glass the glory of the Lord, are changed into the same image from glory to glory, even as by the Spirit of the Lord."* This is a process. The Word of God also says in Ephesians 4:23-24, *"And be renewed in the spirit of your mind; 24 And that ye put on the new man, which after God is created in righteousness and true holiness."*

God saves us through the precious blood of Jesus Christ, and our responsibility is to stay in His Word, His presence, and daily prayer. We are to put on the new man. We must decide to live in His precepts and the fruit of the Spirit. We daily decide to yield to the flesh or the Spirit of God. You cannot do both at the same time. Galatians 5:16-17 says, *"This I say then, Walk in the Spirit, and ye shall not fulfill the lust of the flesh. 17 For the flesh lusteth against the Spirit, and the Spirit against the flesh: and these are contrary the one to the other: so that ye cannot do the things that ye would."* Galatians 5:22-25 tells us, *"But the fruit of the Spirit is love, joy, peace, longsuffering, gentleness, goodness, faith, Meekness, temperance: against such there is no law. And they that are Christ's have crucified the flesh with the affections and lusts. If we live in the Spirit, let us also walk in the Spirit."*

So we are responsible for crucifying the flesh with its affections and lusts. It was not God's job to take romance away from me, but my responsibility to make wise choices to fulfill that dream in God's way and His timing. While many of my friends were dating, getting married, or back-sliding over the opposite sex, I set my sights on the call of God and pursuing Bible school. I knew I was not meant to stay single all my life, but the wrong decision in this area could cost me everything. My parents had a near-perfect marriage even though they were not serving God. I desired to have what I saw in the Bible that marriage should be. I knew it could be heaven on earth or something very close to hell on earth. I saw the latter in some marriages. I vowed that I would be careful and never have to experience that.

I believe that marriage is until death do you part. Romans 7:2 says, *"For the woman which hath an husband is bound by the law to her husband so long as he liveth; but if the husband be dead, she is loosed from the law of her husband."* Marriage is a sacred institution ordained by God. It was not only my Christian instruction that taught me that but my family upbringing. I firmly believed that if I didn't get it right the first time, nothing in life would be quite right. I knew that once I said those sacred vows, I would endure to the very end. I was all the more determined to wait to date and seek God in the matter. I refused to date several young men and was in my last year of high school, preparing for Bible College and the ministry, when everything changed.

It was a balmy autumn evening. I seldom went roller skating. For many years the older saints in the church discouraged it. They mentioned that the music was not godly and that members of the opposite sex held hands with each other as they skated. They believed that would invite trouble. However, this was 1973, and some of that was beginning to dissipate. After telling friends that I would not attend the roller skating party that evening, I had a change of heart. I hurriedly finished my homework and joined the rest of the youth group at the skating rink. Two Pentecostal youth groups combined for this event. I thought, 'This might be an excellent opportunity to meet new Christian friends.'

A friend from my youth group dated a young man from another youth group the previous year. His name was Bruce. She brought him to church a few times, and he seemed like a nice guy. We all thought they would probably marry, but she ended the relationship. The youth group that he attended was part of the fellowship this evening.

I was a terrible roller skater. I struggled every time I tried to skate; I fell down more than I skated. I hoped that no one was noticing. I was so embarrassed by my performance that I wished I had stayed home. At that moment, the young man who previously dated my friend approached me. He asked if he could skate with me, and I sheepishly agreed. At least he could hold me up. After an hour or so, he asked if I would like to get pizza. Who could turn down pizza? I was thrilled to be asked out by a guy with a Christian reputation who went to another Pentecostal church. I felt that the decent church guys always went for the typical pretty blonds and were not looking for a preacher girl. They only wanted to have a Bible study with me. The dates were for the other girls. Yet, we are three-part beings: spirit, soul, and body. I wanted to have all three areas fulfilled. I knew that whoever I married would have to be a dynamite Christian young man to do so. I wondered if this man could be the one.

You may be asking, how do we know who is the one? When I went to Bible school, some of the students had long lists of their requirements for a mate, such as, he must be tall, dark, and handsome. He must be able to sing and play the keyboard. He must like tennis. He must love pizza, etc. Some of them had impossible lists for anyone to fill. I wanted to remind them that they did not have that much to offer someone else, but I thought, 'I better keep that to myself.'

I believe that many people go too far in their requirements. However, the Bible gives us guidelines. We must not be unequally yoked together. I think that is referring to more than just salvation. If one is spiritually hungry for God and the other is not, you are unequally yoked. You are unequally yoked if one is called to full-time ministry and the other is not. If one is Spirit-filled and the other is not even seeking the experience of the baptism of the Holy Spirit, you will be unequally yoked. If one has strong convictions against something and the other wants to participate in those things, you are unequally yoked.

A person needs to date someone long enough and in different settings to be able to see some of these things. It is so important also to pray and seek God about these matters. It is vital to have good spiritual mentors that you look up to and know that they have your best interest at heart. It is important to look at their family values. How does his father treat his mother? How does he react when you have a difference of opinions? Does he have a temper? Does he value your opinion? Does he believe in having a civilized discussion, or does he always have to be right? Does he honor and value you?

If I could go back and give myself advice, I would say, "Listen to the Holy Spirit, Debbie. Do not keep overriding the check you have on the inside just because you are afraid that you will never find someone to love you. Do not be afraid of disappointing him now. That is better than living in heartache for many years."

I enjoyed our time over pizza, and I especially enjoyed the feeling that someone of the opposite sex accepted me as a worthy date. I was looking forward to seeing him again. He asked to see me again, which I accepted. Bruce and I continued to date for the next nine months. What I found most appealing about him was his sense of romance. He was not interested in team sports like most young men. He wrote poetry that would make a girl cry. While most boys talked about football and cars, he brought flowers and chocolates. I thought he was mature beyond his years.

Bruce was an outdoorsman, and his favorite hobby was hiking through the woods. He had a German Shepherd dog that obeyed his every hand signal. The dog came with us on every outing. Bruce's knowledge of survival skills, hunting, fishing, and camping impressed me. My family did nothing outdoors, but I always had a love of the country. One of my favorite things on our dates was to walk through the bluffs that covered the Nebraska, Iowa, and South Dakota borders along the Missouri River. I especially loved getting close to nature in the fall. Watching the trees turn colors filled me with wonder. Bruce built a hut in the woods. He was a natural-born survivalist.

I knew that no matter what happened in life, he would know how to take care of his family. It didn't hurt that he had a hot car. It was a 1967 yellow Dodge Dart, a four-speed with headers and loud mufflers. Bruce would let me drive it to school occasionally. You could hear it rumble blocks away. The best of all, though, was his love for the Lord. He went to church with me all the time. He told me his testimony of how his entire family gave their lives to Christ at a Lowell Lundstrom crusade. He said that he threw all of his rock music away in one moment and had a real conversion. He vowed that he would live for God all of his life. However, I later realized that was only half of the story.

There were signs of personality problems that I should have been able to pick up on if I weren't blinded by romantic ideas and looking for love and acceptance. One night, we planned to go to a revival meeting at my church. He was supposed to pick me up and take me to the meeting when he got off work. The meeting started at seven, and he was supposed to pick me up at six forty-five. He was working on construction with his father, and sometimes they were delayed. I waited until seven-thirty. My grandfather called at that time and asked if I needed a ride to church. I tried to call Bruce to ask if he was coming but could not reach him. I decided that he was detained but didn't think he would want me to miss the service just because he had to work. Grandpa picked me up, and I went to the service.

About an hour later, Bruce showed up at church. He didn't look happy. He motioned for me to walk to the back, and I did. His face looked angry, and he told me that he couldn't believe I would leave without him and that I better not do it again. I apologized profusely and didn't ever want to disappoint him again. A sentence is invented for moments like that: how dumb can you be and still breathe? I was only seventeen years old, dated minimally, was eager to love and be loved, and, most importantly, he was a Christian. He was even a Pentecostal one at that. So, I overlooked his anger, not only this time but many times.

Most of the young people at our church believed that Christians were in such a minority that there were only about three members of the opposite sex genuinely serving the Lord. I thought, 'if I found a young man who professed Christianity, I better snag him before it was too late.'

A few months after our first date, Bruce asked me to marry him. True to form, it was a wonderful, romantic moment. He purchased a giant pink teddy bear. Under the arm of the bear was a long-stemmed red rose. It was beautiful. Inside the rose was the yellow-gold ring with a dainty solitaire diamond. I said yes, and couldn't wait to tell my friends about the romantic proposal. Wedding plans began immediately. I loved how he seemed to take an active interest in making wedding plans.

This time, my parents seemed delighted. They thought we were a bit young but felt they couldn't argue the point because my mother was eighteen when they married. I would be eighteen in April, graduate high school in May, and marry in June. What an eventful spring and summer!

Again, more incidents should have served as warning flags. Just weeks before the wedding, I decided to talk to my youth leader about my upcoming plans. I told him that I was concerned about several things. I noticed that when we spoke after a church service, Bruce didn't seem as excited about the things of God as I was. He was more passive. He didn't raise his hands in worship. He seemed reluctant to express his love for the Lord. My youth leader felt that I was from a perfectionist family and that I just had prenuptial jitters. He said that guys weren't usually as emotional in church as women and that he thought Bruce was just shy. He would probably become more expressive in worship later. He thought I was asking for too much. I decided that he was right and that I was nit-picking and needed to look at the positive, not the negative. I was an eighteen-year-old kid who had never done anything like this before.

The worst moment occurred shortly before our marriage. My mother thought that she was doing me a favor. She made an appointment for me to see our family doctor before the wedding. She knew that I kept myself pure, which was important to me as a Christian. The Bible tells us that sex is only reserved for the confinements of marriage. That instruction was not just for a specific time but for all times. Not only that, but it was important for me that my husband and I only save ourselves for each other. Young people need to understand how precious that moment is for a husband and wife to see one another on the wedding night for the first time.

The Bible is very clear about this important matter. It teaches that sex before marriage is immoral in a couple of different passages. One is 1 Corinthians 7:2, which says, *"But since sexual immorality is occurring, each man should have sexual relations with his own wife, and each woman with her own husband."* This verse presents marriage as the cure for sexual immorality. Sexual union within marriage is commended, but any sex outside of marriage is considered immoral. This includes premarital sex.

Another verse that presents sex before marriage as immoral is Hebrews 13:4: *"Marriage should be honored by all, and the marriage bed kept pure, for God will judge the adulterer and all the sexually immoral."* Here, we have both adultery (sex with someone other than your spouse to whom you are married) and fornication (sex outside of the marriage relationship) contrasted with what happens in the marriage bed. Marriage (and sexual intercourse within marriage) is honorable; all other sexual activities are condemned as immoral and bring God's judgment.

Based on these passages, a biblical definition of sexual immorality would have to include sex before marriage. That means all the Bible verses that condemn sexual immorality in general also condemn sex before marriage. These include Acts 15:20; 1 Cor. 5:1, 6:13,18, 10:8; 2 Cor. 12:21; Gal. 5:19; Ephesians 5:3; Col. 3:5; 1 Thes. 4:3; Jude 1:7; and Rev. 21:8.

God designed sex, and the Bible honors marriage. Honoring marriage is the Bible's promotion of complete abstinence before marriage. When two unmarried people engage in sexual intercourse, they are defiling God's good gift of sex. Before marriage, a couple has no binding union, and they haven't entered into a sacred covenant. Without the marriage vows, they have no right to exploit the culmination of such vows.

Mom wanted to make sure that I understood everything. She was one of those mothers who did not talk to me about the facts of life. It all came through either a book or friends. Now, however, I could tell she regretted her reluctance to talk about the birds and bees but could not bring herself to speak of it. So, she made the doctor's appointment. With that appointment came a physical examination. Bruce found out about it and was furious. I never saw him like that before. He was ranting about my mother's interference and how she should have minded her business. He threatened to cancel the wedding, even on the very morning of the wedding, because he felt the doctor got me instead of him. I was interrogated about the doctor's every move and my reaction to it. I was shocked, cried, apologized, and tried to smooth it over. In retrospect, I had a way out and did not realize it. I have often relived that moment and wished I had seen the writing on the wall.

I overrode every doubt and fear and dreamed of that perfect, romantic wedding day. It came. The sun was bright, and the temperatures were soaring that June afternoon. It was an evening wedding, and over three hundred guests were present. My parents were on a very tight budget but sacrificed to give me the most beautiful wedding possible. As the wedding march began, I felt apprehensive. Part of the way down the aisle, I hesitated, faltered in my step, and shed some tears. Somehow, I knew that I shouldn't continue, but I didn't exactly know why. I remember someone in the audience mumbling, "Look; she's so happy, she's crying." I wanted to tell them that was not why I was crying, but I couldn't. I saw over three hundred people, out-of-town guests, and the money my parents spent, and I believed I could not embarrass my family or his. After all, what would people think? I kept walking.

I wanted everything to be perfect that night. I was brushing my long hair when he began to holler at me and ask what was taking so long. I was hurt but again made excuses for him. The following day, I woke up to an angry, pouting husband. He would not speak. We sat across from each other over our first breakfast as husband and wife, with my husband glaring at me.

We left that morning to head for the Black Hills of South Dakota for our honeymoon, but something was askew. This was not the romantic honeymoon I envisioned. We went to all the typical tourist places in the Black Hills, but he still would not speak to me. You could cut the tension with a knife. We planned to go to Montana after the Black Hills and then to Open Bible College in Des Moines, Iowa. However, he told me he no longer wanted to go to Montana, so we went home early. It took almost two weeks before he blurted out what was bothering him. He was still upset that my mother had taken me to the doctor. He said he should divorce me because I did not have the Old Testament proof of virginity of bed sheets with blood. The doctor stole that. He said, "I should have canceled the wedding or divorced you the day after the wedding." I apologized and begged him to forgive me. I had a nagging feeling that I was in for a lifetime of pain for the next fifty or sixty years. What did I do? How could I have missed God this badly?

Before marrying, I talked to Bruce about the call on my life and Bible school. He said that he would go to Bible school with me. He also said that though he was not called to preach, he would be behind me all the way. At that time, I did not understand his definition of 'behind me all the way.' I now realize it meant 'behind me about twenty feet' with a rope pulling me backward.

One month after we were married, we left for Open Bible College in Des Moines, Iowa. I sadly looked back at my parents as we left that day. Our marriage was off to a rocky start. At least he was speaking to me again. Things would get better. I was sure of it.

I had dreamed of Bible school since the beginning of high school. All of my friends and family knew that. When I announced that I was going to Bible school, my father told me that his friends' children in the Air National Guard would be lawyers or doctors and that he would be embarrassed to tell them his daughter wanted to be a preacher. My friends thought I would be the last one to get married. Instead, I turned out to be the first.

I chose Open Bible College for several reasons. It was close to home, and we would be able to visit both sets of parents often. Open Bible Church was Bruce's church and Open Bible College was the nearest Pentecostal Bible School in the area. So, I decided to attend their career day. The classes were great, the students friendly, and we could secure jobs immediately. However, more trouble was brewing. Bruce was angry all of the time. I could not do anything to please him.

He often got into fights with fellow students over things like parking spaces in front of our dorm. I was constantly humiliated.

After weeks of trying to please my husband, my body reacted to the stress. I developed a nervous stomach and was in a lot of pain. A couple lived across the hall from us in the married dormitory. We became close friends. The man worked for a local doctor. He suggested that I make an appointment to see him. I did and was diagnosed with early-stage colitis. The doctor suggested that I try to get rid of as much stress in my life as possible. After telling my husband about the check-up and diagnosis, he was enraged that I went to a doctor again. He questioned me about the examination. He accused me of enjoying the doctor looking at me. I apologized for seeing the doctor and promised I would not visit a physician again unless I could find a female doctor. I began a lifestyle of cringing and apologizing. I thought that was what submission was. It is not, but I had a lot to learn. I was living to please him, being fearful of doing anything that could upset him, and making excuses to others for his behavior. I walked on eggshells. It became my way of life for the next eighteen years.

I got a job as a teller at a major bank in Des Moines, Iowa. They told me when they hired me that they wouldn't usually hire an eighteen-year-old woman fresh out of high school. However, my report cards impressed them. I received favor and was very grateful for the job. It was added stress, though. I attended school full-time, was involved in a learning curve at work, found myself newly married to an angry man, and was studying to prepare for ministry. My nervous stomach did not go away. I loved Bible school. I was fulfilling a dream I had kept alive since I was young. Yet that dream was about to die.

One day, as I came home from work, Bruce told me that he had withdrawn me from Bible school. He reminded me that the doctor said that I needed to de-stress. Therefore, he exercised his authority as a husband to simplify my life and took me out of Bible school. I was devastated. That was the only part of my life that I enjoyed. It was the place where I could temporarily forget about the other aspects of my life. However, I realized that I had no choice. My husband was the head of the home, and I had to submit to him.

All of this took place in the seventies. There was a teaching that was very prevalent in the church at that time. It was a Biblical teaching that was perverted in a lot of circles. The teaching stated that a woman has to obey and submit to her husband no matter what, with no exceptions. If he was not spiritual, if he was domineering and abusive, or if he was unkind or living in sin, it did not matter. A wife's job was only to submit. The theory was that even if he asked his wife to sin, she was to obey. They taught that obedience would ultimately cause him to come to Christ. This teaching made its way to my ears, mind, and heart. Several well-known Christian books on the subject fueled the perverted doctrine. One was a book titled *Total Woman*. I am sure that was not the intent of the book, but, since I was submissive by nature, raised to never question authority, and was eager to please by personality, I was the perfect candidate for someone to take advantage of.

The more I submitted, the more authoritative he became. He came from a strong German heritage and believed that as he gave the command to jump, my job was to ask, "How high?" He picked out my clothes, friends, conversation, and my hobbies. He swung like a pendulum when it came to his views and opinions. One moment he was going through a jealous stage and threw away all of my knee-length shorts or anything that he thought was too immodest. The next moment, he was angry that I would not go without a bra so he could show me off to his friends.

We took only one vacation in about ten years to see his friend in Colorado. After a long drive, we finally arrived. While preparing to go on a hike, he asked me to dress promiscuously in front of his friend. Shocked and embarrassed, I refused. That made him angry, so he told his friend that I would not obey him, grabbed me, and announced very matter-of-factly that we were going home. We drove hundreds of miles back home without spending time with his friend.

We left Bible school one month before the end of the first year. I was on the honor roll and was not even allowed to complete my first year. We returned home to northeast Nebraska. My first birthday after marrying Bruce was another nightmare, as every holiday would be from then on. We went to my parents' home for a birthday party. My mom baked a beautiful cake, presents were waiting to be opened, and it should have been a very festive evening. We waited to open gifts and eat cake until my grandparents arrived. Bruce was tired of waiting. He announced that there would be no opening of gifts, no eating cake, and that the two of us were going home. I made the mistake of looking at my mother with an apologetic look that said, "I'm so sorry about all the work you've done to prepare for this." I didn't know Bruce noticed the look. As soon as I stepped into our car, he grabbed me around the throat and said, "If you ever want a divorce, look at someone like that behind my back. Now shut up. We're going home." What a birthday, what a marriage, what a life! I cried all night but knew better than to say a word.

A year into our marriage, the Open Bible Church that Bruce grew up in offered us a job as youth leaders. With that position came a church parsonage to live in. I was thankful. Even though we didn't finish Bible school, we would at least be in some ministry. Bruce also worked full-time doing cement construction with his father, who owned his own company.

I knew my husband flirted with all of the girls in the youth group, but I did not know how far that went. We invited the youth to our home many times. Sometimes, we had slumber parties. At bedtime, we kept the girls upstairs and the boys downstairs in our basement. I sensed that something was wrong on many occasions. However, it was not until we were fired from our position that I found out that several of the girls accused him of making flirtatious advances toward them. I defended him and convinced myself that the accusations were made up. Deep down inside, I knew better.

We bought a trailer and moved to the country on a lot across from his parents. Even though we started attending my home church (Gospel Lighthouse) again, I realized that ministry would not be possible. I resigned myself to becoming a better wife. I would concentrate on that. I became pregnant with our first child. He did not want me to see a doctor, but I defied him for once and went anyway. That ended up being the only time I saw a doctor during the pregnancy. The doctor confirmed that I was pregnant.

Bruce was furious about the appointment and the diagnosis. I was heartbroken. I heard his sister tell the story that her husband took her to dinner and celebrated when she found out she was pregnant. Instead, I walked off alone, patted my belly, and said, "Baby, I love you and can't wait to be your mother." I decided to go to my parents and tell them. After all, every potential grandparent gets excited to hear their first grandbaby coming, right? That was not to be the case for me. I received a lecture. "What are you thinking? You have no money, and you're not getting along."

No one was happy but me. It was the first thing I had in a long time that gave me any hope. I knew I would have to be happy all by myself. I wondered why I could never have anyone to celebrate anything with me, like getting baptized in the Holy Spirit, earning good report cards, preparing to go into the ministry, or having a baby.

Bruce told me I would not be seeing the doctor for prenatal appointments or the delivery. He used the excuse of being into natural things and told me he read about the increased mortality rates after women began to give birth in hospitals. I think he convinced himself of that, but I knew what was behind it. He repeatedly said, "No doctor will ever look at my wife." I searched for a female doctor, but none were found. I never saw a doctor for the rest of the pregnancy. I had no prenatal care.

When I was three weeks overdue, we went for a country drive to see Bruce's sister and brother-in-law in another town. We all went to the local Dairy Queen that night. We returned home at about ten o'clock and went to sleep. I woke up vomiting and experiencing cramps. At first, I thought the chili hot dog did not sit well. Then, my water broke, and I realized what was happening. The contractions were hard and fast, about two minutes from the first moment I woke up. I woke Bruce up. He said he had to drive to another city about twenty miles away to pick up a friend who would help with the delivery. I suspected that he was interested in her but I wanted someone to help me. I would be grateful for anyone who had given birth to be at my side.

My parents didn't speak to me for a few months because they were so upset that we would have a home delivery. That added to my emotional pain throughout the pregnancy. I understood how they felt. I felt the same way but was afraid that if I defied him, it would mean the end of my marriage. My baby would not have a father, and the church would feel I failed as a submissive wife. Caught between my husband and my parents, I chose his side, which resulted in isolation from everyone else whom I loved.

Bruce was gone for about an hour and a half while I continued to experience severe contractions. He finally arrived with the female friend. After another couple of hours, they told me that the baby was crowning, and they could see the top of his head. They said that the baby had a lot of dark curly hair. I suddenly had hope and felt that I could endure anything.

I continued pushing with no medication, monitoring, or medical help. After fifteen hours, I was making no progress. The pain in my lower back intensified. My strength waned. I was scared and could no longer talk. I was too tired. I just wanted it to be over. At about two-thirty in the afternoon, my mother-in-law visited us, unaware I was in the middle of childbirth. She was shocked when she walked into the home to find me in that condition, with boiling water on the stove. She could see how weak I was and was furious with her son. She informed him that she was calling a rescue unit and wouldn't take no for an answer. That, in turn, angered him. He said that no stranger would take his wife to the hospital. He would do it himself. He carried me to the back of our car and drove to the hospital over twenty miles on bumpy, graveled country roads. I was more dead than alive.

My mother-in-law notified the rescue squad so they would meet us on the road. My husband refused to stop and transfer me to them. The rescue unit informed the hospital that we were coming and the baby had already crowned. The hospital did not think we could make it to the hospital before the baby was born. The delivery team met us outside in their gowns and masks. I told them I was worried the baby would fall out on the cement if they weren't careful.

After being taken to the delivery room, the team informed me that my contractions were no longer productive. I was too exhausted. Also, the baby was in an unusual position and receded backward toward my spine. No wonder I was experiencing such back pain! They would have to use forceps. It took a few more minutes, but finally, seventeen hours after it started, Joshua Israel arrived at eight pounds, nine ounces. His head circumference was the largest in the nursery, even larger than a ten-pound baby. They said he would never have been born if we hadn't gone to the hospital. He had a temperature, so they placed him in isolation. They were afraid that the hands of his father were not sterile, and Joshua might have an infection. Again, my joy was short-lived because I was concerned for my baby's health.

My father, who never interfered or said anything to Bruce about his abusive ways, had finally had enough. Dad was usually soft-spoken and didn't want to cause more problems. However, when he saw my condition and that of my baby, he said one thing to Bruce. "Son, you're fortunate that your wife and baby are alive." That was all that he said, but it was more than Bruce would take. He became angry and left the hospital. He did not return for several days to see his son or me. That was supposed to send a message to both my parents and me.

Again, I experienced more anguish. I watched our embarrassing trip to the hospital air publicly on television that night. I had no idea that the media followed us to the hospital. It was my first television debut.

After twenty-four hours, Josh's temperature dissipated. They placed him in my arms. As I looked into that tiny, perfect face and those beautiful blue eyes, I no longer cared about the pain of the last few months and days. My world felt right again.

Over the next few years, Bruce and I had two more boys, Billy and Caleb. They became the focal point of my life. I was now the proud mother of three adorable sons who brought joy into my life every day.

I must say that Bruce loved his boys despite his reaction to my first pregnancy. He shared his knowledge of the outdoors and was very proud of them.

Both of our sets of parents were strict disciplinarians. We raised our sons in the same way. They were well-behaved young men. As toddlers, you could take them to anyone's home and would not hear a word out of them. They never reached for anything that they were told not to. No one had to put up their pretties because young children were there. They never made noise. They sat on the floor, playing with their cars or some other toy. People said that they never saw such well-behaved children.

However, Bruce's anger toward me increased. He had no patience and became physically abusive. When the boys were babies, I feared that one of them would get sick and cry. Many holidays were ruined because a baby cried in the car on the way to my parents' home. Bruce became angry and shouted, "We're turning around and going home. No Christmas for anyone!"

My youngest son, Caleb, was colicky. He cried almost any time that he was not sleeping. I was never allowed to comfort or bring him to bed with me. Bruce told me to shut the door and let him cry it out. My nerves strained as I tried to keep my children from irritating him.

On one occasion, my parents asked me to go to Springfield, Missouri, with them to my brother's graduation from Evangel College. We now had all three boys, and I asked Bruce if he thought there was any way we could make this work. He said that it would only be if I would allow a girl from my Sunday school class to babysit. I reluctantly agreed. I went on a three-day trip with my parents. One evening, after arriving at our motel, Bruce called and asked why he had a hard time reaching me at the motel earlier. I explained that my family had gone to Silver Dollar City. We just got back. He accused me of cheating on him. I couldn't believe my ears. He knew me better than that. I soon discovered I was

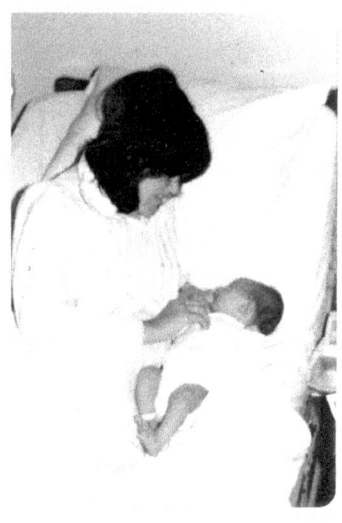

Joshua's birth

My boys as toddlers growing up in Nebraska.

being accused because of what he was doing. Very often, a person full of lust is also a jealous person who thinks everyone else's mind works like theirs.

When I arrived home, I found that Sandy was no longer there. His explanation was that she started acting weird, so he took her home. I wondered if that was the truth. Sometime later, she told me that they were involved while I was gone. She said that it stopped short of the final act of intercourse, and he took her home. Her mother found out and announced it during prayer request time in front of the whole church. I was again hurt, humiliated, and resigned from teaching Sunday school. Ministry once again seemed totally out of the question.

A few months later, my aunt, close to me, took me to dinner. She told me about an incident that she felt I should know about. While pregnant with my second son, Bruce asked her to play ping-pong in our basement. While she was walking down the stairs, he tried to kiss her. She told him that she should slap him. Of course, she refused his overtures. He didn't think she would tell me. He was wrong. When I told him what she said, he turned the whole thing on her and told me that she was the one who flirted with him and that he would never do anything like that again. I forgave him again.

Bruce was a weight-lifter and wanted me to lift weights with him. At that time, I only weighed one hundred and ten pounds. I was tiny all of my life. I never had to watch my weight. In high school, I was the one who could eat anything that I wanted without gaining a pound. Still, I was not shapely enough for Bruce. When he watched television, he openly commented on other women's bodies. This took place in front of friends and family. His sisters asked me why I put up with it. Humiliation was such a part of my life that I grew accustomed to it.

After having the children, I gained five or ten pounds but was in relatively good shape. However, that did not stop Bruce from taking magazines into the bedroom, showing me other women's bodies, and reminding me of what he preferred. I decided that I would do anything he required to get the body that he wanted me to have. At his request, I had surgery to please him. Years later, he told me that he was in a different mood and liked a different look. I had the surgery undone. He also wanted me to be very tan. I sunbathed every day with no sunscreen. I was far too blue-eyed and freckled for that. Several years later, spots appeared all over my arms and legs. To this day, I bear the repercussions of those bad choices. At the time, I was willing to do whatever it would take to become the perfect wife.

At his suggestion, I began to lift weights. I worked out hard. I eventually competed in powerlifting and won twelve trophies over the next few years. At a weight of only one hundred fourteen pounds, I bench pressed one hundred thirty pounds, squatted two hundred sixty-five pounds, and dead-lifted two hundred seventy-five pounds. I became strong, muscular, lean, and defined. I convinced myself that if I looked perfect, he would be faithful, and I would finally please him. I was again striving for perfection to receive love. It did not work. Nothing could please him because he was miserable inside.

A newspaper article about me winning a meet.

Me lifting weights in my basement.

My parents were familiar with his temper and were concerned daily for my safety. My parents must have had many sleepless nights worrying about me. I especially regret that I caused my father that kind of concern. If I would have known he had so few years left, I would not have wanted him to waste precious moments worrying about me. Later, he told me that he often wondered if he would get a call saying I had died.

Over the next few years, we tried many things to improve our marriage, but it was all in vain. We moved out west because that was his dream. My aunt lived in Kelso, Washington. We asked if we could stay with her while Bruce looked for a job. She said yes. She and her family lived only thirty miles from Mount St. Helens. We were there when that mountain erupted with its fury of ash and lava in 1980. Bruce was promised a logging job close to the mountain, and now that would not materialize. We returned to Nebraska.

We were not financially well-off. The bill collectors were our primary callers. I dreaded answering the phone. Even though Bruce was a hard worker, he never had high-paying jobs and could not, or would not, manage money. Our poverty was toward the bottom of my list of concerns though. I wanted a faithful, godly husband above all things.

Finally, after eight years of marriage, we could buy a decent home. We purchased it through a government program. It was a Farmer's Home Administration house in a rural Nebraska town. The boys had a treehouse and a good school. I had hope, once again, for a normal life. However, trouble once again was brewing on the horizon.

FOUR

A DIVINE VISITATION

After every hurtful incident, Bruce quoted Bible verses about wives submitting to their husbands and how much God hates divorce. I was overcome with guilt at the thought of divorce. I also worried about how the church would view it. I knew no one would believe how violent he could be or how much he lusted after other women. I was trapped in a living hell.

Ten years into my marriage, I was in total despair. I couldn't take it anymore. I am ashamed that the girl who came to know Christ at a young age, was called to preach the Gospel, and knew the promises of God's Word, felt such despair. Everything took its toll on my mind and emotions. I went to my bedroom, picked up his loaded forty-five caliber gun, and held it to my head. I was consumed with self-pity. I told God how unfair life was and why I could not go on. I knew that I would never pull the trigger. It was a moment of letting the Lord know how desperate I was. I should have known better than to hold a loaded gun. I knew gun safety. I suddenly came to myself and realized how irresponsible and dangerous this was. It frightened me. I threw the gun down in a hurry. When I did, it went off right beside my head. I thought I was shot. I looked down, expecting to see blood. I had gunpowder burns on my face. I realized that God spared my life. Bruce found the bullet on the garage floor. It went through the bed and the floor of the bedroom before coming to a stop on the basement floor. God is so good, despite our foolishness. But my future did not turn around that day.

Things deteriorated when we found ourselves on the way to church to listen to an evangelist. I didn't want to go to church. I felt like a hypocrite. We argued all the time. I was depressed. I felt like we were going through the motions. We were far from what I knew a Christian home should be. I didn't even understand why he wanted to attend church or quote scriptures. My father lived a far better life without church or professing salvation.

On the way to church, I told him I felt like I was in a desert and would never come out the other side. He told me to "shut up," and that we would go to church anyway. As the evangelist was preaching, he operated in one of the gifts of the Spirit called the word of knowledge (these gifts are listed in 1 Corinthians 12.) and said, "I'm preaching today about the desert place. Someone here just said that you feel like you are living in a desert and never coming out the other side. This is for you." He got my attention. He gave an altar call, but I was too proud to go forward. I didn't want the church to know the state that I was in. No one went forward because it was specifically for me. Yet, as we left the church, I felt sorry for the evangelist. I feared he would think he missed it, and I knew I needed to turn around. I returned to the altar and told him he was preaching to me. He nodded and gave me some instructions before praying for me. He told me that I would be free from depression after he prayed. However, the next day, when circumstances presented themselves again, the depression would try to come back on me. I needed to be prepared to pray and worship God like never before, no matter how depressed I felt. Also, I needed to get into God's Word as never before. He prayed with me. I recommitted my life afresh. The evangelist reminded me that the enemy would not give up easily. He said that if I gave in to the devil again, depression would come back even stronger.

The next day was a trial for sure. Bruce was extra verbally abusive that morning. He left for work, and I felt that darkness trying to embrace me again. I wondered if the night before accomplished anything. I thought about how I could not continue to live this way. Then, I remembered how the evangelist exhorted me. I could not give in to this again. I had to fight the sense of hopelessness. I read God's Word for quite some time. Next, I walked the floor in praise and worship. Lastly, I knelt beside my bed to pray.

I only prayed for a few minutes when I was caught up in the Spirit. I still don't know if it was a vision or if I had left my body. I could see a heavenly city in the background. The Lord Jesus walked toward me. His eyes pierced like fire, yet they were filled with liquid pools of love simultaneously. He was love personified. As He walked toward me, I suddenly had no desire to ask all the things I thought I would if ever given the opportunity. Yet, other questions came to my mind. Before I could verbalize them, the answer shot back from Him like an arrow into my heart. He never opened His mouth or spoke with His voice. The answers were immediately absorbed into my being. What overwhelmed me was His intense love for me! I looked into those eyes and knew that nothing in my life took Him by surprise. He loved and called me and would preserve, restore, and keep me as the apple of His eye all of the days of my life. Nothing would ever again take away my joy. Jesus was all that I needed in life. I knew everything would be all right. I had no understanding of how the events of my life would unfold, but my Jesus would keep me, no matter what.

I decided I would not tell Bruce what had happened that morning. I felt he would make fun of me and not take me seriously. Yet, when he came home from work, he immediately said, "What in the world has happened to you? You look different. You are glowing." I had no choice but to tell him. Much to my surprise, he believed me and asked if the Lord had said anything about him. I had to tell him no, that He didn't mention him. God only let me know how much He loved me.

Bruce had encouraged me to befriend another lady in the town who also lifted weights. She was not saved but attended the local Methodist church. We worked out daily. When she came to work out, I told her what had happened to me. I was constantly witnessing to her. I knew this was a new opportunity. She believed me and came to church with us that night. I told the evangelist and my pastor what had happened to me. I wanted to encourage them. I was called to the platform to testify about my experience.

Several people received Christ as their Savior that evening. Others rededicated their lives. There was not a dry eye in the building. My friend also gave her life to Christ. However, later, her Methodist pastor talked her out of it. Then, several months later, Bruce made advancements toward her. She refused them, but he lied to her about me, ending the friendship. I finally realized I could not have normal friendships without him ruining them. However, I had a new relationship with the Lord. He wouldn't let me die. I would survive, overcome whatever life threw at me, and return from the dead.

I have not shared this experience publicly except for a handful of times. It was too holy to find adequate words for. I hear many people relate so-called spiritual experiences of what they saw so flippantly that I know there is no truth in it.

DR DEBBIE RICH

My experience was so intimate and precious that I never wanted it cheapened. When I try to share it, I begin to weep and sometimes cannot continue. However, it is such a part of my story and why I have been able to continue that it is now time to share it.

FIVE

A FRESH START LEADS TO A DEAD END

While Bruce did have many admirable traits (especially toward friends and people in need), he could be a very psychologically and occasionally physically abusive husband. I endured years of fear, self-loathing, and feelings of entrapment that grew almost unbearable at times.

There were several more instances of his adultery. He always said that he stopped before completing the act. I do not need to go into detail about the several instances of infidelity and what it did to me. My intent is not to crucify him or to get revenge. I only want to point out that God delivered me from a soul-crushing situation. Some people use the word abuse so flippantly that they might be referring to someone just mildly disagreeing with them. I often wondered if I would end up in a mental ward because of the severity of the abuse, but my God set me free.

Finally, after thirteen years of marriage, I could not take it anymore and filed for divorce. My parents agreed to help me with the financial part of the legalities. However, some church ladies persuaded me to give him another chance. They believed he was repentant and saw him distraught and crying. He drove one hundred miles several times a week to attend Born Again Marriages. This was a ministry located in Omaha, Nebraska. The ladies reminded me of how long I had prayed for this miracle. They asked me if I could live with myself if I threw in the towel. Deep down, I knew he was not genuinely repentant but only sorry for getting caught and losing his family. However, I could not live with that nagging doubt of 'What if he really was repentant?' My constant concern reared its ugly head, 'What would people think?' We reconciled one week before the divorce was finalized.

My parents were out of town that weekend. When they got back and found out that we had reconciled, they were very upset, to say the least. They said they would never help me again. I now understand that, but it hurt at the time. I never asked for their help again.

I felt that I had to do what was right. Bruce may not deserve another chance, but it was the Christian thing to do. One of the things Bruce asked me to do was to go with him to the Born-Again Marriage seminar. When I arrived, they asked me to share on their weekly radio program. I was willing to do anything to help others. Little did I know what they and Bruce had planned. They explained that although I was determined to get a divorce, Bruce, God, and these leaders had a covenant together. That covenant would not allow divorce. Because of their prayers, God worked on me, and I had come to my senses. The situation painted a picture in which I was the guilty one – the wayward sinner. They did not mention anything about Bruce's previous sins or his repentance. It was all about my sin in seeking a divorce. I was taken off guard and didn't know what to say. I was humiliated but determined to do anything to make our marriage work.

The one good result of this episode was that Bruce promised to put me in Bible school again. It was an almost forgotten dream. This time, he mentioned a Bible school I had desired to attend for a long time. Rhema Bible Training Center was in Broken Arrow, Oklahoma, just outside Tulsa. It seemed almost too good to be true. I would finally be going back to Bible school. My family was reunited, and I felt that I could now fulfill the call of God in my life. Once again, Bruce said, "I'm behind you all the way."

With no money in our pockets, we needed to move from Nebraska to Oklahoma in a few weeks. We had to sell our house first, which we had bought through the Farmer's Home Administration (a program for low-income people in small rural areas). We sold it to the first person who looked at it for half the price we had paid. The Farmer's Home Administration made up the difference.

We packed three boys (now between the ages of six and ten), our pictures, and clothes into a borrowed pick-up and headed for Tulsa. We arrived one day before Bible school started and the day after our boys' school started. We had ordered a local newspaper from the area before leaving for Oklahoma. From the newspaper ad, we rented an old, two-story apartment, sight unseen. It literally was on the wrong side of the railroad tracks, one block away from the tracks. We took the first jobs we saw that day. I started working at a doughnut shop until midnight every night at minimum wage. Bruce found work as a chimney and duct cleaner. He too, only received minimum wage. Our apartment had no air conditioning to counter hot Tulsa summers. I remember one summer when the temperature registered over one hundred degrees for almost two months. We were so poor that we ate only oatmeal for a week. To borrow a phrase that my pastor uses: "We were so poor that the cockroaches were packing because they could see there was no food." However, I was back in Bible school and happy.

What I received in those classes was like gold to me. I wept through the teaching. Such marvelous revelation. I had never heard anything like it. I kept thinking about how different my whole life would have been if I had heard some of these things earlier. Rhema Bible Training Center was the best one in the country at the time. I was so blessed to have Dr. Kenneth E. Hagin teaching us almost daily. He has since graduated to heaven and is sorely missed. What a champion of the faith. He was a man of both the Word and the Spirit.

It was good that I received such wonderful faith teaching because I was about to be tried in it. The emotional and sometimes physical abuse from my husband became more intense than before. The name-calling began all over again. One night, he grabbed me by the throat, kicked me in the stomach, and threw me on the bed. I called out for my oldest son, Joshua, to get help. He tried, but his father met him at the door and would not let him in the bedroom. The more he heard me call for help but could not, the harder it was on Josh. I hated what all of this was doing to my children. I could see the fear in their eyes the minute things grew tense. Yet, I did not know how to change any of it.

A neighbor lady named Julie was a Rhema graduate working for Kenneth Hagin Ministries. She became a very good friend and helped us with the boys. Julie would often babysit and occasionally take our kids to soccer practice; for me, she was a God-send. She also encouraged me when things were at their worst. Julie believed in the call on my life. I tried to keep the details of our marriage hidden from her. I didn't want anyone in Broken Arrow to know how bad it was, being terrified that I wouldn't be able to finish school.

In many of my classes, I heard this statement repeatedly: "If you don't have a good marriage, you can never have a ministry." They also said they would only do counseling if both parties agreed. I now understand the reasons for these statements, but, at the time, it left me feeling entirely hopeless.

Now that I have been in full-time ministry for over thirty years and have pastored for eight years, I understand why this is taught. When you enter the ministry, you live in a glass house, figuratively speaking. People should be able to imitate not only what you preach but what you live. Ministers are supposed to be living examples of the Christian life, including marriage. 1 Timothy 4:12 says, *"Let no man despise thy youth; but be thou an example of the believers, in word, in conversation, in charity, in spirit, in faith, in purity."*

These are a few more verses showing that ministers are to be an example. 1 Corinthians 11:1 says, *"Be ye followers of me, even as I also am of Christ."* Philippians 4:9 reads, *"Those things, which ye have both learned, and received, and heard, and seen in me, do: and the God of peace shall be with you."* Philippians 3:17 says, *"Brethren, be followers together of me and mark them which walk so as ye have us for an ensample."* Titus 1:5-9 says, *"For this cause left I thee in Crete, that thou shouldest set in order the things that are wanting, and ordain elders in every city, as I had appointed thee: If any be blameless, the husband of one wife, having faithful children not accused of riot or unruly. For a bishop must be blameless, as the steward of God; not self-willed, not soon angry, not given to wine, no striker, not given to filthy lucre; But a lover of hospitality, a lover of good men, sober, just, holy, temperate; Holding fast the faithful word as he hath been taught, that he may be able by sound doctrine both to exhort and to convince the gainsayers."* There are many more.

Marriage itself is supposed to preach a sermon of Christ and His Church. Ephesians 5:22-32 reads, *"Wives, submit yourselves unto your own husbands, as unto the Lord. For the husband is the head of the wife, even as Christ is the head of the church: and he is the saviour of the body. Therefore as the church is subject unto Christ, so let the wives be to their own husbands in everything. Husbands, love your wives, even as Christ also loved the church, and gave himself for it; That he might sanctify and cleanse it with the washing of water by the word, That he might present it to himself a glorious church, not having spot, or wrinkle, or any such thing; but that it should be holy and without blemish. So ought men to love their wives as their own bodies. He that loveth his wife loveth himself. For no man ever yet hated his own flesh; but nourisheth and cherisheth it, even as the Lord the church: For we are members of his body, of his flesh, and of his bones. For this cause shall a man leave his father and mother, and shall be joined unto his wife, and they two shall be one flesh. This is a great mystery: but I speak concerning Christ and the church."* If the ministers cannot show this kind of marriage to the congregation, they will be led to believe it is impossible to obtain.

Also, ministry puts extra stress on a marriage. It takes a lot of time to be involved with others' problems, and there is a devil out there who would love to destroy marriage and bring reproach to the body of Christ. If the marriage is already shaky, everyone is in a dangerous and compromising position. In my case, there was nothing wrong with what they were teaching, but I was left feeling completely hopeless. I think there needs to be something in place for one spouse to come in and counsel, even if the other refuses.

It wasn't long before I saw the usual pattern developing with Bruce's attraction to Julie. He helped her with her car and fixed things in her home. Of course, she thought that he was a kind, helpful, and charming neighbor. She was single and not dating at the time. I knew his intentions were not above board, but I was too embarrassed to talk to her about it. Eventually, he began to flirt openly. I was humiliated again. He asked her to sunbathe in our children's small kiddie pool. She accompanied us on most of our outings, picnicking, swimming, etc. I could see what he was doing but knew that she couldn't. I argued with Bruce about it, but he reminded me he would not put up with jealousy. Every outing ended with arguments and fighting. The day came when she realized he was a predator and refused his advances.

One evening, he became so angry that I ran out of the house. It was raining, but I was terrified and didn't know what else to do. The car was locked, so I took off walking in the rain. After I was soaked, I returned home to find that he had locked me out of the house. I walked around all night in the rain. I managed to get into my house after he left for work, got ready for school, and attended classes. I knew that I could take no more and that I had to leave this marriage. I planned to do so the following day.

Instead of going to Bible school or sending the boys to school, I planned for us to run away to Nebraska. I waited for Bruce to go to work and stuffed a few necessities into our old Ford. I cried and felt close to a breakdown as I told my boys that we had to move back to Nebraska and be close to family. We headed north on interstate twenty-nine. Forty-five minutes into our journey, I saw a familiar sight in my mirror. It was Bruce in our other car, coming up on my tail at high speed. I couldn't believe it! He worked on the other side of the city. How did he know what we were doing, and how could he know what route we took? I later found out that he felt something was up, called Julie, and asked if I had left him. When she told him that the boys and I had left, he decided to pursue us on the highway.

Now, I was faced with a great dilemma. Bruce swerved close to my car, trying to scare me. He succeeded. We looked like two cars playing chicken on the road. He rolled his window down and yelled at me to pull over. Terrified, I pulled over.

He ordered me to go home and told me he would find me wherever I went. He also informed me that he would take my children someplace secret and that I would never see them again. I gave in like a whipped pup and returned home to resume the living hell.

When I went to school the next day, my thoughts screamed at me. I almost couldn't hear what the instructors said. I noticed, more than ever before, that most students were married and attending school as a couple. They held hands and praised God together. They learned and discussed the Word of God together. Unlike them, I sat there alone with tears streaming down my face. I knew that my husband's heart was not with me, let alone with God. What would I do? How could I continue school or even hope for any ministry someday?

While I battled these emotions and thoughts, the woman sitting next to me in class sensed my emotional state. She told me that she knew I was being abused and wanted me to see one of the school counselors. I did not know this woman; we were just sitting together in the same class. I knew it wouldn't be good for me to attend counseling when my husband would not join me. I would also risk being asked to leave school because of marriage problems. She grabbed my hand and said, "Come on, we have to get you some help." I followed. I was used to letting someone else take charge.

When I approached the administrative counter, a woman spoke to me. She did not even look at me. Her voice was monotone as she stated, "Badge number, please." I was crying but stated my number. Then my friend explained the reason for my visit. The office person informed me that I would have to sit and wait for an available counselor to talk with me after he was through with his class. I felt like a complete imbecile. How could I concisely state what my problem was? I didn't know where to begin.

A short time later, I was sitting in front of one of the church's assistant pastors. He immediately asked if my husband would come in and talk with them. I answered that he would not. He stated that there was very little they could do under those circumstances, which was what I expected him to say. I was humiliated. I should have been used to that by then. Now everyone knew my marriage was a mess. I believed that I would never have a ministry. Also, I was at risk of my husband finding out that I spoke to the church, and he would be furious. It unfolded exactly as I thought. I appreciated the motive of the woman who tried to help, but it was to no avail.

Every day, I told myself that I had to concentrate on finishing school, one day at a time. Things continued to deteriorate at home, but my classes went well. I not only finished school but also did so with a GPA of a perfect 4.0. It was so important to me to listen, study, and do well. Even though Rhema was not known to be a highly academic school, many around me were flunking tests. Some of them had parents and churches supporting them with tuition. They were able to attend healing and prayer schools in the afternoons. I had to endure abuse and still hardly ever missed class. I worked a job, got my children off to school in the morning, and still found time to read and study. When I saw students miss classes just because they felt tired or wanted a day off, I wanted to shake them. Everything that I heard was so precious to me. I thanked God every day for the privilege of attending Bible school. Because of the grace of God, I was able to graduate. How thankful I was, and how grateful I am to this day.

During my second year in Bible school, Bruce enrolled in a paramedic school in Tulsa. The reason sounded good. Someday, he would be able to make good money. He said that would help me in the ministry. Meanwhile, he would be able to use his skills to help people. I wondered how that would work when he had to deliver a baby or look at a woman. I remembered what he had told me. "No medical person can look at a woman without lusting after her." I knew better than to remind him of that statement.

When he started school, I immediately saw changes that were not good. He often referred to a young woman he worked with during his internship. They had to stay in a trailer together. He taunted me with remarks about her. To make matters worse, she eventually went to Rhema Bible Church, where we attended. I later acquired a job at the Rhema gym as the aerobics and weight-lifting instructor. She came to work out. She giggled when she discovered who I was and said, "Oh, I didn't know Bruce was married." What an interesting remark!

Every time he came home, his anger and frustration grew worse. I knew it was because of his guilt and lust, although I couldn't prove it. Surely, something would change. I couldn't make the connection regarding what I would have to do for it to change. It would take courage.

By the time I graduated from Rhema in 1989, I was working for Kenneth Hagin Ministries. The ministry had just completed a multi-million dollar gym for the church members and students. They sought qualified male and female instructors. Since I was a weight-lifting instructor in the past, I felt that this was the perfect job for me, and it was. I worked at the gym for over a year. I loved my job. It was my favorite job until I entered the ministry. Eventually, they wanted to add high-impact aerobics classes to weight lifting. They sent me to school to become an aerobics instructor. I created my own routines, which were set to

Dr. Kenneth E. Hagin presenting me with my diploma.

Lifting weights at Rhema's gym, as the instructor.

Christian music. I also took nutrition classes. I loved working for a wonderful ministry, doing something I loved, and being able to help people get fit. If we are going to run our race and complete it, we must be healthy and fit.

I recently held meetings in Tulsa, Ok., and visited Rhema. I was able to go into the gym (called Ninowski Recreation Center), visit with Doug Jones, the Alumni Director, and sit at a classroom desk. It brought back a lot of memories.

It was at this time that we came to know of a couple from Alaska. We heard an announcement in our Sunday school class that they had graduated from Rhema and were returning to Alaska to pioneer a church. Bruce was excited. He was always interested in Alaska and often bought the Alaska Magazine. He dreamed of living there someday, even though he had never visited. He was an outdoorsman, hunter, and fisherman. He loved hiking and observing nature. When we heard the announcement, he asked me to invite this couple to our apartment for dinner. They came to our home and shared their vision with us. They showed us pictures of Alaska and shared stories about the state. We promised to keep in touch.

Sometime later, this couple called us to see if we were still interested in Alaska. They told us that they pioneered a church in a small town but were now called to be missionaries to Russia. They wanted to hand the church over to a new pastor and wanted to know how we felt about that possibility. I was honored but told Bruce we could not pastor a church with a marriage in trouble. He said that he realized that and told me he repented and would stand behind me. He reminded me that he was not called to preach but that I was. He would be the one who would do the janitorial and construction part. He would shovel the snow and do all the behind-the-scene projects. He said it would be a new beginning for us and an adventure for our three boys. I wanted to believe this was true. Despite a good deal of skepticism, it gave me a little hope. In the end, he persuaded me.

Of course, this couple had no idea of the baggage we carried, and I didn't feel I should advertise it. How could we ever do ministry if I told people about our past (his in particular)? Didn't I have to trust God to change him? After all, God called me, knowing that all of this would take place. Maybe this would be our new beginning, and we could finally put the past behind us. Alaska was nearly 4,000 miles away. If we couldn't have a new beginning there, where would we?

We prepared for the long trip to Alaska. We read books about Alaska, studied atlases, and talked to anyone who had been there. We learned that another couple came to Rhema from Alaska, and we became acquainted with them. We exchanged our car for their old pick-up and camper they brought from Alaska. The vehicle did not get good gas mileage. It only got five miles to the gallon on a 4,000-mile trip. It was 1990, during the first Gulf War. The price of gasoline was well over three dollars a gallon, which was a lot for the time. We put three boys, a huge Newfoundland dog, clothing, books, and a few essentials in the camper and trailer and headed up The Alaska Highway in September. We had to hurry before the winter made the roads impassable. We also wanted to give our children a vacation in the process. We stopped at The Black Hills and Yellowstone Park. I should have been excited about our new beginning. However, I had a gnawing sense in my spirit that although the scenery would change, our problems would not. But I had to try.

We arrived in Alaska at the end of September 1990. Winter was already on its way. We tried to save money and sell a few things. Some gave us small offerings to send us to Alaska. We arrived with only $300 to our name.

We stayed with a couple from the church for about two weeks until we could rent a place. We were able to rent a mobile home in the town where we would pastor. Can you guess what the rent was? Yes, it was exactly $300. God's grace and provision are amazing, even when things are not His perfect will. I saw His handy work, even in the middle of challenging circumstances.

The first Sunday service was canceled due to a blizzard. Alaskan church services are rarely canceled, but the blizzard was severe. I believe about two feet of snow came that first weekend of October. The winter of 1990 ended up being one of the harshest winters in years. Eventually, I could not look out my kitchen window because the snow was piled up about six feet. That year we spent more money on fuel oil than rent. We could not get natural gas in that small town of about 300 people.

One Sunday, we were introduced to the church congregation of about 25 people. One lady who was our age seemed very friendly. She was a nurse who sang, played the guitar, and served as the worship leader. She came from another church where she had received good Word of Faith doctrine. I liked her immediately. When I shook her hand, I heard the still-small voice of the Holy Spirit on the inside whisper, "Be careful. She will be Bruce's next love interest." I tried to brush it off and convinced myself that it was my imagination simply because she was a tiny brunette, the type he usually went for. We became good friends. I was the keyboard player at the church, and she played the guitar. We sang together with two other ladies from the congregation. It was a good little group, considering our size.

Connie seemed to be one of the hungrier people in the church. We discussed Scripture, had Bible studies together, and I learned of her desire to attend Bible school. However, her husband was unsaved and gave her a hard time about the things of God. She felt discouraged. She said she hoped Bruce could become acquainted with her husband and help lead him to the Lord.

One of the things that the founding pastor was looking forward to was that Bruce was a man's man. The Alaskan men would respect him for that. He was a good mechanic, an outdoorsman, a hard worker, and a builder and was not merely a city-boy preacher. As such, we hoped he would connect with the Alaskan men in the community.

We acquired some chickens to raise. Connie came over and helped Bruce with that. He went to her place to help with the horses. Bruce and Connie seemed to have a lot in common. She was a nurse while he was a paramedic. They eventually served on the same small-town emergency service. I could see the friendship growing. I thought, 'Surely not here, where we are making a fresh start and sowing seeds in the community. This is supposed to be a new beginning.'

I didn't know what to do. I finally pleaded with Bruce to be careful and not sin again. We had too much at stake. This time it would bring reproach on the work of God. We were four thousand miles from home. We had no family around us. He lost his temper and told me he and Connie were just friends. He told me that I better not mention this again. In whom could I confide? I could not tell anyone in the church about his past and my suspicions. What kind of pastor would they think I was? If I told the outgoing pastor what I suspected, he would be angry and probably remove us. 'What if it wasn't true? What if they were only friends?'

I decided my only recourse was to try to talk to Connie. She trusted me as a pastor. I only shared a little of our past with her. I knew that, as her pastor, I had to be careful. Could I trust her? I let her know that there were some indiscretions on Bruce's part. I told her that I knew the pattern. I shared that I could see a growing friendship between them and asked her to tell me if she thought that he had made a pass at her. She seemed shocked and assured me that nothing was happening or ever would be. She felt he was just a helpful man acting as a good pastor. She didn't believe he was doing anything wrong but would let me know if he ever did. She thanked me for being honest with her. I felt a sense of relief. After that incident, Connie and I went on a mission trip together to the interior of Alaska. We had a wonderful time. I was sure that I was concerned for nothing.

Nearly a year after our arrival, we hosted a summer picnic for the church. The scenery was beautiful, and the food was delicious. We had visitors from other churches. However, I found it difficult to throw off concerns. After a short time of fellowship, Bruce said he wanted to go for a hike and asked Connie to go with him. I saw a few congregation members and some visitors look at each other with questioning eyes. That was an odd thing for two married people to do. I was speechless as the two of them were gone for quite some time. Afterward, he told me I'd better not question him about it. A few weeks later, all three of us were at a Women's Aglow service in Palmer, Alaska, where I was the speaker. Connie sang at the event. Bruce was there to support his wife, or so I thought. After I spoke, the organizers invited everyone to stay for a fellowship dinner. Bruce had been nursing a cold for about a week. Connie sat down and told me how she also was fighting a cold. I told her that Bruce was just getting over one. The two of them exchanged looks that said they had inside information. I knew for sure at that moment that things were not right.

A few days later, Bruce told me he was concerned for Connie because of her marriage problems. I asked him how he knew about her marriage problems. As her pastor, she usually came to me about them, not my husband. He told me that she mentioned it when they were taking care of the horses.

Our oldest son, Joshua, was on the freshman football team. Bruce usually took him to practice. His school was fifteen miles away. One day it was time for Joshua to leave for practice. Bruce went over to help Connie with the horses and did not come home at the scheduled time. I didn't have a car to take Joshua to his school. I asked a friend to take me to Connie's house to see what kept Bruce. I was angry. I had no idea what I would find at Connie's home.

When we drove up, Bruce and Connie were nowhere to be found. The horses could be seen from the road. I approached the barn, but it was empty. I went to the house only to find Connie's daughter inside. She said that she thought they were out in the woods. I could not find them and had to borrow a car to take Josh to practice. Bruce had no explanation when he came home and no apologies. He just forgot.

One day a thought came to me. Bruce always looked after the finances; his philosophy was that the husband made the decisions, handled the finances, and paid the bills. I never saw a phone bill but decided it was time to look at one. He worked as a paramedic in Anchorage, which was 65 miles away. If he communicated with Connie by phone, it would be a long-distance call. (This was in the days before cell phones.) I couldn't find any phone bills, so I went to the phone company and retrieved copies of the last several months. The phone bills listed many calls of significant length to Connie. No wonder he knew of her marriage problems!

While Bruce was still at work, I called Connie and confronted her about what I found. She cried and told me there was an emotional attachment but nothing physical. She also told me that he came into her life at a vulnerable time because of her marriage problems. He was so nice and helpful that, in the beginning, that was all there was to it. Eventually, he flirted, and she craved the attention. She assured me that they had never touched each other. They never kissed. She went on to tell me how badly she felt about all of it. They would not see each other again, and if I wanted, she was willing to go to another church.

I was grateful that the truth was out in the open. I assured her that if she genuinely repented and would have nothing to do with him, I would forgive her, and we would work it out. When Bruce came home from work, I told him the whole story. His response seemed all too familiar. He turned it on her and said that she came onto him until he had a hard time resisting, but they never physically touched one another. He said it was over.

Within a week of this incident, there was a youth event at our church. Bruce was supposed to pick up some of the youth and give them a ride. Once again, he was late. I found his car parked in front of Connie's house. When confronted, he said he was picking up her daughter and just wanted to go in the house and be friendly. I finally told him that either we have marriage counseling or it was over.

I no longer remember the exact sequence of events over the next few days.

Eventually, I told the founding pastor and his wife what was happening. They arranged a meeting with our entire church board, which consisted of them and another pastor and his wife. They all recommended a certain marriage counselor in Anchorage.

Bruce had never agreed to counseling before. Years before, we went to a marriage retreat in Omaha, Nebraska, and it ended terribly. After we arrived and heard one session, he became angry and stayed in the room the rest of the weekend. I attended the sessions alone. This time, he was backed into a corner and had to participate in the sessions. Since this may be our first and last time, I was determined to get it all out in the open. I expected him to have a temper tantrum on the spot. Much to my surprise, he allowed me to give details while he sat in a chair and remained rational and calm. I left the session with hope in my heart. We even made an appointment to return. Bruce insisted on shopping for a new car on the way home. I told him that we could not afford a new car and that it was the worst time to invest in something big. He overrode my judgment and bought a brand-new Chevrolet Cavalier. We drove two cars back home that night. Little did I know that he was planning for the separation.

We went to bed that night without incident. I was dumbfounded that he did not lambast me for what I confided to the counselor. I did not know that he was storing up his anger for the next morning.

I woke up to his shouts. It had been a long time since he called me those vulgar names. He said that because of what I told the counselor, he should never have to live with me another moment. God used that moment to wake me up from a long stupor. It was as though clouds of stupidity, self-pity, and helplessness broke off me, and the shackles were destroyed. Bruce thought his tirade would hurt me, as it had many times before. This time was different. I heard the words strongly in my spirit: 'Enough is enough. You don't have to live like this anymore. I'm setting you free.'

I'm sure that the Lord spoke something similar to me before. However, I was too worried about what other people would think and too concerned about how I could ever fulfill the call of God on my life. But at that moment, I knew that I would never live like that again.

God doesn't expect anyone to live in abuse or repeated adultery. I tell people in my services that God can heal anything. His best is for couples to forgive each other, no matter what has been done. I've seen couples on the verge of divorce fall into each other's arms and become reunited in my meetings. They had a honeymoon that was better than the first one. God is the God of the first, second, third chance, and more. However, He needs two repentant hearts to do what He wants. If one refuses to repent and change, God does not expect the other one to live in that.

The Bible makes it clear that God hates divorce. Moses only allowed divorce *"because of the hardness of your hearts"* (Matthew 19:8). Divorce is the literal tearing apart of a divine union. It rips apart the soul, mind, and emotions. It is never the will of God. However, it is not the legal document that God hates but what people do to one another that causes the divorce. It would never take place if two people walked in love with God and each other. I know first-hand how devastating it is to the emotions of both parties. It wreaks havoc on the children.

The only thing in creation that God pronounced "not good" was man's aloneness (Genesis 2:18), so the woman was created, and the marriage relationship was founded. The woman was made to be in a complementary relationship with the man as his helper. (Genesis 2:21-22) God blessed them and established that the man is responsible for leaving home and setting up a new household with his wife. The two were to become "one flesh"—that is, they were no longer two autonomous, separate individuals, but one home (Genesis 2:24).

Throughout Scripture, we see the idea that marriage represents God's relationship with His people. Marriage is described as a covenant relationship in Malachi 2:14 and Proverbs 2:17. In Hosea 2:19-20, God says He will betroth His people to Himself in marriage. In the New Testament, Paul describes marriage as a type of Christ's relationship with His Church (Ephesians 5:22-32).

Because of the importance placed on the marital relationship and what it portrays, it is not surprising that God would put severe limits on divorce. God gives two clear grounds for divorce: (1) sexual immorality (Matthew 5:32, 19:9) and (2) abandonment by an unbeliever (1 Corinthians 7:15). Paul says that, in the case of a believer married to an unbeliever, if the unbeliever chooses to leave the relationship, the believer is not under any obligation to insist that the marriage continue. The final words of that verse explain why—*"God has called us to peace."* A marriage that remains intact despite one partner's desire to leave will certainly not be peaceful.

In 1 Corinthians 7:12-13, Paul says by the Holy Spirit, *"But to the rest speak I, not the Lord: If any brother hath a wife that believeth not, and she be pleased to dwell with him, let him not put her away. And the woman which hath an husband that believeth not, and if he be pleased to dwell with her, let her not leave him."* If one of the parties is cheating on the other or physically (and possibly emotionally) abusing the other, they are not pleased to dwell with the other. He may not have physically left the relationship or said he wants a divorce, but his actions show that he is not pleased to dwell with his mate. There can be no peace in that situation.

Even then, God's will is for repentance and forgiveness, reconciliation, and restoration. Divorce should only be viewed as the last resort. Strong marriages build strong families, and strong families build strong churches and communities. Although divorce is permissible in some instances, the true biblical course of action would be to rebuke, await repentance, offer forgiveness, and be reconciled (Matthew 18:15-17).

Those of us who have been through divorce know first-hand how devastating it is and that it is not the will of God. Some may think that I take marriage and divorce lightly because of what I have been through. It is just the opposite. I believe God for miracles in people's marriages, and we see them often. Each time, I say, "Take that, devil. You will pay for what you did to my family."

The bottom line is to be very careful about whom you marry and make sure that it is God's will in the first place. If you have made a mistake, continue to believe God for a miracle. That is His business, and He is good at it. However, God needs two believing, consecrated hearts for a marriage to work. If one refuses to abide by God's precepts, God allows the other one to come out of that kind of hell. Divorce would only be the last option in the worst of cases.

It would never be God's desire for a wife to remain with a husband who physically abuses her and/or their children. In such an instance, the wife should separate herself and the children from the abusive husband. However, even in such a situation, a time of separation with the goal of repentance and restoration should be the ideal, not necessarily immediately beginning divorce proceedings. If there is any risk to self or children, separation is a reasonable and appropriate step.

I have heard testimonies of women who hung on and believed for twenty years or better to see their husbands come to Christ. I think that is wonderful. If you have a word from God concerning your marriage, do not let anyone talk you out of it. Faith is a marvelous thing. Only you know what God has spoken to your heart.

However, if God has not told you to hang on, and you or your children are in danger, you do not have to live that way. Adultery can be deadly. Today with HIV and other sexually transmitted diseases on the rampage, adultery could cost someone their life. Also, physical abuse is inexcusable! It only takes one time for someone to die or to become permanently disabled. Only the person who has lived through it can appreciate the disastrous effects of physical abuse.

I believe verbal abuse is the most detrimental of all abuses. You may not die physically from it, but it kills the person gradually. It eats away at the emotions, mental stability, and the very soul of the individual. Eventually, you feel that you are worth nothing. An intelligent person can end up feeling like an idiot, that they're worthy of no one's love, and lose all hope. It was only through the grace of God that I did not lose my mind.

One of the worst things is having to endure the judgment of people who do not understand what you're going through. I learned how cruel people can be when they don't know what is happening. Yet, some can be very compassionate. One couple in our little Alaskan town demonstrated this. They were Lutherans who didn't attend my church. They were school teachers who helped my children when we first arrived in town. They welcomed me into their home for two weeks when Bruce would not leave the house.

When the founding pastor of my church learned of the drama, he decided to meet all three of us. Everyone presented their spin on what was happening. Bruce and Connie insisted that they had never touched and that their emotional attachment was over. He believed them. He had known Connie for a long time. He told me to ask her to forgive me for doubting her. I believe in submission and authority and did what I was asked. He went on to tell me that I made many mistakes in the situation. I should have told them about Bruce's past in the very beginning. I tried to believe my husband when he said he had repented and that we would have a fresh start. Besides, I was the one who would be pastoring, not him. If I always brought up Bruce's past, how would we ever begin afresh?

Then, he informed me that I should not have confided in the people I did confide in once I knew about the phone calls. Again, I'm sure he was right. However, it is hard to make perfect decisions when your world is falling apart, you have been physically and verbally abused for years, and your best friend has just betrayed you. I apologized for not thinking everything through better.

Another pastor on our Board of Directors reprimanded me for wearing my feelings on my sleeve. I went to a service at his church while going through this, and probably didn't look very cheery. This is even more interesting because he fought the move of God and was the one who earlier expressed his concern because of the joy in my meetings. He publicly rebuked me. In a private meeting, he told me how costly divorce is and that we would regret it financially. I already knew these things, and divorce was the last thing that I wanted. I wanted to have a godly marriage to a faithful man. If I didn't believe that marriage is a holy covenant, I would never have endured the last eighteen years, left my family, traveled four thousand miles, and moved to the wilderness of Alaska. I held onto the hope of working our marriage out.

It's so interesting that at a time like this, some tell you that you made your bed and now must lie in it. Others say you were a fool to stay in the marriage that long. Some say you can never leave the marriage or God will never forgive you. Usually, these cheap pieces of advice are given by people who have never had to live one moment through anything like this in their lives.

I filed for divorce and finally persuaded Bruce to rent another place. He came over to my house more than once, determined to reconcile, and tried to get in bed with me. I had to threaten to call the police to get him to leave. He still insisted that he and Connie were no longer seeing each other. However, she left her husband and filed for divorce. It seemed like more than a coincidence. During that time, her husband told me that she admitted to him that she and Bruce kissed, but no more. This was interesting since they told me that they never kissed or touched. My friends witnessed Bruce taking Connie home many mornings.

The Christmas season arrived; I agreed to let Bruce come to the house on Christmas Day to spend time with our boys. I gave them their presents from me early in the day. I fixed a nice Christmas dinner and made plans to leave while he was at the house. I knew he would try to manipulate the situation, but I was not up for it. Neither did I want to put our children through that. I knew it would result in another argument.

The couple from my church, Noel and Edna DeVries, invited me to spend Christmas evening with them. We had a wonderful time. While I was enjoying fellowship in their home, Bruce called. As usual, he tried to bully me. He accused me of not caring about the boys on Christmas. He demanded that I come home immediately. He said he couldn't stay any longer because he had to get up early for work. He didn't want to leave the boys alone, so I needed to get home.

At first, I felt guilty and found myself apologizing and promising to get home promptly. It was a learned response. But something snapped me out of it. I realized that I no longer had to jump at his every bark. I made these plans to allow him to be with the boys. I had no idea that he would want to leave that quickly.

Despite knowing I didn't have to do his bidding, I still agreed to come home. My Christmas was already ruined.

All the way home, I thought about the possible reasons for his wanting to leave so early. That wasn't like him, even if he had to get up early. Also, in the past, he used that kind of guilt and manipulation when he was guilty of something himself. What could it be? Then, the answer came to me. Friends told me that Connie had to work at the hospital on Christmas Day but would be off Christmas night. I realized that they wanted to spend Christmas evening together. I went home and relieved him of his parental duty. After the boys were asleep, I made a trip through mountainous terrain to his cabin. I had never been there before, but the boys told me where it was.

It was a treacherous night. It snowed, and conditions worsened as I climbed. The roads grew slick. It was getting hard to see. On nights like that, it is essential to watch for moose. I almost hit one on the way there. Some can weigh up to fifteen hundred pounds. They seem to wait in the brush for a car to come and then ramble out in front of you on icy roads. Nearing 2 a.m., my heart pounded as I approached my destination. 'What would I find?' I had to know for sure, once and for all.

I finally spotted the cabin. I did not dare drive down the driveway to the house's entrance. That would be a dead giveaway. Besides, it looked as though I was wrong. I did not see Connie's car. The house appeared dark. Perhaps Bruce was already asleep for the night. This long, treacherous drive was probably for nothing. Nevertheless, I was here. I should at least make sure.

I left my car on the main road and walked on foot to the back of the house. I had to wade through deep snow. I was cold, somewhat nervous, and unsure of how to proceed. When I came upon the back entrance, much to my surprise, Connie's vehicle was parked between the house and the garage. No one could spot it from the road. Smart thinking. My heart was racing. Now what?

I banged my fist on the window pane. If I knocked on the door, they would have time to look out the window and refuse to open it. I wanted to take them by surprise. It worked. Bruce came to the door with no shirt, his hair a mess, and his pants unzipped. He opened the door just wide enough for me to slip under his arm. I was the last person he expected. Later, he told me that he thought it was Connie's husband. When he realized that it was me, he never expected me to enter without being invited. He was wrong. In the short time I was away from him, I grew stronger and more decisive.

I marched past Bruce before he could stop me. I ran to the back of the house, where Connie was lying in his bed. She was trying to dress but didn't have time to finish before I found her. She looked mortified. Bruce was already approaching me with determination to throw me out. Before he did, I quickly said my piece. "Connie, you better get up. Your pastor is here." I did not say Bruce's wife, but her pastor. I told her that I was not surprised by his actions. I had lived with this behavior for many years. However, I was extremely disappointed in her. I asked her how I could have been her pastor and yet she did not believe me concerning Bruce's past. I asked her if I had ever lied to her. I already told her about Bruce's past behavior, so she must not have believed me, or she would never have become involved with him. Her head hung low. I told her that Bruce was at my house two nights before trying to get into bed with me, but I threatened to call the police. When I said that, Bruce appeared in the room and denied my story. He was quick to call me a liar to my face. I was shocked. He grabbed me by the arm and escorted me out the door.

It was a long, cold journey back to my house. The tears poured down my cheeks. My husband of eighteen years just looked me in the eyes and blatantly lied. I just found him and my best friend in bed together. This is the friend to whom another pastor asked me to apologize for doubting her word. I was concerned about what was ahead for my children and me. Could I continue to pastor? Would we remain in Alaska? How could I pay for the trailer, heating, and car? How would the church react to all of this? I could not stop crying as I thought about the false promises of a new beginning.

The next day, Bruce visited me and apologized for the first time since we were separated. He said that he was sorry for lying in front of her. He reasoned that he had already lost me and didn't want to lose her, too. He also told me that Connie said that she felt like a prostitute, and he thought that would help me. It didn't. He finally agreed to sign the papers on that day, and we worked things out without lawyers. I followed a formula for child support and used the lowest one possible. I was not out to rob him or to seek revenge. I just wanted him to help me support our children.

Before long, Bruce and Connie moved in together. I never thought he would do that in front of our children. They were eventually married. I made one thousand dollars per month pastoring the church on the Alaskan cost of living. Bruce and Connie made a combined one hundred thousand dollars per year. He was supposed to pay six hundred dollars a month for child support. He rarely did. He came to the house, promising twenty dollars this time, fifty in two weeks, etc. I never knew what was coming or when. You can't pay bills like that. I grew tired of the arguments. I realized my God was providing for me and would continue to do so. I wrote a letter to the court to free him of all child support. It was the beginning of a journey where the Lord gave me incredible revelation about sowing and reaping. I am thankful that I learned these principles early on.

The Bible deals with every situation. We must never forget the New Testament Royal Law of Love. *"Let everything be done by and through love"* (1 Corinthians 16:14). The Bible asks the wife to submit to her husband as unto the Lord (Ephesians 5:22-24).

We must also remember that Ephesians 5 has both sides of the marriage covenant. Ephesians 5:25-33 admonishes a man to love and cherish his wife. You can't have a wife submitting to her husband without the husband loving the wife. It does not work to have one without the other. Of course, God hates divorce. Anyone who has ever lived through one knows why. It is the dividing of body, soul, and spirit. It is the breaking of the most sacred of covenants. God created man and woman to live together in holy matrimony as long as they both live. Marriage should be the closest thing to heaven on earth. Divorce destroys souls, brings untold heartache, hurts children, and is one of the leading causes of the disintegration of our society and nation; make no mistake about it. It is a terrible thing, and it is a sin. God allowed divorce in the Old Testament because of the hardness of their hearts. It is never His best nor His will. He desires for us to live according to His Word and His promises.

I am not advocating for divorce to be taken lightly. The church must teach Biblical standards. We live in a day when the Word of God is being watered down to fit society's standards. The world's philosophy has crept into the church on every side. These days, you hear about divorce inside the church as much as outside of it. These things should not be. We live in a time when many take their marriage vows lightly. Some have no qualms about divorcing just because of irreconcilable differences or because the grass looks greener on the other side.

However, the part of divorce that God hates is not just the courtroom or the piece of paper declaring the marriage to be dissolved. God hates what has taken place long before that day. He hates the breaking of vows, mistreatment of each other, abuse and heartache, lies and uncontrolled temper, and murdering each other's souls while you are still together. That piece of paper is just the death certificate of something that has already been murdered.

This is not a book on the doctrine of marriage, divorce, and re-marriage.

There are a lot of good books and some that are not so good on this subject. I have listed a few good books on the subject in the references section at the end of this book. This is the story of a woman who was brought back to life no matter how many times the devil tried to kill her. God is great. Life still triumphs over death. The sun will rise again and will bring joy in the morning.

SIX

THE MINISTRY IS RESURRECTED FROM THE DEAD

I never thought of pastoring a church in the wilderness of Alaska and certainly never dreamed of doing it as a divorced woman with three children. My total income from my little church was a whopping one thousand dollars a month. The rent for my little home was three hundred dollars a month. The cost of fuel oil to heat it was about four hundred fifty dollars a month. The church consisted of almost twenty-five people before my husband and worship leader had an affair. Now, the numbers decreased; it looked pretty hopeless.

The town where I lived and pastored was bordered by two mountain ranges, the Chugach Range and Talkeetna, with the Matanuska River running through it. We had our share of wild moose coming into town. I knew many people who encountered them in cars or by walking. Some of them unfortunately died, and others were paralyzed. I learned that a person should always avoid engaging with them. Often, there were moose in my driveway. A cow moose with a calf is even more dangerous. Often, I could not even get to my car and had to wait for the moose to leave. Living in this town was very close to what many saw in the television series called *Northern Exposure*.

The town was known for having a lot of rebellious, lone-ranger types. Some moved there from what Alaskans call the lower forty-eight states to grow marijuana, which was legal then (now it is legal in several states). One can find all sorts of people there: those running from the law or child support, drug addicts and/or drug peddlers, and those who loved their independence and wanted a more solitary, independent life. There were, of course, regular families who had nine-to-five jobs, as well. My point is that pastoring in a small Alaskan town or village is not your typical experience. It was a town where cowboys still hung their guns in the saloon. No one messed with these independent pioneers. It was challenging, to say the least.

Moose at Sutton Library

A few days after my divorce, I had the most remarkable encounter with God. I realized that without the help of the Holy Spirit, I could do nothing. I didn't have the finances, equipment, wisdom, or reputation to have any ministry; I felt lonely and sorry for myself after being betrayed by my best friend and husband. I thought about my childhood dreams and how I was believing for a lifelong marital relationship. I thought about my precious boys caught in the middle of it all; I didn't know where to turn.

Suddenly, I looked at the revival books on my library shelf. I thought of the stories I read and heard through the years. I meditated on the multitude of good teaching I was privileged to hear. I decided to talk to the Lord in a very personal way. I told Him I didn't want to read another book about revival. I no longer cared what famous revivalists experienced. I wanted to see those things for myself. If grandma and grandpa could see miraculous healings, why not me? I was not alive when Smith Wigglesworth (a great, well-renowned English preacher) had his great miracles. I wanted to see them today. I wondered why the Book of Acts was still in my Bible. Was it just to make me drool over something that was no longer possible?

I remember asking my grandparents why we were no longer seeing these things. They responded that it was because we were living in "the last days, and we had just to hang on, hoping to be raptured soon from this terrible world." I wondered, 'Why I could not have been born a few years earlier?' I was living in the present and needed a personal experience with God. I knew my Bible said it is *"Jesus Christ the same, yesterday, today, and forever"* (Hebrews 13:8). It also says, *"Greater things than He did, we would do"* (John 14:12). I knew that the powerful baptism of the Holy Spirit was to give us boldness and power. I would not be denied. Somehow, I knew this day would be a turning point. I had two choices: either get bitter at God, run from Him, go to a bar to drown my troubles, as many victims of adultery do, or run to Him and draw closer more than ever. I needed Him now like never before. Thank God that I chose the latter.

I told God how hungry and desperate I was for Him. Like David of old, I thirsted for Him like a deer thirsts for water. I expected to see the miraculous power of God operating in my life. I wanted to have all that was possible. Either all of His Word is true, or none of it is. Either He is who He says He is, or He is a liar. It was time to see the Book of Acts in action in my life and my ministry. I asked God for fresh oil from heaven. I'm not sure I understood exactly what I was asking for. Sometimes we use religious terms and lingo we have heard without comprehending them completely. However, I knew that I needed something. Thank God that I received it. He saturated me with His love and presence. What joy, unspeakable and full of glory! Many hours later, I sat down and wrote a song about what I had just experienced. The song was, "I Ask for Fresh Oil from Heaven Once Again."

The following Sunday morning, I found myself at the piano leading worship. I sang the song the Lord gave me. The spirit of God was brooding over our congregation. I suddenly felt led to sing one more song, "On Holy Ground." As I did, the Holy Spirit graced our little congregation with His divine presence. I fell off the piano bench to the floor. The greatest joy and laughter that I have ever known in my life bubbled out of my spirit. I could feel it washing away hurt, bitterness, and anger from years of abuse and betrayal. I never knew such glory. I could not speak, only laugh and cry. Laughter is the language of great joy. The Bible speaks of joy unspeakable and full of glory. I didn't care what anyone thought for the first time in my life.

At some point, I said to myself, 'I am a pastor, worship leader, youth leader, and everything else that a pastor of a small church is required to do.' Yet, as a pastor, I didn't realize what was taking place in my church at that moment.

I thought, *Maybe I better get up and see what my congregation is doing.* I stumbled to my feet and turned to see that my entire congregation was also on the floor. They were all being filled afresh with the Holy Spirit. Little did I know that this day would be the beginning of a fresh, new, miracle ministry. Signs and wonders would follow. The day would come when I would witness the blind seeing, the deaf hearing, and even the dead raised again. God is so merciful.

It was the beginning of revival in my life. To give something to someone, you must have that on the inside. God will give His power to you if He can get it through you. He must be real to you first before He can be real through you. It all begins with a spiritual hunger.

I was involved with ministry at Palmer Correctional Facility in Palmer, Alaska. God led me into that ministry, completely unaware. Another minister needed someone to substitute for him. I thought I was an improbable substitute for him since I was a female who would be going into a men's prison.

Much to my surprise, revival broke out in the first service, and many were saved. Consequently, I was asked by the chaplain to come to the prison twice a week. Usually, the services only lasted about an hour and a half. However, they decided to give me all the time I wanted. Our services were about three hours. I found some of the most talented and intelligent people behind bars. No wonder the devil tried to destroy the lives of many in prison. One of the men, Dave, could sing the song "He Touched Me" with a beautiful baritone voice like no one I had ever heard. Others were called to preach but became bitter and backslid. Those callings were resurrected in those glorious meetings at Palmer Correctional Facility.

I will never forget that night when we had our best service. A few days before, a pastor's wife called me. She told me that she had heard that I was conducting crazy, wild services in my church and at the prison. She reminded me how I used to be a well-balanced teacher who could be trusted with the Gospel. She didn't think she would ever hear me doing anything in the flesh. Now, my reputation was at stake.

She and others were worried about me and wondered if I had gone through so much that I needed to talk to someone. She had heard that people were falling on the floor and laughing in my meetings and that the services were extremely loud and chaotic. She thought that I needed help.

I found it interesting that when I was depressed, crying, feeling sorry for myself, and almost suicidal, no one thought I needed to talk to someone. Now that I was healed on the inside and full of joy, something was wrong. I guess the religious world finds crying appropriate, but laughing, not so much. It was insinuated that maybe I needed psychiatric help. Sometimes things can get very backward in the church.

I experienced such freedom and liberty in the Holy Spirit. Life had never been better. However, the old problem resurfaced. The desire to appease people threatened my newfound freedom and liberty as I began to think about what that pastor had said. I was respected as a minister of the Gospel. It was one area I had excelled at, communicating and expounding the Word of God. Now, I was losing that reputation. 'Hadn't I experienced enough rejection in my life? Besides, maybe she was right.' I have always tried to examine constructive criticism, crucify my pride, and learn from others. The Bible speaks of the importance of having a teachable spirit. I thought 'perhaps there was some merit to what she said.'

Now it was time to go to prison for another service. I thought about the wonderful Holy Spirit services we were experiencing and decided that maybe things were, indeed, getting out of hand. After all, I was, first and foremost, a minister of the Gospel, and teaching must remain my priority. Tonight would be different, and I would only teach, teach, teach. There would be no wild Holy Ghost services.

I went to the prison with the biggest study book I could muster tucked under my arm. I meant business. Pastor Rodney Howard-Browne often mentions that some people carry a Bible big enough to choke a moose. This study manual was enough to choke a moose. We would cover from A to Z on this night. It would be an evening where I would expound the Word of God. These men would have a doctrinal, theological lesson as never before.

However, God had other ideas. Everyone knows you must begin service with at least some praise and worship. I picked up my guitar and began to sing the song "I'm So Glad Jesus Set Me Free." I never thought about the words to the song I chose. Sometimes, we get so used to the words in a song that we have known for a long time that they no longer hold new meanings. As I continued to sing about freedom, freedom reigned in that room. About thirty-five men fell out of their seats, totally drunk in the Holy Spirit.

Some of you are wondering what in the world I meant by that last statement. You must be asking, "What is getting drunk in the Holy Spirit?" I'm so glad that you did. Before Jesus left this earth, he told his disciples to wait and not do anything until they received power. They had a prayer meeting preceding the Day of Pentecost. (Acts 2) On the day of Pentecost, the Holy Spirit fell on 120 people in an upper room. The Bible says that He fell on them suddenly, and they started speaking in tongues, but that wasn't all. They were so loud that people could hear them all over the city. People came running into that room. The outsiders accused them of being drunk with alcohol. Peter stood up and told them they were not drunk like others thought. In other words, they were drunk, but not how the outsiders perceived them. Instead, they were just filled with the Holy Spirit.

One of the dictionary definitions of drunk is to be overcome with great emotion. Why would there be a comparison between being filled with the Spirit and being drunk with alcohol? In the Book of Ephesians, the comparison is made again. It says to *"not be drunk with wine in excess, but instead, be continually filled with the Holy Spirit."* It is letting us know that to be drunk with alcohol is the devil's perversion of being drunk with the Holy Spirit. It makes no sense to compare two things that have nothing in common. To compare two or more items requires that they have similarities.

Becoming drunk with the Holy Spirit and becoming drunk with alcohol have similarities. God spoke to me about that one day. Why do people go to bars to get drunk? There are many reasons, but we will cover just a few. Small-statured men who often are bullied after consuming alcohol become the biggest fighters in the world. The little 98-pound weakling suddenly feels seven feet tall. Instead of cowering in the background, he becomes bold and ready to take on anyone.

Others are looking for love in all the wrong places. They may have made fun of someone they consider unattractive. Maybe they made the typical ugly jokes like, "You're so ugly, your momma had to tie a pork-chop bone around your neck to get the dog to play with you." However, drunk, they find themselves saying, "You're so beautiful. Where have you been all my life?" When you are under another influence, you see people differently and love those who have repulsed you before.

Possibly, someone else wants to feel happy. They are so very tired of feeling depressed and want to be stimulated. They want a good laugh. Others who are usually shy decide to drink to become the show-off who dances uninhibitedly on the table at two o'clock in the morning.

Someone else is tired of living their life only on pure logic, never able to be spontaneous. They are afraid to spend anything. Maybe they are known as the proverbial tightwad. Yet, when loaded with alcohol, they become the biggest givers. You'll hear them say with a slur, "I'll pay for everyone. It's on the house."

Unfortunately, these people will wake up vomiting over a porcelain throne with a head that is throbbing. They may wake up with a black eye and broken bones to see that everything they have worked for has been stolen. They may have lost their wife, family, money, reputation, and health.

No wonder the Bible has much to say about alcohol being deceitful. We are warned to stay away from becoming intoxicated. Instead, the wonderful book of wisdom, the Bible, answers what we are searching for. It tells us what we need. It says we are to be continually filled with the Holy Spirit. When a person is filled with the Spirit, they are under another influence, but it is a holy influence. Instead of waking up sick, you get healed. Instead of losing your money, you become blessed and prospered. Instead of getting fired, you get promoted.

The shy person becomes as bold as a lion. He will never be intimidated. He can easily share his faith with others and do anything that he is called on to do. This person becomes a giver. He learns to step out in faith. He may say, "I'll pay for the whole crusade."

Maybe someone used to struggle with friendships and relationships. They don't think they like another person. However, when filled with the Spirit, they look up and say, "You're wonderful, beautiful, and talented. You have many gifts to offer. I don't know why I didn't like you. I now love you in the Lord."

Someone who has lived his whole life feeling inferior can have new freedom when filled with the Spirit. When under the influence of the Holy Spirit, I've seen people run in the service, dance in the Holy Spirit, and laugh as they've never laughed. They say, "I've never felt so free in all my life."

Others, who have spent their entire lives feeling weak and letting the devil eat their lunch, are radically changed. Once filled with The Spirit, they say to the devil, "You're not going to run over me anymore. I know who I am in Jesus Christ, and I will resist you. I have power over you. I am more than a conqueror, and greater is He that is in me than he who is in the world" (1 John 4:4). The devil runs in terror from a person full of the Holy Ghost. As you can see, there are many comparisons to be made. Why would we want the devil's cheap impostor that will kill, steal, and destroy when we can have the Holy Spirit and be abundantly blessed?

Now, back to my story of the night the fire fell as never before in prison. The in-mates fell out of their seats, drunk in the Holy Ghost, laughing, crying, shouting, and speaking in tongues, just like on the day of Pentecost. It continued for several hours. I heard one of the inmates singing *The Star-Spangled Banner*. I knew who it was because of his deep bass voice. He was a man whose height was over seven feet. I was still on the floor with my eyes closed, and I could not believe what I had heard. I thought, 'the things they are saying about me are true. It's worse than what they are saying. I have to get off the floor and get some order back in this service.'

The moment I thought this, the door to the room swung open wide. A man stood there, looking disgusted. He shouted, "Who is in charge here?" I sheepishly looked up at him from the floor and answered him. "I guess that would be me, sir." Now, he looked even more disgusted. "Well, how do you expect us to conduct an Alcoholics Anonymous meeting next door with you singing 'I Am Drunk' in here?"

I couldn't believe my ears. I had no idea that an Alcoholics Anonymous meeting was happening in the next room. The humor and satire of the moment hit me with impact. As the men in the next room were soberly repeating their twelve steps, they were interrupted by seemingly mocking words coming through the walls. One was probably saying, "I am an alcoholic and will always be an alcoholic," and then heard the words and melody of *I Am Drunk* echoing through the walls, followed by a roar of laughter. No wonder this man was upset.

In the next few moments, I assured this gentleman that I had not been notified of any meeting in the next room. I apologized for the volume of music coming through the walls. I promised him we would try to quiet down and asked the men to make the same promise. They responded with more laughter. The man did not seem to be impressed. He again slammed the door as he exited.

I picked myself up off the floor, and God continued to move in a big way. I did not know if I would be in trouble with the powers that be. I only knew that I didn't plan for things to go this way and that God was bigger than my puny plans. He reminded me that He did more to change these men's lives in a few hours than my preaching did in months.

A few days later, I received a call from the prison chaplain. My first thought was, 'Oh no, I'm about to get my marching orders.' Instead, he told me that he had never seen or heard anything like our meetings. He could not believe how many men were attending the meetings. He informed me that in all the years he was in prison, he never saw any religious group having more than two men. When two came together, one would intimidate the other with bullying until only one was left. He said that there seemed to be no interest in religious gatherings. However, the men were enthused about the meetings for the first time in his tenure there. They were changing. Their anger was gone. Instead of swearing, he saw them being respectful, praying over their food, not fighting anymore, and showing genuine concern for one another.

He told me we were noisy, and the guards were now making jokes about the men paying their bar tabs for the meetings. He said that while he and others did not understand what kind of meetings these were, there was no doubt about how many lives were being transformed for the better. He then dropped the big one on me by asking, "How would you like to start having two services weekly instead of one? We'll even let you take all the time you want in those meetings." I was overwhelmed and grateful. "Of course, I would." I was ready for revival at Palmer Correctional Center; that was exactly what we had.

I could not believe my eyes at the next service. Men were standing in a long hallway to the room where we conducted the meetings. At first, I could not understand why. Then, the realization hit me that there was no more room where we were supposed to meet. The men had doubled, and there wasn't anything but standing room. Upon asking where these men came from, I was told that we now had the Alcoholics Anonymous group with us, in addition to our previous group. I was thrilled. They said singing "I am Drunk" would be a lot more fun than saying, "I am an alcoholic and will always be an alcoholic." I did not care why they were coming; I was just thrilled they were coming. All these men were born again and baptized in the Holy Ghost in the next service. They asked me if they could testify. I couldn't wait to hear what they would say.

Chaplain Silliman being touched in revival.

One by one, they began to testify about being delivered from alcohol addiction. Some of them were addicted for thirty years or more but were instantly delivered in one moment in that powerful Holy Spirit service. Just one touch of His hand did what classes, confessions, and counseling had not been able to do. Some said they were delivered of homosexuality, witchcraft, murderous rage, and drugs. All I could do was sit there and weep and laugh with joy.

The Holy Spirit reminded me that I was willing to throw away what only He could do because I did not want to endure any more rejection. I was still concerned about what others would think. I was worried about my reputation and almost shut God's power down to save my reputation. Thank God for His mercy and grace! That sweet, small voice of the Holy Spirit on the inside of me reminded me that He healed my broken heart and gave me a message coupled with an anointing to destroy the yokes of bondage. He asked me to take that message to a lost and broken world. He reminded me that if I were ashamed of His power or message, He would take it from me and give it to someone who would not be ashamed. Through humble tears of thanksgiving, I vowed never to care about my reputation again. I would never again deny or attempt to thwart the power of God. As the Apostle Paul said in Galatians 1:10, *"Am I now trying to win the approval of human beings or God? Or am I trying to please people? If I were still trying to please people, I would not be a servant of Christ."*

From that day on, I only cared about delivering the message that He gave me. I would flow with the Holy Spirit and see God's power demonstrated. I would see others get set free the same way that I had been. I did not care what pastors, religious people, or people of the world thought. I knew what God's power could and would do if we dared to let His Spirit out of the religious box many want to keep Him in.

I do not want anyone to misunderstand. I thank God for groups like Alcoholics Anonymous and many others helping people. I believe they have their place in the world. The point that I am making is that there is One that can do far more than the natural programs. The power of Jesus Christ isn't only about discipline and willpower. It's about new life, new hearts, transformation, and relationships.

We soon realized that we had so many new converts that we needed a water baptism service at the prison. The chaplain and I became good friends, and he helped pull many strings on our behalf. I will forever be thankful to Chaplain Silliman, who later attended many of my revival meetings outside the prison. He said that seeing the results of the Holy Spirit's power that night caused him to experience more in God.

The first baptism service was one of the most incredible memories of my life. We see several instances in the Bible of people falling as though dead under the power of the Living God. The men fell under the power of God before we could dip them or immerse them in water.

The other inmates were witnesses to the power of God showing up in a big way. As a result, many were saved that day. The men were unashamed of their stand for Christ, and many witnessed their new lives. There was a lot of shouting, laughing, and crying.

The revival began in the prison. Many of these men were later transferred to other jails. They took the revival with them. I began to minister at other prisons, including women's prisons in Alaska. We saw the same things happen everywhere we went. I also had revival meetings in Alabama Correctional facilities.

A decision was made to build a new chapel at Palmer Correctional Facility because of the revival and the need for more space. I was elated and was asked to participate in the dedication, but I was out of town holding a crusade and visited the new chapel at a later date.

I have always felt that the prison ministry was the official beginning of Debbie Rich Ministries as it stands today. It was in those humble beginnings that I saw the power of God move in a big way to change hardened, criminal hearts into some of the most loving and compassionate ones. Only a true God could do that. Those men were not religious but desperate. They were hungry and thirsty, and God responded to that.

I was honored to be used in such a way. To this day, I remain friends with some of these men. I've heard reports of some entering the ministry due to their conversion during that time. I received no enumeration, applause, or reputation, yet a ministry was reborn in power and glory. I would never turn back.

Sometime after the prison revival, I received a phone call from a pastor's wife. I hadn't heard from this couple in a long time. I was going through a divorce (the big D-word in the church) while pastoring. I began to feel like the proverbial leper regarding ministerial fellowship.

Very few church people, as well as clergy, know how to deal with divorce. I believe that I was an embarrassment to them. There were many times that I longed to hear one word of encouragement. It did not come.

However, one day, I received a call from a pastor's wife. I noted a friendly voice on the other end of the line. She told me their church was hosting an evangelist for a few days and wanted to know if I would like to attend the meetings, play the piano, sing one of the revival songs I wrote, and go to dinner with them after the service. I was elated!

To this day, that woman has no idea what that phone call meant to me. I felt like my time of leprosy was over, and I was again being included in fellowship with fellow ministers. I assured her of my presence.

I had never met the evangelist before or heard him speak, but I heard of his reputation. Many said good things about him. He was a teacher at one of the Bible schools that I attended before I went there. I was looking forward to the meeting. Sure enough, the meeting was excellent, and I sensed a strong anointing upon him. I played a couple of songs on the piano. When the meeting was over, the pastor asked if I would like to join them for lunch. Again, I was thrilled to do so.

When lunch was coming to a close, I decided to ask the evangelist some practical questions. (For the sake of protecting this minister, let's call him Brother Jones.) I told him I knew he travels a lot, both in and out of the country. I also explained that I had begun going to the villages of Alaska and needed pointers about buying plane tickets. I asked him for some practical advice about traveling alone. I did not ask if he thought I was called to preach or what my chances were of succeeding. I only wanted some practical information. However, I received more than I bargained for.

He told me that he felt led to talk to me about my calling in general. To his credit, he did say that he was not prophesying but only giving his opinion. He heard what happened to my family and wanted to know why I didn't realize that this Alaskan thing would not work. He proceeded to give me three reasons why it would not.

First, I was a woman. I have said many times that if I had to do it all over again, I would have gotten up from my seat, proceeded to a mirror, and shouted, "Oh, I am a woman. I had no idea before. Thank God a man with revelation has informed me of that, or I would have been in the dark about it."

Next, he said that Alaska is too cold for a woman. Again, if he had not informed me, I would have gone on thinking that I lived in the tropics. I may have paraded around in a swimming suit or something. I have already traveled to places registering temperatures of sixty-five below zero without the wind-chill factor. I slept on village floors wrapped in only a dirty rug. I did not need a visiting evangelist from the lower forty-eight states, who came for only a few days in good weather, to tell me that Alaska gets cold. However, there was more to come.

The third reason was that I did not have a husband. If I wasn't so shocked, humiliated, and hurt, I would have laughed at the absurdity of the situation. I was not walking around thinking that I had a husband or two. I knew that I was a single lady. I guess he felt that when he pointed out the obvious that I never considered, I would stop preaching in Alaska. To heap insult upon insult, he told me that he believed I was just copying my predecessor in pastoring that church. The previous pastor went on to do village work and eventually became a missionary to Russia. He believed that I was going to the villages to copy him. He told me that I would go to a village someday, and there would be no one there to pick me up, and I would freeze or starve to death. Then, my boys would be left parentless. (This was a faith preacher. I would hate to hear what the doubt and unbelief preachers would say.) When he was finished, I could feel the wind knocked out of me. I was speechless and felt everyone could sense the tension in the air. The pastors who invited me politely dismissed themselves from the table. I sat there devastated.

Part of my problem was that ever since I was a little girl, I looked up to every minister. I put them on a pedestal. If they said something, it was equivalent to God saying it, even if they only gave an opinion. I was in this man's service and knew God anointed him. He preached a wonderful message. It was difficult for me to believe he could walk out of the anointing and say something that was not of God. I could not separate the two. I wrestled with this situation. I grew more discouraged than I had ever been in my entire life about the call of God. I almost threw in the towel.

A couple believed in the call on my life from the moment they met me. You have already heard their names, Noel and Edna DeVries. I went to their office as quickly as I could and told them everything. Edna grabbed me and shook me as only she could. She said, "Now you listen to me. Yes, he's a man of God, but even men of God sometimes miss it. He told you that he was not prophesying but only giving his opinion. He should not have listened to gossip and hearsay. He should not have given his opinion when a minister's opinion carries so much weight. If he didn't get it from God, he should not even mention it. The first time we saw you in our little church, the Lord spoke to us and said, 'This lady is anointed and will go all over the world.' We said to each other that we were going with you. We see the kind of call and anointing you carry. The devil has tried to destroy it, but we won't let him. We want you to go to our house, take the phone off the hook, get alone with God, and write down what He tells you. Do you understand me?" I did just that.

Edna is one of the strongest women I know in every way. She was a single parent (before her marriage to Noel), a state senator, a Republican Party's national committee representative, has served as the borough's mayor (Alaska has boroughs, not counties), and is presently the Palmer City mayor. Edna has served in many other political offices, ran a successful real estate office, a Christian bookstore, and a used clothing store. She is a mother, confidant, and counselor to many people like myself. Edna and Noel found each other and married in Alaska. Noel has been like a father to me. We have had many conversations on long road trips and in their home that have helped sustain me all these years. They are givers of their finances, love, wisdom, counsel, and encouragement like few whom I have ever known.

Consequently, I went to their house, took the phone off the hook, sought God with all my heart, and received my answer. The Lord reminded me that when I was a little girl, He showed me how I would preach to many tribes and nations. He told me He saw my hunger and hurt while suffering through abuse and sustained me through it. He gave Bruce a choice, but he rebelled. This did not negate the call on my life, however. I was in a place where no one but God could raise me up now. I had no contacts, money, newsletters, or notoriety. God would give me favor, and no one but myself would be able to stop me. He would open doors that no one could close. He would do it for His glory to show people that He is no respecter of persons. People would know that what He will do for one

Noel & Edna Devries, with me, at Community Hall.

hungry individual, He will do for others if they demonstrate the same hunger and thirst.

He said He would be my provider and a Father to my children. He told me to trust Him and never look back. I would be amazed. The ministry would increase rapidly in the sphere of influence, miracles, anointing, and provision. He told me to get my approval, acceptance, and guidance from Him, not any man. He reminded me that even the greatest of men would disappoint me.

I wrote down and recorded what He spoke to me. I left the DeVries home knowing I was called and on the right path. I would never look back. How little did I realize that the day would come in a few weeks when another man of God would confirm what the Lord spoke to me, word for word. First, I had to get it directly from Him because I have been too susceptible to what others thought, especially great men and women of God. God can only confirm what He has already spoken to our hearts through people. These are not Old Testament days where we have to go to the prophet to find our donkeys. People have a wrong concept about getting a word from a man or woman, but that is a subject for another book. One mighty man of God told me to forget the call of God. In just a few weeks, another mightily anointed man of God told me to go for it. What should I do now? Find a third one so that I could take two out of three. No, this is not Las Vegas. We need to be sensitive, hear the Lord, and obey Him no matter what word anyone else gives us.

At the same time that God was doing a brand new thing in my life, I found He was doing it in the lives of others. After years of living in Alaska, I received a call from a dear friend named Jean Thomas. Jean and I had kindred hearts when it came to revival. Mutual friends often told us about each other and suggested that we meet. It happened when we were in the same church service, walking toward each other, when the power of the Holy Spirit hit us and knocked us both to the ground. We found ourselves lying on our backs, on the floor. When we got up, we introduced ourselves. We became fast friends and co-revivalists.

Jean called to tell me that a man in Anchorage was conducting meetings. The meetings were powerful, with many people being saved, baptized in the Holy Spirit, healed, and filled with unspeakable joy. She said the sessions were like what people were experiencing in my meetings and that I needed to go and see for myself. I told her I would love to, but I had too many responsibilities. I was still pastoring, required to be at the prison two nights a week, and had a village trip planned. I was supposed to leave in a couple of days. Besides, Anchorage was over fifty-five miles away, and it was the middle of winter in Alaska. It would take me over an hour and a half to drive to the meeting on icy winter roads. I lived in the mountains and had to pass through a valley laden with moose in the wintertime. Those animals can total a car. My car was already totaled, and I didn't know how many more it could take. I had a million reasons that it would be impossible.

Alaskan Ministry Team

Just when I was listing these excuses, she said something that changed everything. She said, "Oh, but Debbie, the glory that is there!" Before she could finish her sentence, the word glory carried the Shekinah glory of God tangibly through the phone wires. It hit me with force and knocked me to the ground, where I lay laughing, crying, and shaking. When I regained my composure, I stood with the phone still in my hand and said, "All right. I'll cancel everything and go." The next day, I rearranged my responsibilities, postponed the village trip, and went to Anchorage to attend the meetings that would forever change my life.

I asked Jean if she knew the name of the man conducting the meetings. She told me that he was from South Africa and his name was Rodney Howard-Browne. Instantly, I recalled the man. When he first left his native nation of South Africa, he came to Rhema, the Bible school I graduated from, while I was still a student. I loved his preaching on hunger and the coming revival. He was my favorite visiting minister while I was at Rhema. I wondered if I would ever hear him again. I had no idea where he was or if he was still in the country. He resurfaced in Alaska, halfway across the world from his native South Africa. The last time I heard him speak, he was speaking of a coming revival, and I wanted it.

I never witnessed the power of God in such a profound way or with such widespread magnitude. The crowds measured about one thousand people every night. Young people were shaking, laughing, crying, and falling out in the Spirit. Entire families were being filled together.

I will never forget one particular family who would later become friends of mine. Their last name was Gugle. They had seven children, five girls and two boys. As the man of God called them to the front, not one of them could speak. They were under the influence of the Holy Spirit. They were speaking in tongues, crying, and vibrating under the power of God. Anyone watching this family knew that God was all over them.

When Dr. Rodney invited those who wanted to accept Jesus Christ as their savior, people came running to accept Him. The crowds grew. We witnessed many miraculous healings. Joy erupted many times, as the entire audience was overcome in supernatural laughter, not because anything was funny but because they were overcome with joy. I never saw that much power displayed in such a big way. Even though I was experiencing the same thing, I did not realize it was happening on a broader scale anywhere else. I thought God was moving in my life in such a way because I had been through so much and needed deep healing. Little did I know that this was a move of God beginning to take place from city to city, nation to nation, and continent to continent.

God, in His mercy, allowed me to taste this revival early, in its beginning stages. Many would come to know of this great refreshing event taking place all over the world. My hunger reached God, and He reciprocated. For this is a move of deep calling unto deep, and God answered the hungry heart with joy unspeakable and full of glory.

Even though I was already touched in such a profound way, I still wanted more. In the meetings with Dr. Rodney Howard-Browne, I became even hungrier. From the very first meeting, I was carried out, lost in the presence of God almost every night. My car was often left at the church while someone else gave me a ride home. Most of the time, Noel and Edna brought me back to their home. Sometimes, Jean and Bill Thomas would be the hosts. Other times, when I could drive, I would ask God for help to get home in one piece while I was laughing, crying, and in tongues. I was like that all the way home for an entire hour and a half. I didn't mind the drive when God was with me in the car. I went to every meeting. There were two a day, morning and night.

Brother Rodney announced that he had a pastor's luncheon on Friday. At first, I had no desire to go. I knew everyone else would be with their spouses. I was the only female pastor, and the rumors were flying. Everyone knew that I was going through a divorce, and I was embarrassed. After all, what would everyone think? Besides, he said that it was for pastors. I just announced that I was resigning from my church to be a full-time evangelist. He did not say it was an evangelist's luncheon. I told Noel and Edna that I didn't think I should go. As usual, they insisted that I should. They said that as a South African, they thought he meant minister's luncheon and just used the term Pastor's luncheon because he was from another nation. They reminded me I had very little fellowship as a woman pastor in a small Alaskan town. They said it would do me good and encouraged me to go. Reluctantly, I did.

Sure enough, everyone was part of a couple but me. I knew very few people in the room and wished I hadn't come. Dr. Rodney was eating lunch, telling funny stories, and not being particularly spiritual. At one point, he looked at me and said, "Lady."

I thought he was talking to someone on my left or right, and I looked at them. He then said, "No, you. Right there."

I looked up and realized for sure that he was looking at me. I questioningly asked, "Me?"

He assured me, "Yes."

He continued to tell me that he had a word for me from the Lord. My first thought was, 'Oh, no. Not again. Let me guess. I am a lone woman. Alaska is cold. I will starve to death, and my children will have no parents. It's too late. Go home, be a mom, and get those kids around grandparents where they belong. Forget the call of God.'

But before I could finish guessing, he began to prophesy. He said, "I don't care who came to town a few weeks ago and discouraged you and told you that you couldn't fulfill the call of God. They were wrong. They looked at you by natural standards, not what God is doing in your life. They are reacting to hearsay. I have been sent by God to tell you just the opposite. God has seen your hunger and heard your prayers. Everything He told you as a child, He is about to do. He's seen how you have been abused but would not bend.

"Your husband could have been at your side in the call but rebelled and chose another way. That's not your fault. The ministry is about to explode and will be an international ministry. You have no contacts, no newsletter, and no money, so God will do it all. He will raise you for His glory, and people will see what He's done for you, He will do for them. He is no respecter of persons. He will be a Father to your children, He will be your provider, and He will give you unusual favor that all will recognize. It will be a ministry of such proportions as others whom you have heard about." (He began to name well-known ministers I will not mention here.)

When he finished, everyone in the room looked at me as if to say, "Her?

You've got to be kidding. I'm the one who should be getting that word, not her. She's divorced, and have you seen her car? It's totaled. She's a mom of three sons and has nothing. There is no way that can be fulfilled." However, it's just like God saying, "You want to bet? Watch what I will do through her!" And so He has.

Needless to say, I left that meeting very glad that I came. Once again, I thank God for Noel and Edna, who would never let me give up.

Pastor Rodney (as I now call him) remained in Anchorage for two weeks, and I knew I would never be the same. I loved the joy, the salvations, the healings, miracles, manifestations of the Holy Ghost, and the presence of God. However, the man did something I wasn't sure I liked. He taught before every offering on giving and stewardship.

It wasn't that I disagreed with anything that he was teaching. It was some of the best teachings I have ever heard. I believed in giving. I knew that it was a Biblical principle that was usually ignored. After all, I graduated from a Bible school that emphasized the blessings of God, and we were taught that He wanted to prosper us so that we would have more to give and share with his people.

I had an entire eight-week course on the subject while in Bible school. I got an A on the test. I already knew this subject and thought that I didn't need anyone else to teach me. My critical attitude had more to do with the fact that it was all right to teach it in a Bible school but not in a church service. I never saw anyone take the time to do that before an offering. I perhaps saw a few people take about five minutes, but this man took 30 minutes to sometimes an hour to teach before the offering. I wondered, "If this is how long his offering teaching is, how long will the real message be?" Also, I couldn't wait to get back to the things I came for joy, miracles, and the presence of God. Besides, my pride said that someone who got an A on the test doesn't need to listen to someone else teaching it.

Have you ever stopped to wonder about how stupid pride can make each one of us? I had double trouble; pride and stupidity, double whammies. I was probably the poorest in the auditorium among the thousand in attendance. The other people had their own homes, and I was getting ready to move into Noel and Edna's home. Others had cars that were not totaled. I came with only fifty cents to my name. When others were putting in one thousand dollar checks, I only had two quarters to plunk. I had three children to feed and didn't have enough for a gallon of milk or gas money for the rest of the week. However, I thought, I didn't need this because I got an A on the test. How dumb can you be and still breathe?

Suddenly, the wonderful Holy Spirit interrupted my stupidity, pride, and religious spirit. He spoke to me in the way that only He can. He said, "I've sent this man from his native country of South Africa to the United States, all the way to Alaska, for you, Debbie!" I knew that no Debbie was sitting to my right or left, so I thought I better pay attention. He further said, "I've called you to go all over the world and preach My Gospel, and you don't even have enough to go down the street. How do you think that you're going to do that? On your A's?" (God has quite the sense of humor. I think that He may have used a double play on words with the A's thing. Just a thought.) "You may have an anointing and a call, but you have to have a natural means to take that anointing around the world. This man has your answer if you surrender your pride and arrogance and repent this moment!"

I began to tremble in my seat, like someone shaking under conviction before they met Christ as Savior. The revelation became as clear as could be. "I have been ignorant. Forgive me, Lord." He did. I remember the moment like it was yesterday. It was as though the anointing of the Holy Spirit was obliterating years of poverty mentality around my heart and mind. The Bible says in Isaiah 10:27 that *"the anointing destroys the yoke of bondage."* It did. I wanted to shout. I knew that I would never be poor again. God set me free, and *"He whom the Son sets free is free indeed"* (John 8:36). As the offering was taken, I decided to give my last fifty cents.

I knew when I plunked those two quarters in the bucket, everyone would hear the change hitting. It was embarrassing when people were writing out big checks on my left and right. I knew that because they ensured I could see what they were writing. I also thought about how my children needed milk, and I needed gas in my car. I could keep that fifty cents until it was enough for either of those things, but I knew I would always be in this condition. Instead, I chose to give it to God like the woman in the Bible with the last two mites and trust Him to multiply it. I did and never looked back. I can tell you that I have lived the last thirty years off my giving, and it began that night.

As I repented, the Lord began to speak to me about how He wanted me to teach on the subject of giving the same way. I was, again, surprised. I protested and reminded Him why that would not work in the places that I went to. The native people are quite poor and survive on subsistence living. I didn't think they would appreciate some white woman coming into their village and teaching them about giving. I could see it wasn't even going over well in the large charismatic church Pastor Rodney was in. Several pastors stood in the back of the church, shaking their heads at him while he taught. He later said that it was all he could do not to administer the five-fold ministry to them (as he showed his fist). Religious people resist change, even when presented with the truth. Many think that there is only one way to receive an offering. They believe we should not mention giving or money, pass the plate quickly before anyone notices that we are doing it, and have Sister Suzy sing while we get this part of the service out of the way. People do not like change!

I told the Lord that I didn't think this would work in small Alaskan villages and churches where missionaries go and refuse even to receive an offering, let alone teach on it first. The Lord responded, "If this Gospel only works in large metropolitan cities and large churches, it is not the Word of God. It must work for the red man and the black man like it does the white man, or it is not the Word of God. It must work for the woman like it does the man, or it is not the Word of God." Then, He said that if I refused to teach it, He would hold me personally responsible for their poverty.

While I had the audacity to argue this point with God, Pastor Rodney walked off the platform in front of everyone and confronted me with what God was saying to me. He said, "God is setting you free from poverty right now." I nodded. He then said, "He is telling me to tell you that you are to teach it this same way everywhere you go. Also, He said to tell you that this Word must work in the Alaskan village and for the red man like it works in the metropolitan USA for the white man, or it is not the Word of God." While I tried to say something, he told me to be quiet and listen to what God was saying. He continued and said that if I refused, I would be held personally responsible for their poverty. My mouth hung open as he told me word for word what God had already spoken to my heart. *"In the mouth of two or three witnesses let every word be established"* (2 Corinthians 13:1). From that day to this one, I have taught it in 46 nations, all over Alaska, and all over this country. I will not be held responsible for anyone's poverty.

Little did I realize that these meetings were just the beginning of a long, wonderful relationship with Pastors Rodney and Adonica Howard-Browne. Their encouragement and prophetic words of instruction launched me forth with holy fire.

I knew I had to take this revival fire to the villages of Alaska, the entire state, this nation, and the world. I remembered that God spoke to me and showed me, as a child, that I would preach to multitudes of people worldwide. I realized that it was time to launch this ministry to the nations.

At that time, Noel and Edna DeVries, my right hands in my church, told me that God spoke to them about my sons and me moving in with them. I thanked them profusely but reminded them that I had never heard of two families living in the same home and still loving one another after a few months. They laughed and reminded me that God spoke to them. I relented and told them of my plans for evangelistic ministry. They offered not only for me to live with them but to help as much as they could with my children while I traveled. It was a God thing. We agreed that it was God's answer to launching this ministry.

I will never forget an incident that broke my heart right in the middle of all the wonderful, miraculous things God was doing. My youngest son, Caleb, was only nine years old at the time. He was given a puppy that we named Wimpy. She was a small dog of mixed breeding, part Schipperke and part Lhasa Apso. She had an underbite that caused her to look like she was perpetually smiling. She was as smart as a whip. I taught her to peel that lip back and look like she was in a full-blown smile when I said "joy." Caleb loved that dog and didn't have many reasons to smile after experiencing his family breakup.

He walked up to me with a worried expression, fighting back the tears. He asked, "Mom, will I have to give up Wimpy when we move?" I didn't want to answer him but knew that we had to. I drew a deep breath and told him we would have to ask someone else to take care of her for a while. He hugged his dog and began to cry. I turned my head and shed my own tears. While I had the supernatural joy on the inside, there were still many natural moments of anguish while watching the pain in my children's eyes. I thought of how I longed for that wonderful Beaver Cleaver family. I thought I was getting that when I waited for God's man of faith and power to marry. I was wrong, but I had to depend on God to carry us through this, as never before.

Noel and Edna had limited space in their home. They were now moving four additional people into their home. They didn't have enough beds or bedrooms. Noel took care of that problem in a very practical, Noel-way. He built beds out of plywood. He made bunk beds for my children.

My room was a small half-bath that they were planning to plumb but never got around to it yet. It would be my bedroom. They put a small dresser in it against the small twin bed. I had to squeeze between or jump over the dresser to get into the bed. It's a good thing that I'm short. If my head came down from the pillow, my feet were touching the opposite wall. I was so thankful to have a bed and a dresser and grateful for my children to have beds and a roof. It was the small beginning of a worldwide, international ministry. No wonder the Bible admonishes us to *"not despise the days of small beginnings."*

Noel and Edna were so gracious that they told me that having me there was like having the ark of the covenant, of the Old Testament, in their house. I appreciated their humor. Noel and Edna's son, Gordon, is the same age as my oldest son, Joshua. They went to school together and were best friends. Gordon and Joshua studied together, skied together, and were in car wrecks together.

Sometimes, when the enemy is trying to stop you, his attacks seem relentless. While the prison ministry was thriving, I knew not to let my guard down with some of the inmates. I had to attend classes to ensure we would follow all the rules and we wouldn't do the wrong thing. Common sense goes a long way. I received a call from an inmate one afternoon, requiring my counsel. I was beginning to trust this man enough to guide him in preaching. He felt the call of God in his life, and I wanted to encourage it. His name was Richard. He worked on preparing a sermon and wanted me to critique it before he delivered it. I knew that it was very important to him. I also knew better than to visit a men's correctional facility alone. Noel and Edna were busy that afternoon, so I enlisted the help of my eldest son, Joshua, and Noel and Edna's son, Gordon.

After a short visit to the prison, we prepared to leave. Joshua asked to drive the car home. He had his learner's permit, and I usually let him drive anywhere with me in the passenger's seat. I already had my hand on the driver's door when he asked if he could drive us back. On the inside, I heard, 'No, not today.' However, I let reasoning interfere with the Holy Spirit's direction. I asked myself, 'Why not? I let him drive any other time. Why should this be any different?' I looked at him and said, "I guess so." We switched places. That was an almost fatal mistake for all of us.

So often, we wonder why God allows bad things to happen to good people and have no idea that our decisions and ignoring His leadership have gotten us into some precarious places. I hated to say no to any of my boys while they were going through so much. I ignored that still, small voice of the Holy Spirit.

We started down that winding, cork-screw road that led to and from the prison. It is a gravel road, and it is slick. Josh was not used to all of those conditions at one time. He had too much speed going around the first bend. I started to tell him to slow down but could not get the words out before he lost control on the gravel, and the car became airborne on that mountain road. I can remember calling his name out at that moment. He still jokes about how loud and how long his name was coming up from my throat in panic as J-O-S-H-U-AAAAAA echoed through the woods.

We stopped when we made an impact with a tree located part-way down the mountain. When we gathered our wits about us, we stepped out to see my totaled car. The worst damage was to the only door where none of us was sitting. However, the car was a mess. People were on the scene within minutes. Someone was driving down the mountain behind us, saw us lose control, heard the impact, and did not expect anyone to be alive. Instead, all three of us walked out unscathed, without a cut or bruise. That's our mighty God at work. Our angels were working overtime that day.

I contacted my insurance company to learn that I had a new problem. The car was recently purchased the night before our separation and against my will. It was a brand-new Chevrolet Cavalier. I was only paying for it for a few months, with nothing down. I no longer remember all the specifics of the choices the insurance company offered me, but none were suitable. I didn't have money for another car and elected to keep it just like it was. They said they would pay it off but not fix it. The roof caved in, the windows gone, the hood smashed, and the grill bent in, but the tires and engine were still running. I found myself saying, "World, here I come in my little smashed-up car. You still haven't stopped me, devil."

That car was a continual source of embarrassment to my three sons. They begged me to drop them off a block or so from their school, even in sub-zero temperatures. My oldest ended up taking it to prom. A man's gotta do what a man's gotta do. It's pretty hard to walk a girl to prom when it's cold outside. I knew the car wasn't the greatest tool for telling people, "God has set me free from poverty. What He's done for me, He will do for you."

Josh, going to prom in the totaled car.

It's good that my parents weren't there to ask, "What will people think?" I went to the junkyard and purchased a black hood for a red car. At least it was now a classy two-toned car. We put plastic in the place of windows. It wasn't a bad beginning for an international ministry preaching that God desires to bless us and make us a blessing. I learned many lessons about humility and dependency along the way. We don't change the Word of God to match our experience. We change our experience to match the Word of God.

While Joshua was doing pretty well, the other two boys felt a little lost. My middle son was much shyer, and I learned many years later how hard the entire Alaskan experience was on him. He was doing well in Oklahoma with school, church, and many friends. This was when I was attending Bible school. He did not want to leave but was afraid to voice that. In perfect 20/20 hindsight, I wish I had spent more time with him and recognized what was happening.

My middle son's (Billy's) high school graduation from Palmer High, AK.

I finally was able to purchase this home for us in Palmer, AK.

I had to figure out how God wanted me to launch this international ministry, where my office would be, and how to get incorporated. I had to learn how to get invitations and how to make a living at this for my children. I needed to feed and clothe my children. I wanted to help with expenses at Noel and Edna's. Some days, it all seemed so impossible that I wanted to pull the covers over my head and go back to sleep. The weather did not help with the temptation to stay in bed. When you look out and see only snow, cloudiness, cold temperatures, and dusk in the middle of the day, you want to stay in bed.

Whenever I heard about Bruce and Connie, their engagement, and subsequent marriage, I just wanted to stay in bed. Then I would hear about a pastor discussing how ministry was over for me. God used Edna to remind me that this ministry would never take off if I didn't get up and face my fears, disappointments, and insecurities and work with God to make this happen. She would simply holler down the stairs, "Debbie, you need to get up and go to the office and call pastors today." I agreed on the outside but felt sorry for myself on the inside, thinking she didn't understand my situation.

Meanwhile, I began to work at the used clothing store, now owned by Noel and Edna. A lady who previously attended my church donated the store to her as a tax write-off. Noel and Edna were registered as a non-profit ministry and were able to add other ministry branches to it. They ran a very successful real-estate business and a Christian bookstore. They helped me with the prison ministry and ran a used clothing store. Their real estate office was in one part of the rented building, the used clothing store in another part, and my small ministry office, in still another. It wasn't long before we didn't know who was working for whom, as all the business and ministry arms intermingled. Instead of forming my own non-profit, I merged with their non-profit. They paid me from the used clothing store, I paid them to help me in ministry, and my son jokingly called it all money laundering. He said I would be fine if ever audited because even the IRS would say it's too complicated to figure out. He still makes jokes about it to this day. However, it all worked for that moment in time by the grace of God.

I saved up the money I made from the clothing store to buy plane tickets to the villages of Alaska. Alaskans call those villages the bush because of the rugged terrain in the interior and coastal areas. I was profoundly touched in revival by the fire of God, much like Moses at the burning bush. I needed a name for the ministry, and Burning Bush Ministries seemed to fill the order for more than one reason. The Holy Spirit met me in such a powerful way at the lowest point of my life. Also, I knew that I was called to go to the Bush of Alaska and many outlying places around the globe. Thus, Burning Bush Ministries became a subsidiary of Noel DeVries Ministries. It saved me the expense of incorporating in the beginning; because of Noel and Edna, I now had a roof over my head, a job, and a ministry. God certainly joined us together.

We placed my first ministry sign with a logo outside Noel and Edna's real estate office in Palmer, Alaska.

A source of income for Alaskans is the yearly dividend. It comes from the interest made from the investment of oil tax dollars. Each Alaskan receives a dividend check that varies in size depending on different factors each year. When I lived in Alaska, the dividend check was about $1,300 per person for each family member. At the same time it came out, usually, in October or November, some of the Alaskan airline companies ran sale specials on tickets.

Miraculously, several people came into the office and offered me their dividends to buy plane tickets to the Bush. It was the beginning of my God continuing to be my provider. He proved Himself faithful to me over and over again. The villages were ignited with revival. The revival continued to burn in the prisons. Word of mouth carried the testimonies of revival to almost every town and village in Alaska. Soon, I had more ministry than I could handle and had to pinch myself before going to sleep to ensure that I was not dreaming. This is what I lived and breathed, taking revival to the hungry and the thirsty.

SEVEN

REAWAKENING THE VILLAGES

My first village trip was to a small village in the interior of Alaska called Venetie. Several other people were with me. We stayed in a hut with no running water, no indoor toilet, and very unique and interesting food. I returned alone later in the winter, without the team.

The airplane trip was quite an adventure. It was a two-seater with no restroom. The pilot suddenly turned to me and said, "What would you do if I had a heart attack right now?" I was taken aback and replied with another question. "Why are you having symptoms?" He answered, "No, but if that were to happen someday, you would be in trouble. I want you to take the rudder on this plane and pull us up over that mountain in front of us." I had no idea how much force to exert or how quickly I should pull back. I was shaking and told him I would rather believe God that any pilot traveling with me would be in perfect health to take me where I needed to go. That was easier to believe than to believe I could safely pull that airplane over the mountain we were approaching.

When we were close to the village, I asked, "Where is the airport?" He laughed hysterically and replied, "Lady, there is no airport down there." I tried to correct my stupidity with, "I didn't exactly mean airport. I meant airstrip." He laughed again and replied, "There is no airstrip. See that gravel road covered with ice? We are going to attempt to land on it." I did not particularly like the word attempt at that moment. I asked him how often he was able to accomplish it, and he said, "Most of the time." I felt like I was in some adventure movie. That was only the beginning of my new missionary experience. Yes, he made a pretty good landing on the icy road.

From Left - Mary Glacier (another minister), myself, and my pilot.

I had made arrangements with the village people before leaving for Venetie. The day I arrived was freezing. I did not know where I was supposed to go when I exited the plane or with whom I was supposed to stay. I walked down the gravel road, dragging my luggage behind. No one greeted me. When I finally saw someone on the road, I asked where to go, and they said, "Oh, you are the missionary? We forgot what day you were coming. I'm not sure that our chief will even let you stay. You had better go get tribal permission." My pilot had already departed and would not return for a week. The situation could get precarious if I was not permitted to stay.

I had a lot to learn. The fact that I had already made arrangements seemed irrelevant to everyone I spoke with. I finally found the chief and asked for permission, which was granted after some persuasion.

I was directed to a hut and found out it had no running water, and a wood stove was the only heat source. I was told that I could light the fire myself. I wondered if I looked like a Boy Scout to them. I had no idea what to do! It was a cast iron stove. I retrieved wood from a wood pile outside and, after several tries, was successful in producing some sparks with matches. Those sparks eventually became a flame. I congratulated myself and thought I could star in the *Survivor* series. Finally, it was a roaring fire, and the outside of the cast iron stove became bright orange. I panicked. I didn't want my first newsletter to read, "Evangelist lights village on fire, literally." I ran outside, scooped snow with my hands to douse the fire, and accidentally put the entire fire out. It was a long, cold night.

I grabbed a dirty old rug and wrapped it around me as I slept on the floor. When I awoke to use the bathroom, I remembered that I had to walk down a gravel road to the outhouse. I hoped that I would not encounter a grizzly. However, my joy in preaching the Gospel to hungry, thirsty people overcame discomfort or apprehension. I had waited for this moment.

After that first night's meeting, I lay on the village floor and talked to the Lord about my dreams for the future. I knew what I was called to do. I was in

RESURRECTED

The stove in Venetie, AK.

How I love the native people of Alaska.

faith and believing for big things. I knew it was important to be grateful for where I was now. I cried and laughed at the same time with extreme gratitude. My mind was filled with the memories of the night's meeting. The Village Council Hall was packed with hungry, precious, native people. They were born again, baptized in the Holy Spirit, delivered from drugs and alcohol, healed from broken hearts and physical ailments, and filled with incredible joy. Young people and children laughed and danced in the early hours of the morning.

This is why I was born, and this is why the enemy tried to detour and destroy my life. But he could not! It did not matter where I slept, what I ate, or if anyone would ever know my name. All that mattered was that they would know the name of Jesus Christ.

I made many mistakes along the way. Thank God that He rescued me time and time again. It is essential not to take yourself too seriously and to have an active prayer life and a good sense of humor. One of my first mistakes was not knocking loudly enough at the door of the only outhouse I could find. I opened it to find the elderly Episcopal priest sitting in it. I screamed, excused myself, and ran. Later, I discovered that I would have services in his Episcopal church. The priest's eyesight was poor, but upon introducing myself later while shaking hands, he said, "Haven't we met somewhere before?" I replied with "Possibly" and went on. Thank God for divine favor. Everything was well worth it. What a revival we had!

These days broadened my taste palate. Early on, I was offered a bowl of soup. They told me that the meat in it was moose. I had no problem with that. I had eaten moose steak, stroganoff, and other moose dishes. I made the mistake of asking what part of the moose. They said, "The head." That was not quite what I expected, but I was even more surprised as they got more specific. My friend, Jean Thomas, was with me on that trip. I turned to her and whispered, "Maybe it's from the nostril." I was only joking but found out that I was prophesying. The person turned to me and said that it was made out of the nostrils of the moose. I hoped that the moose did not have a cold. I noticed that there was an unusual burnt taste and found out why. They use charcoal to burn the nostril hairs off. I found that very interesting. I also noted the broth's floaties and to not find out exactly what they were. Then the greatest surprise came. I was the guest of honor and would receive a second bowl. Yum-yum. I was now a missionary.

I learned of another delicacy in some of the coastal villages, like Bethel. This one is a dessert. Who doesn't like dessert? When I heard the word ice cream, I became even more excited. 'How different could Eskimo ice cream be? Isn't there a brand of ice cream bar named that?' They placed a big bowl in front of me. I excitedly dipped in and went into immediate shock and revulsion. I managed not to gag or vomit with the help of the Lord. The consistency was that of lard. I found out the reason for that. This ice cream was made out of whale blubber (a little fishy tasting), with berries added. It's not the recipe my relatives used for homemade ice cream in Nebraska, but it was theirs, and I was sitting in their home. So, down the hatch it went, with much prayer and supplication. I was told that when they couldn't get whale blubber, they purchased cans of Crisco shortening. I've had it both ways. I prefer the whale blubber. However, with either one, my lips became so slippery that I wondered if I could preach. My upper and lower lips were having difficulty finding each other.

I went to potlatches (the native version of potlucks) and learned to eat *muktuk* (again, whale blubber soaked in seal oil) with the texture of extremely tough jerky. I came to realize that native people have extremely hard teeth to be able to chew. I had to wait until they were not looking and spit it out. Of course, I was always given a new supply. I experienced some of the sweetest times of hospitality and fellowship at those potlatches.

Nebraska seemed a long way away. It was more than worth it, though. One of the nights in Bethel, at a Pentecostal Holiness Church, a literal wind from heaven blew through the place. All the young people heard it and began to run to the altar, shaking under the power of God and giving their hearts to the Lord. A precious elderly grandmother fell to the ground laughing so hard that I thought laughter would kill her.

She was as wide as she was tall. She left the church after midnight but forgot her homemade, furry Eskimo mittens (known as *mukluks*) under the pew. She came back for them but hesitated at the door because she knew that if she went back to the front of the church, God's power would fall upon her again. It was late. She had to walk home. I decided to walk to the back of the church and take her mittens to her. When I handed them to her, the power of God hit her again as she fell to the floor, laughing, rolling, and crying until about 2 a.m. Those were wonderful days and nights; I came to love the native people of Alaska, and they loved me.

One of the women who attended my church in Sutton was originally from the coastal village of Barrow, now called Utqiagvik, the northernmost city in the United States. It borders the Arctic Ocean and is the center of Alaskan governmental activity and jobs. It is in an area called the North Slope, which is the beginning of the Alaskan pipeline. This lady had relatives there and told me about the need for revival in Barrow.

These extremely northern coastal villages have unique problems. It is frigid beyond imagination. Your nasal hairs will freeze in the winter when exposed to the outside air. Facial skin must be protected and covered or be subject to frostbite. Cars are plugged into engine heaters or left running all night. Tires burst from the cold. There are no trees because it is too far north, above the northern tree line. There is nothing but blowing snow in the winter. It looks like a white desert. Even in the summer, the temperature averages only about forty degrees. In the winter, it can easily dip into the minus fifties. I was there more than once in December. One of those times, I stayed for two weeks. At noon, it was still as black as midnight. The sun never comes up in the winter. Domestic violence, incest, drug addiction, and alcoholism are rampant. Wife-beating, suicide, and adultery are commonplace.

The more I learned, the more I became burdened to reach the precious people of that town with the love of God. The lady from my church, originally from Barrow, knew the Assembly of God pastor in the town. She gave me his contact information, and I called him. I experienced something unexpected; he raised his voice so loudly on the phone that Noel and Edna could hear him in the next room. He told me he did not want me to come to his town. He had heard of Rodney Howard-Browne and wanted no part of him or anyone like him and had no desire for signs and wonders. He added he would run me out of town if I chose to come anyway. He was one of the very first pastors that I dared to call. After that day, I didn't know if I would ever make another call.

The Lord continued to speak to me about going to Barrow. I decided to go and scout out the land. I would rent a hall if I couldn't preach in a church. I took

Jean Thomas with me again. We began to have some meetings, but that pastor made it very difficult. He sent spies to the meetings. He did his best to run me out of town. He had a lot of real estate property in the town and a lot of connections. I admit I was a bit discouraged, but some lives were touched, and I vowed to return. I learned a lot on that trip.

Meanwhile, I heard that a huge native meeting was taking place down the coast at Wainwright, Alaska. I bought two more plane tickets for Jean and myself and set out for Wainwright. It was also in the North Slope Borough, about a hundred miles down the coast from Barrow.

I am standing alongside the Arctic ocean, frozen over.

Most people have no understanding of the expense involved in traveling within Alaska. We bought plane tickets from Anchorage to Fairbanks, which is in the interior of Alaska. The next plane took us to Barrow. Usually, the first plane would cost about $600 to $800 in the early nineties. The smaller plane to Wainwright would be another $200 to $300 apiece. If you took someone with you (which is wise traveling as a woman in the state), you have now spent about $2,000 to minister in a small village at your own expense.

But we were determined. No one sponsored us. I only asked to be able to teach and receive offerings for each service. The same lady who had told me about Barrow now informed me that her aunt lived in Wainwright and would be happy to host us in her home. The large "singspiration" (where each village would have representatives sing songs in the evening services, followed by a potlatch) was held at the Presbyterian Church. She told us that we would have the opportunity to meet many native people. Even if I was not allowed to minister, I could make contacts for future ministry. That is an expensive way to do it, but a white woman coming into a native territory uninvited must be very patient and cautious.

We arrived at the airport with no one to meet us or tell us where to go. That was our first surprise. We did not even have a last name for the aunt who was supposed to host us. There was a raging blizzard outside, and we knew no one in the town. I believed that God was leading us. I walked up to the person in the small, rudimentary airport and described the little we knew about our hostess.

He felt he knew the person we spoke of from our description and asked someone to drive us there. Thank God it was the right place and the right person.

The small hut was so hot that I got a new sermon on hell while trying to sleep. These places are often too warm because they only have a wood-burning stove for heat. Those are difficult to regulate, and there is no thermostat. They do not dare let the fire go out. Our hostess, Annie, was elderly, and her internal metabolism was not working properly. It was frigid outside, and people wanted a lot of heat when they finally got inside. It was difficult to sleep in that heat, but I was thankful we were not sitting in the airport or stuck outside in the blizzard. The native woman was extremely gracious and kind but elderly and frail. Because of that, the place was not clean, and we faced some challenges. When you mix wood-burning stoves with what they call honey buckets (inside buckets used as toilets, without water or flushing), you have a very unpleasant odor. However, I was called to these people, and I would endure. Jean was domestic by nature and decided to clean the hut.

We had no transportation, so we asked the direction of the church and set out on foot. It was forty degrees below zero, with blowing snow that blinded us. We felt as though we were freezing. We knew we only had a few blocks to go, but it was more difficult than I had imagined. After a few blocks, a man approached us in a pickup truck with an extended cab. He asked if we wanted a ride. We were desperate and grateful. I started to climb in the back seat when he grunted at us, "No, I said back." I realized that he was not talking about the backseat but the open box. We climbed in the box. I can still remember Jean's look. I knew she was thinking, 'Remind me to have my head examined if I ever agree to go anywhere with you again.' She didn't say it, though. She was a good sport.

Alaskan Singspiration

We finally arrived at the church. We were cold but eager to tell people about God's power and love. The service started at 7 p.m., but I had no idea how long the service would go. I had never gone to a native "singspiration" before, but I would attend many later. Each village had people who sang (or attempted to, I should say). There were solos, duets, trios, quartets, choirs, and testimonies, and it would begin all over again. Many people would start by saying they couldn't sing, and my ears agreed. They just wanted to make a joyful noise unto the Lord. However, I wasn't always sure how pleasing it was. Some of the testimonies were more like pitiful prayer requests. "I have been off alcohol for three days. Please pray for me to stay off alcohol a little longer." At about midnight, I could tell we weren't even close to the end of the service.

Finally, someone announced that a white woman was visiting who sings, plays the piano, and might want to testify. That was my small window of opportunity. The service was broadcast throughout the north slope by KJNP Christian radio out of North Pole, Alaska. I knew that many were listening, and this could mean future opportunities. Just as I approached the piano, a big gust of wind hit the power lines and cables, knocking out our lights, microphones, and radio service.

I could not believe it; after all we went through to get there. Nevertheless, a true missionary will do what one has to do at the moment. Even without power or microphones, I testified and got in as much preaching as I dared. I sang and played the piano, even without a radio audience. A few minutes after 2 a.m., I looked over to see Jean take a candy bar out of her purse and begin to eat. I was shocked but did not blame her. We had no idea that this service would last until after four in the morning. I was learning about Native time, and I needed to learn more if I was going to reach them. When it was over, I found out that the potlatch would be held in the basement. It was my first introduction to *muktuk*, the dried whale blubber soaked in seal oil. However, it was the beginning.

The next day was Sunday, and we went to the Assembly of God church in town. I told the pastor who I was and what I hoped to do in the future and asked if I could testify. He did not allow that but allowed me to sing. So, that's all I did. Many years later, that pastor approached me in another city and was weeping. He apologized for that day and told me he had no idea "whom he had in his midst and has lived to regret that missed opportunity many times." I told him that I forgave him and understood. He was not to be blamed. It is important to remain patient, walk in forgiveness, and keep your heart right. God was watching everything. I made contacts that opened up many doors of opportunity for village ministry later. We also had home meetings in Wainwright and saw God do great things.

One interesting thing about Wainwright involves seeing the fruit from that trip 25 years later. I was a teacher for several years at the River Bible Institute in Tampa, Florida. (You'll read more about that in a few chapters.) One of the couples who attended that Bible school and its hosting church, The River at Tampa Bay, later became missionaries to Alaska. Their names are John and Janet

Turner. The Assemblies of God asked them to take a church other than Wainwright, Alaska. When they were cleaning the parsonage and getting to know some of the church's members, they made an amazing discovery. They found old VHS tapes with my name on them. The tapes were all about revival. They even found some of Pastor Rodney Howard-Browne's tapes among them. Even though I was never allowed to preach in the village (except to testify at the "singspiration", I left revival tapes all over the village and encouraged the people to watch them together. John and Janet Turner were told that quite a revival ensued after I left the village.

It took 25 years for me to discover that the seed sown all those years back took hold, and others I taught are now carrying on the work. That is fruit from both sides. The time we sow in praying, testifying, giving, loving, teaching, and preaching, is never wasted. God will always bring a harvest from it. Sometimes we see or hear of it later. Yet again, sometimes, we will never see the harvest while on this earth. However, God's Word will never return to Him void (Isaiah 55:11).

EIGHT

THE FIRE OF GOD COMES TO NOME, THE KENAI PENINSULA, AND THE PLACES IN BETWEEN

One of my most unforgettable Alaskan village revivals took place in the town of Nome. Nome is a small town south of the Arctic Circle on the Bering Sea. It is the termination point of the famous Iditarod dogsled race. I'll never forget the day I received a call from a lady I did not know. She said she was in one of my meetings in Palmer, Alaska, but was originally from Nome. She told me of the high ratio of suicide, drug addiction, and alcoholism in that town. I never went to Nome but heard about it many times. From 1899 to 1909, Nome was part of the gold-rush era and was a village of about three thousand people. I could hear the desperation in the woman's voice. This lady's name was Bessie Meyers. Before I knew what I was saying, I emphatically declared, "You don't have to say more; I will go." She laughed and shouted at the news.

I told Bessie that I was leaving the next day to hold a revival in another city and that I only had one free week on the calendar for a long time. I was ministering in the Alaskan Bush for only six months, but already my calendar was full. My open week would be the week after I returned from this present trip. I told her that I knew no one in Nome, did not have a single contact and that we needed somewhere to preach and somewhere to stay. I asked her to take care of all those details. We would take off for Nome in a week. I was willing to take Bessie with me but also wanted to take my friend Jean, who was 25 years my senior, half-native, and raised in the interior of Alaska, close to Fort Yukon. Her father was Swedish, and her mother was Athabaskan. Her inside knowledge of

Alaskan villages would prove indispensable in the years to come. I knew Jean's doctrine and prayer life and that she knew how to flow with the Holy Spirit. She also followed my direction.

Upon returning home, I immediately called Bessie. "Do you have a place for us to preach?"

"No, I'm afraid that no pastor knows you, and they all said you cannot preach at their church. However, there is a native corporation that may rent a building to you, but they won't know until you get there and speak with them. They don't usually rent to white people."

I replied, "I see. What about a place to stay?"

"I'm sorry, but the hotel is extremely expensive and already at full capacity."

"What about people to come to listen to us when we get there?"

"Well, my sister said she might come to hear you."

Wow! What a trip this was going to be. I had to return to the definitive direction I felt inside when she first told me about Nome. I witnessed such a strong Holy Spirit leading that it was as if something exploded inside me. So, even if these circumstances did not look promising, I would take a leap of faith. A great man of God by the name of Smith Wigglesworth said, "Fear looks, faith leaps." So, leap, I did.

When we arrived at the airport in Anchorage (a trip that would total $1,800 for the three of us), we discovered that our plane was running late. We ended up waiting for several hours, and by that time, we were quite hungry. I saw someone walk past me with a big plate of Mexican nachos piled high with chili, salsa, tomatoes, lettuce, cheese, sour cream, and jalapeño peppers. I knew that was what I wanted. We proceeded to the restaurant at the airport. I asked for the nachos and was told they didn't serve them there. I thought that was very odd, considering that I had watched someone eat them. Then it was explained to me that he bought them "next door, and we would have to go there to order them."

I did not realize that there were two restaurants at the airport. We went to the next-door restaurant, as instructed. I couldn't figure out why it was so dark and noisy. Then, as we were walking into the place, I noticed that the sign said, "Cheers." I was horrified as I stopped in my tracks. I said, "It's a bar. We almost walked into a bar. How embarrassing!" As soon as I said that, I felt that familiar inward witness of the Holy Spirit nudging me to go ahead and go in. I was surprised and told the others. They prayed and witnessed the same thing.

Now, please pay close attention to this. I've never done such a thing before or since. That was thirty years ago. However, I would do so again if the Lord told me to. I do not drink and have never had a problem with alcohol. Someone who does have a problem should never do such a thing. I knew God was up to something, so we proceeded into the bar.

There were no seats open at the tables. However, there were three unoccupied bar stools. We stepped up and sat on the stools. That was a brand-new experience for me. Before a bartender came to take our order, I told my two friends that I wasn't sure exactly what would happen in Nome but somehow knew it would be extraordinary. I could sense that God was up to something very big. The moment I declared that, the same Holy Spirit that fills us in the church meetings filled us right there. It was at that exact moment that the bartender asked what we wanted.

In Acts, chapter two, we read that "suddenly" the Holy Spirit filled them. I often preach about the suddenlies of God. That was sudden! We had no warning. It was the most unlikely place for God's presence to manifest that I had ever imagined. Immediately, all three of us began to laugh uncontrollably. While laughing in the joy of the Lord, we began to wobble and spin on the bar stools. The lady looked shocked. She sarcastically asked me if we were "having too much fun already." She then sternly told me that I could have no more alcohol for the evening. We laughed harder. Through the laughter, I managed to get out the words. "I've not had any alcohol. This is not what you think."

I realized that I sounded just like Peter in Acts, chapter two, on the day of Pentecost. I began to explain to the bartender that this is how we live. I said, "It is this joy that healed my broken heart." I shared my testimony. She began to cry. I gave her cassette tapes of my meetings that I had in my purse. I was suddenly aware that the noisy bar had become extremely quiet. As I spun around on my stool, I faced many inquisitive faces. I could tell that they wondered why I was already in the condition they were paying to try to get to. Though they had drinks in their hands, they were still empty on the inside and sad. They could see that I was happy and full of joy. I knew that they longed for what I possessed.

I finished my entire testimony to people in a full bar. My only regret, which is a real regret, is that I never gave an altar call in that bar. I would say today, I was less bold in those days. However, a seed was planted that I believe the Holy Spirit will watch over. And I have faith that some of that seed landed on fertile soil.

We eventually ate some nachos and returned to our gate. The plane still was not there, and no one was given any explanation or information. That airline company is no longer in business today, and I think I can guess why. People were not happy. Tempers flared. We sat back and watched people losing their cool, cussing out the people at the gate, and looking like fools. I said to my two companions, "I don't know what will take place in Nome, but it will be something big. I can feel it." When I said that, we had another *suddenly*. Immediately, we began to laugh in The Spirit with great joy for the second time that evening. The woman at the gate left her post and walked over to us. She asked, "Aren't we having too much fun already?" Then she declared rather sarcastically, "I know where you have been. We are not serving you any more alcohol on the plane." That made us laugh harder. She asked the exact question that the bartender asked.

Again, I found myself repeating the words of Acts 2:15. I explained that we were not drunk on wine as she thought but were filled with the Holy Spirit. I gave my testimony and some cassette tapes. When I looked up, the formerly angry passengers at the gate calmed down and listened to every word. I was again preaching to a good-sized audience and was not even at the meeting yet.

Finally, the plane arrived about seven hours late. We boarded, and I listened to the flight attendant give her instructions. While partially listening, I repeated that God was about to do something big in Nome. Yes, we had another "suddenly." Also, these were instructions that I had never before found humorous but now found hilarious. I heard the flight attendant say that we would be "flying at an altitude of 34,000 feet over the Alaskan Mountain Range. In the event of an emergency, you have a safety cushion under your seat." That sent me into an outburst of laughter. I heard myself declaring to my friends, "Well, if we crash from 34,000 feet into Denali, the highest mountain in North America, we have a small safety cushion. No problem." We burst out laughing. I couldn't buckle my belt and slid out of my seat, laughing. The lady left her position and safety instructions behind. She took her responsibility very seriously but now came and stood directly in front of me and asked me an important question. "Aren't we having too much fun already?" You guessed it. That finished me off. She told me sternly that I would not receive any more alcohol on this trip. For the third time in one evening, I explained that I was not drunk on alcohol but filled with the Holy Spirit. God healed my broken heart, and I now live with this joy. These days confirmed that the events in the Book of Acts were not just events of the past. The same power of God and the same manifestations of the Holy Spirit still operate today. We only have to surrender to God and learn to flow with the Holy Spirit.

Suddenly, I was aware that about two hundred passengers were quiet and listening. Again, I should have given an altar call and would do so today. I preached to about three hundred people before I even got to my destination. This happens when you live in such a way that you are filled with His Spirit daily.

When the Assembly of God pastor in Nome told me that he didn't know me and could not let me preach in his church, he followed that with an offer to pick us up at the airport. He also said that he would allow us to sleep in one of the offices at his church. I thought that was very kind of him, considering that he had never met us.

Since we were about seven hours late, I had to call this pastor and tell him that we were coming in the early hours of the morning instead of 7:30 in the evening. I dreaded it and thought that this was not an ideal way to begin a relationship with him. However, he was very understanding and helpful. I could see that this man, Pastor Bill Welch, was very patient and Godly. Even though we were so late, he was good to his word and greeted us at the airport. He told us that we could go to his church and stay in an upstairs room for now. We would talk tomorrow. I was grateful and immediately recognized his sweet, Christian spirit.

The following day, as Jean, Bessie, and I were praying in a room the pastor allowed us to spend the night in, we experienced joy unspeakable and glory. We rehearsed the night's events among ourselves. We did not realize that the pastor was in his office in the next room. Much later, he told me that he could hear us praying, praising, laughing, and thuds when we bumped into the wall on our way to the floor under the power of God. He called his wife and said, "Honey, we either have three very insane women staying in the church or three women who have more of God than we do, and I am going to find out which one it is."

Sometime later in the day, Pastor Welch asked if we could talk. He offered the room to us for the remainder of our time there, which was scheduled for five days. He explained why he could not allow me to preach there. He did not know me and had a responsibility to his sheep. He added that perhaps I could preach sometime in the future. I understood and thanked him for his hospitality in allowing us to stay and assured him that I would rent a building for the meetings. As I walked back to my room, I heard the Holy Spirit inside me say, "You don't even have to go meet with the native corporation. You will be preaching here." I was stunned. However, I knew the voice of the Holy Spirit and told the other ladies.

The pastor asked us to come to their prayer meeting that morning. We were happy to accept his invitation. I was sitting beside a spiritually hungry native lady. I later found out that she was the one in his church who had been praying for revival for many years and declared that revival was on its way. At one point, I reached my arm up behind her on the pew, and she suddenly fell out under the power of Almighty God. I didn't know what to do and tried not to make a big deal out of it. I tried to prop her up in the pew and just smiled. Unbeknownst to me, Pastor Bill Welch saw every moment of that. The very thing that I was afraid for him to see, God used to speak to his heart. We never know what God will use. We cannot be ashamed of anything God does or any way He moves.

Later, Pastor Bill approached me with an invitation. He had a somewhat apprehensive look that said, "I can't believe that I am saying this." He told me that he never does this but was extending me an invitation to preach for just one night.

He emphasized the words ONE NIGHT! He said he knew I planned to be there longer but would have to rent the other building if I wanted to stay longer. I didn't repeat what God told me.

I must admit that I was too nervous that night to look at the pastor. I am a person who walks and moves a lot when I preach, and out of the corner of my eye, I could see his eyes following me like a ping-pong ball. People usually fall under the power of God in our meetings, so most of the time, I have catchers. However, I was very aware of the main-line Pentecostal mindset. I grew up in it. Most pastors do not want catchers because they do not want to predispose the person to fall. The pastor believes, "If it's real, let's let a few of them drop and bounce, and we will find out how real it is."

So, I did not call for catchers. I decided, in my brilliance, that I would handle it another way. I asked everyone to line up against the wall while I prayed for them. I forgot how big God can be and how much smarter He is than me. Everyone that I prayed for fell forward to the floor. I believe it was a great sign and wonder to the pastor. Backsliders ran to the altar to return to Christ, and people were healed and baptized in the Holy Spirit.

Following the service, Pastor Bill told me that it was a wonderful night and that I could have two more meetings, but only two more. That was becoming quite humorous to me. Each night was more dynamic than the one before. The crowd grew. The people were hungry for God, and the anointing was powerful. The glory of God filled that auditorium. No one wanted to leave. After Friday night, Pastor Bill approached me and asked me to stay over for the following Sunday. I was more surprised than I had been since I arrived. I told him I would love to but was scheduled to start a new revival in another location on Sunday.

He said that it was imperative that I stay and that he would pay for the change in my plane tickets and do whatever he needed to do.

Immediately, I got on the phone and arranged for someone else to take my next revival meeting. I knew that Sunday would be a pivotal day, but I had no idea what God was really about to do. On Sunday morning, I made a big mistake. I will never forget it, and I will never repeat it. I told the Lord what would happen and what would not happen that morning. I explained that this pastor was beginning to trust me. I didn't want to do anything to hamper that. I reminded God that we had great things happen the last three nights but that Sunday mornings were supposed to be a more conservative service in most churches. This would be a day for visitors looking for a traditional service. We could go back to a full-blown revival on Sunday night. This morning would be strictly a salvation message to reap the harvest. In prayer, I said, "Let's not have a wild meeting with everyone falling out. We can't have Holy Spirit joy and demonstration. We'll save that for tonight. The pastor and the visitors will be happy, and I will be invited back." That was a terrible mistake that I am still ashamed of.

That morning, I preached one of my best salvation messages. I could feel firm conviction in the air. I gave an altar call and was sure many would receive Jesus that day. Much to my shock and disappointment, no one responded, no matter how many times I repeated the call. I was devastated. After the service, I ran to my room above the auditorium, threw myself onto the bed, and called out to God. "What happened in there? I know we had unsaved people, and no one responded to the message." It didn't take long for Him to respond to my question loud and clear. I heard that inward voice of the Holy Spirit say, "You told me how the service would go this morning, and you have your results. Do you like your results? If not, and if you will do what I tell you to do and say what I tell you to say from this moment on, you will have My results." I repented.

Sunday night was beyond description. Thirty years later, I am weeping, remembering that glorious, holy night. You could feel the anticipation in the air. Everyone was spiritually hungry and ready for God to show up in a big way. I don't remember what I preached, but I remember the power in that altar call. People were saved. Every backslider in the house came forward to rededicate their lives. People were healed. We found out later that a lady with incurable Hepatitis C was totally cured. Someone was supposed to have knee surgery and was healed. A man with terminal cancer was healed. Joy was everywhere. People basked in the presence of the Lord. After prayer, everyone in the church was on the floor except the associate pastor, the pastor, and the cameraman. I never pray for the pastors unless they ask me to. I respect them and walk gently around men and women of God.

The associate pastor's name was Andy, and he was originally from Louisiana. He had an accent and was a Holy Ghost man (as far as he knew). He ran up to me, shouting, "More, more, I want more!" I walked over to him to put my hand on his head and prayed. When I did, Pastor Bill walked over to him to help me pray for him. When my hand came down on Andy's head, Pastor Bill's hand was also on him, and the power of God shot through both of them, and they were airborn. They fell under the front pew. It was like an explosion. Everyone present that night told me that electricity arced all over the place. The minute those two large-built men hit the floor, they were extremely "drunk" in the Holy Spirit. They laughed, cried, sang, rolled, spoke in other tongues, sang in other tongues, interpreted what they spoke, and sang and laughed again. It was hilarious, yet so very holy. It is indescribable.

After quite some time, the blood vessels in Pastor Bill's face began to pop. His face turned as red as a tomato, and his body arched off the floor as he gave a message in tongues. Then his body relaxed, his face turned back to a normal complexion, and he was still again. In a few minutes, that began all over again as he gave the interpretation of the message he delivered in tongues. It honestly looked like he was being electrocuted. Even his cowboy boots pointed in the air and then relaxed again. It went on for several hours.

His wife, Dori, started to get afraid. She had never witnessed anything like this. Even I had never seen anything quite like it, and I thought I was getting pretty used to Holy Ghost meetings by then. Dori was afraid that his head was bent in the wrong position under the pew and that he was not getting circulation. She called for a medical doctor that went to the church. The doctor arrived and said, "I'm not going any closer. I can see that his head is fine. His neck is not bent. The only person that I have ever seen quite like this was someone who was being electrocuted. I believe this is God, and we are on holy ground, and I am not going any closer." Later, she fell under the power and had a vision of Heaven. She even testified of seeing people who were part of the church at one time and graduated to Heaven. It was extraordinary. She is an educated medical doctor who is not given to imagination.

Eventually, people began to get off the floor and watch their pastor experience God in such a special way. It was as if everyone sensed the holiness of it all and would not get very close but gathered at a safe distance. They wanted to watch God at work but did not want to interrupt. This continued for another three and a half hours after the service ended.

Pastor Bill Welch (R) and his assistant pastor Andy (L).

In the middle of this, a lady approached me and asked me to pray for her husband. He was filming the service on a camcorder at the back of the room. I asked her if her husband wanted me to pray for him. This man never came up in the prayer line before. He always looked grouchy. He had a long beard and a flannel shirt with suspenders, reminding me of an Alaskan grizzly bear. He never smiled. I got the impression that he volunteered to run the camera partially to avoid being in the line of fire. He seemed nervous with the moving of the Holy Spirit. However, if he wanted prayer now, I would go to him.

I found out later that his wife had to repent for saying he wanted me to pray for him. It was only she who wanted it. However, God once again had something up His powerful sleeve. As I approached Hank, I saw him smile for the first time. I found out later that it was because he saw a fire in my eyes and thought I would pray for someone behind him. He told himself, "Someone's about to get it." Then my hand started down on his head. The next thing we heard was, "Oh no, it's me!" He hit the floor without catchers. The camera even went to the floor. He rolled, cried, and laughed until he could no longer breathe. He said, "God, stop it. I can't breathe from laughing. Don't kill me." The entire church was astounded. They knew that he would never fake anything like that.

Pastor Bill took me to Hank and Dorcus' home the next day. Hank met me out in the snow in front of their home. He picked me up, squeezed and hugged me (again, like a grizzly bear), and told me he was a new man. He said, "My wife has a new husband this morning. I never knew that you could have this in God. I've been angry and bitter. The man I most hated got stuck in my driveway this morning, and I told him I loved him, forgave him, and helped shovel him out." True revival bears fruit, my friends!

Now, back to Pastor Bill under the pew. At one point, he began interpreting one of the messages he gave in other tongues. However, this message was about him, yet God was using him to deliver it. I have never heard anyone do that before or since. He said, "This vessel that I'm speaking through did not believe this was me, but now he believes. Now he believes." I sat speechlessly and thought, 'I bet he does.'

Finally, he came around. His face was blotchy, tears ran down his face, and he rubbed his eyes. He said, "Why can't I see? I can only see white. Someone help me." Again, I never encountered this. People who are blind should come from our meetings saying, "I can see," not the other way around. After a few seconds, I realized what was going on. I told him that he was seeing the pure, white, holy Shekinah glory of God. A group of his parishioners helped him home. Their parsonage was next to the church. That came in real handy on this night. He could see nothing. He couldn't speak. He was still caught up in the glory.

The next day was my departure date from Nome. We were supposed to go to lunch with the pastors first. He tried to drive. Nome is a small town that he lived in for twelve years. Only about five streets ran east and west, and he got lost. His wife told him to let her drive because he was in no condition. We arrived at the restaurant, but he couldn't order or speak. He just laughed and cried and then sat silent. We ordered a burger for him while the waitress stared.

At the end of the lunch, I tried to talk to him. He could say a few words by then. He begged me to stay. He said, "My people are hungry, and I don't know how to give them what they need. Please don't go." I assured him that he now had the same touch of heaven I had on my life and that he would have plenty to give them. We returned to Pastor Bill's home for a few minutes before leaving for the airport.

The previous night in that magnificent Holy Ghost service, the pastor's son, Billy, told me that when Hank fell to the floor, he picked up the camera and focused it on his father. I mentioned that to Pastor Bill and asked if he would like to see the video. He cried out, "No, I don't want to." That concerned me, and I wondered if the enemy was tempting him with doubts about what had happened.

I asked Pastor Bill if he remembered that he was on the floor. He said he thought that he was out for a few minutes. I explained that he was there for three and a half hours. He was in shock! Then I asked if he remembered giving a word of prophecy or tongues and interpretation of tongues. He said he thought he may have given one for about five minutes. I informed him that he had done that for over an hour. He was shocked again! When I asked why he didn't want to see the video, he tried to explain between tears. "When you came here, I did not want any part of it and would not let you preach. When you were preaching the first night, it was like a religious spirit was sitting on my shoulder telling me that I would lose my church and everything I had built here. It said that I needed to stop you. I was prepared to do so when I heard the Holy Spirit say on the inside, 'This is the revival that you have prayed for for twelve years. It is now camped on your doorstep, and if you do not allow Me to have My way, I will remove you and put someone else in who will go with Me.'" Pastor Bill said that terrified him so much that he decided to let me continue. Then he told me that his wife, who usually has excellent judgment, said she was afraid I was pushing people down. That's why they put a camera on me.

They watched me in slow motion every night after the meeting. They found that I would just be walking toward someone, not yet touching them, and sometimes several feet from them, and the person would fall out. He told his wife, "Well, she didn't push that one." So, they let me continue.

After he confessed to all of this, he said, "I am a third-generation Pentecostal preacher who didn't know what Pentecost was until last night." It takes a humble man to admit that to another Pentecostal preacher. He said he wasn't even worthy of watching what God did in and through him but would watch it someday. With that, I left Nome more aware that I was so blessed to witness God's power in its true manifestation. I was also aware of what the enemy meant for my demise; God was now using it to plunder hell and populate Heaven. The enemy thought that the divorce and betrayal would destroy me and cause me to become bitter toward God. However, it back-fired. The circumstances caused a dependency upon the Holy Spirit as never before, coupled with spiritual hunger and tenacity to see everything in God that I knew was available.

I returned to Nome four more times. Each time was equally powerful, but I would have to write a book just about Nome if I told you all of it. One of those times included a water baptism service that continued most of the night, much like that first Sunday night. We never had to immerse anyone. They all fell in the tank, and the church participated in a water baptism and rededication service. I watched as the line to the baptismal tank grew. I looked out to the congregation, and no one was left in their seats. They all decided to get re-baptized because Jesus became much more real than He had ever been. They had their first love restored to them. That same night, the Holy Spirit drew two men from South America into the church. They heard the noise of joy coming from the church and were curious about what was taking place. They entered the church, were born again, and were baptized in the Holy Spirit.

On another evening, a youth high school dance ended, and the students heard noise coming from the church. It was louder than their dance. That is the way a church should be. Where there is life, there is noise. About forty young people walked into the church at the end of the service, saw everyone on the floor, laughing, crying, and speaking in tongues, and asked what it was. They were especially amazed to see some of their friends and acquaintances from school on the floor laughing, shaking, and speaking in other tongues. They kept walking around them, getting in their faces and staring at them, trying to figure it out. Many never went to church before, had no religious protocol, and did not know that they should not walk up to the altar and look at people being touched by God. They asked, "What is this?" I explained quickly with a five-minute salvation sermon, and they all received Jesus as their Savior. They came back for more in the next few nights. Some of them eventually went to Bible school.

Baptism service at Nome Assembly of God

One young man, dressed in leather, appeared to be the leader of the pack of teenagers. He looked curious but skeptical. He was the only one who would not accept Christ as Savior immediately. The Holy Spirit told me he wanted prayer to see if this was real. Once upon a time, in my by-the-book, religious days, I would have said that it doesn't work that way. You must first be saved, baptized in water, baptized in the Holy Spirit, and someday, you may have a powerful experience like this. But you cannot start by trying to experience this and then get saved later.

However, I thank God that I have come to know that He likes to show people how powerful He is. I told the young man, "All right, that's fair. Do you want to know how real our God is? He will show you right now." Sure enough, he hit the floor under the power of God. When he stood up, his eyes were the size of saucers. I asked him if he wanted to receive Christ, and I was disappointed in his response. "No, but I know He's real." However, guess who was the first in the service the next evening? Yes, the leader of the pack. He said he had some time to think about a God who was that real and was ready to accept Him as Savior, and my, my, my, did he ever have an experience with God!

When I returned the following year, he had watched all of my pastor's videos. Pastor Rodney Howard-Browne is from South Africa. When I returned to Nome,

Mr. Leader of the Pack was in every service, walking around with a South African accent, imitating Pastor Rodney from the videos he watched. Listening to an Inuit young man sounding like a South African was hilarious. I found out that he planned to go to Bible College with a call of God upon his life. Thank God for enough power of God showing up in our meetings to attract young people to the reality of His presence. Our youth aren't looking for dull religious services. They want to see that God is alive and real and will still manifest His power to them.

Little Rodney testifying in Nome.

Another interesting village trip involved a place called Gulkana. A young native couple approached me at a large meeting in Anchorage. They informed me that they were originally from a village north of Anchorage called Gulkana. They frequently went back to that village to minister and wondered if I would consider ministering there. I immediately sensed the confirmation of the Holy Spirit.

I took two ladies with me, one of whom was Jean Thomas again. The other one, Priscilla Cameron, was a woman I came to know from Petersburg, Alaska. Gulkana is on the highway system. Most cities in Alaska are not. It was a rare thing to be able to drive to a village. My friend, Priscilla, volunteered to drive. The night we left held a not-so-welcome surprise for us, an Alaskan blizzard. The snow blew horizontally and blanketed our car. The windows covered more rapidly than the wipers could keep up with. We inched our way through the blizzard over an ice-covered, narrow road. After several hours, we arrived at our destination. We were shaking from the distressing driving conditions when we arrived and were barely on time for the service.

The worship service left a lot to be desired. Something was wrong. The anointing was nowhere to be found. People struggled not to fall asleep. It was hot in the building, as it often was in the villages, due to wood stoves competing against the cold outside. There was a dullness to the meeting. It seemed as if the enemy was determined to destroy any possibility of the power of God changing lives that night.

Finally, I was introduced, and I went to the piano. I began to play and sing the revival songs that I had written. People began to perk up in a hurry. They came alive! They began to shout, cry, and laugh with joy. God came upon the scene in a big way. I preached, and then Jean and I ministered to the sick, oppressed, and bound. Pretty soon, people were dancing, some lying on the floor under the power of the Holy Spirit, and others testified to His great power. It was worth every inch of our nail-biting trip! It was time to retire in our motel, the only one in town.

Many times, I stayed in homes in the villages. In this case, we knew no one in the town who lived there. I was elated when I heard of a motel in the town. We were happy to rent it for the two or three nights we were there. We arrived full of joy but exhausted after the blizzard experience and long service. We walked into the front office and had one of the greatest shocks I have ever had in a motel. I was greeted by a pig! Yes, you heard me. A pig! It was a pot-bellied pig that was the manager's pet. The pig even did some astounding tricks. He reminded me of Arnold, the pig in the old television show Green Acres. The pig's personality was hysterical, but his smell was deplorable. He had a rather large litter box. The stench matched its size and was carried through all the rooms. It made the food that we brought a little less appetizing. Again, I reminded myself that I was a missionary and this was not the Hilton Hotel.

The motel with the pet pot-bellied pigs. That is me in the red coat staring in disbelief.

Upon returning the following evening to the meeting, I was greeted by a very somber expression from the couple who invited me. I was told that while the service was outstanding, somehow, I had the wrong impression about what I was asked to do. The woman continued to explain that I was the guest, not the minister. I could not get up and do whatever I wanted in the meeting. I should only do what I was asked to and no more. I may be asked to sing, play, or testify, but I was not to preach until asked. I couldn't believe what I was hearing! First, they were not pastors; they seemed to be facilitators of some sort in the meeting. We were never introduced to any pastor, and I did not travel through a blizzard at my own expense and stay in a motel with a stinking pig just to testify. However, I learned that a white woman is a guest in native villages, and there is a protocol that I must understand and respect. I was determined to do absolutely nothing the next evening until asked. God had something in mind, as He always does.

The evening began with a greater heaviness than the night before. It was as if the atmosphere was stifling and nothing could happen. The couple who invited me tried to lead the service. They tried praise, worship, and testimonies, all to no avail. Nothing happened. Then, in a moment of revelation that I could see come upon her face, the lady announced, "Debbie, please come up here and do anything you feel called to do. Take your liberty." I did, and it was an incredible meeting. Later, Priscilla and Jean told me they had never experienced anything like it. They said that the first moment my hand touched the piano's keys and I began to sing the song I had written, I Ask for Fresh Oil From Heaven Once Again, it was as if the atmosphere was blanketed with heaven itself. The anointing was tangible, transmittable, and permeated the entire building, and everyone began to weep. The weeping later turned to joy and shouting. God proved Himself so very faithful to me once again.

None of this had anything to do with me. I assure you that my songwriting and musical abilities are limited. It's not that God chose me over others. It has more to do with surrendering to the Holy Spirit and being a conduit for His Spirit. God can use anyone who submits in this way.

Fort Yukon was another exciting experience. The village is located in the interior of Alaska. The tribe of the interior of Alaska is called Athabaskan. I had the privilege of meeting one of the most precious men of God I have ever met. He was an elderly Spirit-filled, native, Episcopal priest named David Salmon.

David Salmon on the left—a godly episcopal priest.

He spoke little but radiated Godliness; I could see Jesus in his eyes. He was in his eighties at the time. He chopped wood daily, walked all over the town, and attended to his duties. His sister's name was Annie. She was also in her eighties and loved Jesus with all her heart. Our services in her home were always filled with adults and children. I will never forget the sight of children drunk in the Holy Spirit every night, laughing, crying, and speaking in other tongues into the early hours of the morning.

Annie had twelve children and countless grandchildren and great-grandchildren. I was able to meet several of them at different moments. One night, I stayed up after Jean and Annie went to bed for the evening. Suddenly, the door opened, and a young man was standing there with a broken nose, bleeding. He staggered in with a stench of alcohol coming from him. Immediately, I assumed that this was another grandson whom I hadn't met. People constantly came in and out of Annie's home. I looked unafraid and said, "You must be another one of Annie's grandsons that I have not yet met." He mumbled yes, and sat down. I got him a rag and asked if I could pray for him. He let me. After a long time, I began to feel uncomfortable because he was only staring at me, not speaking. I said to him, "Well, I believe I am going to bed now. Would you please shut off the lights before you go to bed?" He mumbled and nodded. I went to bed. In the morning, I told Annie what had happened, and she looked troubled. There was no sign of the young man. She asked me to describe him and then looked even more disturbed. Upon going to the refrigerator to prepare breakfast, she let out a small scream and declared that someone had taken all of her food. We realized that a thief and robber had spent the night with us! Once again, my angels were working overtime.

Days later, we enjoyed a Thanksgiving feast at the town hall. At one point, some people pointed out the window and asked me if that was the young man I sat with that night. I declared that, indeed, it was. He was running down the street at that moment with someone chasing him. I was told that he was the only person in the town that we would need to be concerned about, for he was a known criminal. I realized how ignorant I was of my surroundings and how faithful God was to my covenant with Him. He has promised to protect, use, and stay with me.

At one point, I held a revival on the beautiful Kenai Peninsula, one of the most beautiful places on earth. I believe it was my reward for some of the desolate, cold places I served in the middle of the winter. I had the privilege of ministering several times at a church called Kalifornsky Christian Center. The church's initials were KCC, and I accidentally announced that it was good to be at KFC. They laughed at my slip of the tongue. We had some of the most incredible meetings there. They were better than finger-licking good.

There were nights of such holy fire that people cried out all over the auditorium, asking for God's mercy. Young people hitchhiked from all over the peninsula to attend the meetings. No one cared about sports or anything else but the presence of God. Altar calls were filled with people answering the salvation call every night. People were saved, backsliders came home, young people were called to the ministry, many were baptized in the precious Holy Spirit, and people were filled with joy, healed, and delivered. Alaska was truly ablaze with holy fire. We had nights where I sang in the Spirit in perfect rhyme, operated in the word of knowledge, and the glory of God lay heavily in that building. We decided to have a water baptism service where the whole church was baptized afresh because their salvation became real to them.

I ministered in Kalifornsky for seven weeks, and the pastor asked me to stay another seven weeks. He said it would be like Moses going up the mountain a second time. I didn't stay but have often wondered if I missed God. What seven weeks of glory!

My office was located in the Matanuska-Susitna Valley, home to the two fastest-growing cities in Alaska, Palmer, and Wasilla; the office was in Palmer. The two cities have grown together. My boys attended junior high and high school in Palmer. I held many revival meetings in both the cities at Gospel Outreach in Wasilla and Matanuska Assembly of God. In recent years, I have had the privilege of holding a revival at King's Cathedral in Wasilla, pastored by Daniel Bracken.

My, what revivals we had! I was content to hold meetings wherever I could. Noel and Edna DeVries told me about the historic depot building, a former railroad depot, that was for rent in Palmer. It was not fancy but sufficient. We saw people's lives changed forever in that building. People soon came from everywhere in the valley. Many came from a place called Willow Chapel. Others came from Anchorage. The depot building was filled with the glory of God, and word spread that God was showing up in a big way.

The Palmer Depot Building

Eventually, I was invited to hold a revival in a place called Gospel Outreach. Hundreds of people came. Young people came from the two high schools of Wasilla and Palmer. They were shaking, laughing, crying, and lying on the floor in the presence of God every night. I had to move my book table to make room for more people. Young people sat in any available space, whether they had chairs or not. Eventually, the revival spread to Palmer High School, where the study hall became a place of God's revival presence. The young people shook and trembled under the presence of God, much like the Quakers of old did. It became so pronounced that parents and pastors were being called by teachers and principals, asking for explanations. Young people became bold in witnessing and leading other friends and students to Christ.

One evening, unbeknownst to me, a young man, a professing atheist, decided to attend one of the revival meetings. He was annoyed at seeing the manifestations of the Holy Spirit at school and announced in his biology class that this was all nonsense and there was no God. He would come to the meeting to prove it.

He was sitting there in the meeting with all the other young people. He ran to the prayer line, and in moments, he was on the floor like all the others. One of the youths explained to me who he was and what he said in class that day. I told him I believed the young man's atheism days were ending and asked the ushers to pick him up. He cried and shook and said, "I want to know two things, what was that language you prayed over me, and what was that power that hit me?" I explained both, and the atheist saw the light that night. That's why we have revival and not just church. That's why I traveled from one end of the state to the other. We saw revival from the high schools to the homes, villages, and churches, from Point Barrow at the top of the world down to the Southeast panhandle. I was touched to touch others. The life in me would continue to raise the spiritually dead.

Pastor Rodney Howard-Browne decided to have a state-wide Alaskan campmeeting in Juneau with Pastor Mike Rose of the Juneau Assembly of God Church. I flew into it, and so did many others. The church was packed and glorious. We had two meetings a day. My friends from Barrow and Nome were there, and so were my friends from the Mat-Su Valley and other villages. At the end of the week, Pastor Rodney decided to go home a day early and asked Pastor Mike to allow me to do the last meeting. I was honored but trembling at the responsibility of continuing Dr. Rodney's meeting. We received so much, and everyone anticipates the last night to be the best. How could I fill these shoes? Then I remembered that I didn't have to fill Pastor Rodney's shoes or anyone else's. God called me, opened this door of opportunity, and God would meet people where they were. He certainly did. I was humbled and grateful. God was moving in Alaska once again. Alaska would be shaken with the glory of God.

Since then, God brought Pastor Sam Dalin from pastoring in Ketchikan, Alaska, to pastor in Juneau. Pastor Rodney had a great revival in Pastor Sam's church in Ketchikan. I went back to Juneau many times to hold revival for Pastors Sam and Jennifer. We saw the glory flood in Juneau. Now, Pastor Sam goes to any village with an open door. I have another pastor friend, Pastor Mark Spitsbergen, who has started an Alaskan missionary base in the state. My good friend, Pastor Bill Fergusson, invited me many times to minister in North Pole, a suburb of Fairbanks in the interior. Alaska has been given a great opportunity, and I believe the wind of God is about to blow across that state again. I see a fresh breeze and a fresh fire moving across that state.

The day came when I could line up a crusade in Point Barrow for Pastor Rodney Howard-Browne and his team. The entire village experienced the glory of God. I couldn't help but think about my first phone call to the pastor years before. He threatened to run me out of town if I came. I quivered with fear and thought of giving up, but I didn't. I went anyway and was asked to hold revival there four or five times. That pastor, his wife, and I became good friends until she went home to be with Jesus. He ended up loving Pastor Rodney and his ministry and had him in his church. Just weeks ago, that same pastor and I were reunited in Washington State. He has remarried since his first wife died and brought his new family to be with us for a day at a church picnic. That was a great reunion. God is the great restorer if we refuse to quit, refuse to die, and refuse to feel sorry for ourselves. God will raise us up time and time again; He is the God of the second chance.

Me preaching in the Assembly of God church, in Barrow, AK.

Many were saved, baptized in the Holy Ghost & delivered.

Bessie Meyers, myself & Jean Thomas at Pt. Barrow.

NINE

FROM THE VILLAGES TO MADISON SQUARE GARDEN AND THE WORLD

My first year of pastoring in Alaska was from 1990 to 1991. It was a test for me in many ways, teaching me many lessons. Noel and Edna DeVries were my right hands in the church. They were both married before and had children from their previous marriages. Noel had a daughter and a son. His son, Gordon, came to live with him and Edna at a young age, shortly after he and Edna were married. Katie, his daughter, lived with her mother and stepfather in Montana. Noel desired to be with his daughter more but trusted God to take care of the situation. Eventually, Katie came to Alaska to visit her dad in the summer of 1991.

I found out later that Katie dreaded the summer. She was a popular college girl majoring in international business and was involved in the typical college party scene. She had no desire to attend a little church in the middle of the wilderness, let alone prison services, which her father told her she would have to do. She thought she would just have to endure it. She told herself, 'at least it's just one summer.' She had no idea that summer would change her life by one hundred and eighty degrees.

Almost immediately after coming to my church, Katie was radically saved, baptized in the Holy Spirit, and called to ministry. While attending one of the prison services, she was healed of a tailbone injury that she acquired while skiing. I baptized Katie in a very cold Alaskan lake. I did not tarry with a long sermon.

Baptizing Katie at Lucille Lake in AK.

Just a few months after experiencing salvation, she announced that she would not finish her college program in Montana but wanted to attend Bible school. She had heard much about Rhema Bible Training Center from me, her father, and her stepmother. Noel and Edna attended Rhema for a year and found out we were there at the same time but never met. We were delightfully surprised at Katie's announcement. God put it on my heart to have my church pay her tuition; I never dreamed at the time that I would reap a wonderful assistant. She served me and my ministry for several years after graduating from Rhema.

Katie returned to Alaska in the summer between her two years at Rhema. A woman from my church had given Katie's parents a used clothing store. I worked in the store between my village trips. Katie worked with us at Used A Bit for the summer. I will never forget one particular week. A Baptist church had a rummage sale and evidently could not sell much of their junk. They brought what they couldn't sell to our store. Noel jokingly said that people felt it was too far to take their junk to the local landfill, so they dropped it off at Edna's store. Instead of being used a bit, most of it was used a lot.

The church brought truck-load after truck-load to the store. Katie and I had the job of sorting the junk. We had puzzles without pieces, dolls without heads or arms, dirty underwear (yes, you heard me), and holey socks. I spent my time asking questions like, "Katie, do you have Ken's leg or Barbie's arm anywhere?" If it were not so sad, it would have been hilarious! I emphasize this because it is still how most churches live, in poverty mentality. We will never see a Great Spiritual Awakening by trying to finance it through selling junk, having youth car washes, and a bake sale. That's why some of us teach the church to change its perspective and walk in what God has provided for us.

One day was an unusually hot summer afternoon, with no air conditioning in most of Alaska. We were both perspiring, and Katie looked depressed. I looked at her and said, "Don't despair, Katie. You are only doing this for one summer; then, you will graduate from Bible school and hopefully go into the ministry and never have to do this again. On the other hand, I graduated from Bible school with a perfect 4.0, and this is what I am doing." We burst out laughing. Katie and

I became best friends, even though she was fifteen years younger. Little did I know at the time that we were about to share adventures worldwide.

I was Noel and Edna's pastor, but after I went through what I did and moved in with them, they became spiritual parents in a way. It was an unusual relationship. God poured His love through them to heal my broken heart. They brought my family into their home, provided me with an office, became my board, and traveled with me from time to time. I couldn't imagine them not traveling with me. We made a great team.

One day, Edna told me that because of their other responsibilities in real estate and politics, they felt they could not travel with me much longer. She told me that she was sure Katie would love to take their place upon her graduation from Bible school. As much as I loved Katie, I couldn't imagine her becoming a replacement for the couple whom I came to depend on so very much. However, God had other things in mind. Also, He never wants us to get too comfortable or too dependent on any human, a lesson that I was about to learn over and over again.

While Katie was at Rhema, a fiery evangelist from South Africa came and turned Rhema and Tulsa upside down with the presence of God. You guessed it. It was Dr. Rodney Howard-Browne and his wife, Adonica. Katie experienced first-hand what we had told her about his meetings.

Katie never knew religion before she was born again at my church. She was saved from the world and came directly into revival. She never knew the religious poverty mentality. She heard great teaching on the subject of giving from the very beginning. She only knew how to be a giver. She was drunk in the Holy Ghost many times in our church, the revival meetings, and the prison ministry. Yet, she was hungry for more and received greatly from Pastor Rodney's ministry. Little did we know how God strategically arranged to bring all these ministries and people together in the revival. We couldn't have done that ourselves if we had tried.

Upon graduation, Katie came back to Alaska and traveled and worked for me. What glory, what fun, and what friendship!

One day a group of us sat in the office. Noel, Edna, Katie, myself, my secretary Shirley, and Edna's son, Keith, were all there. We were looking through Charisma Magazine, and I remarked, "Hey, do you suppose we will ever be in here?" We all laughed, and I was suddenly convicted and could sense that God was not pleased. I stopped abruptly and said, "I repent. Look at what God has already done. Anything is possible."

The next day I was at home, and the phone rang. When I answered it, a male voice told me that he represented Charisma Magazine and they wanted to do an article on my ministry. You can only imagine my disbelief, especially regarding what happened the previous day. I answered (like a fool), "Sure, you're from Charisma, and I'm Billy Graham. What do you want?" I was sure that it was only my staff having fun with me.

Shillong, India

There was dead silence on the other end of the phone. I had the same sense that I had the day before when I mocked the possibility of being in a Christian magazine. I apologized to the magazine editor on the phone and found out the rest of the story.

Charisma magazine did an article on Dr. Rodney's ministry, in which they inquired if any pastors ever stood against him and later repented. Dr. Rodney told them that he had just received a letter from a pastor in Nome, Alaska. (That pastor was Bill Welch of the Assembly of God Church in Nome.) Pastor Bill wrote to Dr. Rodney and asked for his forgiveness. He believed the things about Dr. Rodney even though he never attended any of his meetings. Pastor Bill explained that a lady named Debbie, touched by Dr. Rodney's meeting, came to Nome uninvited and brought such a revival that he and his church would never be the same. In fact, they changed the name of their church from Nome Assembly of God to River of Life. He asked Pastor Rodney to forgive him. That led Charisma magazine to me; I was speechless.

Charisma magazine did an article about Dr. Rodney Howard-Browne. They also did a sub-article about Pastor Bill Welch in Nome, Alaska, who I held a revival for.

As a result of the article that Charisma printed, I received letters and invitations from many pastors. One letter was from a man in Seattle who said he was desperate for revival and wanted to know if I would consider coming to his small church of only 300 people. That was hilarious to me after ministering in homes, staying in villages without running water, using outhouses, and being told that ministry was all over for me. I said, "Yes." I didn't have to check my schedule.

We had a great revival. Many churches in the Seattle area came together, and eventually, we had six to eight hundred people for weeks at a time. God again showed me that He could resurrect anything, in ways we couldn't imagine.

That was not the only time Charisma did an article about my ministry. They later published an article about my ministry to the Arctic. Many Christian magazines from around the world did articles on the ministry as well. Those articles hang on my office walls, showing the favor and goodness of God. Never despise the days of small beginnings (Zech. 4:10)!

Charisma article about the Alaskan Bush Ministry

When Pastor Rodney was in Anchorage, he mentioned that he would have a summer campmeeting in Louisville, Kentucky. He said that I should come. Wild horses couldn't hold me back. However, I never dreamed that he would remember me. I was wrong. I believe it was the first meeting that he called me out. "Debbie, from Alaska, I see that you are here. If anyone wants to have a fiery evangelist in your church, this is the lady that you need to have." I was overjoyed. Many ministers were there. 'How did I obtain this kind of favor once again?' I didn't tell anyone that I knew him or that he prophesied to me in Alaska. I did not try to get a special seat or inform him I was there. When God anoints and appoints, your gift makes room for you (Prov. 18:16). You don't have to try to push doors open yourself. I desire to get that through the heads of young preachers!

I never missed a campmeeting after that. Dr. Rodney scheduled two of them every year, summer and winter. He also began to have a ministers' conference in October and New Year's Ablaze in January. I never missed one for the next fifteen years, no matter where I was in the world. I always came home to receive more. I knew how important that was, and I was never disappointed.

January of 1994 brought me to the winter campmeeting at Carpenter's Home Church in Lakeland, Florida. The church could hold 10,000 people, and it was full. More important is the fact that it was full of God's glory. That was an unforgettable night, impossible to describe, but I will try. Ten thousand people heard the angels of Heaven join in with our worship on earth. Heaven and earth came together that night. The atmosphere was charged with the holiness and the glory of Heaven. I will never forget it as long as I live.

Once again, I did not try to sit in the reserved section or tell Pastor Rodney I was there. I saw people trying to talk to the ushers about special seating. I found that repulsive. I was there for the glory of God. I was hungry and thirsty and would not be denied. I would go away different from how I came, in Jesus's name.

Promotion doesn't come from the East or the West but from God Himself. The day came that week when Pastor Rodney called me to testify. People wept, laughed, and fell out of their seats because of the power of God. I would never be the same.

When I finished, I went to the bathroom. You can imagine the line for the ladies' room in a building that holds ten thousand people. It was wrapped around like a queue at Disney World. While waiting, I saw people pointing and heard them whispering, "Look, it's her. She's here." I wondered who was there. I saw Marilyn Hickey in the meetings, the Happy Hunters, and another famous minister or two, so I turned around, trying to figure out who the famous person was. I couldn't see anyone who fit that description. I turned back to see them all staring at me, and then I heard, "Oh, how I loved your testimony. There is such an anointing on you. How quickly can you come to my church? When can you come to my nation?" I couldn't believe my ears. I mumbled. "I think I can fit it into my schedule."

Katie and I were on a jet headed back to Alaska after that campmeeting. A man and his wife sat in front of us. Katie and I were talking, and the man turned around and said, "Honey, we have someone famous sitting behind us. I know you. You were the lady who testified at the campmeeting. I want you to come to my little church. Would you?"

He told me that his church was in Georgia and that he wanted to have a true faith person who had achieved something in life come to minister to his church. Little did I know that Pastor Mirek Hufton would serve on my board for many years. I said yes, and we planned a revival. When my plane landed in Atlanta, I could not believe my eyes. I recently left the Nome revival, where everything was frozen in April. Here, the sun was shining, everything was green, the weather was warm, and the countryside bloomed with beautiful flowers. I felt like I had died and gone to Heaven. It seemed that I went from severe winter to hot summer. I lost the spring entirely.

The pastor told me that I would stay with some rather well-to-do people. I wasn't used to that in the villages of Alaska. I didn't care at all where I stayed. I only cared about having a wonderful Holy Ghost revival. On the way to this couple's home, I saw many beautiful homes that I called mansions (you must remember what I was used to at the time).

As we were on route, I felt like Granny on the Beverly Hillbillies television show. I could have said, "Which mansion is ours, Jed?" My mouth was ajar as I saw large estates, waterfalls, bridges on private property, etc. I slept on a queen-sized bed instead of a dirty rug on the floor, and my bathroom was elegant. I remembered Alaskan outhouses. I had steak instead of moose-head soup and a beautiful church building instead of a village hall.

Upon arriving at the church, I was taken to a backroom, often known as the green room. It is a room where ministers can relax, wait, study, and pray before going out. It serves several purposes, including protecting the minister from many distractions. I was never ushered to a green room before and was not used to the protocol.

Upon entering the green room, I saw a beautiful bouquet and was offered juice and fruits. People serving in hospitality asked if I preferred another kind of fruit or juice and if I needed anything else. The tropical wallpaper gave the illusion of being in The Caribbean or Hawaii. I recently came from frigid temperatures and snow. I was in awe as I was introduced to my usher, who would escort me by the arm when I was ready to go to my front-row seat. By that time, I couldn't hold back my laughter and exposed myself to be the country girl that I was. I asked them if they had me mixed up with Gloria Copeland, Marilyn Hickey, Joyce Meyer, or some other well-known female minister. I reminded them I was just an Alaskan missionary who was never given flowers, juice, or fruit. I never sat in a back room and certainly never had a personal usher before.

As I was laughing, the pastor told me that he knew exactly who I was but didn't think I knew who I was. He said this was the first time I would be treated like that, but it would not be the last. He was thrilled that they could be the first to do so. I made the adjustment, put my arm out for my usher to escort me to my seat, and told him that I was ready.

They have built a new church since I started going in the 90s. I prophesied that he needed to build bigger than he was planning on and now they have acquired more land and are building again; they are on the move.

When the revival was over, my gracious hosts ordered a limo to take us to the airport. They had a wedding to attend and could not take Katie and me personally, but they wanted us to go in style. As we sat in the back of that limo with the television on and fresh sparkling cider on ice waiting for us, I again laughed and said, "Well, look what the Lord has done."

I have told this story many times as an illustration while teaching stewardship from the fourth chapter of Philippians. I believe it so aptly applies to Paul saying that he knew how to be abased and abound. He knew how to be content in both sets of circumstances. I have learned the same.

Whether on the village floors or in a king-sized bed in an affluent part of town, I was content with my Jesus. In both places, we had a wall-to-wall Holy Ghost revival. In both places, I told the Lord, "Thank You for what You did tonight, for the people saved, baptized in the Holy Ghost, delivered, healed, and filled. How I love what I do! I am so thankful that You gave me another opportunity for the ministry. Religion told me it was all over for me, but You are not a God of religion, but relationship and You are the God of the second chance."

I also told the Lord, "While I am thankful and content, I am not staying here. I believe You for great things; to build churches, put people through Bible school, feed the hungry, clothe the naked, hold big crusades, and do television and radio. It's not about limousines, hotels, prime rib to eat, and elegant back rooms. Neither is it about poverty mentality and only believing for enough to get to the next village. It's about being blessed to be a blessing, and I'm content now while believing for much more to bless Your people and build Your Kingdom."

God heard that, and much more was on the way. I remember the campmeeting where a man invited me to go to Pennsylvania to do television for three days. His name was Russ Bixler. He told me that he had a three-day event every year where he brought in very well-known ministers. He told me he had never heard of me but was impressed with my testimony and knew I was the woman to do it this year. I accepted and was excited. He told me that satellite would broadcast the meetings all over the country. Then he gave me the dates. I was so disappointed. The dates clashed with Pastor Rodney's next campmeeting. I explained that I could not do it. He was perplexed, reminded me of the opportunity I was foregoing, and told me to miss one campmeeting. I told him I was not like many of the ministers that may or may not come to the campmeetings. I told the Lord that as long as it was at all possible, I would always be at the campmeeting to support Pastor Rodney. I offered to help him if he needed me, and I needed to be there for myself to continue being refreshed and grow in the things of God. I asked Mr. Bixler if he could change the dates; he said it was impossible and sealed in stone. He already began to advertise and spent thousands of dollars on it. I told him I understood but hoped he would remember me for another time. We said goodbye.

I left for my next revival. When I arrived, I received a call from Mr. Bixler. He told me that he had changed the dates and asked if I would consider coming. Of course, I would! God will part the waters for you and me if we remain hungry, faithful, and teachable.

This was the first of many television opportunities. I eventually was on Sid Roth's program three different times. I have been on television in Norway, with the potential to reach 160 countries. I was on Lester Sumrall's television station for three days. Later, I had my local television program in Washington State and did a weekly program on three continents through Faith Broadcasting. Only a big God could have done this. Without Him, I have nothing, but in Him, I have all things and can do all things.

The Lord has allowed me to meet many wonderful ministers of the Gospel. Many of them are ministers to whom I grew up listening. I never thought I would have the opportunity to know them personally, let alone minister with them. At one of the campmeetings, Marilyn Hickey told me to call her if I ever needed anything. I have looked up to that lady for many years. I never called her, but just to know that she offered meant so much. After a campmeeting, I ran into the Happy Hunters at an airport. Francis Hunter came to me and said, "Aren't you the young lady who testified from Alaska? There is a strong anointing upon you. Please let us know if we can do anything for you." Years later, I became friends with their daughter, Joan, at a women's conference in Minnesota where we ministered. Some years later, she invited me to sit on the platform where her parents were honored for their many years of ministry. When I looked around at the other ministers on the forum, I was astounded at the group of God's generals sitting with me and remembered my father telling me to give up ministry, for I would starve to death. I thought of the other minister who said it was all over and that I needed to give up this missionary idea and go home. I thought of my ex-husband, who said I would starve to death without him. Then I thought of my big God!

After Pastor Rodney started the church in Tampa, Florida, he decided to have an evangelist's conference called "Calling All Evangelists." He called and asked me to be one of the speakers and informed me who the others would be. He listed T. L. Osborn, Reinhard Bonnke, R. W. Shambach, and Mike Francen. I read T. L. Osborn's magazines when I was still a child. I listened to Reverend Shambach on the radio at my grandmother's when I was a teenager. If someone had told me back then that I would be ministering with them on a platform someday, I would have laughed. You never know what God will raise you to do.

When I was a student at Rhema, Norvel Hayes came to speak several times. He was a good friend of Dr. Kenneth Hagin. I loved his ministry and wished I could shake his hand and talk to him for a minute, but I didn't dare to try. There were lines of students waiting to do just that. Years later, I had the opportunity to minister with him more than once. He came to the River at Tampa Bay to minister for Pastor Rodney. I was asked to do the teaching on giving before Dr. Norvel's offering.

He so enjoyed it that he invited me to travel and minister with him regularly. I knew I could not, but to be asked was a compliment and a dream come true! One of the times that he came, Pastor Rodney was out of town and asked me if I would host Dr. Norvel and his wife, Maggie, to dinner. I enjoyed conversing with them at length. His wife, Maggie, and I became friends. We had some great conversations. We also had mutual friends in Georgia and met together there. Only God can put people together like that.

As each door miraculously opened, it made room for the next door to open. It was amazing to watch God do it step by step. I never tried to push a door open. God just opened them. I have had the privilege of ministering in 46 nations, many of them numerous times. I loved each country in its unique way. I fell in love with the people of each country and wept when I had to leave. There are hungry and thirsty people all over the world. I have ministered in almost every continent, including Europe, Asia, South America, Africa, Australia, and North America. God has been so very good.

In 1999, Pastor Rodney launched the largest soul-winning crusade he had ever done up to that time. It was held in New York City, at Madison Square Garden. He called it "Good News, New York." It was a great leap of faith, and God rewarded him accordingly. I canceled everything to be a part of the crusade for one week. Never did I dream that I would have the opportunity to preach there. Yet, just moments before the service started one night, he called me to the platform and asked me to do the teaching on giving. He did the same thing the next night. Standing in that great auditorium, I was overwhelmed by how miraculous the favor of God had been. It has taken me from the village floors of Alaska to Madison Square Garden. Truly, He has raised me to proclaim His great grace and restoration to the world.

Royal Albert Hall, London, England

I remember when Pastor Rodney announced that he would go to London, England. He had gone there before, and I never felt the impetus to go, but this time I did. Several friends of mine witnessed the same thing, and six of us decided to go at our own expense. I never attended Pastor's overseas crusades without his permission. However, this time, I just knew I needed to be there.

On the way, I was reading a book about Aimee Semple McPherson, the fiery woman evangelist who formed the Foursquare denomination. I was nearing the end of the book when I noticed something. The last place she ministered before she died was in London, England, at Royal Albert's Hall. That was the same building where Pastor Rodney would be ministering. What a coincidence, or was it?

Like I did with the Charisma magazine article, I began to joke. "Hey, do you suppose I will ever minister there too?" Again, I was convicted and stopped joking. Pastor Rodney greeted us in the lobby when we got to the hotel. We all checked in and found our various rooms. I believe it was the second or third day, as I stepped out of an elevator before going to the morning service, Pastor Rodney stepped into the elevator. As we saw each other, he told me he was coming for me. He wanted me to know that he wasn't attending the morning meeting and felt I should have the entire session. I was speechless. It was only two days after reading about Aimee preaching at Royal Albert's Hall, and now I was preaching there myself. Big God!

I am not sure what some of those ministers thought about that. Most had never heard of me and were expecting Pastor Rodney. I could tell that they were looking at me with disdain. I believe some of them even held doctrinally to the notion that a woman is not supposed to preach. It makes no difference what they thought before the meeting. By the end of the meeting, I believe God convinced them that I was the lady for the hour. I still remember people running all over that auditorium, shouting, "I didn't even know a woman could run with the fire of God until today. I want that fire!"

One day Pastor Rodney asked me to go with him and the team to Indiana, to Lester Sumrall's church. Pastor Rodney would be ministering there but also needed to fly to New York in preparation for the Good News, New York crusade. The plan was for him to preach the first night, then take the jet to New York the next morning while I preached at Dr. Sumrall's church in his stead, and then he would return. I was thrilled to be preaching in the church of another one of the great generals of God's army. Even though Dr. Sumrall was now in Heaven, I was escorted to his office, where he was writing his last book when he was called to Heaven. I had the privilege of looking at his notes and touring his church. I didn't take it for granted. God's hand and favor were on me, and I was eternally grateful.

Another time, I was invited to go with the Howard-Brownes to Melody Land in Los Angeles, California. After Pastor Rodney finished ministering, we were invited with them to participate in food and fellowship after the service. While enjoying a snack, Pastor Rodney pointed at a chair in the room and suggested I sit in it. I thought that was odd, but I knew there must be a reason. I sat in the chair for several minutes. Later, I stood up to get some punch, and Pastor Rodney said, "Don't get up for a while, Debbie. Someone else can bring you the punch. Sit in that chair longer."

I was suddenly struck with the revelation of what was taking place. I looked up and stated, "This was Kathryn Kuhlman's chair, wasn't it?"

He smiled and said, "Yes, it was."

Anointing can be stored in cloth. The Bible tells us that the aprons and handkerchiefs taken off Paul's clothing drove out sickness and disease. As I sat there, I began to think about the healings and miracles in Kathryn's ministry. I mixed faith with the moment. I knew in my heart that I would see many greater miracles than before. Those things began to take place.

While holding meetings in New Jersey a couple came to my meeting and asked to meet with me. They were brought into the green room. They looked familiar and I realized that I saw them at Pastor Rodney's meetings. I recognized that they carried the anointing and were hungry for God. They introduced themselves to me and told me that they heard me teach in Pastor's meetings several times.

Odd, Lisa, Debbie & a Philippine pastor flying to another island in the Philippines.

Their names are Odd and Lisa Frustal. They are originally from Norway but immigrated to the United States when they were very young. Odd was a businessman who owned several furniture stores called House of Norway. God blessed them, and they determined to use their blessing to take the Gospel to several nations and build churches. They heard enough of my testimony to know that I was a missionary at heart and could endure tough circumstances in the foreign field. They invited me to go to Ukraine with them. I sensed that I should go. They bought my ticket on several trips. We became close friends and co-revivalists. We took many trips together after that; Philippines, India, Cambodia, Vietnam, and several more trips to Ukraine. They have been a tremendous blessing to me, my ministry, and the body of Christ. We know how to minister and flow in the Holy Ghost together.

I am so thankful for them. I ordained them to the ministry and now they have preached in many countries.

TEN

THE RIVER AT TAMPA BAY

One phone call, one letter, or one invitation can change a person's life forever. I will never forget the invitation that came from Dr. Rodney Howard-Browne. I was living in Alaska while continuing in the village and prison ministry. I flew into Dr. Rodney's meetings whenever possible. It was the ministry that changed my life, transformed my ministry, reaffirmed my call, and the ministry that encouraged me and believed in me. The letter explained that he was calling several ministers to come together for a minister's conference in Tampa and inviting me to become his associate evangelist. Would I consider it? Well, is the pope Catholic? You get the picture. I almost fainted. I honored, respected, and appreciated this mighty man of God and his wife. Could it be that he felt my ministry could be a good addition to his? I couldn't wait! He also asked if I would consider moving to Tampa because the Lord established that as his base city. They were putting down roots and buying a home at last after living out of hotels for so many years.

I knew immediately that I would be honored to be his associate evangelist. I knew I was completely aligned with his doctrine and immersed in the intimate presence of the Holy Spirit, much like he was. Dr. Rodney and his wife have a heart for our country to be saved and were patriots. That was my heart, as well. I answered with an affirmative, "Yes!"

However, regarding the second question, I was not yet sure it was time for me to leave Alaska. My heart was there, my boys were in an Alaskan school, and

Noel and Edna were such an important part of my life. I just purchased my first little home there. The village and prison ministry were flourishing. God was blessing. I knew I could not be too hasty, even with such an honor. I flew into the meeting in Tampa and became his associate evangelist, but I operated from Alaska for another year. I waited on God to release me from Alaska. I knew how important it was to hear from Him and not move too early. It is also important not to lag behind God. I don't want God to have to kick me in the behind. I wanted His perfect timing.

I continued to fly into every campmeeting, winter and summer. I went to every minister's conference, no matter where I was. I would not miss one of them, even when I was given exciting invitations. I knew that God put my ministry together with Revival Ministries International. I knew I must continue to be filled and receive direction, revelation, and fellowship with like-hearted people. We are people of the Holy Spirit. We are men and women of God and people of faith. I needed to return to "my own company", as the Bible speaks of in Acts 4:23. Religious spirits don't like us; sometimes, we come back wounded from war and need to have that precious Balm of Gilead poured over us once again. I was never disappointed.

I remember so many precious moments. It is difficult to only refer to a few. I was at Carpenter's Home Church on that incredible night when the angels of Heaven joined the worshippers in that auditorium. I can't even write about it without feeling awe, reverence, and holy fear. There is no way to describe it, and I almost feel like I am debasing the moment while trying. Ten thousand people were caught up in the holiest worship I have ever experienced. We stepped in and stepped over into that sacred realm. We were in a glory realm so indescribable that I could not put it in words.

The atmosphere of heaven broke into the earthy realm. It became difficult to distinguish between the two. It seemed like a holy, harmonic melody was coming over our heads. It grew stronger, louder, and more sustained as if it were one long divine note that would go on forever. I remember thinking, "I've never heard anything like this. It's as if, no it can't be, but it must be... It's as if an angelic choir has joined us. No, I've never heard of such a thing."

I finally opened my eyes and looked at other people's faces to see if they were hearing what I was hearing. Part of me was almost terrified to open my eyes. However, I knew I must. When I slowly opened them, I looked at people who were all looking at one another. It was as if you could read each face and know they were asking themselves what I was asking myself. Then, we all realized what was happening. The angels of Heaven joined us in worship. Every instrument stopped. Eventually, the crowd closed their mouths as the beautiful song continued to crescendo. No one moved, and I think no one even breathed for a few seconds. We were on holy ground.

There have been many moments similar to that one. There were nights that many refused to leave, even at 2 a.m. A holy hush came over us, and no one said anything. Then, as if a conductor was there, waving his hand, the joy of the Lord came with another fresh wave. Then, as if the conductor raised his hand to signal stop, everyone stopped and sang in the Spirit simultaneously. After a while, everyone wept, and then another wave of joy came. There was a holy, perfect conductor among us, and His name is the Holy Spirit. I thought of all the people who left too early and weren't spiritually hungry, thirsty, or desperate enough. God comes to those who hunger and thirst after righteousness (Matt. 5:6), not those who are full of themselves and satisfied with the world's pollution or religion. One thing I always took away from those special meetings was getting hungrier and thirstier. I did, and God did!

There was another call that changed my life. Of course, it was from Pastor Rodney again. I knew that he started a church in Tampa. He told me that he had to be away on a Sunday to fulfill some of his evangelistic responsibilities. He pondered who should fill his pulpit for the first time that he would be away. He said to me on the phone, "Debbie, I could have anyone from anywhere in the world. (That was a true statement because he had close relationships with many of the world's most renowned ministers.) I believe that I am supposed to have you fill the pulpit while I am away."

Can you imagine what that sentence did to the heart of a girl whose parents told her, "Forget that stupid missionary idea. You're going to starve to death." I thought again of the minister who said, "It's all over for you. Go home, be a mother to your kids, and forget your crazy Alaskan call." I was speechless but managed to get out a "Thank you very much for your trust, Sir. I won't let you down." What a Sunday we had in Tampa! I still remember that message. I titled it, "What is your glory temperature?" I knew that this would be my church soon.

The day came that the Lord gave me a very specific "Go now to Tampa." I told Katie that it was time. She was very excited. I dreaded telling her parents, who were my spiritual parents, my confidants, advisors, and encouragers. They helped raise my children, helped me financially, traveled with me, and provided me with a home and an office. I couldn't imagine being separated from them. However, God doesn't like it when we let anyone take His place in any way. He is a jealous God. Even though they decided to stay home to pursue Edna's political call and not travel with me, I knew this would be a difficult transition. However, when you truly love one another and have the heart to see each fulfill their respective callings, God heals the hurts and restores relationships.

One of the times I was asked to testify at the minister's conference was most special. I finished telling everyone how my big God did great things for me. The people exploded in shouts and applause, rose to their feet, and continued to praise God for several minutes. I was amazed at how much encouragement my testimony brought to others.

After the meeting, Pastor Rodney and Pastor David Sumrall (nephew of Lester Sumrall) approached me to ask me if I could go to Manilla, Philippines, to hold a revival. Pastor David was needed in Tampa to help Pastor Rodney. Pastor David's church had a membership of twenty-thousand people. It was a Holy Ghost church, and I had no hesitancy about going. I again thought of the village floors from where I came. I not only had a wonderful revival in their church but was asked to go to the island of Cebu and hold another revival the next week.

I will never forget the summer of 1995 before leaving Alaska. I felt that Noel, Edna, Katie, and I should bring the ministry van from Alaska to travel across the United States all summer. We began the journey on the Alaska ferry system. I spent the entire summer ministering across the country. When I left Alaska, I had only one invitation. I trusted God that more invitations would supernaturally come; they did. That was an unforgettable summer! I ministered in Washington State, Idaho, Montana, Oklahoma, Arkansas, Nebraska, and Kansas. Every week, a new place opened to the ministry. In the daytime, our team enjoyed some relaxation. On one occasion in Montana, we rented horses, while on another day, we went white-water rafting. God was allowing me some refreshment as I was giving out spiritually. I never had any of that in the villages.

The main appointment for the summer was to be at Pastor Rodney's summer campmeeting in St. Louis, Missouri, in July. God opened doors along the way to the campmeeting and back to Alaska after the campmeeting. It was a summer of outstanding revival everywhere we went.

When we arrived at the campmeeting, I had a special excitement on the inside. I stood in the registration line after a long trip from Alaska. Pastor Rodney began a ministerial association for revival ministers associated with him. They were given special seating closer to the front. However, if they weren't recognized at registration, they were asked for their credentials.

I never asked for special seating in any of his meetings, even though he introduced me and asked me to speak at most of his campmeetings. I watched people try to manipulate and maneuver to get close to him and was determined not to be one of them. If I had to sit back a few rows, so be it. I forgot that he started the ministerial association and did not bring credentials with me. It was the first meeting in which Revival Ministries International (RMI) asked for the documents. Almost anyone who had been around for any length of time knew who I was. However, I was about to encounter someone who did not.

When I registered, I told the volunteer lady I was a minister and came to his meetings frequently. She looked at me skeptically and asked for my credentials. I told her I drove from Alaska to St. Louis and did not bring my credentials. She looked down her nose at me and stated, "I don't believe that you are a minister, and you cannot sit in special seating." I put down my flesh and answered that I would do whatever I was asked to do.

I believe there were about 10,000 people in attendance. Pastor Rodney was ministering when he asked for me. As I stood up near the back of the nose-bleed section, he said, "Debbie, what are you doing back there? You need to be close so that I can call on you." He asked me to come to the platform and testify. I couldn't help but think about the lady who was probably crawling under her seat about now. I never addressed her or told Pastor Rodney about her. She was just a volunteer doing her job, although doing it with a rather snotty disposition. The point is that we don't have to make room for our gifts. They make room for us. Again, God had exalted the little lady from the Alaskan village floors. What can He do for you?

Later in the week, Pastor Rodney announced that too many people had their eyes on him instead of Jesus. Thus, he would not pray for anyone but asked certain well-known ministers to pray in his stead. He laid his hands upon them. He called upon several men and then asked for me to come forward. I was at the end of a line of black, blue, brown, and gray suits. I was standing in my pink skirt with all the men, getting ready to run through that auditorium praying for people and calling out "Fire." God made way for me once again.

The summer of 1996 was just as exciting but different. The Howard-Brownes invited me to go with them to their native country of South Africa. I had never been there before. Upon arrival, I had some difficulty with customs, and they almost sent me home. It was a misunderstanding about offerings and officials thinking I was working for Pastor Rodney. It was not a good beginning, but things were about to get even more interesting.

Just weeks before, I finished a revival in Tulsa, Oklahoma. It was another glorious revival with signs and wonders following the preaching of God's Word. At the end of the revival, the pastors informed me that a young woman was mightily touched in the meetings and wanted to meet with me. She explained that her grandmother left her an inheritance, and she was an heiress to a fortune. She decided to bless the church, pastors, and my ministry with some of that fortune. I was promised two million dollars after completing the required paperwork. Needless to say, I was beside myself with joy. All I could think of was the people and ministries I would be able to bless.

The first one on the list was the ministry that had impacted my life, Revival Ministries International. I couldn't wait to tell Drs. Rodney and Adonica. I called them and told them I was tithing from the amount. They sent flowers to my hotel room and told me how happy they were for me.

I saw them a few weeks later and gave them the check for $200,000. I should have waited until it was in my hand but was told again that it was imminent. I wanted to see their faces. It was a moment that I had dreamed of, and brought me great joy. They had given so much to me, including the key to a breakthrough. Now, it was my turn to give back.

There were some delays in receiving my funds that were explained each time. They seemed reasonable, and I still expected what was promised. I explained all of it to Pastor Rodney and asked him not to cash the check until my check was in the bank and cleared.

We were all together weeks later at his South African campmeeting. I waited for the call from Tulsa to tell me everything had cleared. I will never forget the morning that my call came. I celebrated my 40th birthday with the Howard-Brownes and Katie. I thought this call would be the icing on the cake, so to speak. Upon answering the phone, I heard the voice of an associate pastor from the church I ministered at in Tulsa. Today, he is married to Katie, and they have pioneered a wonderful church in Tennessee. Pastor Todd told me, "Debbie, I don't know how to tell you this, but the woman has turned out to be a fraud and a flake, and none of us are receiving anything." I was speechless. Katie and I were supposed to go to the hotel dining room for breakfast and then to Dr. Rodney's meeting. How I dreaded seeing him and Dr. Adonica! It would be sooner than I thought, for they, too, were eating in the same dining room that morning.

When I walked in and saw them, I wanted to run and hide. How could I tell them I gave them a hot check with nothing to back it up? How could I apologize for being stupid, gullible, not checking things out first, or having any discernment? If things weren't bad enough, Pastor Rodney told me that this check would be used as a major part of a down payment on a plane he was about to buy. I didn't even have enough money to buy him a toy airplane. I finally told myself, "Well, whatever is about to happen, I deserve it. Let the chips fall. I have to walk into the dining room."

I walked over to their table and told them I had news for them. He immediately said, "Is the money through?" I looked at him with dread and said, "Oh, it's through all right," and made a motion with my hands that showed it was finished. He looked up, stared at me for a few seconds, and began to laugh one of those famous Dr. Rodney belly laughs. I couldn't believe what I was hearing. I also began to laugh but my laugh was more of a nervous laugh. He said, "Debbie, I had a feeling that this might happen, so I have not cashed the check. However, you have proven to God that you are faithful and have shown Him what you will do with it. This is just the counterfeit before the real. It will happen someday. What would people do if something like this happened to them? They would get drunk, wouldn't they? Well, let's go to the meeting and get drunk in the Holy Ghost right now." Then he laughed some more. I believe about a hundred tons of shame, regret, embarrassment, and feeling like a fool rolled off of me. I realized the character of the people I had the privilege of being associated with and how much I learned from them.

After that campmeeting, I was booked for two solid weeks across South Africa. I didn't know any church or pastor, so I just said yes to every pastor who asked me to come. I found out later that I turned down the second-largest church in South Africa because I was booked up by the time they invited me. However, I believe that was the plan of God all along. I have never enjoyed being another "who's who in the charismatic zoo." I want to go where I can make a difference, where people are hungry, thirsty, and desperate. We had meetings that were incredible in places most would not go. How I wish we had a video camera in those days!

One church was a Dutch Reformed church that had never seen the power of God demonstrated like that. They had no ushers, no catchers, and only a cement floor. I could be there only one night. Only one woman from the church had been to Pastor Rodney's meetings. They were not predisposed to expect anything. However, the joy broke out immediately. The sound man turned my microphone up, and I still could not be heard over the sound of joy, laughter, and shouting. People began to drop all over the building to the cement floor without catchers. Yet no one was hurt. It was holy chaos. Oh, what memories! By the time I left

South Africa, we had an open invitation to come back all over the nation. The nation's Christian magazine, Joy Magazine, printed an article about the small Alaskan woman setting South Africa on fire.

A leading South African Magazine did an article on my ministry.

In 1997, I traveled to Australia and New Zealand for four glorious weeks. I went to several cities in both countries. We had a women's conference in Brisbane, Australia, that I will never forget. I was asked to do the women's state conference for the Assemblies of God. I had never been to Australia before and was looking forward to ministering on the famous Gold Coast. We had about 1,000 women in attendance at the first meeting. Before the meeting, I was given a copy of the schedule, or as the Aussies call it, the *shedule*. I had never seen so many tea times in all my life. I noticed that we would have tea time, then a meeting, then tea time, a meeting, and then tea time again. The services were tightly sandwiched between these infamous tea times. I didn't like the idea, at all, of breaking women free, and then I would have to stop for tea. The idea seemed preposterous to me. I finally mustered up the courage to ask if I had to stop for tea if the Holy Spirit was moving in a great way. The lady in charge looked at me strangely and said, "Perhaps if He is R-E-A-L-L-Y moving, we can post-pone tea." I felt a degree of relief. The whole thing was quite humorous to me.

I remember thinking that they didn't know whom they had invited to do this conference. I was not your typical women's conference speaker who would talk about beauty secrets, how to be a good wife, and how to conduct women's ministry. I was a Holy Ghost revivalist who was there on a mission. They were about to find out what that mission was. There would be no tea time that week, for they were all too drunk in the Holy Spirit to remember they even drank tea, which is saying something for an Aussie.

The very first evening was a Holy Ghost blow-out. Women were lying everywhere; nothing was as humorous as watching women catching women in a prayer line. They had not been trained as ushers and catchers and were not used to people falling. They allowed petite, hundred-pound ladies to stand behind very robust two and three-hundred-pound women. The small catchers and the larger women being prayed for were equally drunk in the Holy Ghost. I saw the situation getting interesting, and I prayed for their safety. It all ended up just adding to the hilarity of the evening.

After the service, I was taken to a waiting car. I could not believe my eyes. Women were hanging onto the light posts, swaying, singing, laughing, and announcing to the world what joy unspeakable they were having. They were witnessing to anyone within earshot. "Come and see how good our God is. Come, and witness for yourselves this incredible joy." The next morning session was packed.

I laughed as I entered the waiting vehicle. I stated that I wished I had a video camera. That is not the first time I said that. The best moments of my ministry have unfortunately escaped the recording. However, they will forever remain etched in my memory and the hearts of the people who were touched.

When my vehicle pulled up to the lovely hotel where I would spend the next several nights, I again could not believe my eyes. Women were lying on the sidewalks in front of the hotel. They had succumbed to the wonderful power and glory of the Holy Spirit and could not walk into the building. I did what any respectable minister of the Gospel would do. I walked past them like they were not there and acted as if I did not know them.

Upon entering the elevator (which they call the lift), I had yet another surprise. When the door opened, it was packed with some ladies from our service who were still drunk in the Holy Ghost. They were laughing, crying, singing, and speaking in tongues and could be heard from quite a distance. A couple was waiting to get into the elevator, but when they saw the ladies, the woman remarked, "I'm not getting in with those women," while her husband retorted, "I am." I almost fell to the floor laughing. He got in, and his wife stayed behind. I'm sure he was quite shocked when they brought out their Bibles and explained what they were experiencing.

When I finally crawled into bed, extremely happy, I thanked my Lord for the call on my life and the privilege of witnessing lives being touched in such a profound way. I heard hilarious outbursts of laughter coming through the walls. This continued all night as other women from the conference were on the other side of the hotel room wall. What a glorious way to drift off to sleep, knowing that women who had been depressed and hopeless were filled with ecstatic joy. They would never be the same. Neither would I.

When I left the United States to travel to Australia, the ministry was having a tight month financially. I decided long before to pay for my travel, including airfare, hotels, and meals. I would not be dependent upon churches to take care of me. My trust was in God alone. Also, if I paid my expenses upfront, I could preach whatever God laid upon my heart. I would not be a hireling. I would be free to receive whatever came in the offerings. That also meant that the church should allow me to teach and believe God. However, I would be in a difficult situation if God did not come through. However, He always has, and He always will.

Normally, I put the two tickets (for myself and my assistant, Katie DeVries) on the credit card. I trusted that the offerings from the women's conference would be wired at the end of the week. My first surprise was to be told by a phone conversation that they were surprised that I was even offering to purchase my tickets. However, they had a different way of doing things. They told me they would buy my ticket, and I would have to pay for my assistant's ticket. Also, they would receive several offerings for their fellowship in the first few days. I would be allowed to receive my offering in the last service. I realized that I would have to believe God for a great offering, but I had seen Him do it many times before. He would do it again.

RESURRECTED

We had outstanding meetings, and a miracle offering of $13,000. The women who were in charge of the conference were astounded. They told me that Marilyn Hickey was the speaker at the national conference the year before and received less with more women in attendance.

Me preaching to over 1,000 women, 3 times a day.

The women in the congregation rejoicing.

Me with a Koala Bear

I gave all the glory to the Lord. I couldn't wait to share with my office staff the good news. I was asked how I would like to receive this offering. I asked them to please wire it immediately. They agreed. I told no one that the account was empty when I left the States. We had bills and staff to pay, office rent due, and I was responsible for paying students' tuition for Bible school at the River Bible Institute. I was also helping to build churches. I needed God to come through in a big way.

I was told by the woman in charge of the conference that arrangements had been made with the four churches that had invited me. They all agreed to allow me to receive the entire offering for every service of each week. They were also given my wiring information and would send it promptly. Their word was enough for me.

I assumed that the offerings would be wired immediately. After the women's conference, I went to the next church. While in Australia, I ministered for several days in Brisbane, a week in Sydney, and then in Melbourne. I also did a fourth week in Adelaide. When it was time to leave the first church, the pastor was called away for an emergency. He asked his secretary to drive me to the airport. I expected her to mention the offering for the week, give me an idea of how much it was, and ask me about wiring instructions, but she never said anything. It was awkward. Yet, I felt I was a visitor in another country and should trust God to remind them to send it. I went to the next church.

At the second church, we had another great revival. I was also asked to preach at the Assembly of God Bible school, where we had a glorious revival. The offerings were not mentioned again upon leaving the church and the city. However, I assumed they would be wired, as promised.

When I went to the last church before returning to the United States, I developed a special rapport with those pastors. We become close friends in a short period. They loved the teaching that I did on giving. It was setting them and their church free.

On Sunday morning, I taught on the subject of the tithe. I emphasized that the tithe does not come to me or any traveling minister. It goes to the local church, where the person receives their spiritual food. I told them that I would not receive an offering for myself until Sunday night. I later found out that a man was convicted over that message and ran into the pastor's office after church and wept and confessed. "Pastor, I have lied to you about my income. My business took off greatly, and I have not been tithing from the income." He repented and wrote out a huge check to the church. He gave a couple of years of unpaid tithes. The pastors were incredibly grateful for the teaching.

At the end of the week, I was told what my offering was. It was an incredible blessing! God, indeed, came through. By that time, I was given unexpected news; however, that was not so good. My office staff in Alaska called me and asked what was happening in Australia. They wanted to know if I was preaching or goofing off. Of course, they were joking, but it was their way of announcing that no offerings were received. They wanted to know what I wanted them to do about paying staff, bills, etc. I told them that while I was shocked, I was not discouraged. I told them they were to stay in faith with me, trust God, and believe it would come quickly. They agreed.

I did not feel I should call and talk to any Australian pastors. I was a visitor to their country and would respectfully wait, pray, and trust God. However, I did feel that I could tell the story to the pastors of this last church. I explained my situation and asked them to wire the offering from their church immediately. They understood and agreed but asked if I would like them to communicate with the pastors of the churches where I had been. I thanked them but told them I would trust God to take care of it.

After the last service, Katie and I returned to the hotel where we were staying. I was exhausted after preaching two and three services a day for four weeks. I went to sleep immediately. I was awakened in the middle of the night by the inward voice of the Holy Spirit. I heard on the inside of me, "Give the pastors back all of the offerings so they can go to Pastor Rodney's campmeeting." I shot straight up in bed. "What? Surely, Lord, you mean that I should give them the morning offerings and keep the evening offerings or vice versa. Besides, I haven't even heard them mention wanting to go to the campmeeting. I don't even know if they have any desire to go. Lord, your Word says we are to come and reason our case together (Is. 1:18). You know that the other churches have sent nothing. You know that when I left my country, we were broke. I have given offerings when we needed them desperately. You know that I put Katie's plane ticket on our credit card. You know that I have just been told that we can't pay our staff, bills, office rent, or anything. I have been sowing, trusting You, and staying in faith, and now the reward and harvest have come, and You are asking me to give all of it again. How will I explain that to my staff or to Katie, who is waiting to receive a check? How will I say that I just gave away her check? Am I hearing from You, Lord? There is a lot at stake here." I was perspiring and knew that I had to wake up Katie.

"Katie, you will never believe what God just asked me to do!" I secretly hoped she would argue with me and tell me that I had no right to give away her paycheck. I wanted her to say that I probably only thought I should give it all, but did not hear it from God. She did not. She responded, "That's awesome, Debbie. We need a great miracle. So let's do whatever God asks us to and believe Him." What an assistant!

Katie was saved into revival, giving, and joy. She never knew religion. She had simple faith, the God-kind of faith. I was never more proud of her, my spiritual daughter in the faith.

The pastor's wife had been designated to take us to the airport the next morning. She arrived on time, and I could not wait to talk to her. Part of me still felt it was necessary to make sure I heard from God. Too much was at stake.

After greeting the pastor's wife, Lynn, I decided to inquire if they were interested in attending Pastor Rodney's campmeeting. After all, what if I didn't hear from God correctly and wasted this offering on something they were not even interested in doing? So, apprehensively, I approached the subject. "Have you ever been interested in going to Pastor Rodney Howard-Browne's campmeeting?" She answered, "We have never been before." Relief began to sweep over me. Then she continued. "Until you came and began to tell us all how wonderful those meetings are. We began to get hungry to go to them. You do not know this, but we so love your teaching on giving that my husband and I have been sowing heavily into your offerings. We came home after the last meeting and named our seed. We said, "Lord, we believe that we will be able to attend Pastor Rodney Howard-Browne's campmeeting." Why do you ask, Miss Debbie?"

I swallowed big and answered her, "Because God just spoke to me to sow the entire offering back to you so that you could go to the meeting. Has your husband wired the money yet?" She told me he was just about to do so, even as we spoke. I instructed her to call him quickly and ask him to keep the money. She did, and I witnessed both of them ecstatically rejoicing. Oh, what a morning! Do you know what it is like to be used in such a way? It is thrilling to be an instrument in God's hands to make people's dreams come true. There is nothing like it.

The enemy comes immediately to steal our faith. He likes to use the term "using wisdom." I was now faced with having to call my office and tell them what I did. We were all waiting for this offering. I had to tell them I had given it away before it even hit our bank. I was trying to figure out the easiest way to break it to them.

When we arrived at the airport, I made the call. As Edna answered the phone on the other end, I said, "I have news for you." She said, "We have news for you, as well. Who should go first?" I replied, "I think you should." She then told me about the financial breakthrough just minutes before the call. The wire arrived from the women's conference and the three previous churches in one day. Also, we received an offering from my prison ministry for the first time. Then she informed me of the biggest shock. I ministered in the Philippines the year before, and they just sent a second offering. That never happened before. Also, a church I previously attended in Canada sent a second offering. Edna told me that more money had come in one day than ever before in the history of our ministry. Then she asked, "Oh, by the way, what was your news?" I was smiling ear-to-ear and replied, "My news is that I just obeyed God. I took a big leap of faith, and look at what He has done! Once again, we cannot out-give God, and we can never afford to disobey Him."

Immediately following Australia, Pastor Rodney hosted the summer camp-meeting in Tampa. I was asked to continue in Australia and New Zealand both. The revival was burning in both nations. The largest Pentecostal magazine in New Zealand wrote an article about my ministry and the mighty revival there.

The article about me in the New Zealand magazine.

I was asked to hold meetings on both the north and south islands. On the south Island, I had a women's conference and revival in a city called Christchurch. The women were healed from much abuse there. They received joy unspeakable and full of glory. Many had been raped or were victims of incest and yet totally delivered in the meetings. Later, upon holding a revival in the local church, I had some of them testify. Many denominations were represented: Baptists, Catholics, Presbyterians, Episcopalians, Pentecostals, and more. The joy of the Lord was so pronounced that I almost could not be heard.

I saw that almost all of the denominations were responding except for one group. The Holy Spirit revealed to me who they were. They were the Pentecostal group. The same Holy Spirit showed me what to do about it. I called up about five women to testify of what the Lord did for them at the conference. Each tried but was overcome with joy and could not speak. Each fell out under the power of God and only erupted with laughter. I could see the Pentecostals become angrier. I called up five more with the same results. Eventually, I called up about 25 women, but not one could speak. Their faces lit up; they displayed joy unspeakable and then fell out.

Suddenly I said, "The Lord knows your thoughts. You are saying that God wouldn't have the evangelist call people up to testify, and then they can't testify. That is not God." I saw the group nod in the affirmative. I then said, "Oh, they testified all right. I could hear them. They said, 'I would love to tell you what the Lord has done for me, but when I think of it, I cannot, for it is joy unspeakable and full of glory.' You all grew up singing the song 'It is Joy Unspeakable and Full of Glory' and think you know about it. However, you are singing about the author's experience. He wrote the words that were experienced. The words conveyed that this joy is too wonderful and too deep to express in words. You clap to it, you sing it, but you never had it. Don't think your Pentecostal denomination and name on your church make you Pentecostal. It does not. These women are living what you grew up singing. This joy is too great to speak of. It only comes out in the language of joy, which is laughter." Finally, they understood, repented, and received true joy, unspeakable and full of glory. We had a wonderful time all over the beautiful country of New Zealand.

Several pastors asked me to extend my trip to these nations. However, I told them I must return to Dr. Rodney's summer campmeeting. They reminded me that I had never missed one in all these years and that he would surely understand if I missed this one. They believed it could become a national revival. I knew that Dr. Rodney would realize that. After all, that's what he's all about. However, I knew the importance of staying filled up and on fire. The more a person gives out in revival, the more we have to continue to receive. Many do not realize that and start believing they have something on their own. We do not have anything except what He gives us. I told the Australians that I would come back again someday and that they now had enough to carry revival on. That's the key—giving away what we have received. *"Surely you have received, surely you must give"* (Matthew 10:8).

By now, I had a message from the Holy Spirit to move to Tampa and become Pastor Rodney Howard-Browne's associate evangelist. Shortly after the Australia trip, Katie, myself, and my youngest son, Caleb (the other two were now in college), packed our clothes, pictures, and books and flew to Tampa. I didn't take a dish, a piece of furniture, or even a curling iron.

We arrived in time to attend the 1997 campmeeting. What a week! I planned to stay in Tampa for an extra week to buy a house. I never had a beautiful home and lived almost every week in someone else's house. It was time for me to have my first new home. I looked at homes and realized I could have one built for the same price as the existing ones. I secured a builder, obtained a loan (which was difficult since I had no work history in Florida), saved to go to the bank with a down payment, and then... you guessed it. God asked me to sow the down payment into an offering that week. By now, I was used to Him asking large and difficult things of me. I knew I was being tested, and God wanted me to show others how big He could be in their lives.

The next day, someone I did not know called me from a bank and offered me a one hundred percent loan. The person mentioned that he knew I had given my down payment. To this day, I do not know how he knew. The loan officers gave me special favor, and the move was on. In that one week, I established an address, reincorporated my ministry, was given a loan, ordered furniture and appliances, and secured a builder. Then, as usual, I had to fly out once again. I did not even get to watch them lay one brick.

I will never forget walking into the home for the first time. I secured a company to build the home and met with builders in a brief two-week period. I obtained a post office box for an address, started the re-incorporation process of my ministry from Alaska to Florida, secured a loan, picked out colors, and flew off to my next revival meeting. I could not oversee the workers or observe the house as it was being built. I was in revival meetings and couldn't even go to my house closing or inspection. I arranged for someone from Pastor Rodney's ministry to go in my stead. I saw it for the first time the night that I occupied it.

Katie and I walked through the furniture-bare home, crying with excitement and gratitude. We slept on the floor, but I was too excited to sleep. I thought of the days ahead and about what the Lord had done. My thoughts were taken up with the faithfulness of my big God. I came from the cold, frigid state of Alaska to hot, humid Florida. I was now a baked Alaskan. I knew that God had directed me thus far and would continue to guide my footsteps.

My new home had four bedrooms, an office, a family room, a formal living room, a formal dining room, a kitchen, two and one-half bathrooms, a swimming pool and deck, and beautiful landscaping. I was far from the village floors with no running water and the outhouses. My God certainly is no respecter of persons. He wants to give His children the desires of our hearts. He asks only for us to believe Him, step out of our comfort zone, and go after Him!

I will never forget the first time my father visited my new home. I saw him walk into my bedroom and start pacing off the width and length of the room. I asked him what he was doing. He smiled and said he couldn't believe how large my bedroom was. He said it was as big as his house. Now, this was an exaggeration! However, the house that he built when I was in kindergarten was only a little over nine hundred square feet.

My home was not extravagant, but it was far beyond anything he thought I could ever have. He had reminded me years before that I needed to "forget this stupid missionary idea before my children and I starved to death." So, this was quite a witness of my Big God's provision.

Not long after moving into the home, my oldest son, Joshua, came for his first visit. He was on spring break from the University of Nebraska. Upon arriving, he saw my new sports car in the driveway. It was a brand-new red Pontiac Grand

Prix and was given to me by a couple in one of my meetings. He walked into the home, looked around, and walked out to the swimming pool. He looked at me with tears in his eyes and said, "Mom, when we were staying with Noel and Edna, and I watched you giving when we needed it so much, I remember you telling me that you couldn't out-give God. You were right. I see what He has done for you." It was a special moment that I will always treasure. My boys had watched me sacrifice when it looked like we would never get ahead. Now, they could see first-hand what my God had done.

My beautiful Tampa, FL home with my sons.

My home became a hotel, and visiting ministers used my car. I was able to bless them so that they did not have to rent a hotel or a car. The home and car were tools used by traveling ministers, pastors, evangelists, missionaries, Bible school students, secretaries, and people who needed vacations and honeymoons. I have counted at least seventeen people who lived in my home at various times and many others who visited. We are only stewards of the material possessions that God entrusts us. They belong to God.

Pastor Rodney started a Bible school in Tampa to train revivalists for the twenty-first century. One of my greatest privileges was to be a Bible school teacher.

I loved teaching in the Bible school and training revivalists. I knew our goal was to duplicate the spirit of a revivalist in students. My calling was to spark a spiritual hunger in them, which they would take worldwide. I knew how important it is to teach them the fundamentals of good, Biblical doctrine. They needed to be ministers of the Word and the Spirit. This would bring about a worldwide revival.

When the Bible school became accredited, I looked into furthering my education. At that time, River Bible Institute was accredited through Life Christian University, with Dr. Doug Wingate as president. I eventually obtained my bachelor's degree, master's degree, and finally, my doctorate in theology. The night that I received my degree at the River Bible Institute. Dr. Wingate and Pastors Rodney and Adonica Howard-Browne officiated, and my heart was full of gratitude.

Receiving my doctorate in theology.

My degree is an earned degree. Some of my credits were earned through life experiences. I have pastored, ministered on the mission field, been involved in prison ministry, traveled for thirty years, and taught internationally in many Bible schools. I have many years of theological notes from sermons, books, and studies. I wrote my thesis on stewardship for my doctorate. I was always a good student in secular and Bible schools and kept a 4.0 average. I have known ministers who allow themselves to remain illiterate. Some send out emails with misspelled words and no understanding of basic grammar. Some have never tried to study and improve. I am not one of them. I continue to learn and explore.

Teaching Bible school was right up my alley. To this day, I enjoy hearing the reports of what the graduates from the River Bible Institute are doing all over the world. They told me countless times they were discouraged and tempted to quit. They said that my teaching, testimonies, and examples of overcoming caused them to persevere. Today, they pastor wonderful churches in many nations. Some are outstanding evangelists and missionaries. Even Pastors Rodney and Adonica's daughter-in-law, Jessica, told me that she was tempted to quit Bible school and I walked up to her and encouraged her to stay put. The rest is history. She is such an integral part of the ministry at RMI. This is what I live for. As they shared these testimonies, tears of joy ran down my face.

Me teaching the charter class of RBI.

Me teaching at River University many years later.

Tampa, Florida, holds wonderful memories for me, aside from the River. I love the swaying palm trees, the smell of ocean beaches, and the memories of my Corvette with the top down. I had great fellowship with wonderful friends. Every memory has a story, and I cannot tell them all, but there are some special ones that I must share.

My greatest honor while living in Tampa was ministering at the River, sometimes with Pastor Rodney present, and other times, I took his place while he ministered elsewhere. The campmeetings were the highlights of the year. People flew in from all over the world to do nothing but bask in God's glory and be forever changed. Every campmeeting was glorious and indescribable. Each one was unique, yet they all had a commonality of the extraordinary presence of God.

I never dreamed of becoming a regular campmeeting speaker alongside Pastor Rodney. Quite frequently, I was asked to give testimony of God's great provision and teach on stewardship. Sometimes, I was given notice, sometimes not. It's all part of the *"be ready, in season and out-of-season process"* (2 Timothy 4:2). It was a great honor and responsibility. I did not take either lightly. It was very important to me for Pastor to trust me implicitly. If he asked me to testify, I did not prophesy. If he asked me to teach, I did not testify. If he asked me to prophesy, I did not teach. When he asked me to take 15 minutes, I did only that. If he told me I could take my time, I did. This is something that the present generation needs to understand. He said more than once, publicly, that he could trust me to do only what I was asked to do. More importantly, I knew that meant he could trust me.

Praying for pastor Allyn at RMI.

Preaching at RMI.

Ministering at Revival Ministries International Headquarters, Tampa, FL.

Pastor Eric Gonyon, one of Pastor Rodney's associate pastors on staff, introduced me at one of the campmeetings as the greatest preacher in the world, in his opinion. I nearly fell off my seat. Not only did I not feel worthy of such an introduction, I thought of all the wonderful ministries that came through that place. I realized the special favor that God had given me and refused to take it lightly.

I was asked to take full services when Pastor Rodney was out of town. I often did Sunday mornings, Sunday evenings, and our mid-week Tuesday evening service. I loved my church and being able to serve in it.

On one occasion, I knew that Pastor Rodney was believing for a miracle in the area of finances. When he needed it most, he pledged a $100,000 offering to a church in South Africa. I knew that he wasn't in a position to give that kind of an offering but was trusting God. At the same time, I had a special need and was given a miraculous offering at the River for ministering. I thought, 'If he can give that, I can give this offering back,' and I did. It was several thousand dollars, and guess what? God took care of both of our miracles. I learned from a great teacher.

After being gone for several months, I flew into Tampa from an Alaskan trip. I was tired and couldn't wait to rest a week and then get back on the road. As the plane descended, I sensed the still, small voice of the Holy Spirit speaking to me. I heard, "Cancel all your meetings for the next two months." My budget was now $10,000 a week, and I had nothing in reserve. How could we be taken care of financially, and why would I do such a thing? It made no sense to my natural mind. However, the things of God seldom do. I again heard, "Do you trust Me? Have I ever failed you? Will you obey without knowing what is on the other side of your obedience?" I knew the voice of God and told my secretary sitting beside me, "Cancel all of my meetings." She was stunned but agreed.

The very next morning, we were in the middle of canceling them when Pastor Rodney called me. "Debbie, what are you doing for the next two months?"

"Funny you should ask. Why?"

"I need you to take my meetings for the next two months while I finish some business I am working on."

I laughed and told him what I had just heard from God and had acted upon that word. God is so very good. The next two months were exciting as I took all his crusades. At times, the crusade team decided not to tell the pastors that I was coming instead of Dr. Rodney until we were on the ground.

Substituting for the world's greatest revivalist is no small assignment. I walked into the office of pastors who did not know me and said, "Hello. Dr. Rodney can't be here this week, but he sent me." Sometimes I was met with rude remarks like, "Well, that's just great. I'll give you one night and see if anyone comes back." It is hard to walk into a crowded auditorium of people expecting Dr. Rodney Howard-Browne, while wearing a pink skirt and saying, "Hello, there's been a little change, as you can see." But each one of those churches asked me to stay on for weeks. Some pastors told Pastor Rodney and me, "Now that I've had Debbie in, I don't have to have you anymore." Of course, they were just joking, but I had the time of my life. Again, what an honor, trust, and responsibility!

I have had many celebrations in Tampa—parties, Christmas, birthdays, weddings, graduations, and showers. One that stands out is my birthday. Pastors Rodney and Adonica had recently moved into their beautiful home in the country, north of Tampa, called River Manor. The fact that my pastors were throwing me a beautiful party at their new home was over the top.

Me with Pastor Rodney.

The entire story of God giving them that home should be included in another book because it is miraculous. They had lived as a family with three children on the road in hotels for many years, building God's house. Now, He built theirs. When God gives you something, it is very special. The first time I drove out to their new home, I stopped and wept at the magnitude of what God had given them. I knew firsthand of their sacrifice, their giving, and their faith. Now, I was looking at the results of all of the above.

As I sat on their patio, eating from a wonderful barbecue buffet and fellowshipping with the best people in the world, I reflected on God's actions in my life. Never far from my mind was my past, the abuse, some pastors' negative remarks, living with other people, my father's remarks about my imminent starvation, my children's sacrifice, the village floors, my regrets, and then, the completely gracious favor of our Lord Jesus Christ. Only God could have done this!

ELEVEN

THE DEVIL TRIED TO KILL THE CALL AGAIN

Right about now, you probably think, could life get any better for me? I was asking the same question. I pinched myself to make sure that I wasn't dreaming. I felt like Cinderella in a movie. I went from rags to maybe not millionaire riches, but riches compared to where I started. I came from abuse and depression and now lived in joy unspeakable and full of glory. I had friends all over the world, traveled to different nations, and was getting paid for what I loved to do. The only way it could be any better was to have someone to share it with.

I enjoyed my friends, assistants, secretaries, and single pals in Tampa. We went to dinner and an occasional movie and had great fellowship. However, that romantic nature was surfacing. I have always desired to love and be loved. Every time I stood in front of one of the world's great waterfalls, rode an elephant, went on a safari, or stayed in a nice hotel room, I couldn't help but brush away a tear at the thought of not having that special one.

On several occasions, Pastor Rodney and others prophesied and encouraged me not to give up; they reminded me that God would bring him. They all recognized that I needed someone special and deserved to have him after what I went through. I must admit that after seven years of being single, at the prime of my life, I was starting to wonder if I would meet him.

Pastors reminded me that I was in a difficult position and was already aware of that. I was never in one place long enough to begin a relationship. Most single men are afraid to approach the evangelist, fearing she would think he is a flake. He would also face the fear of a possible reprimand from his pastor.

I knew that it would take a supernatural intervention of God for this to come about. I should have known how easy that was for God after everything He had done for me. For some reason, however, I thought that this area of my life would take a little help from me. Many of us find that while our faith can be great in some areas, it lacks in others; this was my other.

There was a church in Tulsa, Oklahoma, that became very dear to me. I went there every year for some time and absolutely loved the pastors and the community. People came from far and wide to my meetings; one man drove eight hours to come. It was very easy to flow in the Holy Spirit at this church. The meetings were outstanding.

When I first came to the church, I was assigned an usher to help set up the book table. He was kind and served with a spirit of excellence. However, as he helped, I noticed that he seemed to make some effeminate gestures. A few minutes later, I whispered to Katie, "That man is gay." She giggled but looked at me like I was, perhaps, being a little judgmental, considering that I had just met him. Later, I felt guilty for making such a statement.

There seemed to be several young, single men and women in that church in proportion to the size of the church. It worked out well for Katie and me since we were both single and usually only had married couples for fellowship. We enjoyed going out after the meetings to a restaurant with them and befriended many of them. It didn't take long to realize that the usher assigned to care for me seemed pretty fond of me. He constantly tried to get near me for conversation and tell me of his ministry call. On one occasion, I had a few throat problems, and he put a scarf around my neck, brought me tea, and started my rental car for me. I deeply appreciated his help and found myself thinking how handy it would be to have someone to take care of me. My next thought was, 'Not this someone, though. He's too effeminate. I still think he's gay.'

His pastors asked me if I could ever be interested in him. I realized that they saw the attention he was giving me. I told them that I suspected homosexuality. They assured me that was not the case and explained he was adopted and his adoptive father never treated him like a son. Therefore, Patrick gravitated toward his mother and female relatives and friends. His pastors believed that he just needed someone to masculinize him a bit.

Eventually, over the years, he and I became close friends. I did not keep my guard up because I knew I could never be attracted to him. However, feminine or not, he made a good friend. He frequently called me on the phone to encourage me. It seemed as though he knew when I was experiencing a difficult situation or trial. He called the day that I lost a close pastor friend to cancer. He said, "I just felt you were going through something today and needed encouragement." I felt that God must be talking to him about me.

There were times that I joked about him with Noel, Edna, and Katie. I said, "Don't let me get so desperate that I turn to Patrick." We laughed. They assured me that they wouldn't allow that.

On one of the trips to Tulsa, I took my good friend, Jean Thomas, with me. She observed Patrick looking at me and smiling while I preached. She heard his voice as he sang specials, observed his ushering, and the special attention he gave me. After the service, she said, "Debbie, that man is in love with you."

I said, "I suspect he is, but he's not my type."

She said, "You could do much worse and should be ashamed of yourself for joking about him. He seems like a very nice young man."

I did, indeed, feel ashamed. Jean was a spiritual, trusted friend, and I had just been spanked. I knew that he was nice, treated me well, and seemed to love God and the ministry, but wasn't I supposed to have an attraction of some kind?

After some time, Katie began to date a young man whom she had met at another church where I ministered. He was a youth leader, and they began to get quite serious. He was even talking about marriage. I realized that Katie could soon be going off to her own life, and once again, I would lose someone I had become very close to. It was like losing Noel and Edna all over again. I thought about how nice it would be to have a husband to love me and know we could share everything forever.

At this same time, I heard Pastor Rodney talking about how wonderful it was to have a good wife at his side. He said he couldn't go through the things he does without her. Ministry throws so many things at you because the Devil always tries to find new avenues to stop us. He said it was so good to come back to a good wife who could help him fight the battles. Once again, I began to feel sorry for myself in that area and wondered if I would ever have someone to share my life with and to encourage me.

I told Noel and Edna shortly after my divorce from Bruce that I had a fear that constantly barraged me. 'What if I ever married the wrong person again? Not only would the ministry be at stake, but I don't think I could live through that again.' I told them there was nothing worse than the hell of a bad marriage.

They assured me I was in a different place with the Lord and would know this time.

However, I was lonelier than anyone knew. Loneliness can be dangerous if you aren't diligent 24 hours a day. I faced crowds of hundreds and sometimes thousands daily. I ate, talked with them, and then returned to an empty, lonely hotel room. I looked out the window at the beautiful scenery and felt so alone, and then I was ashamed for feeling alone; God should be enough.

I had seven years of no dates, not even one kiss, in the prime of my life. I was not having such a battle on the physical end of things as the emotional end. I simply wanted to love and be loved. I saw in the Word of God how marriage should be and how it was designed to be. I realized that I never had one moment of that. I knew that it should be the closest thing to heaven on earth. However, I had only known the closest thing to hell a person could know on earth. I longed for the heavenly part. The more I was around godly marriages and could see their marriage preaching a sermon of Christ's love for his church and how she honors and submits to Him, the more I desired it.

Valentine's Day was approaching. Katie received flowers from the young man she was dating. He turned out not to be the one for her, and she realized it. But at that time, I thought that she would be receiving a proposal soon.

I began to think about the only possible, available person for me. I began to reason (so did Eve in the garden). 'Maybe I'm not all that attracted to him, but maybe that's for the best. I've heard that the best marriages are based on friendship first. Maybe I don't have to have the sparks flying. We're more mature than that. He loves ministry and encourages me. So what if he's not Mr. Macho? My first husband was, and look where that got me. My first husband was Mr. Bodybuilder, who thought he was God's gift to women. Wouldn't this be refreshing? Patrick is just the opposite. He doesn't flirt. I would never have to worry about that. Look how long he has waited for me to respond. He is patient and kind. Just think how thankful he would be if I were to return his love. Yes, I think I could love him in time. I think I'm starting to. I'm going to call him. Won't he be surprised?'

Oh, yes, he was. He sounded stunned when I asked him if he had feelings other than friendship for me. He seemed to stutter a little. Eventually, we talked again and decided to pursue more than friendship. I offered to fly him to my meeting. He lectured me about being practical. That should have been my first flag. A man in love, who has waited to hear these words for a long time, won't pass up an opportunity like that. However, I decided that I was being emotional and needed that balance of a practical person in my life. I was still reasoning instead of praying.

Eventually, I returned to Tulsa. The excitement mounted as my plane descended. After all these years, has true love been under my nose, and I didn't recognize it? I reasoned, 'Well, one thing is for sure. We have been friends for a long time and know each other. This relationship has not been built on attraction, youth, or spontaneous emotions. It has been built on a two-year friendship, a love for the Lord, revival, and ministry. That sounds like the right kind of beginning, so surely it will end happily, right?'

I noticed that he did not seem too eager to kiss me. However, again, I thought that meant this relationship was so very godly. He didn't want any lust to have the slightest opportunity. Neither did I, but I thought we could kiss if we were talking about marriage, but I would wait. A few weeks later, in April, he proposed to me in beautiful Woodward Park. I asked him if we could seal the engagement with a kiss. I was somewhat concerned about asking him, but I heard of several people who decided they would not kiss until their wedding night. I thought that he just wanted to do things as holy as he could. I cannot resist quoting my pastor once again. It is too apropos. "How dumb can you be and still breathe?"

Now, I needed to call Pastor Rodney and tell him about my engagement. I was a little nervous. I knew he had believed God with me, but would he believe Patrick was the right man? I made the phone call to tell him of the events that had transpired over the last few weeks. He interrupted me with, "Debbie, you don't have to sell me on him. I know that you know how to hear from God. I trust you, and we will be happy to meet him." He should have been able to trust me with that after the way I have known the Lord. I am quite sure that he has regretted trusting me in that area. That makes me sad because I never wanted to let the Lord or him down in any way.

We both flew into Tampa the next week. I remember taking Patrick to meet Pastor. The River at Tampa Bay was meeting in the Sun Dome then. Pastor Rodney hesitated as he looked at Patrick for a moment, then smiled and said, "Let's go out to the meeting, and I will announce your engagement." The crowd cheered. They loved me and wanted to see me happy. After the service, we discussed wedding plans. I was going to have a longer engagement, but we all decided that shorter engagements are better once a person knows it's right. It leaves less temptation for the flesh, and it is difficult for ministers who are traveling to be able to date. We decided to have the ceremony in the middle of the

July campmeeting so that I could have ministers from all over the world at my wedding. Pastor Rodney agreed to marry us and even sent us to Hawaii for our honeymoon. Finally, I would have the storybook wedding, honeymoon, and life.

Many years later, Pastor told me that when he saw Patrick, he was not happy. That is why he looked at him oddly for a few moments. He almost said something but knew that I had waited so long and was so happy, and he overrode what he thought he was getting on the inside.

The wedding was as beautiful as I had hoped. I had some of the best musicians and singers in the world sing and play at my wedding. They were at the campmeeting and agreed to do that for me. Everyone talked about how holy the service was, how anointed our vows were, and how happy I looked. I could not help but think that Patrick didn't look as happy as I did, but then I thought, 'He's not as emotional, and I'm sure that's all it is.'

After a beautiful reception, we went to a nice hotel in Tampa. It was already late, and we were tired. I walked onto the terrace. Patrick's best man and friend decorated the room with rose petals, which I thought was a very romantic thing for a best man to think. I waited for Patrick to join me on the terrace, which he eventually did after having some refreshments from our room. The terrace had a hot tub. He was not interested. I had to approach him with the first kiss. I decided that he was very shy, having never been married. Looking back now, the handwriting was on the wall.

The next day, we were off to Hawaii for our more official honeymoon. We flew from Tampa to Atlanta and then Maui, Hawaii, for six days. I had no idea that a dangerous near mishap would only be the first of the marriage.

Within moments of take-off from Atlanta, there was a loud explosion. All talking came to an abrupt halt. It seemed as though the air was sucked out of the atmosphere. We all waited. After what seemed like an eternity, the pilot's voice came over the overhead speakers. "Ladies and gentlemen, we regret to inform you that there has been an unfortunate incident. A tire exploded at take-off, but our wings seem to be okay." We were stunned. 'Why would the wings not be okay?' I thought that maybe the latter part was a joke to relieve tension. We were informed that the plane was returning to Atlanta for an emergency landing, where fire trucks and ambulances would be waiting. We were also told that the plane would have to eject fuel from both sides of the aircraft before landing. I had never seen fuel expelled from a jet before. It was a steady stream from both sides of the aircraft. After a relatively smooth landing, we exited the aircraft. As we did, we saw that the wing had a gigantic hole through it. At least one tire shot through the wing. Fire trucks, ambulances, and news teams were all present. Thank God we made it to the ground safely with no more incidents. However, it looked as though the marriage had begun amidst the turmoil.

Maui, Hawaii, was the most beautiful place I had ever seen. We were blessed with a week at the well-known Grand Wailea Hotel. Upon pulling up to the hotel, we saw many waterfalls landscaping its terrace. The hotel had fountains and pools running through it, with underwater bars where you can swim up to a counter and order a coke. It was a romantic paradise for sure. The sunsets, scenic roads, and waterfalls were more than I had even dreamed they would be. What a location for a honeymoon!

I was at a point of exhaustion from pushing too hard without taking a rest. I felt that I could never take a week off. I was able to trust God for anything financially when I was working but had not yet learned to do so personally or if I needed to rest. I needed two weeks, not five days, for a honeymoon.

Not only was the financial pressure of the out-go of the ministry large, but we had been blessed with a free hotel stay for five days. I knew it would be over before I wanted. I wanted to relax, enjoy my new husband, lay on the beach, swim, get a massage, sleep late, and go for excursions in the car. That was not my husband's plan, though. Most women would celebrate if they had a husband who liked to shop. However, I doubt that they would celebrate it if that was what he wanted to do on a honeymoon. He informed me that he did not like the beach, swimming, or getting sand on him. He did like to shop, though. The more expensive the item was, the better. It did not take long to know that he had a high-class taste, especially with my money. He loved jewelry, furs, nice furniture, and nice cars. The problem was that he was in the process of bankruptcy when I married him, and now, he was not working.

With the bankruptcy, some of his bills were written off, but he still had to pay others. Guess who that now fell on? Yes, I was the woman who paid off his car and student loans. I knew that when I married him, but I did not expect him to continue pushing me to work harder and pay for nice things. It did not take long to see that he had a real need to look like a big shot. I was his ticket to do so. His interest was in shopping, jewelry, and art. I was on my honeymoon but already feeling lonely again.

We hit the road running after the honeymoon. Not long after we were married, my pastor extended his campmeeting in Tampa, Florida. It went on for nine weeks, and I helped him preach at those meetings. I taught on giving almost every night. The meetings went late, and we fellowshipped late most of those nights. That part was fine, but Patrick pushed for even later nights with people.

I was experiencing some health symptoms. I had fought a bladder condition for some time. The doctors told me that it was nerve damage. It could have been caused by the traumatic childbirth delivery I had with Joshua or the years of weight-lifting. Either way, I needed a miracle. The bladder would not empty all the way. I was constantly carrying a full bladder. Also, it would go into spasms. I could get a signal that I needed to go to the bathroom now, and it may or may not be true. There was no way I could know for sure. I was getting those spasms about every fifteen minutes. I was usually in two daily services, each lasting from four to five hours. During that time, I felt like I would have an accident in public every fifteen minutes while preaching. I thank God that I never did. It wasn't easy to concentrate on what I was preaching with that taking place in the background. While I was continuing to see miracles all the time in my meetings, I needed my own. Yet, I was determined not to quit and continued to believe God. I did not tell anyone else about it.

I begged my husband for a rest. I asked him if he could get a job for a little while, just long enough for me to rest and believe for my miracle. He not only refused to get a job but pouted if I asked to come home after church instead of going out to eat with everyone. He called me a party pooper and told me to quit talking about it and that I would be all right. He even asked others to go out after the services. I begged to go home.

My mind reflected on a time when Noel and Edna told me that they would be glad when I got married someday so that I would take care of myself physically. Edna said, "Your husband won't like you being in a big crowd of people every night. He will want to take you home to be with him. Then, you'll finally get some sleep." I had been looking forward to that day but now realized that my husband didn't want to be alone with me.

Every once in a while, my pastor, friend, and fellow evangelist Richard Moore invited Patrick to golf with them. He told me he was not interested in going with the men. Yet, he always insisted on being a part of the girls' night with my friends. He made an excellent girlfriend, but I needed a husband.

I invited several people to live in my home in Tampa through the years. I was home so infrequently and needed someone to watch the house. Shortly after Patrick and I were married, I talked to my pastors about how things were going. They suggested that I ask the friend who was living there to leave so that Patrick and I could be alone. Instead of being elated, he was disappointed because he "enjoyed having my friend, Candy, live there." That was another red flag.

Almost every night, he wanted to stay up and "search the web." The internet became almost his sole interest. He never seemed to be looking for anything in particular that he wanted to share. Yet, I never suspected pornography because he had little interest in women. I just thought it was a distraction from sleeping with his wife.

Eventually, I sought counsel. I talked to my pastors. They assigned an assistant pastor to meet with Patrick. He finally agreed to meet with him. Things improved for a week but later returned to how they were.

I continued to battle health symptoms. I was rapidly gaining weight and knew that it was from stress. I knew that God was always my source and still was. I continued to trust Him.

The day came when we were supposed to leave on another ministry trip, but I was very troubled about the circumstances. I was desperate and talked to Pastor Rodney. He told me to have Patrick stay home and travel alone on this trip. He told me he would talk to him sternly while I was gone. He would get to the bottom of this. When I presented this to Patrick, he was noticeably upset and told me that the marriage would be over if he could not go on this trip. I should have stood my ground, obviously, but I did not. I bowed to the fear of another failed marriage and told him he could come. I continued to pray that things would change.

There were times I was awakened in the morning to hear a young boy making race car or cartoon sounds. When I approached the living room, I saw him sitting on the couch, watching cartoons and getting involved like a small child. I couldn't believe it. I remembered reading about children who had traumatic experiences that sometimes became that age again. I wondered about it.

We became good friends with a pastor and his wife from Oregon. They were a couple who met the two of us together after we were engaged. Most of my pastor friends met me first and knew me much better than him. However, this was not the case with these pastors. We eventually went to their church many times, and the pastor became a part of my ministry board.

Patrick and the pastor's wife became friends. He liked to decorate, she liked antiques, and they worked on projects together. We bought chandeliers and put them in their church building. I invited them and some other pastor friends to go to Ukraine with me. We had a fruitful week, great ministry, and precious fellowship. However, it was tainted by the problems between Patrick and me. I was preaching at two meetings a day, as usual. We all went to lunch every day after the morning meeting. I needed time to study and rest. However, Patrick wanted to go shopping. We walked everywhere we went. One afternoon, some of our party discussed visiting a flea market and shopping for rugs. He wanted us to go. I was exhausted and told him he could, but I would not. After we got back to our apartment, we got into an argument. I tried to tell him how bad my physical body felt. I told him everyone else could shop and rest, but they were not speaking in the services. The argument eventually became heated. I was at the end of my rope and didn't care anymore about trying to stay calm. Both voices were raised, and our pastor friends could hear us arguing; their room was directly above ours. They had no idea what had taken place behind the scenes for so long. They later told me that they thought I was unreasonable for trying to get through to him and how much I needed a rest.

Patrick told me about his best friend, Terry, who pastored in Texas. They went to Bible school together at Southwestern Assembly of God Bible College. Patrick lived with Terry in his parents' home for several years. They traveled in a special singing group together and remained close even after Terry's marriage. Terry was Patrick's best man at our wedding. He and his wife seemed to be top-notch people. They were exceptionally outgoing and friendly, and I was eager to get to know them better.

Eventually, Terry invited us to hold revival meetings in his church in Texas. I couldn't wait! We would be with good friends and a new church; I felt it would be the beginning of a growing relationship with them. I thought that Terry could help with our marriage. If Patrick didn't trust my pastors or friends, he might allow his friends to help. I didn't care about the helping source; I just knew we needed help.

We had a great revival. People were saved, healed, baptized in the Holy Ghost, and set free. They received "joy unspeakable and full of glory." We had a wonderful time in the presence of God. We also had a great fellowship time in Terry and Janice's home. I even felt Terry made headway in encouraging Patrick to be more romantic. I did notice a couple of things that bothered me, however. One was the fact that Terry, too, had effeminate characteristics, which sometimes were more pronounced than others. I thought it was a little strange that both Patrick and his best friend had these tendencies, but maybe they were bullied by the more macho types. That may have helped form the friendship. I couldn't dwell on that. Besides, Terry seemed happily married.

The other thing that troubled me was a particular incident that took place while we were in their home. After church one night, we decided to have ice cream at their home. Terry offered to go to the store to get the ice cream. Each of the couples drove cars separately to the church that evening. Terry suggested that his wife and I ride home in one car, and he and Patrick would take the other. I thought that was a little unusual, but I shrugged it off. It seemed to take an unusual amount of time for them to pick up the ice cream and get home. However, I thought maybe Terry had taken him for a scenic ride.

When the revival was over, we gave our parting farewells. Terry told me that he had a surprise gift for me. He loved my teaching on giving and had never heard anything like it before. He wanted to sow an extra seed and decided to give my ministry his computer. I knew that it was a very sacrificial seed. I thanked him and assured him we needed more computers and would believe for a harvest with him.

As we were leaving, I realized that Katie needed my computer. She had moved to Tulsa after marrying Pastor Todd Holmes. She was still working for me but using Todd's computer for our ministry work. I was going to buy a computer and send it to her. Now, I had one to send. I didn't look at the computer before I sent it.

After some weeks, Pastors Todd and Katie called me. They were now doing marriage counseling with Patrick and me over the phone. The marriage was deteriorating. I also thought that Katie, being my best friend, and Patrick and Todd being from the same church would make it seem less threatening for Patrick. I thought that they were calling to encourage us. Instead, I heard this, "Debbie, I don't know how to tell you this, but the computer that Terry gave you is full of homosexual pornography." The wind was knocked out of me. Katie went on to explain, "Not only is it full of horrible pictures and movies, but it even has explicit messages between Pastor Terry and other men. He used the worst four-letter swear word you can use in some of these messages." I could not speak. I had her on speakerphone, looked over at Patrick, and expected to see a man devastated and in shock. Instead, I saw a man sitting and listening as if he heard someone say, "It's a nice day, isn't it?" He was absolutely unmoved and non-emotional. I was getting used to seeing no emotion in his eyes or face, but this was incredible. After I hung up the phone, I asked him what he thought, and he had nothing to say. I told him we had to call his friends and tell them what we found. I also reminded him I had to revoke my invitation to Terry to preach at my next campmeeting. Patrick finally responded with, "I don't see why." I was in even greater shock.

I no longer remember if it was that night or the next one before we called his friends. I dreaded confronting Terry and telling his wife. I knew it would devastate her, but I felt I had no choice. When I informed him of what Katie disclosed, Terry gasped. He told me that this had taken place over a year before. His brother-in-law, a practicing homosexual, had visited their home and bought homosexual pornography on Terry's computer. After the brother-in-law left, Terry saw the pornography, and it brought back Terry's addiction. When he was a boy, he was raped and had to fight the spirit of homosexuality. After he was sucked back into it, he confessed the whole thing to his wife (she backed up his story) and then to his board. He had offered to resign. His board forgave him, prayed with him, and would not accept his resignation. He said that it was all behind him. Nothing like that would ever happen again. I was somewhat relieved.

Again, Patrick did not seem surprised by any of it. He said very little. When I called Todd and Katie, they asked me for the dates that Terry gave me. Katie said, "I'm sorry, Debbie, but this filthy chat box was dated just a little while ago." Again, Patrick said nothing. I thought about Terry and Patrick's excursion to get ice cream and was again quite troubled. I was determined not to give up and get help.

My friend Richard Moore and I decided to have a joint campmeeting in Houston, Texas. It was a great step of faith for both ministries. We had to rent a building, bring in a worship team, send my secretary ahead of us, and do advertising. We asked Pastor Rodney if he would come and minister for us one night. We believed God to bless him with an offering, pay all the bills, and hope to have something left to split between our two ministries. We were not used to doing neutral venues. We were usually in churches.

Patrick was spending more and more time on the computer and less and less time with me after meetings. I begged him to communicate with me. I asked him about his past. I assured him that it did not matter to me if he had been molested as a child or even wrestled with it now. If I only knew the truth, I would know how to pray and get help for us. He closed up even more, denied any problem, told me he did not want to talk about this and was tired of me asking him. I asked Richard to talk to him and found out some things I had suspected about his disinterest in me. After talking for hours with Richard, we decided that it was best for me to come back to Tampa when the meetings were over. I told Patrick that he needed to go to Kansas, his hometown. I needed time to think, pray, and seek counsel from my pastors.

We had an awesome meeting in Houston. No one would ever guess the personal hell that I was going through. I cried alone in my room with every new revelation about Patrick. I then walked out in front of a crowd and allowed the Holy Spirit to touch them and me with great joy. The more dependent I am on the Holy Spirit, the more He has shown Himself strong on my behalf. Those were some of the most anointed meetings I have ever attended. Richard told me that he had never seen the anointing stronger on me. What a faithful God!

Patrick was sitting at the computer when I entered my hotel room after the last meeting that Friday night. He was surprised when I walked through the door and abruptly closed and clutched the computer and put it behind his back. I asked him what that was about, and he just looked at me. I told him that I was going home without him. I also told him that I needed the computer. It belonged to the ministry, not to him. He was adamant about keeping it for a while. Suddenly, everything came together and made sense. I will never forget the moment of revelation. I brought the computer back to Tampa with me. I cried most of the way home, sitting by myself on a jet. I didn't even try to look at the computer, for I was almost computer illiterate at that time. My staff did my emails. I only typed sermons.

When I reached home, I asked my middle son, Billy, to help me. He attended ITT in Tampa, a computer tech school. I asked him to look wherever anyone would hide anything they didn't want someone to see.

It only took minutes for homosexual pictures, movies, books, and chat boxes to appear. I almost fainted. I could not look at it after seeing the first couple of pictures. I didn't want my son to keep looking at it either. I called my pastor. He told me to bring my computer in. He had some of his staff take a look at it. It was unbelievable. I was done. Another marriage was dead!! I felt dead!! Could God raise me up again?

I called Patrick and told him. He couldn't deny what was found on the computer but denied practicing any homosexual activity, either in his past or recently. He denied being molested. He denied anything between him and Terry. He did say he would get a job. However, I was finished. My first husband wanted other women; my second husband wanted other men. I had found both husbands in the church, and people had prophesied about both. I wondered if love and marriage had eluded me forever.

Shortly after this, I received a phone call from the pastors on my board from Oregon. Patrick called them. They wanted me to do over-the-phone counseling with someone they knew in another state. I told my pastor, and he said, "No, tell them you are already in counseling with your own pastors." I agreed. They had no idea what I had been up against or for how long. They thought I was throwing in the towel too quickly. How easy it is for outsiders to step in when they have not walked in your shoes. It would be years before they apologized to me. That would not be the first time I would be disappointed by church folks, but I knew I had to keep walking in love and forgiveness. I still love them greatly to this day.

Not long after this, my pastor offered to pay for Patrick's car and belongings to be shipped to Kansas. I did not destroy anything. I have heard stories of angry wives burning their husband's clothes, but I packed up all of it and sent everything that belonged to him. I remained firm in my resolve to end the marriage. My emotions and hope were destroyed. I knew he obviously preferred men to me, and I could never compete. I was sure that he had been molested at some point. For that, I was sincerely sorry and had compassion. What I found inexcusable was his dishonesty, refusal to acknowledge anything until caught, and even then, denial to admit his past. I could not forgive that I had told him everything about my life and knew very little about him. I knew he did not love me, but only what I could give him; ministry, a nice home, a reputation, and a steady income. There is no deeper loneliness than being with someone and still being alone. I was betrayed and considered it to be adultery. He was involved with people on the internet, and I was in bed alone, night after night. He was not with me emotionally or physically. He did not seem to care if I lived or died. In fact, he asked me to take out life insurance to ensure he would have the house if anything happened to me.

Just weeks after I decided to end the marriage, Dr. R. T. Kendall, from England, came to our church in Tampa. He ministered on the subject of forgiveness. It was the best message I have ever heard on the topic. He has a book about it called *Total Forgiveness*. It was such a moving message that almost everyone answered the altar call to forgive and release others for what they had done. After that service, my pastor called me and asked if I thought we should forgive Patrick. I was shocked because, although I agreed that we should forgive, I thought he meant I should stay in the marriage. I was devastated that day because, once again, I felt I was letting my pastor down.

I already was living with terrible guilt at being stupid and naïve enough to marry Patrick in the first place. Now, I felt that everyone, from the pastors in Oregon to my own, felt I should reconcile. Yet I knew in my heart that he had not changed. He didn't even want to be delivered. He only wanted the cozy lifestyle. Later, I talked to my pastor about how I felt, and he said they did not expect that and would back me up no matter what. He just wanted me to be sure that I was doing what I had in my heart. Several months later, we were divorced. We were married for three and a half years. At the age of 45, I felt like a total failure.

I will never forget the night I sat in my home, thinking about the mess, the call of God upon my life, a second divorce, the public humiliation, the embarrassment to my pastors and church, and how I let everyone down. At that very moment, when I was succumbing to discouragement, Pastor Rodney called. He said that he called to encourage me. He said, "It's not over yet, Debbie. The greatest glory is yet to be seen in your ministry. Wait and see." I wept and felt the presence of God envelop me. The comfort, joy, and hope of the Holy Spirit flooded my soul. The enemy dealt a hard blow to the call on my life. The call of God was lying at the bottom of an abyss and looked lifeless. But, at that moment, it began to push forth like a seed from the depth of the soil. It would live, grow, and flourish again with greater strength and anointing. I knew that God forgave me, but would people? Only time would tell, and thank God, they did.

TWELVE

THE GLAMOROUS LIFE OF THE TRAVELING EVANGELIST

After that horrible chapter of my life, God was faithful again. There was a monumental shift in the ministry in many directions. Secretaries and assistants got married, some moved, and I needed more help. One of the River Bible Institute graduates caught my attention. Her name was LaShawn Wetzel. I knew she was studious, quiet, diligent, and spiritually hungry. She stood out to me when I taught in the Bible school. She yielded easily to the Holy Spirit. She volunteered with a spirit of excellence. Pastor Rodney's administrator at the time was a good friend of mine. She recommended LaShawn become my traveling assistant. I had one concern. She seemed to be an introvert, and I am an extrovert. Would we get along?

Exploring Uganda's Wildlife with LaShawn.

When you are a single minister, your traveling assistant can become your confidant, close companion, and friend. LaShawn and I did not know each other at all, and I wondered if we would be comfortable with one another. I found out that Candy gave LaShawn advice about her decision whether to accept my job offer or not. She said, "Debbie is in transition right now. She is very focused. This is a new beginning for her, and she is going far. You have the opportunity of a lifetime to go with her and help her achieve all that God has for her." LaShawn agreed and took the job.

LaShawn, myself & Katie in Olympia, WA.

I will never forget LaShawn's first months with me. We were on the road for over four months before returning to our Tampa base. We went to five cities in Finland. We constantly packed and unpacked. We stayed in some apartments where we had to carry our luggage up three flights of stairs. LaShawn learned quickly. The last leg of that three-month journey brought us to a city in Washington State. I will not say which, and I have changed the names to protect people. I met these pastors in another state about a year before. I had no idea what we were about to experience.

When we arrived at the church building, I had quite a surprise. They rented a building that had unfinished walls with drywall exposed. I asked where the women's restroom was and was told I would have to use an outhouse. I wondered if I was back in the Alaskan villages. It was the middle of the winter with snow on the ground. Each night after the offering, I took a quick break to run through the snow to the outhouse in open-toed shoes.

I am an Alaskan missionary who knows how to rough it. However, it helps to know that you will have to do so ahead of time. I didn't know that I was on a mission trip. I was in the middle of a metropolitan city in Washington State. This was not supposed to be the Alaskan bush.

What made it worse was the lack of respect for God or His servants. I stood in line to wait my turn for the outhouse. The women knew that I had to rush back to preach after the offertory but made no overture for me to use it first. I stood in the snow, hoping that the music team would keep playing while they awaited my arrival. However, that was just the beginning of an unbelievable week! Despite it all, we continued to have great meetings only because of the grace of God.

Later that week, I walked down the prayer line to lay hands on people and pray for them. In our meetings, we have catchers. They are ushers trained to stand behind people in case they fall under the power. The Bible speaks of people falling like dead men under the power of God.

The Old and New Testaments tell of those who fell to the ground when they encountered the strong presence of God. Here are some Biblical examples.

Genesis 17:3 records that Abram collapsed when God spoke to him. Joshua 5:14-15 tells us that Joshua collapsed when he experienced the presence of the Lord. Ezekiel 1:28 and 3:23 say that Ezekiel collapsed when the glory of the Lord appeared to him. Daniel 8:17 and 10:15 state that Daniel collapsed on the ground when he encountered the glory of God. Matthew 17:6 records that when God's glory was manifested to Peter, James, and John, all three of these men collapsed to the ground. Acts 9:4 and 26:14 reveal that Paul collapsed to the earth when he saw Christ on the road to Damascus. Revelation 1:17 tells that the apostle John collapsed at the feet of Jesus at the beginning of his vision on the island of Patmos. Revelation 1:17 says, *"And when I [John] saw him [Christ], I fell at his feet as dead..."*

The word "fell" is from the Greek word *pipto*, which means to fall from an upright position. It is used occasionally to describe those who fall in battle — which, of course, could mean falling forward, backward, or crumpling to the ground. In John's case, he fell at Jesus' feet. It says that John fell like a dead man. The word dead is from the Greek word *nekros*, which is the word for a corpse. In other words, in one split second, it seemed that all the life had gone out of him, and he crumpled forward (*pipto*) at the feet of Jesus. As in many cases where people experience God's glory, John's legs buckled under him, and the strength was drained from his body as he fell in the presence of God.

There are a lot of scriptural examples of people falling or collapsing when they come into contact with God's supernatural power. Sometimes God's power can be so strong that when it is manifested, people's legs cannot withstand His great glory and buckle underneath its weight. Our bodies are not yet glorified; that's why we will need new bodies when we get to Heaven.

One of the definitions of glory in the *Strong's Biblical Concordance* is the heavy weight of God. Churches that invite us to hold meetings are familiar with God's heavy presence and power. Ushers stand behind people, just in case. God can and will protect His people from hurt, but people are people, and not everyone is in the Spirit. So, just to be safe, we prefer to have catchers behind people.

In this church, their catchers stood too far back. Some of them were not paying any attention and were holding casual conversations with each other.

Many times, they looked away while I was praying for someone. Unfortunately, what I feared, happened. While the ushers conversed with each other, they dropped several people. I politely asked one of the catchers to stand closer and pay attention. Much to my shock, he looked at me with disdain and said in a voice void of any respect, "Lady, don't tell me what to do. I've been an usher for five years. Mind your own business."

I could not believe my ears! His pastor was standing close to him when he said it. I looked at the pastor, fully expecting an apology and for him to rebuke his usher. Instead, I heard him reply in a somewhat timid voice, "I'd rather you don't talk to her like that, and could you please stand closer?" The usher had a snide remark for his pastor, and the pastor shrugged and walked on. I did not say anything further to either of them. In the next moment, the inevitable happened. I heard a crash as a little elderly lady hit her head on the cement. The same disrespectful man was the one who dropped her. She screamed with pain and was taken to the hospital, where she later recovered. I remember thinking, "This is going to be a long week."

A couple of nights later, in my hotel room, I was awakened by a phone call at about 2 a.m. I was concerned that there was an emergency in my family. I was surprised to hear the pastor's wife's voice on the phone. "Get up; we have an emergency. My husband and I will be there to talk with you in a few minutes." I told LaShawn that we needed to wake up, get presentable, and be in the hotel lobby in five minutes. We could not imagine what this emergency was. After they greeted us in the lobby, she explained about the emergency. "I see the prayer lines are crooked, and we need you to tell us how to straighten them." Once again, I could not believe my ears! Disheveled prayer lines were the least of their problems. Disrespect was a much bigger one. Either way, these were things that could be discussed in the daytime. However, I bent over backward to please the pastors and did not rebuke them. I talked to them about the prayer lines and went back to sleep. There was more to come, however.

One night after the service, LaShawn whispered to me that one man had given $14,000 on his credit card. We didn't even see that very often in large churches, let alone small ones. What an outstanding miracle! I thought the pastors deserved to know about this financial miracle and would be thrilled that their church was used for it.

I have learned many things since that time. Pastor Rodney advised me not to tell the pastors when large amounts came in. I could not understand that at the time. I thought everyone had pure hearts and would rejoice with me about the blessing of God. I thought they would want to know that they were helping to pay for overseas crusades, building churches and Bible schools, and feeding the hungry. However, that is not always the case.

I made the mistake of telling the pastors of our tremendous blessing, and it became apparent immediately that the wife was not pleased. I believe jealousy overtook her at that very moment, much like it overtook Judas when Mary lavished Jesus with the alabaster box offering. We could see her disposition change. The enemy planted a seed of dissension and jealousy in her that took root, and she tried to cause great problems for me later. She also told me negative stories about other ministers who came to their church. She asked me to tell Pastor Rodney about them so he would not use them. I refused and said I was not a tattletale, which added fuel to the fire.

Shortly after, I saw her at one of Pastor Rodney's campmeetings, and she would not even speak to me. I remembered everything I had put up with there and could not figure out why she was treating me like that. The Lord told me that I might as well get used to it because there would be many times that people would judge me from a position of guilt in their own hearts.

Yet, God proved Himself so very faithful in the middle of difficult circumstances. It pays to keep your heart soft before Him.

Even with the hardships of ministry or the pain of dealing with difficult people, God always shows Himself strong. We had extraordinary meetings at that church. A couple I knew previously was having marriage problems. They drove over two hours to come to the meetings every night after they got off work. They began their day at 5 a.m.; they were desperate, and God met them at their point of hunger and desperation. The result was a marriage saved, and their callings reaffirmed.

After the last church service there, as we were packing, LaShawn looked at me with big, brown eyes and said, "All of those stories you told us in Bible school were true, weren't they?" I laughed and asked her if she doubted those stories when I was her Bible school teacher. She explained that she thought that I might be embellishing them a bit. Now, however, she believed that I had not told even half the story of what we occasionally encounter on the road. LaShawn was beginning to understand road life.

The last night was a sleepless one. We didn't finish the meeting on Friday night until very late, went back to our hotel, packed, and waited for the pastor to bring the check. We had a two-hour drive to the airport and a car rental to return. In those days, we were required to be at the airport four hours early. The event of 9/11 blessed us with that special privilege. I seemed to be selected every week for special security checks. I later realized that all of my multi-city plane tickets must have looked suspicious. Airport security employees took everything out of my luggage and did not bother to put it back as they found it. We had to lift the luggage onto tables where airport personnel with gloves and a wand went through our belongings. They even checked my protein powder for anthrax.

In the nineties, we were allowed three pieces of luggage. Each had a limit of 70 pounds. LaShawn and I both carried as much as we could, with the largest carry-on allowed.

Our plane was scheduled to leave at 6:30 a.m., which meant we had to be at the airport by 2:30 a.m. We were over an hour away from the airport. We did not even have a moment to lay our heads on a pillow. We simply packed, proceeded to the airport, and returned our rental car after a sleepless night.

We reached our gate and realized we had a few minutes to spare and bought a few snacks. We were sleep deprived as we walked onto the jetway. We could barely hold our eyes open. A pleasant flight attendant offered us lunch bags from a cooler as we stood on the jetway. We accepted that and walked onto the plane, dragging large carry-ons, oversized purses, lunches, computers, and a portable printer. (You can see that the luggage requirements were not nearly as stringent in those days.) We were relieved to find enough space to store our multiple devices and carry-ons. As we walked to our row, an announcement was delivered. "We have been informed of a mechanical problem, and everyone must exit the aircraft. This mechanical problem is expected to take about five hours to fix. We believe this plane will be able to fly when the problem is corrected, so please stay at the airport. You can enjoy breakfast, shopping, or whatever you like. We will inform you of the re-boarding time."

I could not believe my ears; we could have slept for five hours! Now we were asked to retrieve all of our things and sit at a gate for five hours. Oh, well, this is part of the glamorous traveling ministry. I told myself to wake up, put on my big-girl pants, and do what I had to do. Remember that this ministry trip was LaShawn's first. She experienced all possible scenarios in these three months. We were almost Tampa-bound. In five hours, we would fly to Chicago for our connecting flight home. We could not wait to be refreshed in our own church, the River at Tampa Bay. We were so blessed to be a part of a church where we could be refueled before going out again. We missed our own church and pastors, and nothing would stop us from being in church on Sunday morning.

We retrieved our belongings from the plane and pushed past our exhaustion.

I couldn't wait to sit at the gate and, hopefully, take a nap. That is difficult, sitting upright, no matter how exhausted you are. I was tempted to lie on the floor. I had no pillow, knew that the floor would be very hard and that I would look a little out of place. So, pride prevailed, and I decided to nap from a sitting position.

LaShawn opted for coffee at Starbucks. She offered to find coffee and bring me back a treat. I thought that was a great idea. I could rest and watch our things. She was gone about five or ten minutes when the flight attendant ran to our gate. She picked up a microphone and announced the good news. "Our mechanics have managed to locate the problem and correct it in record time. We will take off in about 20 minutes, and everyone must re-board in five minutes." I could not believe my ears. For a moment, I was elated until I awoke from my semi-comatose state and realized that I had to find LaShawn. I was unfamiliar with the Sea-Tac airport then and did not know where Starbucks was located.

I could not leave our things behind while I looked for LaShawn. Neither could I carry that much. It was a dilemma that even my alert brain would have struggled with. My sleep-deprived brain was completely stumped until moments later when the obvious solution came at lightning speed. I had to carry it and do so quickly. I had to find and retrieve my assistant.

It was the middle of winter. We each had long, heavy winter coats with us. "What to do? I will have to put on both winter coats inside a warm building and attempt to run while wearing them." This was a layered look beyond imagination. I didn't think I was making a new fashion statement. Next, I must quickly assess how to carry two purses, strap a computer and a printer on each shoulder, carry our two lunch bags under my chin, and pull two large carry-ons, one in each hand. I searched for LaShawn as one would search for gold in the streams of Alaska. I was focused and had tunnel vision because I could not see. Since the lunches were carried under my chin, I could only look down and see the floor. Instead of running to find LaShawn, I could barely move from the weight and delicate balance of both of our belongings.

I was weighted down and overheated from wearing two winter coats (one of which was more than a little snug). I could not run. I could barely walk. Staring at the floor in my narrow line of vision, I was taking turtle-speed steps, huffing and puffing, when I heard a scream of shock. LaShawn ran into me almost head-on. She could not believe what she saw! To this day, I wish we had a picture of what I looked like, but this was a day before cell phones. I can only imagine. LaShawn later told me that she had never seen anything so hilarious in her life. She immediately fell to the ground, laughing hysterically. I was still holding the bags under my chin but attempting to talk. "Get up; we don't have time for you to lay on the floor laughing. We are about to miss our plane. We have less than five minutes to re-board, or we will miss our connecting flight in Chicago. Help me carry this stuff; we must run faster than we've ever run."

LaShawn spilled the coffee when she fell to the floor. Now we had a mess on top of everything else. We had to shuffle what I was carrying and run. We were the last two people to re-board. They told us that they were not going to wait any longer. We had to rush down the narrow aisle of the plane, knowing that we had detained everyone. Our fellow passengers did not seem to find any of this humorous. They must have also had a sleepless night, judging by their grouchy faces. I believe that most of their sleeplessness came from parties and hangovers, not the glory. We seemed to be the only ones who were amused at our predicament. LaShawn was still laughing, and now the contagious laughter affected me. It was a mixture of being tired and delirious and having a carry-over of joy unspeakable and full of glory from the previous week. What many do not understand is this: When you live in that glorious presence and have a continual spiritual river of God's presence springing up, it is easy to find something funny in the natural, and often it turns into supernatural joy.

We were laughing until the tears were running down our faces. We also were trying to walk down the narrow aisle with our oversized carry-ons, purses, lunches, computers, printers, and coats. We were trying desperately to walk a straight line and not bump into the grouchy people but found that impossible. We were constantly saying, "So sorry; please excuse us." I don't know why we bothered because no one was excusing us. They acted as though their sleeplessness, the mechanical problem, the de-boarding, the delay, re-boarding, and now being bumped into was all our fault.

Some people just need to get a life. They glared and swore at us. The more they did, the harder we laughed. There is nothing quite as funny as people being in the flesh when you are caught up in the joy of the Lord. We laughed, and they glared. They glared, and we laughed. Finally, we found our row. Now we have another problem. We were the last to board, so no one had the courtesy to leave us any carry-on space. What were we to do? We couldn't fit all of our belongings under the seat and were forced to push the call button for the flight attendant. She arrived, glaring, much like the passengers. Upon hearing of our dilemma, she reminded us that we were detaining the entire plane and passengers. She informed us that the plane could not take off until we were seated. That was not a revelation to us. We reminded her that someone needed to find us a place for our things. It took a while, but the mission was finally accomplished.

Now the passengers glared even more, sighing in total disgust and swearing again. I realized that life was not much fun for most of them, and we remained sweet. As I finished buckling my seat belt, I noticed that LaShawn seemed to be in somewhat of a panic. She told me that she could not find her seatbelt anywhere, to which I answered, "What do you mean you can't find your seatbelt? Everyone has a seatbelt. It must be between the seats. Look harder."

"I have looked everywhere. Then you find it, Miss Debbie." I searched frantically for the missing belt while she stepped out in the aisle; you guessed it. The passengers all began to notice that she was standing in the aisle, which meant the plane could not take off, and they moaned and cussed some more.

We laughed and had to push our call button again. The flight attendant appeared with her hands on her hips as though saying, of course, it is you two again. "Now what?" she said.

I attempted to explain the new situation while trying to stifle my laughter, to no avail. She was not amused and insisted that a seatbelt was hidden somewhere under LaShawn's seat. I suggested nicely that she was welcome to find it. She could not, much to her shock and disgust, and acted as though we had purposely stolen it. She said that she had never had this happen before and that someone before us must have ripped it out of the seat. She would have to call a mechanic to install another one before we could depart. She did so over the intercom system. You can imagine the outbursts when people looked back and saw who were the culprits. I thought I must be having a dream. By now, LaShawn and I were laughing so hard that we couldn't breathe. We were doubled over, shrieking with laughter. No one was joining us.

Finally, the new seatbelt was installed, and we were on our way. It looked like it was going to be touch-and-go with our connecting flight. I called for a flight attendant, who did not want to bend over backward to give us much information. I asked her if we would make our connecting flight from Chicago to Tampa. She assured us that most planes were running late that day because of the weather and we would have no problem.

When we arrived in Chicago, we literally had to run again. I felt my heart pounding in my chest as we ran through O'Hare airport. Most of you know it is not some little country airport with only a few gates. I thought we were running a marathon when I was in no shape to sprint a block. It was no way to keep blood pressure down or cortisol levels and adrenal glands in check. However, it seemed that I had become par for the course every Saturday of my life. LaShawn, however, was still being groomed for the traveling minister's life. I think she must be wondering if it was more than she had bargained for. She was a great sport, though, and we were forming memories that we still laugh about many years later.

After running until our legs felt like they would buckle, we arrived at our gate to watch our plane ascending into the sky without us. Now what? We found out that we would have to leave the airport, rent a hotel room, and be back at the airport by 6 a.m. We would not arrive in Tampa until just in time to go to church, with no time to unpack. By the time we dragged our belongings behind us one last time, called and made reservations, asked for tickets for a new flight, and waited for a cab, we realized that we should have just stayed at the airport and slept in a chair again. However, it was too late now. I remember waiting at the revolving doors for our cab. Every time a cab or bus arrived for someone, the doors opened, and a gust that felt like an old-fashioned Nebraska tornado would engulf us. It was February, and there is a reason that Chicago is called the windy city. We were frozen by the time our cab arrived. We put our luggage in the cab and retrieved it again when we arrived at the hotel. By the time we unpacked, washed up, and finally got something decent to eat, we realized that we could only sleep about four hours. That would not have been bad if we had not already had a sleepless night. As I lay on my bed, I told myself to hurry and go to sleep. But before I knew it, the alarm clock was ringing, and it was time to start over again.

LaShawn and I managed to wake up, get dressed, repack, and take a cab back to the airport. We finally arrived in Tampa on Sunday morning. We were exhausted and dreamed of sleeping until we woke up. However, there was something we dreamed of more than sleep. It was to be at our wonderful church, the River at Tampa Bay; how we missed that place! The more I gave out in my meetings, the more I knew I needed to receive the Holy Spirit's refreshing presence. You can only give out what you have experienced. He can only be as real through you as He is to you. I knew I needed to be spiritually refreshed more than physical sleep. Every other evangelist or traveling minister I knew took time off when they arrived home. That was not the case for me. I was always at the River. I would never miss church if it could be prevented.

We had not yet unpacked and found getting ready for church somewhat difficult. Even though I was spiritually anticipating the service, my body was rebelling. I was so exhausted that I barely knew who I was. I thought of taking toothpicks to church that morning to give my eyelids some much-needed support. However, I decided it would be slightly embarrassing while sitting in the honored first row with cameras bearing down.

At some point in the service, Pastor Rodney called upon me to teach about giving before the offering. I heard my name being called in the distance as though I were in a tunnel. I believe the announcement jarred me out of a semi-conscious state. I found my way to the platform, and thank God, the anointing kicked in and enabled me to deliver the Word of the Lord. I was very thankful for God's help and realized that soon, I would be in my bed, sound asleep.

After the service, I was invited to join Pastors Rodney and Adonica for lunch at the church. I was always honored to be included in the list of people to spend quality time and fellowship with them. I was also eager to catch up on everything. However, I was so physically depleted that I, again, called upon the grace of the Lord to keep me awake during dinner. As it ended, Pastor Rodney looked at me and asked a question. "Debbie, why don't you come with me and the team to Tennessee today to attend a pastor's conference that I preach at?" I didn't know which inward response was screaming the loudest. One was, "What an awesome honor to be asked to go and preach part of the service," or, "You have got to be kidding! I can't even hold my head up for another moment. I haven't unpacked, and now I must repack. How long can I keep going like this?" However, the first response won out.

I looked up and heard myself say, "I would love to go. What time do I need to be back at the airport?" He replied, "We are chartering a jet and will be meeting at a small airport near here in a couple of hours." I told him I needed to repack, and he mentioned that I only needed to throw a few things in quickly. At that moment, I remembered that pastor or not, he is certainly a man, and a man just doesn't understand what a woman has to take. I assured him that I would meet him in two hours. On the way home, I looked at LaShawn, and she looked at me. We burst out laughing. We realized that our lifestyle certainly was one of a Holy Ghost adventure. I started in Nebraska, and she began in North Dakota. We came from families that lived in the same place almost all their lives. They are people who plan for months just to go somewhere for the weekend. Our families could never live the way we were living. "We ain't in Kansas anymore, Toto!"

THIRTEEN

THE BREAKING OF AN ALABASTER BOX

This was my first trip aboard a chartered jet. I found it fascinating, even though I spent countless hours on commercial planes. I was sitting exactly opposite Pastor Rodney, facing one other. We are usually only together in services or a room with multitudes of people at lunch or dinner. I didn't have much opportunity to converse with him one-on-one. At some point, he looked up and asked me a very surprising question. "Debbie, I heard you say a while back that since you were a child, you dreamed of owning a Corvette. Why don't you buy one?"

I forgot that I mentioned that when I was with a group of preachers. Several of them had purchased Harley Davidson motorcycles, including Pastor Rodney. Being a lady, I said that I would wait for my Corvette. I was only joking and never gave that any serious thought. Yes, it was a car I always admired and thought of as my dream car. However, it was not something that I sat around talking about, wishing for, or planning to buy. By this time, I had bought two new cars for others and was living to bless others.

I replied that I looked at the price tag on them and asked the salesman how many bedrooms the car had. My attempt at humor did not dissuade him. He said, "Debbie, you have given much to the kingdom of God and others. You have kept nothing back for yourself. I believe God would let you have the car you like." I said that the Lord probably would, but to do that, I may have to cut back on blessing someone else, and I did not want to do that. He asked if I would consider it if someone gave me a car to trade off for a down payment. He also asked if I had considered a used one with low mileage.

Before I knew what was happening, Pastor Rodney was praying. "Father, you know how Debbie has sown to your kingdom over the years. You know she does not consider herself, is not selfish, and has bought others their dream cars. I believe you want to bless her and have prompted me to pray this way today. I believe you will make way for her to have the car she has always wanted. I believe this in Jesus' name. Amen." I was so shocked that I could not say anything except "amen." I never heard him pray a specific prayer for material things for me. I believe that he was prompted to do so by the Holy Spirit.

When I arrived at the church, I was ushered to the front row, and Pastor Rodney walked to the platform. Later, he introduced me, and I taught on giving and gave part of my testimony. The offering was received, and Pastor Rodney began to preach. A man approached me. He was a minister who was originally from Australia. I preached with him at his campmeeting in Houston, Texas, a few years previously. He sat down beside me in Pastor Rodney's chair while Pastor Rodney was preaching. This made me a little uncomfortable. I thought, 'If you wanted to greet or fellowship with me, you needed to wait until after the service was over, not while Pastor Rodney was preaching.'

Little did I realize what was coming down the pike, or should I say the race track. Chris told me that while I was ministering, God spoke to him. He told him I was believing for a vehicle I had always dreamed of. God told him to give me his Mercedes-Benz as a down payment on the dream car I had always wanted. I almost fainted. Could this have happened so quickly? I believe that not more than an hour has transpired since Pastor Rodney prayed for me. I said, "Thank you so much, Chris. This means more than I can say, and I have to tell you the rest of the story after the service."

He told me that he would either sell the car in Texas and send me the money or drive the car to Tampa at a later date for me to sell. I agreed that we would do whatever was easiest for him. The next day, I received a call from another minister friend who was a mutual acquaintance. He heard that Chis had given me his car. Chris was his spiritual mentor and best friend. He wanted to buy the car. He told me that he would send the check out that day, and it would be waiting for me in Tampa when I arrived home. Our God knows every desire of our hearts and wants to supply it before we ask Him. He knows how to work out every single detail.

I searched the internet for red Corvettes with low mileage. I found blue, yellow, and silver, but not red. A red Corvette is quite popular, and not many people want to let them go. I almost decided to compromise with a yellow one when the Holy Spirit spoke to my heart, "Do you think I would do all of this and yet come up short on the color? You don't know how I long to give you every detail the way you want it. Check again." I looked again, and there it was, only 100 miles from my home in Sanford, Florida. It was one year old and had only 6,000 miles. It was a candy-apple red with gold metallic specks. It was a convertible with a black leather interior. It was a mean-looking machine.

I was on the road again when I made the final arrangements. I could not even pick it up. I had to assign that to my secretary. She drove it back to my home, called, and told me that it was in my garage, and we talked about the fact that I wouldn't be home for about another month to see it. I called Pastor Rodney and asked him to take it for a spin. I explained that I wouldn't have the car if it were not for his ministry, encouragement, and prayers. If he drove it first, it would be like the first-fruits principle in action. He thanked me for the offer but declined. He said that he didn't have time, didn't want to put a scratch on it, and that I should be the first to drive it. I was disappointed, and I think he could hear that in my voice. A few days later, I received a call from him, and I could tell he was trying to talk above some sort of wind noise. He asked, "What do you think I am driving right now? It's a beautiful car, Debbie, and has a lot of horses under the engine." We both laughed. I hung up and thanked God for His wonderful, unexpected, over-the-top blessings.

The day came when I landed at Tampa International Airport. I knew that the car would be there waiting for me. I picked up my luggage, walked outside, and the most beautiful Corvette was in front of me. My secretary already had the top down. It glistened in the sun like a brand-new one on the showroom floor. I stared, choked back tears, and eventually gave in to those tears. They came like a mighty waterfall, running down my cheeks, chin, and onto the sidewalk. I stood there, speechless, and it took a while for me to take a step toward the car. Do you think I was crying over a car? If so, you have missed the whole thing. A car is only a machine, a tool, or an object. It is not worth that kind of emotion, no matter what make and model the car is.

I cried because I was looking at God's incredible love, grace, and restoration. I remembered a totaled vehicle in Alaska. I remember my father telling me I would starve to death with this stupid missionary idea. I remember my ex-husband telling me that I would starve if I didn't have him. I told my children that we cannot out-give God. I thought of the half-bath that had been my bedroom, working at the used clothing store, the village floors, the outhouses, and the touch of God. My life was being replayed before my eyes, and God told me He was delighted to do even beyond what I asked. I was overwhelmed with the goodness of my God.

As I sat behind the steering wheel of that shiny, red convertible, I pushed the pedal to the metal, experienced the wind blowing through my hair, and was elated. Could I be the same woman who was forging through blizzards, living with other people, driving a totaled car, and working in a used clothing store? How did I end up in sunny Florida, watching the palm trees sway in the wind, driving my Corvette convertible, and flying worldwide? I knew there was only one answer. My big God had blessed me in every way. He is a God of restoration. He raised me to be a blessing and display His glory in every way. Tears were rolling down my face as I contemplated His goodness!

I loved that Corvette. I'm an American girl.

I didn't have the car very long when I was once again at Pastor Rodney's camp-meeting, enjoying the presence of the Lord. On this particular evening, Pastor Rodney again taught the subject of stewardship. He chose a passage from the scriptures I had heard him teach many times. It is from 2 Chron. 29. In this story, King David desperately wanted to build God's house. However, God told him that he couldn't. There was too much blood-shed in David's kingdom. His son, Solomon, would build it. David accepted that, refused to pout, and made an astounding declaration. He told God, "All right. Maybe I can't build it, but you didn't say I can't pay for it."

His godly attitude was so very different from many today. Some would say, "If I can't lead the choir, I'm not even going to sing." Others would say, "If I can't be chairman of the bake sale, they won't get my brownies this year." David lived to love and please his Lord and King. He not only had the kingdom contribute heavily to the project, but he led the way in giving himself. He said that he would give millions of dollars. By today's standards of gold and silver, it would be equivalent to $187,000,000 worth of gold. This was from his private treasure, or today, we would say his savings account. What a giver! He led by example.

I heard Pastor Rodney teach this many times. I even knew what he would say next. I heard him ask the question that I knew he would. "Does God have your private treasure?" I knew that many in the audience must be struggling with that question. I felt somewhat smug in my assurance that God already knew He had my private treasure. I reflected on the many times God asked me for what was most dear to me, and I obeyed instantly, without reservation. This was an area I felt I had been tried often, and proven faithful many times. I did not expect any conviction to rise within my heart or that God would want to try me further. I was very relaxed in examining my heart. However, I was about to be caught off guard. Pastor Rodney asked the question, not once but twice.

I sensed something taking place in my heart. I knew the voice of God. He was speaking to me. The question bellowed out a third time. "Does God have your private treasure?" Does He have your all? I defended myself within my own heart. "Lord, You know You have my all. I would withhold nothing from You." The next question was not coming from the mouth of Pastor Rodney but from the Holy Spirit. He spoke again by that still, small voice on the inside. "Would you give Me your new car, your dream car?" I was in shock!

"Lord, of course, I would, but that makes no sense. I didn't ask for it in the beginning. You gave that to me supernaturally. It's not even paid for, so it does not seem like it is mine to give. I don't think anyone else can even get insurance if I am paying for it. I haven't driven it but a few times because of traveling so much. I don't see why You would give it to me just to ask for it back. Also, it's my only car, my only means of transportation. I don't have an extra one to take me to and from the airport, buy groceries, etc. I can't sell it and give the money since I will be paying for it for another six years. Surely, I do not hear from You." But then, the question came again, only quiet and peaceful this time, almost as a whisper. "Does God have your private treasure? I don't know what your treasure is; only you and God know that."

My heart was pounding. No one in the auditorium could have guessed the battle waging in my heart. 'Am I hearing from God?' I don't want this to be one of those crazy emotional things people do at the moment, only to regret it later. I don't want it to be something I do to challenge myself to do more all the time. I don't want to be doing it to be a show-off the way some do when they give publicly. However, I know the voice of God. It is Him and only Him who asks, "Do I have your private treasure? Do you trust Me completely, and can I trust you completely?" The battle was over.

I knew I should not run to the altar and throw my keys down. This would not be done in front of an audience or at the height of frenzied emotion. I knew I had to talk to the Lord about this all week. I had to have my heart exactly in the position of gratitude, worship, surrender, and faith. I knew my mind had to cooperate with my spirit and be firmly settled so I would never look back.

I purchased the song by CeCe Winans called The Alabaster Box. It expressed how I felt perfectly. I taught the breaking of the alabaster box many times. I had become known for bringing truth and revelation in this area. I first heard Pastor Rodney teach on it and borrowed many of his points. However, I had ample opportunity to live the teaching of this story. I felt I became the Mary of John 12 many times. I had been broken and poured out. I had been forgiven much and challenged to forgive others, as well. I am passionate and want to worship my Lord with everything within me. That is why people are so touched when I teach on it. I now listened to the song repeatedly before the day that my alabaster box would be broken yet again.

I drove the car more that week than I ever had the opportunity to before. It was a typical sunny Tampa week. The convertible top was down, and the air blew through my hair daily. I drove while listening to CeCe sing, "Don't be angry with me. You weren't there the night He found me. You did not know what I felt when He put His loving arms around me, and you don't know the cost of the oil in my alabaster box." Tears flowed down my face as I attempted to sing with her. I was not crying more about giving away this beautiful car than I cried in the airport because I had a Corvette. Both times, I was only thinking about the goodness of my God, His restoration in my life, my love for Him, and my total dependency upon all He is. The moment was quickly approaching when I would break the largest alabaster box I had ever broken.

I formed a plan. I asked my friend Candy if she would drive her car behind me as I drove out to Pastors Rodney and Adonica's home. I texted them and asked if I could drop by for a few minutes. I never went there without an invitation before or since. They must have thought that was strange but answered that it would be fine.

Before leaving my house, I took down a Thomas Kinkade painting from my wall. It was my second most prized possession; I love his paintings. This was the one with the chapel in it. I knew that I wanted to give the painting, as well. The Lord would have both of my dearest possessions. I would go over the top in worship and give Him the double portion.

Pastors Rodney and Adonica had recently moved to their beautiful God-given home about 40 miles north of where I lived. Going to their home required taking many countryside roads. My heart was pounding with excitement while driving to their new home. I didn't have any sadness or regret in giving this. I felt like

Abraham when he called sacrificing his son worship (Gen. 22:5). I couldn't wait to worship my God and thank my pastors, all at the same time. I had a plan, and the anticipation was building all the way to their home. I knew that I would be coming home as a passenger in my friend's car, never to drive mine again.

When I arrived, I was surprised and disappointed to find that I was not their only visitor. They had company, and I felt awkward. I did not want to break this alabaster box in front of anyone else. I had to bide my time and trust that the company would eventually leave. I waited somewhat impatiently, and finally, they left. We had some small talk, and I knew it was getting late. Also, I felt that I could not wait any longer, or I would burst. I still remember the emotion coursing through my heart, soul, and body.

Part of me was afraid this gesture could be taken the wrong way. It could be seen as me trying to bribe them for a relationship through what I give. I didn't want to be seen as a show-off. Also, it was so very important that they know once and for all of my love and gratitude to them. They are the ministers God used to preach the Gospel with a fresh anointing that changed my life. I wanted to say thank you for that and their belief in the call of God on my life. I wanted to say thank you for the times they defended me, imparted to me, gave to me, and trusted me with their church and ministry. This gift was holy worship to my Father, but He uses obedient, humble people to change our lives. They were His instruments in not only my life but the lives of so many.

It was time to thank them in a way that words couldn't do. Much was at stake. I didn't plan what I would say because it was so important to me for the words of gratitude to come directly from my heart spontaneously. Yet, I knew that I could end up looking and sounding like a blubbering idiot who might regret saying too much or not nearly enough because of the intense emotion.

I finally told them I wanted to thank them for all they had done for me. I said that I had a gift for them for their new home. I knew they had plenty of artwork and decor, but I thought they might enjoy this. I asked them to come outside. I could tell they were curious. I retrieved the painting from the trunk and told them that it meant a lot to me, and for that reason, I wanted them to have it. I did not care if they ever displayed it or not. It was just important for me to give it to them. They humbly received it, thanked me, and then I knew the moment had come. I muttered something about how the painting was partially a distraction from what I needed to give them. They looked puzzled.

I handed my keys to Pastor Rodney and said, "A long time ago, a missionary and his wife left their native land of South Africa and came to the United States with three small children, four suitcases, and only $300 in their pocket. They obeyed God and came to Alaska, which was halfway around the world. A broken, rejected, and betrayed woman with three children was sitting there without hope. Her family had been destroyed, her confidence and call shattered, and no one gave her much hope. Then, these missionaries came to Anchorage in November of 1992, called her out of the audience, prophesied, prayed for her, and gave her the key to breakthrough. I said, "These keys are nothing compared to the spiritual keys you gave me. They are only a small, symbolic token of gratitude for the true keys."

That was the only time I saw Pastor Rodney look somewhat confused and bewildered. Finally, he said, "No, Debbie, I can't take your car. I am even busier than you are. I don't have time to go driving when I am home. Besides, God has blessed me with some nice cars, more than I can drive at the same time. This is your only car. I don't even have room in my garage for another car."

I was shattered. This was not part of the plan. I must convince him that I have heard from God. I must break open this alabaster box tonight. I told him all of that. Finally, he said, "All right. I'll take your car. I receive it. It is my car." I felt elated and relieved. Then he said, "However, since I don't have room for it, I feel I should give it to someone I know."

'What? That's even worse. It was important to give it to them because of what they had done for me. I was not giving my only transportation to anyone who perhaps didn't pay the price, maybe were not givers, and would not appreciate what was behind this. I wanted to cry.' What could I say, though? If I were truly giving a gift, that means I must lose control of it and place it in the hands of the rightful person. They can destroy it, give it again, let it sit, wear it out, and it is none of my business. I said, "All right, I am just so happy that you are receiving it. You are free to do whatever you wish with it."

He smiled and said, "Great. She's a wonderful woman of God."

I thought to myself, 'She? Who on earth is he giving it to?'

My mind listed several of his male friends, some of whom were close friends of mine that he might be preparing to give this to, but who in the world is she?

"Debbie, it is now my car, and I will come and get it on occasion and take it for a ride. However, I have no room in my garage for another vehicle. I want you to take it back home, park it in your garage, and use my car whenever you need it."

What? This was certainly not even one of the possible scenarios that I had considered. I protested, and he reminded me that I had already agreed to his terms. I was not the only one crying. I could see tears in their eyes.

A few minutes later, I was driving my car back to my house, again playing the Alabaster Box in my CD player, with the wind still blowing through my hair. I was disappointed and tried to figure out what had just transpired. This wasn't the way it was supposed to go. All this driving around and praying, worshipping, deciding, and planning had been for naught. I cried out to God, "Lord, I thought You wanted me to break open another alabaster box. I listened to You and obeyed. I wanted to do it. I wanted You and my pastors to know that I could be trusted with Your anointing, the call upon my life, Your Word coming from my lips, and that I would obey no matter the cost. I wanted to break another alabaster box but didn't get to."

As soon as I said that, the presence of the Lord engulfed me. I heard as distinctly as I have ever heard anything on the inside, "You did break it. Heaven watched it, hell watched it, and the angels witnessed it. Your pastor was there for it. Most importantly, I, the Lord Your God, know it, and I am well pleased. The promotion has just come to you. Your heart has been laid bare and broken before me. I know that I can trust you with anything. You will withhold nothing from Me. I can get it to you because I can get it through you."

I wept and worshipped God in that Chevrolet Corvette convertible underneath the stars of Heaven that night. When the wind blew through my hair, I knew even the wind had witnessed my worship and gratitude for the things God had done for me.

God has blessed Pastor Rodney recently with a beautiful blue Z06 Corvette that he did not ask for or purchase. A few weeks later, he was blessed with a vintage red Corvette. He gave mine back to me, and the double portion blessing chased him down.

I must ask you one question because God is asking it. Does God have your private treasure? He wants all of you, your heart, motives, dreams, and desires.

For those of you who would like to hear or read the teaching that I do on the Alabaster Box, I suggest you go to my web page, debbierichministries.org, and order it, or get my book called *Giving: Your Key to Breakthrough*.

FOURTEEN

THE DEATH OF ANOTHER MARRIAGE

From the moment I began in Alaska, the ministry took off beyond what I could imagine. God continued to bless and open doors. My friend Candy Mills told me that after my divorce from Patrick, she sensed the ministry was going to a new level. Indeed, it was. I had now preached at Madison Square Garden, Royal Albert's Hall in London, England, traveled to over 40 nations of the world, been on television and radio across the nation, and had become the associate evangelist of Dr. Rodney Howard-Browne.

I remember one unusual meeting where six different people approached me, saying they thought I would be the next Joyce Meyer. I was so surprised that each used the same phrase and name. They were people from different states who did not know each other. I wasn't out to copy Joyce or anyone else, but I knew God was letting me know the scope of what He called me to. I went to sleep that night, thanking God for His favor, grace, and mercy. I also told Him that I only wanted what He wanted, nothing more, and nothing else. However, I also reminded Him that even though I loved my call and the privilege of serving Him, I was hanging onto a promise for complete restoration in my personal life.

Much to my surprise, even Pastor Rodney encouraged me to believe God for a mate. He said that he and God knew how much I needed that. I had not sinned, kept my integrity, and God would still do it for me. At first, I felt so ashamed for making another mistake of judgment with Patrick. My heart found it hard to believe God wasn't mad at me. Part of me believed He would punish me by letting me remain single for the rest of my life. Theologically, I knew it wasn't so. God is good all the time. He's the great restorer, forgiver, and oh, so merciful and gracious! Yet, my natural inclination is towards guilt and beating myself up.

Eventually, I realized that, yes, God wants me happy and fulfilled in every area and has a good plan for my life. Jeremiah 29:11 says, *"For I know the thoughts that I think toward you, says the Lord, thoughts of peace and not of evil, to give you a future and a hope."* I wondered how long I would have to wait and how it would all happen. Meanwhile, I had a wonderful God, a wonderful ministry, and great friends and family to keep me more than busy.

My divorce from Patrick was final in the fall of 2001. Four years had gone by since then, without a date, having anyone put an arm around me, and being unable to just hold a hand. I emphasize that because those who have such things forget to be grateful and forget how lonesome it can be for others who don't have that. Everyone around you seems to be happily married, and you are the odd one at family functions, dinners, and even church. You cannot go home at night and share your innermost thoughts with anyone. There is no one to hold you and say, "I understand, darling, and will always be here to love you through thick and thin." Sometimes, that is all that is needed when you are a woman.

Also, in ministry, there are added pressures, challenges, and spiritual battles to overcome that the average person cannot imagine. In my case, there was even the added dimension of being a woman in a male-dominated profession. I would like to say that there are no intimidating bullies in the ministry, but I would be lying if I said that.

Interestingly, bullying is about as far from a Christ-like attitude as you can get. Intimidation is the Devil's game, not God's. I still am trying to work out some of the things I have experienced through the hands of supposedly anointed individuals. Many of them I sacrificed to help. After some of the greatest meetings, I came back to the hotel room, crying myself to sleep. No one knew what I was battling to see people saved, healed, baptized in the Holy Spirit, delivered, and filled with God's presence. Should it be this hard? One would think not. However, we have to deal with not only the Devil (that's the easy part) but also the flesh of human beings.

I will give one example. I was asked to come to a certain nation to hold revival meetings in two cities that were close to each other, where I previously ministered and had wonderful meetings in both places. I went to the first place, and God more than met us there. It was being televised across the nation and in other countries. The power of the Holy Spirit was being manifested in a big way.

We had great healings and miracles. Every night, we saw a wonderful harvest of souls and people so refreshed that it was being talked about everywhere. Within days, people were driving from every direction, coming by motor homes, trains, and anyway that they could; they wanted to experience the power of God. Eventually, the building was full, and it continued to build.

One of the couples who came spiritually hungry from the other side of the country (Bergen, on the west coast of Norway), stood out to me in every service. I could see the hunger in their faces. I called them out and prophesied over them. At the time, they barely spoke English but I knew they had a call of God upon their lives to preach the Gospel. They were so open to the anointing of The Holy Spirit. I knew that God was doing something very special. He spoke to me to pay their way to come to the United States for one of Pastor Rodney's campmeetings. We became very close friends and co-revivalists. Over the years, they visited several times and stayed in my home for as long as their visa would allow. I eventually ordained Eirik and Edit Gussias to the ministry. They traveled as evangelists throughout Norway for a few years and were eventually led to pioneer a church in Bergen. It is called Faithlife, and I have held meetings there. I am so proud of them. They have been a large blessing to me. They have taken me on a beautiful sightseeing trip of their country, remodeled my home in Washington state, and hosted me in their home many times.

Bob, & me with Edit & Eirik, on a fiord in Norway.

I knew that I would probably be asked to extend the revival and was preparing my heart for that event. However, I knew it also meant postponing or canceling the revival in the next city. I anticipated going there, and the pastor is a good friend.

A day or two later, I was asked to extend my stay where I was at. I knew that was what God, the pastor, and the people wanted. There was no doubt about it. However, somewhere in my heart, I felt that the next pastor might not see it that way. I prayed and asked the Lord to give me the courage to call the pastor where I was supposed to go next. I am a peace-loving person who agonizes over disappointing people, and I hate conflict, but I finally made the phone call.

My assistant and a couple who were dear friends were with me. Even though I had the phone tight against my ear, they could hear this pastor yelling at me over the phone. For the sake of privacy, "Pastor, I have been looking forward to coming to hold revival for you. However, I'm sure you have heard about what God is doing here or seen it on television. The meetings are building. I believe this could be the beginning of the revival you and many others have believed God for. The pastor here asked me to extend, and I believe that is what God wants. It breaks my heart not to be able to come to you at this time, but we can work that out later. The good news is that you are so close to this city, and I hope you and your church can come and join us here, at least some of the evenings. You are only one and a half hours away. We have hungry people coming from eight hours away. I ask you to forgive me for not coming right now."

Edit & Eirik and me in front of their church in Bergen Norway.

His response was, "No, I will not forgive you. If you don't come now, I'll never have you back, and I will tell people everywhere that you have no commitment, integrity, or character. I am still angry with Pastor Rodney for not coming the last time. All of you better get some character! So, are you coming or not? Make up your mind."

As I hung up the phone, I was in shock and tears. Was I talking to a Spirit-filled pastor with whom I have had a good relationship over the years or the Devil himself? I was trying to make the right decision under pressure. To those of you reading this, it would be an apparent, easy decision. Things are not always that easy. It would probably close a door (a door that I had enjoyed and developed a relationship with the church, congregation, and Bible school for many years). This pastor would spread his lies about me having no integrity and character. These are two things I make sure that I maintain, no matter what I have been through in life. For I believe enough people are running around without character or integrity.

Also, I felt like I was letting him down. I hated canceling meetings after people had worked hard, advertised, spent money, prayed, and anticipated the meetings. I always try to look at everything through other people's eyes. I knew he was hurt because he felt several of us had done this to him lately. It just happened like that; I was torn. The friend who accompanied me on the trip was called, anointed, and ready to preach. He always felt a call to Scandinavia. That is why he and his wife paid their own expense to come on this trip. I wondered if he could continue the revival where we were now while I went on to the next city. We could have the fire burning in both places at the same time. I asked him. He told me he would be happy to continue if that is what God, myself, and the pastor desired.

The pastor where we were was gracious and agreed to it. My friend did a great job. However, many people stopped coming as soon as they heard that I would not be there. The momentum was destroyed, and the moment in time was lost because of my fear of man.

When Pastor Clyde came to pick me up and take me to his town, I greeted him the way I always had. I smiled, and we even hugged. We still had great revival meetings there. That is the grace and mercy of Almighty God in action for the sake of His people.

My American friends were watching, as well as my assistant, and they remarked later that they didn't see how I could do that. I told them that I have always made a point of forgiving quickly and easily, and besides, I have had a lot of practice. If I held a grudge or did not go back to churches where pastors practiced bullying and intimidation, I would have very few churches to preach in. That is a sad fact that does not please the Lord. We need to change some things. Ministers need to remember that they are not CEOs of a corporation. This is not business nor a machine; this is serving Jesus Christ, the King of kings and Lord of lords. It is about servanthood because we love God and love people.

I remember telling Pastor Rodney a little of this when I got home. He said, "Just tell Clyde that you are not going back." I know that both God and Pastor Rodney were trying to grow me up. He can't fight my battles for me. Yet, I knew that most Pastor's wives, including his, would not have to deal with men like Pastor Clyde. Her husband would take care of it. It was these behind-the-scenes scenarios that were chipping away at my emotions and leaving me vulnerable. I thought, "When my husband gets here, you macho men will be sorry. You think you can intimidate the little lady by being a bully, and you know that I have a soft heart, but you won't be able to do that to my husband." I prayed that God would bring him quickly.

Eventually, Pastor Rodney teased me about my future husband. One night, while visiting Pastor Adonica and him in their hotel room in Finland, he called me over to the computer to ask if I had considered getting to know someone online. I began to think, "Well, I've made fun of looking for someone on the internet. However, with a full-time traveling schedule and never getting to stay in a church for more than a couple of weeks, it's hard to meet anyone. What if I could search through qualifications, interests, callings, hobbies, and family history myself? There is no sin in meeting people online. It is just another form of communication that previous generations did not have access to. It is not much different than old-fashioned letter-writing, a friend introducing you to someone, or a blind date. Yet, people automatically look at you like if you go online, you deserve whatever happens to you." However, I have met several couples who met online and are extremely happy. You can miss God or hear from God with any of the methods. Do not associate this with online pornography and any other online sin. The internet can be used for good or evil; it's just a tool. I understood that.

In my off time, I joined a well-known and respected online site that I had heard many wonderful things about. The questionnaire is more detailed. That gives you the best opportunity to get connected with the right person. After many months of no one even being introduced to me, I was sent a letter saying that I was too strict in my answers.

I was asked to consider changing some of my answers, like "no alcohol on any occasion, for any reason, in any amount." Would I not consider an allowance for a little alcohol on a holiday or celebration? "No, I would not." Eventually, they expired my membership, and I gave up.

In August 2005, I was invited to hold revival meetings in northern California. It was beautiful there. In my off time, I entertained the idea of trying the internet one more time. Someone told me about a specific "Christian" dating site called "Christian Mingle." I reasoned that perhaps more Christians would use that site. As soon as I submitted my application, including a picture of me standing beside my Corvette under a palm tree, I had several responses. In retrospect, that was not too bright. One response stood out immediately.

I loved the fact that he was from West Virginia and loved mountains, nature, scenery, fishing, and camping. Those are some of my favorite hobbies. I was too busy in the ministry to do most of these for years. I loved that he had a well-groomed beard and seemed to be a man's man. I was not interested in a husband who liked to shop for my clothes more than I did, enjoyed having a girl's night out, or liked to do my nails and discuss jewelry. This man was a rugged "Take me away, Rocky Mountain" kind of man (although it would be the Smokies, not the Rockies). I sent a little note, and the next thing I knew, he called, and we talked. My assistant said that she enjoyed seeing me giggling like a young girl. This man had a slow, southern drawl that would put anyone at ease. He said that he was camping with his grandson in the mountains while he talked to me. He sounded like a real family man.

I dreamed of that kind of lifestyle, far away from jets, cities, hotels, rental cars, bullies, and phone calls. I would be happy if I could just have that for a week, about once every six months. I had traveled every week of the year for years. To kick back, enjoy nature, and get my body restored from sleepless nights, traveling overseas, lost luggage, and some health symptoms sounded like a good thing. He told me that he was a simple, hard-working family man. He said he only wanted to love and be loved.

'Am I dreaming?' This sounded like all I ever wanted, as well. No wonder the computer matched us up. He said he was extremely romantic. I was beginning to fall fast and hard. There was one problem that would have to be addressed. I noticed that his application said simply, Christian, without getting specific with a denomination. I had to ask because this could be a dealbreaker.

"What denomination are you, and what do you believe?" I asked.

In a sweet drawl, he answered, "You probably have never heard of this, but I believe in speaking in tongues."

I was elated.

We spent hours talking on the phone daily, even while I had a heavy traveling schedule. I felt I was getting to know him and asked about his divorce. His wife cheated on him. I thought, 'Poor guy, I know what that's like.'

I asked about his children and grandson. I asked about his work and church, how long he had been saved, and what he wanted to see in ministry. I forgot that a person could tell you anything they think you want to hear, especially when that person has already studied your profile. Interestingly, no matter how often I have been betrayed and lied to, I still believe whatever a person says. I have a hard time believing that people can flat-out lie to get what they want. It's especially hard to believe coming from someone with a sweet, southern drawl who loves the simplicity of life and country.

When would I learn that the enemy was out to destroy me and would withhold nothing or no one who would yield to him to accomplish it? This was about to become my costliest lesson yet.

I finally got the courage to present my thoughts to Pastor Rodney. He asked, "Does he realize that he will have to move to Tampa?" I said yes, and that he already wanted to move to Tampa. It was one of the cities he was considering. He had a government job and told me that he was in charge of a two-million-dollar budget for the state of West Virginia in some sort of rural development. I thought about how handy it would be to have a businessman who understood budgets help me with the financial budget of the ministry. I also liked the idea that he had never been in ministry and was not coming after me to have a ministry, as Patrick did. He was a simple countryman, and what you see is what you get. I would soon find out that the situation was anything but that. There was so much hidden under the surface. He was the most complex and troubled man that I have ever met.

In October, we had our first real-life meeting. As my plane flew over the Appalachian trail, I viewed mountains, brooks, forested trails, and the most amazing colors. God's easel was stretched out before me as the autumn hues of yellow, gold, red, and orange brilliantly lit up the sky. I have always loved autumn, my favorite season of the year. However, to gaze upon this display of nature, knowing I was about to meet the man in person with whom I was falling in love over the phone, was a double blessing. My heart began to race. I told a good friend I would know for sure the moment I laid eyes on him.

As I walked through the airport in Charleston, I saw a man standing. He was holding a bouquet. My first reaction was, somehow, he didn't seem like the man in the picture. Even his face looks different, and I can't put my finger on it. I felt a tinge of disappointment and had already forgotten about "I will know when I see him." Besides, it is not the outside package that matters but the inside. I only wanted and needed this: someone who loves and serves God and will love me and allow me to love him. I'm not like the people with their lists—'he needs to be six foot two, has dark hair and blue eyes, has this many kids, a home like this, and this much money in the bank.' I have always believed that my list is simple, not hard, and fairly unselfish. So, I asked repeatedly, 'Why have I had such difficulty seeing it fulfilled?'

Something seemed very wrong, and I couldn't put my finger on it. Today, I would say to myself, "Hello, Debbie, wakey-wakey." At one point that first evening, I said, "I don't think this is going to work, and I have to protect the call of God on my life at any cost." I could not even give him a definitive reason for saying that. We have had no arguments or disagreements so far. I just couldn't shake what I was getting on the inside. I finally said, "I'm not sure, but I think this could be our first and last meeting." I was headed to Finland in a couple of days, and he had to go back to his work.

He replied, "All right, but don't you ever forget this. You will never find anyone who will treat you as well as I would. I will love you, massage your tired feet at night, cook for you, take care of you, and put you first. Isn't that what you have always wanted? It is right in front of you. Don't let fear or the past keep you from what God is sending your way."

Later, he dropped me off at the hotel where I was staying, and I said I should get a taxi to take me to the airport. I went to bed crying that night. I just wanted a Christian, loving husband. I tossed and turned, replaying his words over and over in my head. "You'll never find someone who will treat you as kindly as I will." I had built this romantic notion in my head and could not believe it was over in an instant, and I wasn't even completely sure why. I wondered if he would give me another chance if I called him. I was possibly just fearful of making another mistake. There was only one way to find out. I called, and he would not answer. I knew he was going straight home and realized he was purposely not answering the phone. I tried several times until he finally picked up the phone.

That incident should have told me something that I would soon find out. He is a pouter and a manipulator who thrived on punishing me if he felt that I did him wrong. However, being who I am, dealing with constant guilt that something is always my fault and that I didn't handle it right, and I was always trying to see things from the other one's perspective, I decided it was my fault. I profusely apologized and tried to explain my fear. After a while, he said, "Well, if you are sure, but I don't want ever to be put in this situation again."

Life was about to take a turn. Unfortunately, it was not quite the turn I had been anticipating. We decided to be married in November 2005. This wedding would be much simpler. He already had a chapel picked out in Gatlinburg, Tennessee. He dreamed of being married there for some reason. When I saw it, I was disappointed. From how he described it, I thought it would be a country chapel, but it looked more like a cheap Las Vegas, Elvis-impersonator kind of chapel. Oh, well. It wasn't worth disappointing him.

I must admit that the wedding day itself was beautiful. Everyone rejoiced to see me finally happy.

We spent a few days in a nearby cabin that I paid for. I love cabins and rustic, but it was not quite what I envisioned for my honeymoon. The first thing he wanted to do after the reception was to buy groceries. I asked myself, "Am I going to a grocery store in my wedding dress?" I pictured room service, not grocery shopping. However, I didn't want to say that out loud. Just before exiting his truck to go into the grocery store, he said, "I have to tell you something that I have been afraid to tell you."

My heart dropped. 'Already?'

"I have false teeth and was too embarrassed to tell you. I have been trying to leave them in all the time instead of taking them out to rest my gums. I think an abscess has formed, and I need to buy some medicine." I don't think I was as shocked at the idea of him having false teeth as much as the fact that I was just now hearing about it. I was an open book to him, telling him about everything so he would not be surprised by anything. However, I quickly dismissed his lack of forthrightness and felt sorry for him. He was in fear of rejection. I poured understanding on him, and we went grocery shopping and gum-healing shopping on our honeymoon night before seeing our cabin.

During that week, I was surprised at how quickly he forgot about wanting to cook for me. I noticed that he wanted his wife to do her domestic duties on the honeymoon. I had just come off the road to get married and would return in a few days, and I dreamed of room service and restaurants at least part of the time but did not say anything. I cooked and did the dishes.

Shortly before we were married, he took me to his home. He seemed reluctant, but I was eager to see where he lived and meet his family. Upon arriving at his home, I could see why. He was renting a very simple little home in West Virginia. The furniture was fairly barren except for a large television screen. He quickly explained that he shared his home with his son, David, daughter-in-law, and new grandson. He explained that he had adopted his older grandson, who was not living with them, and he was paying child support for him. That was a shock. What would I find out next?

On our honeymoon, I immediately knew I was in serious trouble again. He had a unique mental problem, isolating himself in rooms after locking the door for days sometimes. I almost walked off to call someone on my honeymoon to rescue me and take me home to Tampa, but I was too ashamed and was determined to tough it out and hope for a miracle.

I paid for the honeymoon, rings, wedding, and everything after the wedding. He left his home in West Virginia and came to live in my home in Tampa. He promised to attend every church meeting with me, both in Tampa and in my meetings on the road.

As a teacher at the River Bible Institute, I went to every banquet as a single woman for many years. It was a big event. I loved getting dressed up and seeing all the wonderful students who were almost at the end of their Bible school journey. The teachers, including myself, were honored with gifts. Funny stories from throughout the year would be shared. I longed for the day I would have a godly husband who would put on a tux, or at least a suit, and escort me to this event.

Dennis knew I had been looking forward to that night for several months. On the day of the banquet, he informed me, after sitting in a chair all day, doing nothing, that he would not be able to go. He needed to work on an old mustang car that he was restoring. He wanted to do it while it was cooler at night. I was shocked again.

"What? You're not going with me to the banquet that is the finality of all the teaching I have done with these students over the last two years?"

He said, "Yes, that's right. Some of us have to work for a living."

I knew I had to keep my thoughts to myself, or we would have a huge escalation, and I refused to enter into a verbal fight with the man I had pledged to love and honor. I was the peacemaker and cried myself to sleep. I had no idea what I would tell the students, the other teachers, the dean, and especially Pastors Rodney and Adonica.

I wondered if I would spend my entire life making excuses for him or being embarrassed by his actions. I knew I could not continue to make excuses for his lack of spiritual hunger. He left my first revival meeting in Georgia after being there for only one or two days. One man wanted to marry me only for hobnobbing in the green room with famous preachers, and the other refused to even meet with them, which is part of my work. I wondered why it seemed so difficult to find someone who shared my love for the Lord and yet loved me for me, not because of what I do.

Dennis promised to look for work in Tampa and said getting a government job would be no problem. He was on government disability from an army injury. He supposedly went to the employment agency most afternoons and came back jobless. Eventually, I found out from someone who worked there that he never went once. Months after we were married, I had ankle surgery and the infamous blood clot I discussed at the beginning of this book. His first comment in the hospital was, "What if you would have died? I can't pay for this house. I don't even have a job. We need to get life insurance on you." Thank God that I didn't have insurance when the incident happened.

It wasn't long before he asked me to sell my home in Tampa and move to Tennessee. He said that he had always wanted to live in Tennessee. We soon put my house up for sale. I wanted to cry. This was my dream house that God had blessed me with. I allowed many missionaries, pastors, and evangelists to stay there. My sons loved coming home from their respective colleges to swim in the pool, drive the souped-up Pontiac, and, later, the Corvette. But most of all, I loved the River, Pastors Rodney and Adonica, my friends, and my position in the church and Bible school. I made it clear that any man who married me would have to move to Tampa. He agreed.

Just weeks after my near-death experience, I loaded all my belongings into a truck for Tennessee. I had to house-hunt and lift heavy boxes and furniture up two stories. Dennis said his old back and knee injuries were acting up, and he couldn't help much.

I could write an entire book on the details of the worst deception of my life. Suffice it to say that as soon as we were married, I found out nothing that I had been told was true. I have edited this book and taken out about fifty pages explaining what I endured that year. I decided to shorten it with a summary. Instead of his wife cheating on him, he was the cheater. I had a long conversation with the woman he had an affair with. I discovered that he had a previous affair with a married woman, threatened her with blackmail, and she committed suicide. I then conversed with her widowed husband. I discovered that Dennis only made half the income from his job that he told me he made. No wonder he never let me visit his job and meet his fellow employees. He quit his job as soon as we married to travel with me on the road but refused to travel with me. I found out that he was on illegally prescribed medication for bipolar disorder, and the doctor who prescribed it went to jail. He coaxed me into buying cars he said he could restore, to find out that I had to hire others to do most of the restoration. Later, he sold three restored cars I had paid for and pocketed the money.

I hired a private investigator to learn that my home had women living in it while I was abroad ministering. I even found that he had asked foreign women to marry him on computer sites while being married to me. He, too, filled my computer with pornography and accused my secretary of it. He tried to get me to fire my secretary and put him in charge of the ministry finances. Thank God I refused! My secretary later discovered that he was searching for the passwords to the ministry accounts on the ministry computer but could not find them. He drained all of my accounts the day after he left me stranded in Tampa. He managed to get me to buy him a new pickup, motorcycle, and land. He ended up selling the pickup and motorcycle and kept that money.

He refused to help with anything that involved physical labor. I purchased a new home and worked hard on getting it just the way we wanted. This was only three months after experiencing that saddle embolism that almost killed me. Someone had to do the work. I cleaned, painted, hired someone to take out the dirty carpet, and put in hardwood floors. I shopped to find new furniture, decorated it, and was relentless in trying to finish it before it was time to be back on the road. I had been off too long, recovering from the foot surgery and the blood clot. A couple of minister friends helped me for a few days. I borrowed the money for the house. It was a one hundred percent loan. This was in 2006 when the banks still loaned that much.

Dennis had nothing to contribute but everything to gain. I had the home put in both of our names because I was still the trusting wife. I also put much of the new furniture on credit cards or installment plans. I was still paying for the restoration of the cars he bought. I was off work for several weeks, and if not for the grace of God, I would not have been able to pay for any of it. The house was the most beautiful one I had ever owned, located on two and a half acres. It was a two-story home with dormers and a big western-style porch, to which I added a swing and yard lanterns. It had an abundance of tall, hardwood trees that were ablaze with color in the fall. They also shed their leaves and left about a foot of leaves over the two acres. I realized I needed to buy a large riding lawn mower and hired people to remove the leaves. Dennis seemed to think that I was an endless cash cow.

I will never forget our Thanksgiving holiday in the new house. My son Joshua, and his wife, Stacie, came from Virginia (where he was stationed in the Navy) to be with us. They also helped us move in a few months previously. They brought with them an underground electric dog fence system. Dennis surprised me with two six-week-old puppies. I loved dogs and wanted one, but Dennis decided to get two. I asked for a golden retriever, but he also bought an Alaskan husky. He was an adorable silver, black, and white fur ball with crisp blue eyes.

I immediately loved him, but he was a natural-born hunter and was already teaching the retriever how to get out of every fence and chain. We decided to try the electric shock system. Joshua not only furnished the system but offered to dig around the perimeter of the entire two-and-one-half acres to place it. His hands were calloused and bleeding as he approached a small problem. There was a large tree root in the way of where he was digging. He felt he could make the hole slightly more shallow to avoid the root. However, Dennis came out and pointed at it and said, "You need to dig out that root." Josh replied that Dennis certainly was welcome to dig it out himself. Dennis went into the house to pout for the rest of the holiday. I knew I was in a lot of trouble.

By now, I understood that the atmosphere in meetings made him nervous. He was not living the way he proclaimed to live and was under conviction. I was finally married but still traveling alone.

My pastor's winter campmeeting would be the next week, following my Texas revival. My secretary and her husband invited both of us to stay with them. Dennis refused to go with me to Texas. So, our plan was for Dennis to meet me in Florida at my secretary's house and attend Pastor Rodney's meetings with me.

When I arrived at the airport, Dennis was there to pick me up. I noticed that he seemed more distant than usual. By then, I sold the Corvette (which God helped me pay off early) to pay for other bills, mostly Dennis' bills. He came up with the idea to sell the new Chevrolet pickup I bought for him and get two junker cars in its place. He made friends with a used car dealer in Tennessee. I have never figured out why he would want to sell a good vehicle for those two pieces of junk. One quit on me on my first road trip with it. Two older ladies whom I had befriended in ministry had an old Lincoln continental that they had no desire to keep any longer. They bought new vehicles and offered us the old Lincoln. Dennis was happy to take it. One side drooped almost to the ground. That is the vehicle that he drove to Florida in.

I was awakened at LaShawn's in the early hours of the morning. Dennis said there was something urgent he needed to discuss with me. I could not imagine what it was but felt my heart rate speeding up and a knot tightening in my stomach. He told me he used my ministry computer at LaShawn's the night before I arrived. He found it to be full of disgusting pornography. He said that LaShawn, my secretary, must be involved in porn.

I suddenly realized everything. I thought back to the reflection in the glass door of our Tennessee living room. I could see that Dennis was looking at pictures late at night. I thought of his growing distance and the medical drugs he was on. I thought of his refusal to travel with me or go to meetings. I suddenly knew that he had a pornographic addiction. My stomach tightened. I was glad that it was dark and that he could not see my face or the tears beginning to fall. I had such a rush of mixed emotions simultaneously: anger, betrayal, hurt, embarrassment, rejection, and near hopelessness. I was so angry to think that he would dare blame it on LaShawn.

Yet, in some ways, there was humor involved. Accusing LaShawn of pornography was somewhat equivalent to accusing Mother Theresa. I knew that was something she would not even consider and that it ranked high on the list of the most ridiculous things I had ever heard. Part of me wanted to laugh at the ludicrousness of it, but I could not even speak, for my heart was breaking. I told him that we would deal with it in the morning. Needless to say, I had a sleepless night.

I got up early that Sunday morning. As I walked toward LaShawn's bedroom,

I had a plan. I knocked on her door. When she answered, I put my fingers to my lips, letting her know we had to talk quietly. Her husband, Will, had already gone early to church because he played on the worship team. LaShawn planned to join him later for the second service. Dennis and I were also planning to attend the latter one. I warned her that this was going to be an ugly story. It was coupled with a terrible accusation that I did not believe a word of, but we had to do a bit of acting for this to play out. I explained the entire last night's scenario, including the fact that I knew he was trying to cover his tracks.

Evidently, he could not erase some things that he had done, and this was the story he concocted. I told her I thought we should all go into the living room when her husband got home. We would simply ask one another, "Have you been, or are you now, involved in pornography?" Of course, everyone answered with an emphatic "no." Dennis said to me in front of them, "Well, you certainly don't think it's me, do you?" I refused to answer. He stomped into the bedroom. A few minutes later, he left the house. A few hours later, he returned with a list of demands I had to comply with to remain his wife. A few will always remain etched in my memory: 'Don't ever ask me to wear dressy clothes, do not expect me to sit in the front row of meetings. I don't want you to have any more to do with Rodney Howard-Browne. Do not ever question anything that I do again. I don't want you to go to big churches, only small ones.' He refused to counsel and added, "I will divorce you if you even mention the word counseling."

Once again, I could not believe my ears. How dare the man who just put pornography all over my ministry computer issue me a list of things I had to change without even an apology or any kind of repentance! I knew that we were at the end of a short marriage. We were only married for one year and two months. My heart sank. I could not believe that I was in this position once again.

I stared at him in disbelief. After the ultimatum, he left the room, slammed the door, and took off in the car that my friends gave us. He left me in Florida without a vehicle or a goodbye. I tried calling him all evening and the next day. He refused to answer his cell phone. I called Pastor Rodney the next day. He advised that I close all bank accounts immediately. I told him that Dennis would take that as an aggressive move and that he would believe that I was divorcing him. I did not want him to think that I was accusing him of stealing. I wanted to believe that Pastor Rodney or someone could get through to him and that it was not over. I hoped that he would come to his senses. Once again, I was wrong and underestimated how low he would sink.

One day later, I found that he had emptied all of our personal accounts. He knew someone had just paid me back $30,000 from a loan. I planned to use what was paid back to pay off credit cards from everything Dennis purchased. He knew about that check and withdrew it quicker than I could imagine. He also withdrew everything from our savings account. He knew I had household bills that had to be paid immediately. He did not care.

I was still reeling from the shock when LaShawn delivered more news. She could see on the computer and in a notebook where she kept passwords and accounting information that Dennis had snooped through the notebook. He was searching for password combinations to get access to the ministry accounts. However, he had failed. Thank God!

My mind immediately went back to the many times we argued about him becoming the ministry financial administrator. He told me that LaShawn could not have that much to do, was overpaid, and that we could save a lot of money by hiring him to do what she did. I knew in my heart that it was not a good idea for many reasons. Yet, I never dreamed that he was asking so that he could steal it. I felt nauseous to think of him trying to break into those accounts. Was he truly capable of touching God's money and stealing it? Apparently, he was.

The next news that I received was that of Dennis filing for divorce. The same day, he cleaned out accounts, found a lawyer, and filed. He got the jump on me. He knew that the charade of his lifestyle was over. I suddenly felt that we should check out the computer that I bought for him, but it was still in Tennessee. How would I retrieve it? I needed to go to Tennessee to hire a lawyer and take care of business.

Over the next few months, I learned how corrupt our legal system is in this country. Again, I am sparing you with many details of my fight against his lies and legal corruption. I endured car chases on a country road. I had three Tampa friends with me on that trip, and Dennis was chasing us with a loaded gun. I went to the courthouse and obtained a restraining order to go to my own home and take a few things back with me. I only had hours to do so. My lawyer left his office early that Friday. I could not reach him, so I went before a judge to obtain the order. I only had one weekend to get my things out of my own house. I was the only one paying the mortgage and all the utility bills, and he was the one living in the home and not working.

Later my lawyer's assistant called me and said I made a mess out of everything and should not have obtained a restraining order. She said that poor Dennis had visited their office, crying. He stated that he had to stay in his car all night in the cold because he had nowhere to go. That was laughable. I went by the used car lot, where I knew he hung out with a friend. We caught him staying there. He glared at us, and we sped off. He had been there all night, not out in the cold. I could not believe that my lawyer's assistant had taken his side.

Another time, two pastor friends worked on my house so that I could sell it. Dennis put a sunroom addition onto the house when I was on a ministry trip. He did not ask me about it and put thousands of dollars on my credit cards for the materials. When it was time to sell the home, an inspector and a realtor told me that Dennis was no carpenter (that was not news to me), and the room was crooked and would have to be removed. I was only allowed to be at the house for limited hours in the daytime to work on it. My pastor friend, Steve Bilsborough, took the glass off, laid it on the ground, and told me I could get some money back by selling it. We had no vehicle to transport it that evening, and places we could sell it to were closed for the evening. I thought that surely it would be there in the morning. I was wrong. Dennis sold it all before we could get back the next day. He also took every painting that I had purchased. He sold everything before we could come back the next morning. Dennis sabotaged the sale of the Tennessee home so that he could live there for free while I paid all the bills from Tampa. Eventually, I was invited to live with LaShawn and Will.

After hiring a private detective, I received pictures of women in my house and riding with Dennis on the motorcycle I purchased for him on his birthday. A realtor called to say that our loan had been approved for several acres of land that Dennis had asked me to buy. I now owed seven hundred and fifty thousand dollars from his purchases, and Dennis had all the money from our joint accounts.

If things could not possibly get any worse on this day, I received a telephone call. The man on the other end was a pastor from another country. He and his family were good friends, had once been students of mine at the River Bible Institute, and I held a revival in their church. He said in a very religious voice, "Is it true what I hear about you getting another divorce?"

"Yes, sir, I'm afraid it is."

"Then I want you to know that you are a disgrace to the body of Christ, and you will never be welcome in my country again." As if he owned the country.

He never asked what caused the divorce, how I was doing, if he could pray for me, or anything else. He simply hung up. It was one of those moments where you almost can't breathe from the pain and hurt.

I turned to LaShawn, her husband, and my assistant and told them what he said. I also told them that I needed to go for a walk. On that walk, I reminded myself of Kathryn Kuhlman's testimony about how she walked down a street and died a thousand deaths. I did so, as well, that night. My friends became worried about the length of time that I was gone on the walk and began to look for me.

Meanwhile, I returned to the house and waited for them when they arrived. I was fine. I joked and made them laugh. LaShawn said I received so much bad news that day that it made her cry. "How can you joke and laugh like that, Debbie, when you are going through so much?" I reminded her that you could never take yourself too seriously, only God. I also knew that this joy on the inside was for moments like these. You don't need joy in the middle of joy or peace in the middle of peace. You need them in the middle of a storm.

Yes, I made mistakes, and plenty of them. Yes, I was in a mess, and it looked like there would be no way out this time. However, I served a big and good God. My God has only plans for my welfare, not my destruction. He would see me through and show me the way out of the situation. He would stick by me even if no one else did. He is faithful and wants our total dependency upon Him. The arm of flesh had proven unreliable to me. People can love you when you are on top and drop you when you are at the bottom. People are fickle and undependable.

The interesting thing about that day was that it was not over yet. How quickly things can change when you give them to God! Our mid-week service at the River was held on Tuesday evenings. I was determined to go, despite the day's events. That night was a special night with a guest speaker. I had heard him before and knew of his background and ministry. He operated in the office of a Bible teacher and a prophet from time to time. His name was Drummond Thom.

That night, when he finished preaching, he walked up to me and began to prophesy. I was the only one he prophesied to that night. That was unusual. He knew nothing about my separation or looming divorce. He knew nothing of the day's events. Yet he prophesied about how everything looked over for me but that God would see me through it, and I would be raised from the circumstances stronger than before. Through him, God reminded me not to be disappointed in people because people are often wrong. I was to keep my eyes on God. He said that I was going through things not because of what I had done but because of the sins of others and not to feel guilty or beat myself up. I would learn much from this. Subsequently, the anointing upon my life and ministry would increase.

I knew God watched me die to my dreams, ambitions, failures, guilt, and more. This evening, He gave me a personal word to help me hang on.

Regarding my legal proceedings, my lawyer convinced me that mediation would be the most prudent way. Dennis was filing for temporary alimony until we could go to trial, and since my lawyer knew the judge, there was a good chance alimony could be granted. Settling for mediation would end things quickly, instead of waiting a year or more for the court date. My lawyer knew the judge was liberal, and a lot could go against me. I wanted my maiden name back, especially for ministry purposes. I didn't want to explain to everyone what was going on. I could not keep dragging this out, traveling back and forth to Tennessee.

Dennis and I agreed to pay half of the cost of the mediation. I paid to travel to Tennessee again, rented a cabin, and brought three ladies to help me. I met my lawyer in his office. His assistant was always rude to me and was even harsher than usual. My lawyer grabbed my file in a hurry and reviewed the case on the way to meet Dennis' lawyer and the mediator. It seemed as though my lawyer never read my file. I hired a private investigator who had a thick folder of proof of all the things Dennis had been up to: women, sabotaging the sale of the house, and more. I also did my own investigation and had documents proving that almost everything I had been told was a lie. The lawyer did not read any of it. He did not seem to care. When asked if he knew Dennis' lawyer, he replied, "no." Yet when they greeted each other, they did it on a first-name basis, and one of the ladies with me heard them talking to each other about their earlier golf game. I found that very interesting.

At first, the plan was to evenly divide all assets and have this mediation over quickly. I bought all the assets: the house, the vehicles, the furnishings, and everything, including most of his clothing. To divide everything in half would be more than fair to him. However, the mediator told me that Dennis wanted more. In the end, he wanted the motorcycle, the three cars that I had paid to restore, more than half of the furniture, the riding lawnmower, and even the massage table that he had bought for my birthday. (Of course, he asked me for the money to buy it.)

When I tried to hold out for the last vehicle that I'd paid cash for and had just finished getting restored (a beautiful '56 Chevy), the mediator said that Dennis was firm. He asked me if I wanted to call an end to the entire mediation over one car and reminded me that if I had to pay alimony for a year, it would come out to more than the car was worth. He also told me that Dennis decided he would not pay for half of the mediation and that I would have to pay for it. He double-crossed me once again. He knew that I would not go back to Florida without finishing this. Then, the mediator said that Dennis demanded I pay for his lawyer and my own, or he would walk away from mediation. I could not believe what I heard, but I wanted to be free of him. So, I agreed to it all.

It is still difficult to believe I was taken by the corrupt legal system. It is one thing to have married a con man who practices deception for a living. However, I was always a patriot who believed in America and our judicial system. When I observed the two lawyers, who supposedly didn't know each other, talking about meeting for golf as they shook hands at the end of the day, I knew I had been tricked. Later that day, my lawyer said, "I'm sure you are disappointed, but at least you are finished."

I paid full price for my lawyer and Dennis'. We never went to court; I had to give Dennis almost everything and did not see where my lawyer did a single thing to protect me. I found out that he went on to become the president of that state's bar association. He must have done better work for someone else than for me.

I had some friends in Tennessee who actually said to me, "You need to let us take care of this the Tennessee way. That's the only thing bullies like him understand." They were serious and volunteered to teach him a lesson he wouldn't forget, but I knew that I had to do things in a godly way and keep my eyes on Jesus.

Even though I was in big debt and lived in my secretary's house, I felt free. I took my maiden name Rich back. My main concern was selling the Tennessee house. My realtor for the land deal eventually relented and allowed me to pull out. He said he had compassion for me and became convinced that I was telling the truth and not just having buyer's remorse. God enabled me to pay off the lawyers. My debt was being eliminated. However, owning an expensive home in another state without being able to live there or rent it out was a pain, especially when Dennis was sabotaging every effort to sell it.

I realized that Dennis had no income, retirement, or assets and was planning on using women to secure all of the above. In fact, years later, his next wife (the one who had been living in my home while we were still married) called me. She said that he never worked the entire time they were married and took her home and all of her assets the same way he did mine. She was a nurse and owned a nice home in Florida before he stole it. (There should be a way that women could get together and ensure that never happens to another person.)

I realized that for the house to sell, I would have to find a way to get Dennis out of the house. I paid more money to my inept lawyer. I asked him to issue a warning to Dennis about neglecting the house and lawn. That did nothing. I prayed desperately about this matter; the Holy Spirit gave me an idea. I would have never thought of it on my own. I heard in my spirit, "Offer $5,000 for him to move out of the home." I could not imagine that he would go for it. The house payments came to more than that in just a few months. However, I forgot how greedy he could be for immediate results. He agreed. I found out later that he used the money to buy his girlfriend an engagement ring and move to her home in Florida. Doesn't history have a way of repeating itself?

The house finally sold for the third time. I did not go to Tennessee for the closing. I had someone represent me. I lowered the price and sold it at a great loss. I cashed out my credit cards to pay what I owed; it took two years to pay them off. Many advised me to negotiate a short sale or file for bankruptcy, but I still believed that God, Jehovah-Jireh, was my provider. I teach that. I have seen the results in my life, and I would take responsibility for my actions and watch God bring me out again. I would be a person of integrity. Meanwhile, I learned lessons that I would never repeat.

Finally, the nightmare chapter of Dennis was finished, although the scars in my heart would have to be dealt with. Also, the fallout in the ministry was another matter. I am a minister of the Gospel who made mistakes but sincerely sought God. I knew that I still had a message to give.

I found myself caught between different ministry friends with opposing advice. I had no idea what to do, where to go, where to live, and how to fulfill my call. I would have to walk this out, one day at a time. I knew my Lord would never leave me or forsake me.

FIFTEEN

RESTORATION, AT LAST, MY KNIGHT IN SHINING ARMOR

After I moved to LaShawn and Will's home, I was busy traveling to Europe for many weeks. LaShawn, Will, and I had great times of fellowship. It seemed so odd for the table to be turned. LaShawn lived in my home for several years. Now, I was living in her home. This was a strange scenario for me.

The couple from Alaska, who traded vehicles with Bruce and me for our trip to Alaska, was now living in Tampa. We kept in touch through the years. Priscilla volunteered to be my secretary for some time. What a blessing she and her husband, Gene, were to me! God laid it upon their hearts to give me $10,000 for a down payment for another Corvette. They said they wanted to be a part of the restoration of my life.

I searched for another low-mileage, red convertible Corvette. I found one in Atlanta, Georgia. It had only 1,000 miles on it with a black leather interior, a navigation system, and a power roof. It had more perks than my previous Corvette and was only one year old. It was delivered to me in Tampa, and I realized that God was once again doing more than I could ask or think.

I had great meetings where people were touched and healed by the power of God. I still had precious and loyal friends. I still had my health. I could have been dead, but by the grace of God, I survived and was feeling good. I even lost quite a bit of weight and was near my weight goal. God was more than supplying my every need.

In December of 2007, I flew to Honolulu, Hawaii, to spend Christmas with my three sons and my daughter-in-law. My oldest son, Joshua, was stationed in Hawaii at the time. My other two sons flew there to be with us.

While there, I received an unusual phone call from a long-time pastor friend named Bob Rester. He never called me before unless he was inviting me to come and hold meetings for him at his church in Washington State. He said I had been on his heart for a few weeks, and he could not shake it. He asked if I was all right or in any trouble.

I assured him that things were going well and I was recovering from the trauma of the divorce and all the legalities, shame, financial upheaval, and hurt. I was with my children and having a wonderful time.

In the middle of the conversation, I remembered that LaShawn told me that he had called the office recently and asked about me. She said he sounded strange, unlike the Bob Rester she usually spoke to. She added, "I think he has a crush on you, Debbie." I scolded her and said, "Shame on you. Bob Rester and I are only friends. He is old enough to be my father." I had been close to both him and his wife, Mary, before she graduated to Heaven a little over a year previously. I brushed off what LaShawn said. Now, the man was calling me directly. Could it be true that he had more than just feelings of friendship for me? I just thought he was a dear friend making sure I was all right. I also thought it was a very sweet gesture.

I told him he should attend Pastor Rodney's upcoming winter campmeeting in January and mentioned I was paying for tickets for several people from Norway and would like to pay for him to come from Seattle. I knew that he was in deep grief. His wife of many years had graduated to Heaven. He needed to have his heart healed and to be spiritually refreshed. He said he was already planning on coming but would not allow me to pay his way. He thanked me and told me that I would see him in January.

My middle son, Billy, was sitting within earshot of the conversation. He asked who it was. I told him it was an old pastor friend I had known for years checking on me. My son, with his usual mischievous grin, said, "Oh, is it time to get out my suit?" I told him that was not funny. The last thing that I wanted or even thought about was romance. I was taking inventory of what could have caused me to be susceptible to the deception of the enemy and what I needed to allow God to do in me to make sure that it never happened again.

The January campmeeting was more than wonderful. I bought plane tickets and hotel rooms to attend the campmeeting for several people from Norway. That was very sacrificial, especially in light of the financial ordeal I had been through. However, I have learned that the more difficult the circumstances, the more important it is to be a giver. I gave my way out of poverty before and would do so again. The same faithful God who honored my faith the first time would honor it again. I loved all these people and wanted them exposed to greater anointing than they had ever experienced.

Many of us stayed in the same hotel, including LaShawn, Will, and me. The distance between Spring Hill and Brandon was too great to drive every morning and evening. Brandon, Florida (where Pastor Rodney's church is located) is about an hour from Spring Hill. I also had several friends in the hotel who were from different parts of the United States.

Bob Rester was one of them. He asked if he could meet with me on one of the days for lunch to catch up and talk. I informed him that while I would love to, I had so many guests and responsibilities that it was improbable. I also had lunch with Pastors Rodney and Adonica and other visiting ministers at the church on many of the days. I told him I would let him know if I had any free time. Meanwhile, I saw him a few times, entering and leaving the hotel, but I never had time to say more than hello or goodbye.

Early in the week, another minister friend met with me. Pastor Mirek Hufton has been on my board for many years. I held revivals in his church many times. I told Pastor Rodney about him and encouraged them to meet. Pastor Mirek helped me greatly through the divorce. He sent his son and another man from his church to work on the Tennessee house before I sold it. He also was the one who went with me to hire my lawyer in Tennessee. He even tried to reason with Dennis, to no avail. One evening, after the campmeeting service, Pastor Mirek, his wife, Linda, and a church member came to my hotel room. He told me how proud he was of my repentance, my dedication to make things right and encouraged me to "hold the fort steady." He suggested I take a couple of years off from ministry, be careful, and watch God restore me. He and his wife brought great encouragement to my heart that evening. I never mentioned Pastor Bob to them because there was no Pastor Bob in my future as far as romance goes. I had no intention of dating anyone. We had not even talked in the hotel at that time.

As the week continued at the glorious campmeeting, I saw almost all of the friends that I wanted to, except Bob. I felt somewhat bad about the fact that he had been ignored. I found a moment to tell him that I thought we could have a quick lunch on Friday after the morning meeting. I asked him if he minded that it would be a drive-through lunch and Corvette ride combined. My time was limited. He said that he understood completely and realized that I had many friends to see from other countries. I found him to be completely understanding. He didn't apply any pressure; I appreciated that.

I was touched very deeply on Thursday night of the campmeeting. I wept in the presence of the Lord. I knew nothing was more important than God's perfect will in my life, and I reconsecrated myself to the Lord and His will afresh.

I saw Pastor Rodney sitting in a chair, basking in the presence of God in the afterglow of the powerful meeting. I felt to go to him and tell him how sorry I was for bringing any reproach upon him or the River at Tampa Bay by my divorce. I asked him to speak into my life if he saw me making another mistake. I told him that I had prayed and asked God to burn any idea of romance out of me. I also said that from now on, I was only concentrating on the call of God. He agreed to speak to me if he sensed I was making a mistake again.

When I woke up Friday morning, I forgot that it was the day I was supposed to meet Pastor Bob for lunch in my Corvette. I suddenly remembered during the service and kept my word. As we drove and talked, he told me how much he and Mary (his wife who graduated to Heaven) always thought of me as a minister and friend. I felt the same way about them. We had a lot of mutual respect and godly love for one another.

He said that over the course of the last few months, he often had me in his heart. At first, he thought he was only to pray for me. Eventually, he felt the friendship in his heart deepen until he thought of me more often. He told me about the grief he experienced after his wife died. He didn't see how he could go on like that. Eventually, he cried out to the Lord, "Either set me free from the grief or take me home because I cannot live like this." God set him free from his grief, and he knew that someday he would marry again. He added, "Debbie, I know there is a large difference between our ages, and I don't know if you think you could ever consider me in this way, but I must let you know what I am thinking." As he said this, his hand briefly rested upon mine, and I felt a stirring in my heart. I had great respect and admiration for this man of God. I knew how he treated his family, daughters, and grandchildren. I knew what kind of pastor he was and what a loyal friend he was to me and others. I held him in high esteem. However, I never considered him romantically and was quite shocked at the thought.

Besides, I recently spent a night in my hotel room crying to God to burn all ideas of being happily married out of me. I told the Lord I didn't understand why he made me such an over-the-top romantic. I want to share everything with someone I love. I cry watching Hallmark at Christmastime. I love watching sunsets and dream of having someone to share them with. However, like Kathryn Kuhlman, I died a thousand deaths and promised to do whatever I had to do. Why would a man of God finally come along now? I had a lot to think about but had no time to do so now. I told him I would have to think and pray, and he was fine.

In the back of my mind, I thought about how I had just spoken with Pastor Rodney about my heart and calling. How could this be happening the next day? Was it a temptation from the enemy? Was it possible that because I was sincere in my repentance and willingness to give up any idea of romance, God could now bring a godly man to me? What about the age difference? He was a pastor based in the Northwest, and I was an evangelist based out of Florida. How would that work? How could we date so far apart? What would his church or Pastor Rodney's church think? What would Pastor Mirek think after I promised I would not do anything stupid? Most importantly, what would Pastor Rodney think after what I had just told him the night before? Would he think I had planned this and deceived him? What strange timing!

Bob rented a car after the campmeeting and drove it to Alabama to minister to his niece. He went there for a few days and was coming back to Tampa the following weekend and would be flying out of the Orlando airport to Seattle on Saturday. I was home for a week after the campmeeting. I had tickets to fly from Tampa to Seattle the same day that Bob was flying there. I was going to hold a revival for Pastors Jason and Hannah Gillick in Silverdale, Washington. We were going to the same airport on the same day.

The night Bob returned to Florida, Friday evening, He called me to ask if he could take me to dinner in Tarpon Springs. I hesitated a moment. Then I thought, "What is wrong with two old friends going to dinner? We have been good friends for many years, we are both single, and we won't be seeing each other for a long time. I also wanted to know how things were with his church. I said yes. He said that he would pick me up at LaShawn's.

I felt nervous and excited as I dressed for dinner. I thought of how many years we had been friends. I also was very close to his two daughters and granddaughter, who sang on his worship team. I loved his entire family. I thought of how kind he was to me as an evangelist. He came to love my ministry, and he and his wife trusted me completely.

When I finished getting ready for dinner, LaShawn looked at me and said, "Debbie, something about you looks like you're ready for a date, not a dinner with a pastor acquaintance. Are you sure you are not falling for him?" I asked myself the same question.

I enjoyed Bob opening the car door for me. He was so polite. He told me that he loved a certain Greek restaurant in Tarpon Springs. He and Mary went there whenever they were in Florida. Greek food is not my favorite, but I did not tell him. I loved Tarpon Springs, the beach, the wind blowing through my hair in a Corvette, and the smell of the ocean water. I ordered the seafood pasta, and Bob ordered his favorite leg of lamb. When I lifted my fork to my mouth, he said, "Debbie, I know God is putting you on my heart. We both fly out tomorrow. After this Washington trip, you are going to Europe for a couple of months, and we won't have any opportunity to see each other for a long time. When I was a boy in Alabama, my family was extremely poor. My sister and I went somewhere with our dad. He bought her an ice cream cone because she asked for one. I never got one. I learned that day that if you want the ice cream cone, you have to ask for it. I didn't plan on saying this tonight, but I'm pretty nervous and am just going to say it. Could you consider marrying me?"

I'm pretty sure the pasta, the seafood, and the fork dropped onto my plate with a clang. I was shocked and did not know what to say. I thought I was dreaming. "Did he just say what I thought he did? Did I just get a proposal?" Before I could say anything, our waitress rushed across the floor to our table and said, "I've never seen a couple so in love. This is a special occasion, isn't it?"

"Well, yes, ma'am. He just asked me to marry him."

"Oh, I knew it, and you said what?" she said with a large grin on her face as though she had just received the proposal.

"Well, I said I will have to think about it."

Her beautiful smile faded into embarrassment as she mumbled, "Well, when you make up your mind, come back here, and we'll officially celebrate." We went back several times, and no one seemed to know who she was.

I don't remember finishing my meal. We were both pretty quiet after that. However, after dinner, we walked on the deck along the water. Sailing boats were at the pier. The wind and temperature were just right for a slight chill. Bob took off his leather jacket and offered to put it around me. I remember the smell of the leather, the breeze, the sky, his gentle blue eyes, and the face of a man who has lived long, loved his wife and family well and lived for his God with all of his heart. He put his arms around me, and for possibly the first time in thirty years, I felt protected and loved by a godly man. I felt like I had come home. I felt like I belonged there.

We walked back to where the Corvette was parked. He got into the driver's seat. I sat in the passenger's seat. We brought the top down. The breeze and ocean fragrance flooded the car. He told me he wanted to play a song for me that a Christian singer sang at his church. I believe Dolly Parton recorded it first. Bob had the Christian singer's CD with him. He said the song described me perfectly and should be called Debbie's Song. I had never heard it before, but as I listened, it brought tears to my eyes, and I felt that he understood what I had been through. The song refers to a woman who has been wounded but is like an eagle when she flies.

When the song finished playing, my mind was racing. I found out later that after Bob dropped me off at LaShawn's, he missed his Orlando exit. He said that he was on cloud nine and didn't even remember that he was staying in Orlando until he had gone out of his way about one hundred miles. He knew he would get very little sleep but did not care. He was happy. As for me, I was miserable because I felt a storm brewing, and I wasn't sure it was going to be the perfect storm.

Pastor Bob had already offered for me to use his car when I landed at Sea-tac Airport. This was not the first time. He offered me his car other times when I held meetings at his church. He told me there was no use spending that extra money on car rentals when he had an extra vehicle that I could use. So, as soon as he heard that I would be holding a revival in Silverdale, Washington, he offered it again. I accepted. That would save the ministry unnecessary expenses. The plan was to have his family bring an extra vehicle to the airport when they picked him up. He was due to land at the airport about an hour before me. Then, he would give me the keys and tell me where it was parked. I was very appreciative.

After the dinner and proposal, Bob brought me back to LaShawn's home. I had a swirling mass of thoughts descending upon me. I knew that I wouldn't get any sleep that night. I was beginning to have feelings for this man. While the romance idea was new, my understanding of Bob Rester was not new. I knew his convictions, doctrine, love for God, and his love and dedication to ministry. I knew how he treated his previous wife. I knew his generous heart. Now, I knew he cared for me. Women are meant to be responders when they are loved. I knew that I was genuinely loved.

However, I also knew that Pastors Rodney and Adonica, Pastor Mirek Hufton, and others did not know him or any of this. All they knew was that I had made two mistakes in marriage and divorce since they knew me, and I asked them to speak into my life. I promised them just a week ago that I would be very careful and not do anything foolish. How would I ever explain any of this?

I was in quite a predicament. I gave him hope for a possible future with me. I didn't say yes, but I didn't say no. I allowed him to hold me. He was on his way home, thinking we could fall in love. He will be telling his family when he sees them. He will be waiting at the airport, thinking we will pick up where we left off.

I realized that the hour was late, and LaShawn and Will had been asleep for hours. However, I needed to bounce some things off my trusted friend. She is the only one who knows all the parties involved. I woke her up and said, "I need to talk to you."

I poured out my heart to LaShawn and added that I thought I had made a mistake. I felt like I gave Bob false hope. He left thinking that I would meet him in Seattle. He told me he would drive to my meetings in Silverdale with some congregation members. I told her that I was so afraid that my minister friends would not understand, did not know what a good man he was, would believe it was too soon after my divorce, that we had too much of an age difference, and that my ministry would come to an end. Yet, I told her that I could not face him and tell him that. I respected and had deep feelings for him, and if I continued to see him, I knew I could love him.

I tried to phone him before he boarded his plane. He did not answer. I knew that I had missed my opportunity to talk to him before his take-off. I hated leaving a voice message but felt I had no choice. I tried to explain things the best I knew; I apologized profusely and hoped he could find it in his heart to forgive me.

I thought of all the things he had been through in the last few years; the death of his beloved wife of over 50 years, his youngest daughter had been diagnosed with cancer, burden of his church, and more. I felt like I added grief to his list. I felt ashamed and sad. I didn't expect to ever hear from him again. However, I was wrong.

In between my flight connections, I noticed that I had a message. I dreaded listening. I expected to hear a sharp rebuke. Instead, I listened to the voice of a very understanding man of God. He told me he understood and asked me to forgive him if he overstepped. He thought he heard from God, but if I felt he missed the plan of God, would I please forgive him? He did not want to side-rail my ministry in any way. He hoped this would not affect our friendship or his ability to call on me as a minister to his church in the future. He reminded me of how much he respected me as a minister and hoped we could remain friends. He said that he did not understand why I did not accept his offer for me to use his car because it was offered before anything happened between us. There were no strings attached to his offer. It was a gesture from one friend to another. However, he respected my decision and told me he would not be waiting at the airport.

As I listened, I fought back the tears. These were the words of a very mature and godly man. I had only known threats, manipulation, anger, and control from men who didn't get their way. This was the first time for me to hear an understanding man humble himself and willing to apologize. I heard a disappointed but strong voice. This was the voice of someone who would go on with God, with or without me. I just wasn't sure that I wanted it to be without me. I was more confused than ever. My heart told me one thing, and my head another. I tried desperately to be strong and do what I thought was right for my calling. Yet, my heart said that this man was God-sent to me. How could this be?

When I arrived at the airport, I thought Bob would be there, waiting and pleading with me. I looked around, but he was nowhere to be found. Bob Rester was a man of his word in every way. I rented a car and drove to Silverdale, Washington. My heart was still on the man of God that I had crushed. However, if there is one thing I have learned through the years, it is how to compartmentalize my personal hurt from my calling and the anointing upon my life. I had a job to do this week. As I unpacked, I tried desperately not to think of him.

I had another sleepless night. I felt like I had just made one of the biggest blunders of my life in letting Pastor Bob Rester slip through my fingers simply because of my fear that people would not understand.

We had a great Sunday morning service. God was faithful, and His presence was so rich. The moment that service was over, though, I felt that I should call Bob. I knew that his church service would be finished by now. I also knew he usually went to dinner with his daughters and sons-in-law. The phone rang many times, but he did not pick up. I knew I could leave a message, but this was not something I wanted to leave to chance. I called Charlotte's phone, his daughter. She answered and said that her father's phone was still turned off from being in church. I asked her to have him call me. He did.

I nervously beat around the bush. "Bob, I believe that I made a mistake yesterday. I was wondering if you would consider attending these meetings this week."

"Well, Debbie, what are you trying to say? What kind of a mistake did you make? How do you feel about me? I need to hear you say what you are feeling." Bob has a way of asking a person to be honest.

I felt my face turn red and was glad he couldn't see it. "Well, I believe that I am falling in love with you, and I have just been afraid that no one else will understand and that it could cost me the ministry as I have known it."

He assured me that he was a man of God and that the people I was concerned about were people of God. They would hear in their spirits what God had put in his heart, and everything would be all right. He would be at the service that night.

He arrived shortly before the evening meeting with his daughter. The moment I saw him, I had that same reassurance of protection and love that I had witnessed on the docks of Tarpon Springs, Florida. I knew at that moment that this would be the man I would marry.

That week was heaven on earth for me. I loved the pastors and church where I was holding meetings. I also loved the scenery of the northwest and this man of God. The pastors knew nothing of what was happening, but the pastor's wife told me one afternoon that I seemed to be glowing. I was very tempted to tell her what was going on. I am very open and transparent and do not believe in hiding things or giving only half-truths. However, I knew before anyone else knew my pastors needed to know.

Bob drove to Silverdale every day. It was a trip of almost two hours. We spent afternoons together, talking about our feelings, our pasts, and our callings. Bob asked if he could drive me back to Aberdeen to meet with his associate pastors and his secretary. He felt that he should tell them what God was doing with us. I agreed. The secretary was elated, and though she is usually a very reserved woman, she sang Bob's praises for about 15 minutes.

She told me that after everything she had been through in marriage, Bob had restored her faith in men. She told me what a man of integrity he was, how he always kept his word, and how much he could be trusted. I already knew it. However, it was wonderful to hear it from the person who worked closely with him for many years. I did notice, however, that his associate pastor and his wife became unusually quiet. I could tell that they did not like the idea at all. Yet, I felt to say nothing to Bob about that.

Bob's daughters and their husbands knew we were falling in love and thinking about marriage. They were ecstatic. They loved their mother deeply, but she was no longer here, on earth. They watched their father suffer immensely through her years of sickness and death. They saw him collapse when she breathed her last. They stood by and watched helplessly as he sunk further and further into depression and loneliness. Now, they watched his face light up with new hope. They only wanted him happy. They knew me from holding revival over the years. We had dinner together, and Charlotte and her husband took me to the beach and shopping.

I later discovered that three people secretly hoped that Bob and I would get together. They were Charlotte (Bob's oldest daughter), Kathy (his younger daughter), and Jennifer, his granddaughter (Charlotte's daughter). They never spoke to each other about it or to their father. They felt that it was too weighty of a subject and must remain in the hands of God. They did not pray a manipulative prayer but decided to just wait and see. Now that their hope was becoming a reality, the family quickly gave their approval and congratulations.

February 8th was Bob's birthday, and it was rapidly approaching. The family decided to have a combination of a birthday party and an engagement party. We met at a restaurant a few hours before my meeting began. Bob's daughters and sons-in-law were there, as well as his granddaughter, her husband, and their little girl. They gave us gifts. We had cake and ice cream, received beautiful cards, and enjoyed laughs and hugs. It was a perfect party. We knew that the day was coming when we would share the news, but these days were precious to have it only known by the family and Bob's assistant pastor and secretary.

Bob told me one afternoon that he had been looking for a nice engagement ring. He wanted me to know that it would not be before I left Washington for my next revival in Alaska. However, we planned to meet somewhere between trips and make it official.

As I preached that evening, the pastor's wife stood up and asked if she could say something. It was almost at the conclusion of my teaching on giving. I always taught on stewardship before I received the offering. It was highly unusual for someone to stand and ask if she could speak. However, this was the pastor's wife, and I trusted her. I said, "Of course. You are the pastor, and this is your house."

"Miss Debbie, I know you were not quite finished, but God has laid something on my heart that I need to be obedient and do. I heard you speak about the breaking of an alabaster box several times. I feel that I am to break one tonight and give you one of my most precious treasures. My husband's grandmother gave me her wedding ring set several years ago. It is not only beautiful and valuable but sentimental to us. I don't know why the Lord would ask me to give them to you since you are a single lady, but God said I had to do it tonight." She ran up to the altar area where I was standing, with tears streaming down her face, and placed that wedding set in my hand. I saw one of the most beautiful and unusual wedding sets I have ever seen. It had a row of red rubies wrapped around the diamond. Red is my favorite color, and rubies are my favorite gem. At the moment that Pastor Hannah brought this ring set to the altar, I saw Charlotte, Bob's daughter, fall to the floor by the power of God. I had never seen her do anything like that before and knew she was not the kind of person to fake anything. She stayed on the floor, under the power of God, for quite some time. When she got up, she was crying and shaking. She was touched deeply. She told me that since her mother died, she lived with nightmares of her mother related to her sickness. She had a lung disease that robbed her of oxygen. Bob and his daughter got her ready for church, bathed her, did her hair, and dressed her. However, on many occasions, she convulsed because of the lack of oxygen. The vivid pictures of Mary in distress continued to haunt Charlotte's mind. God told Charlotte that he delivered her on this night from that torment.

He also told her that people who know Christ are connected in eternity. Bob and Mary planted seeds for a great harvest of souls, and that harvest would be reaped by Bob and me. Yet, her mother would also share in the harvest.

It was an incredible moment for Charlotte, Bob, & me. We knew that God gave us that ring set. The pastor's wife knew nothing about our engagement or discussion about a ring that very afternoon. She was not even aware that Bob and I were seeing one another. The entire thing was miraculous and orchestrated by God. My new engagement ring was the most beautiful one I had ever seen! To this day, every time I look at it, I remember the grace of the Lord as He smiled down on us that day.

Earlier, at Pastor Rodney's campmeeting, a lady approached me who worked for me a few years previously. Our working relationship and friendship did not end well. There were a lot of hurt feelings. She had not spoken to me in about two years. As she approached me, I was guarded. Then I noticed tears streaming down her face as she said, "Miss Debbie, I know this has been a long time coming, but I was totally wrong and want to ask you to forgive me." I embraced her and told her that I had forgiven her. She added, "Do you remember that you gave me a large diamond ring given to you in an offering?" I had to think about it for a moment, and then I remembered. She went on. "God told me I needed to give it back to you this week and ask your forgiveness." I forgave her anyway, but I loved to hear her say those words. The diamond was a one-carat yellow diamond that was very valuable. The band was not to my taste, but the diamond was extraordinary.

Later I had a jeweler take out the larger diamond and put it in the new set. He also took the diamond from the set given to us by the pastor's wife for me to use on Bob's ring. God had arranged for both of those women to share something very valuable at just the right time to give us our special wedding sets. We will never forget it.

The next few months were very interesting. Those months involved much misunderstanding between Bob, myself, friends, and many whom I look up to. The Bible says in Proverbs 15:22, *"Without counsel purposes are disappointed: but in the multitude of counselors they are established."* It also says that pastors, leaders, and shepherds will have to give a higher account of our lives with greater responsibility. Hebrews 13:17 says, *"Obey them that have the rule over you, and submit yourselves: for they watch for your souls, as they that must give account, that they may do it with joy, and not with grief: for that is unprofitable for you."* According to the Word of God, they should speak into our lives, and we should respect and submit to that.

I am a firm believer in submission and authority. I have always felt that I have been an example of that to the utmost. This is the first and only time that I struggled with it. I knew Bob but knew that no one else in Tampa did. Bob can be very outspoken and sometimes says things too roughly, especially when he has a strong opinion. Friends got involved who did not know the situation and misconstrued events. They put events together in the wrong timelines, making things look different. Bob and I did not respond as we should have, and for that, I have asked the Lord and my pastors to forgive me. Thank God they are people who practice forgiveness.

I asked my pastor to tell me if I ever were to do something stupid again. He was concerned that this could be one of those times. I am sure that the short time span since my recent divorce (it had been one year), the age difference, and the fact that I was on the east coast and he was on the west coast had a lot to do with it. Nevertheless, they were only doing what I asked them to do. I knew at that time that my own stupid mistakes of the past were to blame for this moment. Wise people were now being protective. I am so grateful for pastors who love and protect me, but it was difficult then.

Because of the council I received, I took six weeks away from Bob and did not even allow him to call me or communicate with me in any way. I asked God to burn this out of me if it wasn't from Him. It was an agonizing six weeks. After I finished the Great Awakening Crusade in Florida with my pastors, I scheduled a long European crusade. I spent weeks in Norway, followed by Latvia, Sweden, and then back to Norway. I had two meetings a day, every day, for those six weeks. I thought, 'Surely I would be able to wash that man right out of my hair.' The crusades were tremendous, some of the most successful to date. Multitudes were born again, baptized in the Holy Spirit, healed, and delivered. I experienced some of the greatest financial miracles in those weeks I have ever had in ministry.

Everything was just as I had hoped for regarding ministry. However, I cried a bucket of tears every time I was alone in my hotel room. I am surprised that a new river was not found in Europe named "Debbie's Agony." Every day, I quoted Scripture and told myself that I could rise above this and Bob would be forgotten. However, every day, I seemed to love him more and felt more lost without him. I cried out to God to heal my heart and give me fresh vision and direction.

However, the day came about six weeks later, when I felt I had to call Bob.

SIXTEEN

PROPOSAL, WEDDING & HONEYMOONS

I had no idea how Bob would respond when I called him. I had not communicated with him for six weeks after telling him it was over. I explained to him that I set my face like flint to obey God and had to ensure that I was not out of the will of God. However, he was gracious and told me he knew I would call; he forgave me. I was not used to that either.

Bob offered to meet me in Tampa and help me move my things from Florida to Washington. We rented the largest available truck, retrieved my stuff out of the storage unit, sold the Corvette, packed my clothes, and left Florida on April 2, 2008, my birthday. It was a wonderful birthday present. I left with the man of God who was already demonstrating the love of Christ to me.

Bob met me at the airport. Our smiles and tears intermingled as we embraced for the first time in six weeks. We held onto each other in that airport, knowing that God had brought us full circle since our engagement, break-up, and silence. Now, we were making wedding plans. We knew that we had a huge workload in front of us, but we also knew that we needed time to sit, look into each other's eyes, and get re-acquainted. We decided to go to a nearby park and sit on a bench for a couple of hours before our move began.

We talked about the last several weeks. We discussed everyone's motives in all the decisions that had been made. I felt that God brought him back to me because I was willing to lay Bob on the altar and sought God with all of my heart. We talked about wedding plans and both of our families. We spoke of his church and my traveling ministry. We talked about where I could live until the wedding ceremony and what size of wedding we wanted.

We talked about the Corvette that God had just blessed me with. Bob urged me to keep it and tow it to Washington. I knew that was not practical. Even though I had been blessed with a $10,000 down payment, I still owed the bank for most of it. Western Washington (home to a rainforest) is known for a lot of overcast skies and drizzling rain. This car was a convertible, and I would have only a short season to enjoy it. I did not want my husband to be responsible for making those payments. I was still paying off credit card debt from closing the house in Tennessee and did not want to burden Bob with additional debt. I felt that trading in my dream car for my dream man was a small price to pay. I decided to sell the 'vette.

I already gave so much away when I first left Florida to go to Tennessee. I could have sold those things but chose to give them. I blessed friends with much of it and did so again when leaving Florida. Because I had made mistakes and I knew that many were afraid I was making one again, I felt I could not ask people to help me move. My husband was no longer a young man. Yet, we decided that he and I would do it by ourselves. LaShawn's husband did help us load the things into the truck. The heat and humidity of Tampa, Florida, were not on our side either. By the grace of God, we moved furniture, boxes, clothing, pictures, keepsakes, and books.

One of the more pressing problems was selling the Corvette in only three days. I put an advertisement in the newspaper. It looked like it came off of a showroom floor. It had only 6,000 miles on it and was loaded with the top package of equipment; power roof, navigation, and more. I bought it for $15,000, under what a new one cost. I already put $10,000 down and made about four months of payments. I owed exactly $40,000, and the new ones were going for $65,000. I should have been able to sell it at a profit or at least get back my down payment. I would have if I could park it in someone's garage and have time to advertise it. Again, I felt I could not ask anyone. I decided to sell it for what I owed. I took it to a Chevrolet dealer that carried a lot of Corvettes in Clearwater, FL. When I presented my offer to the manager, I think he nearly jumped out of his chair to shake my hand and present me with a check for the payoff. I should have gone back the next day to see what kind of sticker price it was wearing. However, I didn't have time to do that. My guess is that they placed a $65,000 price on it; he had bought it from me for $39,700.

I have learned that when you or people around you make bad decisions, you have to be able to sever the past, learn, and go on. You cannot lick your wounds and think about the what-could-have-beens. The alternative is bitterness, depression, medication, and possibly a mental institution. Some backslide, get mad at God, and turn to drugs and alcohol. I never looked back at the Corvette one last time with a tear or thought, 'that is my dream car going down the drain.' I left with my fiancée on my arm.

I regret not meeting with my pastors before leaving, though. I didn't want to leave Tampa or my church, but I wanted to be loved. I was afraid the meeting wouldn't end well, and I was terrible about confrontation. I have realized that confrontation in the past meant being hit and called names. I needed to let God go in and take care of that, as He had so many other things. The Lord has done that today, and while I still don't like confrontation (I don't think anyone does), I can and will deal with it.

I got up early (not usually one of my favorite activities) with excitement and anticipation. We took off in that huge Penske truck and headed for Washington State. I felt like I was going to another country. In many ways, I was. I have found that north-westerners have their own way of thinking. I had to revert to remembering Alaskan culture to understand it.

The trip took five long days. We seldom stopped to rest. I had to drive part of the way. I did not tell my husband-to-be that I feared driving big vehicles and driving in heavy traffic. It was leftover from a series of car wrecks in Alaska, none of which were my fault, but they left their mark. Also, I did not have much practice in driving in heavy traffic due to living in a sparsely populated area in both Nebraska and Alaska. Even when I moved to Florida, my assistants drove most of the time. I was the navigator and enjoyed that.

I believe in facing your fears and conquering them. So, when Bob suddenly announced that he was tired and asked if I could take over, my response was a resounding "yes, of course" (while my stomach was already forming knots and my head was yelling at me with "say what?"). Little did we realize that within five minutes, I would be facing a construction zone with nowhere to pull off and only about three inches to spare on either side. We had concrete guards on both sides with red cones. If that wasn't bad enough, the cross-wind suddenly picked up to almost gale strength. That huge truck was swaying in the wind. Perspiration ran down my pale face as I gritted my teeth and felt my heart begin to race. Everything within me wanted to cry, but I refused. I decided to pray under my breath with all fervor. If there had been any place to pull over and exchange places with Bob, I would have. I was glad it was dark, and he could not see the sweat running down my forehead. He told me later that he was amazed at the great job that I did and that it didn't seem to bother me at all. He said, "I wouldn't have wanted to be driving in that, and you did just fine." I confessed that it was only the Lord who got me through it.

The long drive gave us a lot of time to speak of our dreams, ministries, upcoming wedding, and families. We discussed our pasts and our callings, and what brought us together.

We stopped along the way to meet with some of Bob's family and friends. One of the first stops was Alabama, where he grew up and was married to Mary. I finally met the Alabama relatives he wanted to introduce me to. I met Bob's brother, Clyde, and two living sisters. I was introduced to nieces and nephews and saw the home Bob grew up in. I enjoyed meeting his family.

We made another stop in Colorado. A couple who had been part of Bob's church for many years moved to Colorado. He called them and asked if we could spend one night with them. We had a lovely Mexican dinner and were serenaded by the Mariachi. We had a wonderful evening of fellowship as Bob's friends congratulated us and were happy for us. We drove through a mountain pass. Bob knew that I love mountains and made sure that I saw Silverton Pass. We saw elk, deer, and other wildlife going through the pass. I could not have been happier!

We arrived in Washington State, knowing we had to store my furniture somewhere until we could fit it in his home. He asked his granddaughter and grandson-in-law (who had previously been saved under my ministry at Bob's church) if we could put it in their basement. They graciously agreed. Several men from Bob's church were willing to assist us. There were many narrow stairs that they had to navigate large furniture through. They accomplished the difficult task. I felt like I had been moving for months. First, from Tampa to Tennessee, from Tennessee back to Lashawn's in Spring Hill, Florida, and then to Washington, all within a little over a year. I longed to stay in one place to call my own for a while. However, that was still a few weeks away. For now, I would stay with Charlotte, Bob's daughter, and her husband, Gary. I felt that I could not stay with them indefinitely. We decided to marry in a few weeks.

Bob had a plan. He wanted the church to be very much a part of our plans from the beginning. So, even though he had blurted out somewhat of a proposal in Tarpon Springs, to which I gave him no reply, and had officially proposed in Silverdale, Washington (of which very few knew about, and I later broke that off); he wanted to do an official proposal at his church. He desired to do so on bended knee. He did not tell me the bended knee part. It was a surprise. We decided that I would preach at his church the next Sunday. I felt called to preach on the blood covenant. When Bob realized my topic, he approached the pulpit after me, expounded on the covenants, and read from the book of Ephesians about marriage. He also expounded on a text found in the Song of Solomon. He knelt on bended knee and asked me to marry him in front of over two hundred people. I cried and said, "Yes!" The church erupted in shouts, cries, and laughter, then rushed to the front to congratulate us with hugs, tears, and smiles. It was a glorious moment!

Bob proposed on bended knee in front of his church.

This moment was one that I will forever cherish, as the majority of his church rejoiced at the idea of their pastor (whom they watched grieve over his deceased first wife) and one of their favorite evangelists (whom they also knew had gone through so much in my personal life) being united and happy. The celebration continued for quite some time. The only thing that concerned me was that I noticed two couples not rejoicing.

We set the wedding date for April 27, 2008. That gave us only about two weeks to get ready. Bob wanted his family and church to be there but did not desire a large wedding. I agreed, yet it was very important to me to have some traditional things. I'm that kind of girl. The next two weeks were full of invitations, shopping, dinners, a surprise shower, and rehearsal. I was ecstatic. What made it even more fun was to have two soon-to-be stepdaughters, who were close to my age, go shopping with me.

I have already mentioned Charlotte, whom I stayed with until the wedding. Bob's second daughter, Kathy, was just one year older than me. She had been diagnosed with cancer while her mother fought for her life. At first, the breast cancer diagnosis did not seem quite so grim. She was never told what stage it was. However, later we found out that she was stage three when diagnosed. Her doctor decided to do an experimental treatment. Cancer spread to the other breast and then to the bone. At one point, both Kathy and her mother, Mary, were so sick that they could not visit each other's homes. After Mary's death, Kathy was still fighting for her life. By the time I got to Washington, her prognosis was not good. She already had a hip replacement, and the cancer had spread. She had regular chemo treatments, platelet replacements, blood transfusions, and surgeries. She never complained, never felt sorry for herself, and wanted to be such a part of these wedding festivities.

She was a person who was larger than life, was outgoing, and had a real sense of humor. I remember one day in particular when the three of us went shopping; I decided to look at beautiful nightgowns for the honeymoon. I picked one out and laid it on the counter as Kathy announced to the sales clerk, "She's gonna be my new momma."

The clerk didn't know how to respond and finally said sheepishly, "Well, I guess if you're all okay with that."

I felt my face blush as all three of us burst out laughing. There was never a dull moment with Kathy. I was so happy that she was feeling good enough at the moment to do this kind of shopping.

Later, Kathy was a big part of my personal shower. I thought I was just going out for dinner with Kathy, and she asked if she could blindfold me. They took me to another town, to a home belonging to one of the ladies from Bob's church. We stopped the car, and the blindfold was removed. I found myself at a shower in my honor. It was a wonderful night with the church ladies spoiling me.

This was just days before the wedding. My mother flew in from Nebraska for the shower and wedding. I noticed that one of the leaders of the church was not there. She is the same one I had noticed who did not look happy when Bob proposed. On that day, she grabbed her husband by the arm and rushed out of the church instead of congratulating us. I tried to think it was all a coincidence, but it proved to be something much more than that.

I found a beautiful mauve-colored dress that had a train. It was perfect. The girls offered me the beautiful tiara their mother wore at her and Bob's fiftieth wedding anniversary. They ran away, married at sixteen, and renewed their vows on their anniversary. Charlotte agreed to be my maid of honor, and Bob Junior agreed to be his father's best man. Two of my sons flew in from Alaska for the wedding. Unfortunately, my oldest son, a naval officer, was stationed in Hawaii and could not attend. His wife had given birth to his first child five days earlier. Gary Standridge, Bob's son-in-law, agreed to walk me down the aisle.

The church was filled to overflow capacity. Some had to watch from the foyer. Bob's new church auditorium was still in the process of being built. The ceremony was perfect. We had communion, lit the unity candle, used Kenneth Copeland's blood covenant marriage ceremony, exchanged vows and rings, and, of course, he kissed the bride

We had the reception at a place called The Log Pavilion. We danced to the tune of From This Moment. It was a perfect moment. I could hear Bob's church, our friends, and family saying "awwww" as we danced. Then, unexpectedly, Bob's head usher and close friend, Paul, tapped him on the back and acted as though he was interrupting and wanting to dance with me. It was hilarious. Bob also acted his part. He raised his fist as though he was going to hit him. Everyone loved the humor. It was a perfect day, minus the rain. I must admit that I was hoping for sunshine on my wedding day. That would have taken a miracle since our wedding was near a rainforest in April. However, there were no clouds on my horizon that day. I was inside, dancing with a godly man, with the rest of my life before me.

Our Wedding

We had the usual pictures, toasts, bouquets, and garter tosses. We fed each other wedding cake and opened gifts. People offered their well-wishes, and we were off for the honeymoon. Bob told me he was taking me to Whidbey Island, off the west coast of Washington State. I looked forward to the scenery. It was located on the sea. The landscape surrounding the cottage was beautiful. It had a gorgeous flower garden. Everything was perfect.

My new husband insisted on carrying our luggage up the stairs to our room. He wouldn't let me help with anything. I watched him bound up those stairs and realized what a young man he still was for his age. I would not have been able to do that. He built a fire in the fireplace. I loved

Our Wedding Dance

watching him build a fire and knowing that he was a man who could do anything.

The island was beautiful, and spring was in the air. We went sightseeing in the stunning Deception Pass, stood on the beach, and watched kayakers. Some people were flying kites in the wind as we watched. We ate by the fire, walked hand in hand on the quaint streets, enjoyed small restaurants, and stared into each other's eyes. We thanked God for the restoration and joy we were enjoying after the long night we had each endured. All we could say was how good our God had been to us.

My husband anointed me with oil and said it was now like I had never been married to anyone else. I was his, and we believed that God sanctioned our marriage. Bob promised me that he would do everything in his power to see that I was completely healed from all the years of being mistreated. He felt God gave me to him to help with that healing process. It was the sweetest thing I had ever heard in my life. We danced, held each other, and he called me Mrs. Robert Rester. Nothing had ever sounded more perfect!

Deception Pass

Unfortunately, the honeymoon was a little shorter than I wanted. We had to return to Aberdeen because Bob promised to do someone else's wedding the following Saturday. We only had four and one-half days before returning home. However, another honeymoon was coming.

Before we married, Bob told me he had bought two tickets to visit Greece in June. Bob had a lifetime dream of walking the steps of the Apostle Paul and had been planning the trip.

After we were engaged, he told me he invited Charlotte to go with him but asked her if she would mind being bumped for me. She was gracious, and I still feel like I need to take her to Greece someday to make up for it. Bob told me that we would have an immediate honeymoon to Whidbey Island, and the one that he considered our real, over-the-top honeymoon would be to Greece in June.

Just before the wedding, Bob told me about his dilemma. He was credentialed with The Assemblies of God. He loved The Assemblies of God. They were good to him, and vice versa. They used to have a rule that nobody who has been divorced and remarried, or anyone who marries a divorced person, could be credentialed with them. After many years, that was overturned at the general council of the Assemblies of God. Now, they take each case individually to see if there are Biblical grounds for divorce. Bob was confident that I had Biblical reasons for each of my divorces. However, he had to present this to the northwest district for their approval before he could be credentialed again. Their office is about two hours from where we live. He decided that we would marry, and then he would go to their office and face this. He said that whichever way it went, he was satisfied in his own heart that we were both within our Biblical rights to marry. He would face the consequences of them possibly not credentialing him. The matter concerned me. I did not want to be responsible for him losing his credentials, but we decided to cross that bridge when we came to it.

Bob called the district and made an appointment with them to settle this matter. Meanwhile, we received paperwork from them that I had to fill out for each marriage and divorce. I had to verify dates, places, and proof of what each spouse had done. I needed to provide witnesses and documents. They wanted to know if we had counseling, who did it, the counselor's input, where I was going to church at the time, the pastor's remarks, and more. That would be difficult enough with one, let alone three marriages. As I began filling out the paperwork, I felt shame trying to choke me. I wondered how this could have happened to me, the girl who wouldn't date unsaved men, and only married Pentecostal men (two of whom I met in church, went to Bible school, and promised to go into the ministry with me). All three claimed to be tongue-talkers. I wondered how this could happen to a lady who believes in submitting to her husband and is willing to go to any lengths to make it work.

I thought of all the nagging and domineering women I know. I watch their husbands put up with it. I was not one of them. Yet, I must look like I am difficult to live with or someone who thinks lightly about her marriage vows. I felt like I was wearing a scarlet letter.

These men I would be facing did not know me, never heard me minister, and were total strangers. They had no idea how much of an effort I made to make these marriages work. I put enough paperwork into their hands to sink the Titanic. I hoped they would believe me. Worse, before marrying Bob, I could have had many witnesses sign affidavits and come to plead my case. They could give plenty of evidence of what I had been through. However, I knew, because of my previous mistakes and how people were feeling about the suddenness of this marriage, that I could not ask them. It seemed hopeless to me. How would Bob ever be credentialed again? I was sure the northwest district would feel that Bob had lost his mind and was marrying some stained girl. I thought of what Bob said on our wedding night about my purity, that he was anointing me, and that God saw it as though I had never been married to anyone else. The enemy was trying to steal that and make me feel dirty and unclean.

I did my best to get statements from friends and people who knew the truth. I called someone who previously worked for Pastor Rodney. When Patrick filled my ministry computer with homosexual pornography, Pastor Rodney asked me to bring the computer into his office. The staff took pictures for evidence, in case I ever needed it. I never needed it before now. I located the man who worked on the project. The man's son also worked on the case as one of the ministry's IT people. The father told me he was taking his son off the case because the information on the computer was too horrible for his son to see. He didn't want him exposed to such things. I knew the father would remember this, even though he no longer worked for Pastor. I called him, and he said, "Well, Debbie, I don't remember anything about this. Yes, that sounds like something I would say about not wanting my son to be exposed to it, but I just can't help you out." "Wow, thank you so much." This wasn't looking too good for me.

In the end, a few friends and some ministers told the truth, and I had a few documents. I recall the day that Bob and I were on our way to meet with the northwest district of the Assemblies of God. Those two hours seemed like five. I walked into a room of eleven solemn-looking strangers. They asked Bob not to speak. They told him that it was about me, not him. They asked many questions I tried to answer to the best of my knowledge. It was humiliating to talk about homosexuality, adultery, wife-beating, perversion, court cases, and more. I almost felt like it was someone else talking. God had done such a work of healing in me. I hated drudging up the past and relating horrible details of my stupid decisions.

As the meeting drew close, one of the gentlemen looked at Bob and asked this question. "Pastor Bob, if we decide not to renew your credentials today, what will you do with that church auditorium you are building?" (referring to the new addition to his church that was near completion).

He replied, "Gentlemen, I know you are facing a difficult decision today. You don't know Debbie. You have to simply take this paperwork, pray, and make a decision to the best of your ability. If it goes the other way, I will not be bitter. I will understand, and I will hand the church over to my associate and hope that you will allow me to keep pounding the nails and finish the building."

They said, "That's the Bob Rester we thought we knew. Thank you. We will let you know our decision in a few days."

I had no idea what that meant. Those next few days were some of the longest of my life. I had to depend on them to look at the huge file, read information about a woman they had never heard minister, and feel that she was the innocent victim of three husbands who sinned against God and her. Would it be possible for them to overlook my stupidity three times and hear from Heaven and grant my husband his credentials? A month was a long time to wait.

I no longer remember how many days before we received the news that they decided unanimously to renew his credentials. They also said in their letter that I had been hurt by three men. They hoped that their decision would aid me in my healing process. I cried with joy. However, it was short-lived. Their letter also stated that they had to send their findings to the general counsel of the Assemblies of God in Springfield, Missouri. They added that, unfortunately, because of the time of the month, they missed the date for turning it in to the executive presbytery this month. It would be docked for another month before the general counsel would make their decision. Wow! That was going to be a long month.

Finally, Bob and I both received their letters. Mine started with "Welcome to the Assemblies of God!" I cried with joy. You talk about rejoicing! My husband would retain his credentials and his relationship with The Assemblies. He would be able to continue pastoring his church, and it was also a victory for me. This board had no idea how much they ministered to me and how much I would learn important lessons from this. My shame vanished with this letter. I felt exonerated, like someone must feel at the end of a long trial. To think that this board heard from God and understood what I had been through was like God Himself had reached down and said, "I understand. You are forgiven, and the call upon your life still stands." What a day!

The invisible scarlet letter hanging over me had been ripped apart. I had never heard of a Pentecostal organization even using the term ecclesiastical annulment. It would be a miracle to be granted one, let alone three.

My mind went back to when friends suggested I ask my lawyer for an annulment from Dennis. We were married for a short time, and I found out that almost everything he told me was false. Yet, my lawyer's assistant made fun of me for suggesting it. She actually said that I watched too many movies to think I could get an annulment. Now, a much more important body had granted me three annulments. I felt like God repeated what my husband told me on our wedding night. I was clean at last! God saw it as I thought I had never been married to anyone but Bob. The blood had done that. It erased those marriages that took place under false circumstances. Men had professed to know God but lied to both God and me. However, my God restored me again.

I have had some unusual meetings with the presbytery of the Assemblies of God. Several years before this, when I was in Nome, Alaska, they asked my forgiveness. Now, it was my turn. I judged the Assemblies of God as always being a religious institution, void of flowing in the Holy Spirit or being sensitive to His voice. I made some jokes about them, as some of them have about us. Most of that was based upon a few churches and pastors, not the fellowship. Yet, it is easy to form a prejudice that is based on things that are not facts. The fellowship that I called religious now ministered to my hurt and pain. Sometimes, you never know who will hear from Heaven. I learned not to group everyone into the basket of what a few do. God can use whomever He chooses to bring our help. It may not be how we expect it, but it will come.

I have held more revival meetings in Assembly of God churches than all the rest. Every one of them has been outstanding meetings with some of the hungriest, sweetest pastors. Are there religious pastors in the Assemblies? Yes, just like there are in any other fellowship or denomination. Are there pastors who only consider it a job and have lost their first love? Yes, as there are in every denomination. Are some Assembly churches full of fire and others as cold as glaciers and dried up like a prune? Yes! Yet, it was the Assemblies who sought the Lord, heard from God, welcomed me, and granted me ecclesiastical annulments. They were there for me when I needed them, and I will never forget that. Most of us are where we are because this fellowship was formed. They have taken the fire of Pentecost all over the planet and done more for missions than most. Many denominations that began in the fire ended up in a glacier. What it takes to get, it takes to keep. The Assemblies of God and every movement must remember that.

The second honeymoon that Bob had promised me came. We flew from Washington State to Dallas, Texas, and then onto Greece. We explored those beautiful islands for ten days. The blue and green seas were dotted with white waves. We preached at the famous biblical city of Corinth. I found it ironic that I was preaching in the city where so much confusion and misunderstanding arose over the verses about women remaining silent in the church.

We visited the Isle of Patmos, where the Apostle John wrote the book of Revelation, and we put our hands on Paul's judgment seat. We went to Athens, Ephesus, the islands of Ios, and Mykonos (where I had the privilege of leading a storekeeper to Jesus). We went to Santorini, one of the Cyclades islands in the

Aegean Sea. It has a beautiful and rugged landscape. The whitewashed homes cling to cliffs above an underwater crater. They overlook the clear Aegean. The beaches are made up of black, red, and white lava pebbles. I could have stayed there the entire time.

I preached in Corinth.

Unfortunately, the heat was excruciating. We climbed the steps of old ruins. I thought the steps would never come to an end. A humorous incident took place on the cruise ship. One of the young ladies in our tour group told us that she was a previous amphetamine addict. She seemed to have endless energy and never sat still. On planned bus tours, she would disappear to go off on her own. Her endless chatter was somewhat annoying and yet funny.

We did not know that her ship quarters was next to ours. The beds on the cruise ships are about the size of a twin bed. Neither my husband nor I were small. When one of us had to get up in the early morning, we accidentally caused another to be dumped onto the floor. We could not help but laugh hysterically. The next morning, on my way to breakfast, I saw Suzie come out of her cabin and walk down the hallway. I ran into my room and told Bob she was staying next to us. We had no idea that someone from our group was next to us. Most of us were separated from each other in different areas of the ship. After arriving at breakfast, Suzie could not wait to tell her funny story.

"You won't believe the people next to me. I hear thump, thump, and then laughing all night long. They must be having quite a great time. They must be on their honeymoon."

I felt my face blush and give me away. I tried to stare straight ahead. Then she announced, "Oh my goodness, it's you two, isn't it?" Our group burst forth with laughter. Then she added, "Didn't you go on a honeymoon a couple of months ago on an island called Whoopee Island?"

I could not believe that she thought that was the island's name. I told her it was called Whidbey, and she laughed and said, "This whole time, I thought for sure you were saying Whoopee, not Whidbey." It took us a long time to live that down.

SEVENTEEN

THE END OF A MINISTRY CHAPTER BRINGS FORTH NEW LIFE

After all that I had been through, I felt it was time to simply enjoy happiness in my personal life. I longed for this my entire life. Others wanted it for me. My husband had been through so much with a sick wife for many years. He mourned her death, and it was now time for him to enjoy happiness, as well. However, the enemy never desires us to have a free ride up the side, so to speak. He will do everything in his power to steal, kill, and destroy. Unfortunately, many people unknowingly allow him to use them in the process. We experienced pain in the middle of our joy.

The worst pain was losing my husband's baby girl to cancer. She fought long and hard for about seven years. When we married, she stated she wanted to live long enough to see the wedding. I only knew Kathy for a short time, but I feel like I've known her for so much longer. The family shared numerous stories with me.

Kathy was Bob and Mary's youngest daughter. Bob was not able to be there for her birth. He was stationed in England. He did not see her until she was fourteen months old. Mary did a good job of keeping his picture before Kathy's eyes daily. When Bob finally arrived home, she came running into his arms, calling "Daddy." She was the apple of his eye. She was beautiful in every way, hilarious, outgoing, and everyone's friend. You knew where you stood in every situation with her.

We spoke faith and healing to her. We watched her undergo transfusions, chemotherapy, experimental drugs, surgeries, and hip replacements. She made jokes through it all. Toward the end, I helped take care of her when the family had appointments. I saw the wounds from chemo and dressed them. I helped her walk to the bathroom as my heart broke. It was only days later that she succumbed. Bob's sweet, beautiful baby girl went home to be with her Savior in September 2008.

Bob preached at her funeral; I had no idea how he could get through that. I will never forget walking into our office and seeing him. His head was in his hands, wrestling with his thoughts. I felt like I had entered a place where I did not belong. Many know the agony of loving someone so much that we want to take the pain for them. However, we cannot, no matter how much we try. He told me that the only thing that helped him was that he knew where she was for all eternity. He knew that he would see her again.

We know that healing belongs to the child of God. It is part of our covenant. I can't give you all the answers to why some don't receive it, but we still believe in the Bible. We must continue to do so till our last breath.

Another painful storm was brewing on the horizon. When Bob proposed to me, almost the entire church rejoiced. However, there were a few who did not, and they were influential people. I had an entire chapter that explained this in detail. I was going to include it only because it was one of the most painful moments of my life. If God had not helped me, it might have been the trial that derailed God's assignment for my life.

I overcame horrible abuse in marriages, a physical attack that threatened my life, and the betrayal of a close friend. However, there is nothing that can hurt like church hurt. We do not expect it to come from the safety of the church and fellow believers. When you look at Matt. 26, you realize that Jesus' betrayal did not come from a distant friend or a parking lot attendant. It came from the one he was having a close, intimate supper with. We cannot walk around being suspicious but need to realize that anyone has the potential to disappoint and even betray. Perhaps this situation would not have penetrated my heart so much if my husband was not battling cancer at the same time.

The enemy tries to attack from all sides to wear us down. He knows that while our faith is strong in some areas, it may not be as strong in others. He hopes that we cannot stand against several attacks at the same time. The enemy mounted an attack from several fronts, believing that we would say, enough is enough. However, he underestimated the power of the Holy Spirit inside us. When we feel weak in and of ourselves, we need to remember that we are not in and of ourselves. The Greater One lives within us, and we can overcome anything.

This chapter originally detailed the events that took place in the church that my husband built and pastored. However, I decided to remove most of those details. You need to realize the depth of the hurt so that you can see that God wants to deliver you from all pain. If details are removed, it is difficult for the reader to understand the depth of the pain. Consequently, you may think your pain goes much deeper, and God cannot set you free from it. That is the only reason I considered sharing it.

However, I concluded that I could not be a part of further hurt and misunderstanding. I love the people involved dearly, and my husband loved each of them with the unconditional love of a pastor and spiritual father. He walked in total forgiveness beyond anyone I have known. He refused to defend himself or say anything that could possibly divide the kingdom of God. He said over and over again, "Debbie, you and I are expendable, but the kingdom of God is not." He hoped that if we remained quiet and prayed, people would turn. As we continued to hear reports of things being said and done, he ignored what we heard and said nothing.

The storm was not blowing over, though.

Many things were taking place as my husband was struggling with his voice. He told me that for some time, he had problems with his voice getting weak when he was stressed or overly tired. We had no idea what was causing it. Eventually, we sought medical help. At first, they diagnosed him with something called leukoplakia, a plaque-like coating that is pre-cancerous. They scraped his vocal cords and said that he needed constant monitoring. A few months later, we heard the big C word, cancer. They removed the tumor, but it grew back, and they had to get more aggressive. The surgeon took almost the entire right vocal tube of his larynx.

His voice was pretty hoarse, but we were thankful that he still had a voice and did not have to have his entire larynx removed and replaced by a mechanical voice. Some months later, they saw a tumor again and said he needed six weeks of intense radiation.

My husband's family has had more than their share of battling this disease. I can't help but wonder about the fact that he made a career in the Air Force, and they lived on many military bases. I wonder what they were exposed to. Cancer is something he thought he would personally never battle after seeing his first wife and daughter battle this disease from hell. However, we found ourselves there.

It's amazing how many things we have been healed of, and how many people have been healed in our combined ministries. However, it is more difficult sometimes to believe for yourself. We believed that God would guide all the doctors involved and that the radiation would succeed without side effects. God came through for us. He was eventually pronounced cancer-free; we celebrated twelve and a half wonderful years together. We could have enjoyed these years more without other people's actions that caused heartbreak.

My husband resigned from his church after twenty-three years of ministry, and only one week after he was cleared from cancer, we found ourselves churchless. We definitely did not plan on that. Bob still refused to divide the kingdom or the church. The man I married was, at times, gruff around the edges but was a man of integrity, humility, and honesty!

Bob endured six grueling weeks of radiation until his neck looked like a raw hamburger on the outside. I couldn't even imagine the inside. He couldn't eat or swallow. I heard him moaning as he changed the bandages. He still insisted on going to Alaska with me for revival the day after his last treatment. He couldn't even button his collar. What a trooper!

We searched for a good Word of Faith church that also would flow in the Holy Ghost. We needed a revival church in our area, which proved difficult to find. We visited several churches; some seemed to want revival but were flaky. They wanted more than God's glory. They also wanted a cheap imitation of it, such as gold dust and supposed angel feathers. I've tasted the real and will not settle for the counterfeit. I want the supernatural, not the sensational.

We also visited churches that don't believe it is always God's will to heal. They think that God may or could, but He might not. Healing is a part of our redemption. Jesus already bought and paid for it; I will not compromise that. We traveled one hundred miles to attend a church with great worship and preaching The Word. However, it was too far away for us to get very involved. The task of finding a good church was turning out to be much harder than we anticipated. When you are used to solid teaching and a powerful flow of the Holy Ghost, it is impossible to settle for less. I didn't know what we would do and was tempted to stay home and watch Pastor Rodney on television. Yet, I knew we needed to be a part of a physical body.

Bob's family asked if he would consider doing a Bible study in our home. Meanwhile, they tried churches in other towns, as well. One couple who also left

Bob's church asked if we would start a church. I emphatically told them that I had no desire for that. However, we agreed to start a Bible study at Bob's granddaughter's house on Sunday nights. It was only for our family.

Sometimes Bob or I led the Bible study. Sometimes, Bob's grandson led it. We never thought about it becoming anything else. Eventually, the couple who left Bob's church asked if they could be a part of the Bible study with Bob's family. At first, my husband did not allow them to come. He did not want to be divisive or encourage anyone from his old church to leave the church. In fact, a few others came to our home and said they were called to follow Bob's vision when they came to his church, not the congregation. Bob still encouraged them to stay in the church and pray for revival. However, he finally allowed this one couple to come to the Bible study because they convinced him that they had already left the church. They said they missed solid teaching and the move of the Spirit.

One day, as I was praying about what we were all to do, I found myself saying, "Lord, we need someone to start a church in this town that will contend for the move of the Holy Ghost. We need someone who preaches faith and has solid doctrine. Why don't you send someone to start one here? I know it's a difficult place for many reasons, but surely someone is willing to pay the price. The darker the place, the more anointing and grace are there to break it open. Lord, how hard is it to send someone full of the Holy Ghost with solid doctrine?"

I no sooner prayed that than I got an unexpected answer in my spirit. "You're here. You are a Word of Faith minister and a Bible-believing minister of the Gospel. You know how to flow in the Holy Ghost. You have been saying for years that you were transitioning and would be pastoring. You said it would be wonderful to raise a congregation to speak the same things, believe the same things, worship with all their heart, and know how to yield to the Holy Ghost. You are the answer."

I was shocked and began to laugh. When my husband came home, I told him what I had heard from the Lord. After discussing it, we agreed that "it seemed good to the Holy Ghost and us." I was eager to announce it to our little Bible study group on Sunday night.

Consequently, in December 2013, our church was formed. We moved the meetings to our home. After a few weeks, Jackie and Javier Moreno offered to hold church in their home since it was larger. Eventually, another man who was a good friend offered his home. Their home included a huge fellowship room they used for other social activities. We met there for several months. The problem was that it was located in the country, and very difficult for anyone to find us. We could not advertise the location. Also, the area flooded in the springtime, and the roads were closed. That wouldn't work long-term for a church.

The day came when that inward voice of the Holy Spirit spoke on the inside of me. "It's time to believe for a building." We had about fifteen people and no money. Aberdeen is very limited in buildings that are for sale or lease. However, the gift of faith fell upon me. I called for a prayer meeting that night and declared we had a building. I had not even looked for one yet. A couple of days later, I sent some of our family to scout the land. They discovered a building for sale that was in excellent condition. It was a carpenter's union hall, and since carpenters built it, it was built very well. It was a little too small for a church but bigger than the others available for lease. Instead of renting a building for $2,000 to $3,000 a month, we could buy this building for a little over $500 a month. Within days, someone approached us and gave us $50,000 for a down payment. Our God is truly Jehovah Jireh!

We closed on the building in May 2014. We painted, put in a platform and big-screen television, bought a sound system and new appliances for the kitchen, and had our first service in June. The building could only hold up to 70 people comfortably, but it was a great beginner building. Also, we could build equity for a larger building in the future.

We had over fifty people in the building by Father's Day. I thought that we were rapidly on our way. However, we quickly discovered that the majority were never with us. Some wanted to continue to live together in sin without getting married. Some looked to us as a social institution that could help them with rent and food. It didn't take long for a great sifting to take place.

We had out-reaches, and in-reaches, where we offered beautiful prizes for those who came. We did soul-winning in a variety of ways. We invited some of the best evangelists, went door to door, and fed the community. We hosted hot chocolate and cookie stands at Christmas.

Many came through the doors. There were services when a dozen or so people came to the altar for salvation. Tears were streaming down their faces. Some said it was the best day of their lives. One visitor broke out in tongues while I was preaching. After church, she said she knew God as a young woman but had backslidden. She was still shaking and crying while testifying. She said it was the best day of her life, yet we never saw her again. I could tell that Aberdeen, Washington was a unique place.

We exercised our faith and did some water-walking financially. We purchased an LED sign for the church. It was a huge expenditure for such a small church, but I felt it was necessary. We were sandwiched between an office supply company and apartment buildings. Our building was set back from the street, and many drove past it without realizing it was a church. This sign proclaimed the love of God and pointed people to our location. We had an immediate response. People came and said they did not realize it was a church until they saw the sign going up. They thanked me for starting the church, answered the altar call, and promised to be a part. Still, we never saw many of them again. They did not return our phone calls.

We were in close proximity to the bus station and the downtown area where drug dealers and prostitutes roam the streets. I felt that it was an excellent location to see people come out of darkness and into the glory of God. The enemy tried to discourage me, but I never gave up.

I knew the city needed a faith-teaching, Bible-preaching, Holy Spirit-demonstrating church. Many people came and were born again, but they didn't stay for long. Some were visiting from other countries, and others were in the military and transferred shortly after they were saved. The reward shall be on the other side. People don't necessarily have to come to my church; at least they heard The Gospel.

We began a yearly conference called Northwest Ablaze. I continued to believe that the liberal state of Washington would become the new Bible belt. Another church in Bremerton, Washington, became our sister church. Jason and Hannah Gillick pastored it. They were touched in my meetings in Silverdale many years ago. Later, they attended River Bible Institute (RBI, now River University) in Tampa, Florida. They became the associate pastors of Pastors Rodney and Adonica Howard-Browne. Eventually, Pastors Jason and Hannah returned to Washington to pioneer a work. I held revival for them several times. We went to each other's meetings and partnered together to see the state come to Jesus.

I remember the first campmeeting we attended since I left Tampa. I did not expect to have a special seat and did not desire one. We only came to partake of the anointing and did not want to be acknowledged. We tried to sit toward the back. It did not take long for an usher to approach me. "Pastor Debbie, we have special seats for you upfront." I was in shock. I shook my head and replied, "No, that's okay. We're fine where we are and don't want to disturb anyone or interrupt the service." Only a few minutes passed when we were approached again with the same statement. Once again, we gave the same reply. However, moments later, the youth pastor (whom I knew very well) approached us and said, "Pastor Rodney has seen you and wants you in the front row." We quickly moved to our new seats. This was much more than I had desired.

We ended up being invited to dinner with Pastors Rodney and Adonica and many other guests. While we didn't get alone time with them, we were very honored to be included at all. It seemed much like old times. I did have some tough moments. A greeter asked if it was my first time at the River. I never thought I would be asked such a question. She was new, and I had not been there in a while. That is very understandable. Yet, it was a difficult moment for a woman who used to preach there and teach in the Bible School frequently. At dinner one day, another guest asked me my name and if it was my first time at the River. I wanted to reply with, "I used to be Pastor Rodney's associate evangelist, take the church when he was out of town, hold crusades with him, and teach in the Bible school." However, I simply said, "No, I've been here before."

We did get an opportunity to ask Pastor Rodney's forgiveness. My husband told him that I never spoke disparagingly about them but always was loyal and defended them. Bob mentioned that he said one thing about them that he shouldn't have and deeply regretted it. He asked Pastor's forgiveness. Pastor Rodney said, "That's all in the past and forgiven." It was over. I didn't know if it would ever be the same, but it was more than wonderful to know that we could go and participate in the anointing. I dreamed of this moment.

Since then, we have attended many meetings together. We went to Washington D.C., to Pastor Rodney's "Celebrate America" crusade in July 2015. We went to most of the campmeetings and minister's conferences after that.

In January 2015, I was enjoying the service when Pastor Rodney called upon me to come to the pulpit and teach about giving before they received the offering. I could not believe my ears. I had no warning. It had been seven years since I had been asked to teach at the River. I wondered if I would ever teach on that platform again. Now it was happening. I had so many emotions going through me that I didn't know if my legs would hold me up as I walked to the platform. I taught five times that week. Each time I did not know that I would be teaching until I heard my name called. What an honor! What restoration! What forgiveness! What a good God!

On Saturday of that week, I was called upon to teach again. This time, Pastor asked me to teach a particular message, The Alabaster Box Breaking. My text was John, chapter 12. That is my favorite stewardship teaching. I have taught it many times at The River, and the glory of God comes every time. Occasionally, Pastor Rodney could not even preach afterward because the glory rolled into the auditorium in such a powerful way. People fell to the floor weeping before God. Many of them piled their gifts for the Lord on the platform.

However, this time I preached under the heaviest anointing I had ever known. An Australian evangelist named Tim Hall was supposed to follow me and teach about end-time events. He walked to the platform after I took my seat and repeated "wow" five times. That was all he could say. He was overcome with emotion. He said that he didn't think he could minister after that. Eventually, he recovered. After he finished his "wows," he commented on my teaching. He said that I had been through much and was broken before God. That allowed me to minister this passage in a way very few could. He said, "Debbie, the Devil hates you. He really hates you. I believe I could say prophetically that he hates you." Pastor Rodney came to the platform and prophesied, "the attack on your life from the enemy is over, and God is restoring." He continued with, "You have not seen anything yet. Get ready to run." Now, it was my time to say, "Wow!" This was above all that I could ask or think.

The interesting thing is that my friend Tina, who lives in Switzerland, called me before I went to this campmeeting. She said, "Pastor Debbie, I dreamed that you were teaching at a campmeeting. I think you better be prepared." I just smiled and put it on the shelf, so to speak. However, I did not expect that at all. I thought she had a natural dream and had eaten too much pizza before sleeping. I knew she loved me and would enjoy seeing that come to pass, so I thought she probably dreamed it up. Now, it was fulfilled. I was home and could once again receive the anointing that changed my life. All that I could say was, "Thank You, Jesus!"

Pastor Rodney has invited me to teach several times since then. It is always the highest honor. I thank God every day for allowing me to meet the Howard-Brownes. That would have been incredible in itself, but the ministry and friendship over the years is an over-the-top, God thing.

The Holy Spirit eventually brought supernatural restoration between myself and many of my friends. I am so grateful. We love each other and have forgiven one other. Out of the smoking embers of Bob and I's ministries, a new ministry came into being in Washington State. God truly is the Great Restorer.

EIGHTEEN

COMING BACK FROM THE DEAD AFTER TERMINAL ILLNESS

In the fall of 2014, a vicious stomach attack came out of nowhere. It was like a cyclone from hell. My husband and I went for a pleasant car ride earlier in the day, and it came to a close with a beautiful dinner by the water. I had no symptoms until an hour or so later. I wondered if I had contracted food poisoning. However, my husband ate the same food and seemed fine. The pain was like nothing that I had ever experienced before. It was all-encompassing and unrelenting. It centered in my upper abdomen but radiated to my back. The intense pain refused to give me one second of relief. It came with an onslaught of nausea and continued for eight hours. I walked the floor all night. I could not sit or lay down. The pain was so intense that I almost could not breathe. My husband woke up to see tears running down my face, even though I was not crying loudly. I was taught to bear physical pain on the inside while not making a sound on the outside. I knew that it would do no good to scream or moan. I suspected that it was a gallbladder attack.

About three months later, another attack came. This one didn't last quite as long. The pain coursed through my body for about six hours. It ended the same way, with vomiting and diarrhea. I knew that it was not the flu or food poisoning. Something was not right in my body. However, between the attacks, months went by with no symptoms. I noticed a pattern forming. The attacks came about every three months and then every two months. I had something different to eat each time. The attacks lasted from one to four hours after I ate. I told myself I would never have another one when I lost weight and became more health-conscious. However, they continued.

I also experienced another problem. I tried to work out. Walking on the treadmill, I was out of breath within the first minute. My heart rate climbed to over 200 beats a minute. My face became beet-red, and my energy plummeted. I thought that I was just out of shape. That was true, but I was about to find out that it was not my only problem.

In April 2015, I traveled to France and Switzerland for ministry. I was excited to go to these nations. My first evening at the women's conference in Paris did not begin well. The pastors hosted a welcome dinner for all of the speakers. I was the key-note speaker, and several other women were also invited to speak. The dinner was great, but I immediately experienced a stomach attack. I was in severe pain and discomfort. To make matters worse, the only available bathroom joined the fellowship room where the other ministers were. It was an extremely small bathroom. Every time I had to run there (literally), I had to pass the other guests.

I asked for a place to lie down. They offered the pastor's office. There was a mattress on the floor. Unfortunately, it also joined the fellowship room. To go to the bathroom, I opened the office door and ran through the fellowship room to reach the bathroom. This took place every few minutes. I was experiencing so much pain that I wanted to moan but tried to remain silent. The healing evangelist was lying on the floor in excruciating pain before my meetings even began. I could not believe what was happening! The pastors discussed who could fill in for me. This was the first meeting. I made up my mind that I would preach if I had to crawl to the meeting.

When I arrived at the meeting, just a few minutes late, everyone looked surprised. We had a great service, and my pain subsided. It is interesting to me how symptoms leave when the anointing is strong.

I experienced minor bouts the entire week, but the grace of God was there for me. We had a wonderful week; I loved the pastors and the people. They were very gracious. I also received an invitation to preach in the largest charismatic church in France. We had another wonderful meeting there.

I hoped the worst was behind me, but that was not the case.

After France, I went to Switzerland. Tina, my friend since River Bible Institute days, and her Swiss husband, David, rented a school building to conduct the meetings. Tina invited me to visit Switzerland and hold meetings years before. She continued to believe that I would come, and finally, the day arrived. When she attended RBI (River Bible Institute in Tampa, FL), I was her favorite Bible school teacher. Years after she graduated from Bible school, she confessed that she had written in her Bible, that her greatest hope was that she and I would become friends one day. She also wrote that her second desire was for me to come to Switzerland to preach. God heard that, and both were granted.

The anointing and presence of God were strong. I ministered for three nights. People were born again and filled with joy. When the meetings concluded, Tina told me she had several surprises for me. She planned a mini-vacation, knowing I loved nature, especially mountains and water. She and her husband went out of their way to bless me. They sacrificed their finances and time.

Tina took me to one of the most beautiful views I have ever seen, Hotel Seeblick, facing Lucerne Lake. The hotel and spa were located on the top of a mountain. I enjoyed a Swedish massage in Switzerland.

After the massage, we ate ice cream sundaes on the terrace overlooking a breathtaking blue lake in the Swiss Alps. I wondered if life could get any better. I thanked God for His goodness. I could have stayed right there the entire time. However, she told me that the next surprise was even better. She would take me to see the famous Matterhorn Mountain in the Swiss Alps.

We would go by train to a village called Zermatt, at the base of the mountain, and then take a tram up to the infamous Matterhorn. I couldn't wait! The train ride was so extraordinarily beautiful. It took us through Swiss cities, meandered through quaint valleys, wound around rivers, and ascended slowly up the mountains. I experienced views of rushing streams pounding their way over boulders. The sky was blue, and the mountains were topped with white, glistening snow.

However, the train ride was not without some minor stress. The trip required us to take four trains before we arrived at our destination. Every time we stopped, we were rushed through terminals. We had to figure out which track we were to be on next, inquire from people who spoke Swiss-German, and drag our carry-ons behind us as we attempted to make our next connection.

Tina was born two months premature with cerebral palsy. I tried to help her with her coat and carry-on, as well as my own. Unfortunately, she misunderstood some directions, and we ended up on the wrong train on one of our connections. This lengthened the trip considerably. We were tired and more than anxious to get to our destination.

When we arrived at the beautiful village below the mountain, we had no time to waste. We walked some distance to find lockers for our bags. We succeeded in our search, then walked to the other end of the village.

Eventually, we boarded a tram and ascended the Matterhorn. When we stopped at a station, I realized I was not feeling well. I was not having another abdominal attack but felt light-headed and was facing difficulty breathing. I blamed it on the rush of boarding trains and the long walk.

When we finally arrived at our last tram stop, I could see that we were only a few feet below the top of the Matterhorn. It was fascinating. There were a few steps we could still ascend to get to the highest point we were allowed. I thought I would do that and pose for a picture after touring the visitor's center. I was told that we were at an elevation of over 14,000 feet. As we walked into the visitor's center, I knew I was very ill. I felt like I could faint, but I didn't want to tell Tina and hoped it would pass. She had planned this just for me and was anticipating my reaction. We were too close to the top to turn back now.

We walked up an incline for quite some time. It was not very steep, but I felt worse by the moment. I even stopped at a room where they showed an informational video about the Matterhorn. I needed to catch my breath and rest. It did not seem to help. After we climbed a few more feet, we came to a restaurant. I asked Tina if she could order us a coke while I rested. She agreed. I hoped the fainting sensation would pass if I put my head down for a few minutes. It did not. It was getting worse by the minute. Everything was spinning. I became nauseous. I suddenly could not breathe. I had never had that sensation since the blood clot incident almost ten years previously. I was frightened and did not want to tell Tina. I didn't want to ruin her plans. When she brought the food to the table, I could not eat a single bite. I knew that I had to tell her.

My heart pounded in my chest. Something was terribly wrong, and I was sitting in a restaurant 14,000 feet above sea level, thousands of miles from home. I had a moment of revelation that I was in serious trouble. I almost could not speak. I finally blurted out, "Tina, something is wrong. I can't breathe, and my heart is racing. We have to get down." I wondered if I was having some altitude sickness. I couldn't figure it out. I have been at high altitudes before without any problems.

When a person at a high altitude struggles with a lack of oxygen in the United States, there are available oxygen stations available. I thought Switzerland would be the same. I asked Tina to ask for oxygen for me. She told me there was none available. I asked her to tell the man in charge of the tram that I needed help and must get down the mountain quickly. As we made our way out of the restaurant, I managed to pose for one picture with the top of the mountain in the background. I wanted proof that I had been there. I only had to climb a few more steps to reach the highest point, but I knew that was out of the question.

The man in charge asked the people to exit the tram for me. I could not have people crowding me. That would make breathing even more difficult. I was so thankful to be descending at last, but I also knew that the tram would stop at every station. I wondered if each person in charge would be so gracious and understanding.

We arrived at the next station in only minutes. There were two medics waiting for us. I asked for oxygen but was told they do not make it available without a doctor's prescription. That would involve a lot of red tape. They asked me if I thought it was absolutely necessary. I regret to this day that I did not say, "What part of 'I cannot breathe, and my heart feels like it's going to explode' do you not understand?" Instead, I responded with a typical Debbie-do-not-rock-the-boat-sentence. "I don't want you to go to all that trouble."

Tina told me that she arranged for us to spend the night in a beautiful hotel called Gornergrat, with a direct view of the Matterhorn from our window. It was the highest place people could lodge to view the mountain. Again, I knew this trip was extremely sacrificial for her and David. Mine and Tina's birthdays are in the month of April. Her husband told us that it was a birthday present for us. I did not want to disappoint her and ruin this. I asked the emergency workers what they thought about the hotel stay. One said, "You definitely need to cancel it." The other one spoke up and said, "I don't think you need to cancel it. The hotel is located lower than we are right now, and you are already feeling better. This is an once-in-a-lifetime thing. I think you will be fine." Can you guess which one I decided to choose?

We had to go all the way down to the village to retrieve our carry-ons and buy tickets for the bus that would carry us back up to the hotel. I thought that descending to the bottom would fix everything. I was wrong.

I was told later that the worst thing you can do if you are suffering from altitude sickness is to go down to the bottom and come back up again. By the time we reached the village, I was feeling much better and looking forward to having dinner at our hotel. We had some difficulty with purchasing our tickets. Tina was quite upset because they gave her the wrong information. We almost did not make the trip, but eventually, it worked out. By this time, we had to move quickly. We literally had to run to catch the last bus of the night to the hotel, even though neither of us was up for it. We were huffing and puffing as we climbed onto the bus.

The ascent was a long one, but oh, so beautiful again. I had time to reflect on the day's events and was thankful to be alive. I could not help but wonder what had brought all of this on. I decided to schedule a check-up when I returned to the States. However, at this moment, I only wanted to enjoy the rest of my vacation.

We finally arrived at our hotel. The view was incredible, even from the bus window. I grabbed my carry-on and exited the bus. When I stepped outside, I began to have problems breathing again. I was distressed as I watched the last bus drive down the mountain. 'Surely this will pass. Maybe I'm just anxious or imagining it because of my experience at the top of the Matterhorn. After all, this hotel is only about 9,000 feet above sea level, not 14,000. Maybe I'm just tired.' I didn't say anything to Tina. I thought it would pass.

We found our hotel room. We ordered, waited for the food to arrive, enjoyed the view of the Matterhorn from the dining room, and began to eat. I was fighting the temptation to panic. I wondered, 'What is wrong with me, and what do I do about it?'

Eventually, I knew that I had to say something. "Tina, how I hate to tell you this, but I have been having breathing problems again since we got off the bus. I need you to insist that someone get me oxygen." I will never forget the look on Tina's face as the realization hit her that she was with a desperately ill person and there was no way to get down this mountain tonight.

Tina asked for the manager, explained the situation, and was told that there was little that they could do. They explained that they could not give anyone oxygen without a doctor's prescription. There were no doctors at the hotel. They would have to spend hours trying to locate one. They also reiterated that there was no way off the mountain. The last bus had left. The earliest that we would be able to leave would be 7 a.m. This was not good news. I realized it was the perfect time for a prayer meeting, except that I needed maximum effort to talk.

We made it back to our room. I told Tina that I would be quoting Scripture in my heart but could no longer talk, except if I had to. I told her to get some rest. I knew that I did not dare to lie down. It would exasperate the breathing situation. I sat in a chair all night and meditated on the healing promises of God.

Tina was more concerned than she let on. She later told me that she hardly slept and kept an eye on me the entire night. At one point, I asked her to text a few friends whom I knew were people of prayer and faith. I did not want my husband to be notified because I did not want him to worry when he was thousands of miles away. Eventually, I decided that was the wrong decision. I would want to know if the situation was reversed. I asked her to text him. After only an hour, I knew that I needed to have oxygen. I told Tina I didn't care how much red tape there was, how much the staff didn't want to call a doctor, or how much the doctor didn't want to be disturbed. This was now life and death. She called, and God gave her the supernatural ability to explain everything in Swiss German. Normally, she can only speak a few words in that language. This was a miracle! They understood everything and brought a small tank of oxygen.

I was so grateful for even a small tank. Before the night was over, they brought me four more. They weren't very happy about it, but, for once in my life, I didn't care. Those eight hours were some of the longest of my life. I had no desire to even look out the window at the view of the Matterhorn. I was literally fighting for my life. I continually reminded myself to breathe slowly and deeply. I knew if I started gasping for breath, I would hyper-ventilate. It was difficult to discipline myself not to gasp. I rebuked fear and anxiety, claimed my healing, and asked for the peace of God.

Eventually, I saw the beautiful sunrise and was so very grateful to be alive. I still had difficulty breathing and told Tina there was no way I could pull a carry-on. She explained the situation to the staff, and they assured us they would send them to Tina's home.

It was difficult for me to walk out of the hotel and board our morning bus. However, by the grace of God, I managed it. I was thrilled to watch the bus descending the mountain, even if at a snail's pace. I dreaded the four or five trains we must take to get home. I dared not think of that right now. God had kept me alive through the night, and He would help me do whatever I had to finish this.

The rest of the trip was pretty much a blur for me. Each time we transferred from one train to another, I told myself, "Just do this one more time. You shall live and not die. You shall finish your race and fulfill your call. You can do it, Debbie. You've been through worse."

Tina informed me that she had planned another surprise. We were scheduled to take a boat ride on beautiful Lake Thun. That would have been a perfect ending for the trip had I not been fighting for my life. I hated disappointing her again, but we both knew that was out of the question. I just wanted to return to their apartment, pack, and leave the next day for America.

When we arrived at the apartment, Tina called a few friends to get their advice about my departure. They believed I should go to the hospital and be checked; I refused. I knew they would want me to delay my flight and stay in

Switzerland to get tests and that I would be there indefinitely. I needed my husband's support, prayers, and arms. I packed. After having no sleep the night before, I was looking forward to a good night's sleep before leaving for the United States.

I was in the middle of packing when another stomach attack began. Tina and her family were already asleep. I thought, "No way, this cannot be." It was only moments before a full-blown attack hit me. I continuously expelled everything from both ends. The pain was overwhelming. It did not help to walk, stand, lay down, vomit, cry, or breathe. The excruciating pain spread from my upper stomach to my back. Once again, I was not able to sleep the entire night.

When the Bruderer family woke up, they discovered I had not slept and had to leave for the airport in a few hours. We also learned that my carry-on had not followed me to their apartment from the hotel. After much inquiry, we were told that it was lost and they were trying to locate it. How much worse could it get? We were finally told that the bag would be in my possession by the time I left for the airport. My attack subsided, and I was comforted that I would soon be in my husband's arms. Things were looking up.

When it was time to depart for the airport, I still had no carry-on. I wanted my computer and iPad close to me on the plane, so I borrowed a carry-on from the Bruderers. When I reached the airport, we said our goodbyes, and I thought I was finally almost home and would have no more difficulties. I walked through security, and buzzers went off everywhere. People descended on me from every direction and were not sporting friendly faces. They informed me that my borrowed suitcase had some white powder that their sensitive machines could detect. I was taken into an interrogation room and asked multitudes of questions I could not answer. "Where has this suitcase been? Where was it purchased? What was the powder?" I thought, 'This is not happening, after two nights of no sleep, losing my carry-on, a night of not being able to breathe, and fighting a terrible stomach attack. Now, I am being looked at as some sort of a United States terrorist suspect.'

It would have been hilarious if it were not so unbelievable, and I had just a little sleep. However, I had not, and it wasn't. After what seemed to be an eternity, they told me that I could go, and perhaps their machinery was overly sensitive.

I was grateful to be alive, not hurting or vomiting, and that I was not sent to prison. I was wondering if I was in the middle of a nightmare. I couldn't help but think about all the eager, vision-filled Bible school students who think an evangelist's life is all glitz and glamor. They have no idea at times. However, I was headed home, and oh, how I was looking forward to seeing my husband! I also knew that when I got back, I needed to have some tests done to know exactly what my enemy was. I knew who the enemy was (the Devil), but I was not sure what exactly he was attempting to do to my body. I am a person who wants to know what I am up against as I prepare for battle.

My reunion with my husband was extra sweet. I told him I never wanted either of us to travel alone if it could be helped. The Bible says, *"one can put a thousand to flight, but two will put ten thousand to flight"* (Deuteronomy 32:30). I always needed him, but I needed him more in the battle.

We agreed I should make a doctor's appointment to see what was happening. It took a few weeks before I could see a doctor. Then, weeks of tests began. They did abdominal tests to see what the attacks were all about. Then they started lung and heart tests to ascertain the cause of breathlessness and altitude sickness. Meanwhile, I didn't have time to sit and babysit myself. I did what I always do, keep busy in the kingdom of God.

Two months later, in July, I still had not heard the test results. We joined Pastors Rodney and Adonica Howard-Browne for their Celebrate America Crusade in Washington D.C. They took the Gospel to every member of Congress, brought a team to witness on the streets, held nightly crusade meetings, prayed for our nation, and made people aware of how much was at stake. We felt that it was vital to be a part of it, not only with our prayers and financial contribution but to be there physically. Our nation is hanging in the balance, and too many Christians are burying their heads in the sand.

However, no one knew what I was fighting just to be there. I did not tell anyone. It was hot, but I was determined to join the soul-winning team. We walked all over the halls of Congress and the streets. I exerted great effort to keep up with the team. I led most of the soul-winning activities on our team despite how I felt; breathless, overheated, and exhausted. We attended nightly meetings, returned to our hotel late, and tried to sight-see a bit in between. I had never been to our nation's capital and felt that it was important to see the Holocaust Museum, hear the history of all the memorials, and more. No matter what, I would not give in to the enemy's plan for my life.

Some people give up far too easily. They resort to self-pity, baby themselves, slip into a negative confession that does not line up with the Word of God, and give up and die. I knew that no matter what was going on in my body, the Word was true. *"Let God be true, and every man a liar"* (Romans 3:4). *"His promises are*

My husband served at the end of WWII at the occupation of Germany, the Korean War, and the Vietnam War. He served his country in the U.S. Air Force for 22 years as a flight engineer.

yes and amen" (2 Cor. 1:20). *"Who his own self bare our sins in his own body on the tree, that we, being dead to sins, should live unto righteousness: by whose stripes ye were healed"* (1 Peter 2:24). That is the truth. That is reality, not my feelings and symptoms. I would fight, proclaim, and see this victory to the end.

At the end of the event, I received a call from my doctor. She said, "Well, we know the source of your stomach attacks. It's your gall bladder. It is full of stones and very diseased. It has scars where stones have been passing. It needs to come out; however, we don't know if your heart is strong enough for the surgery. We'll talk about that when you come home."

I replied in shock, "My heart? I have never had a heart problem, and no one in my family does." That's the last thing that I expected to hear.

She answered, "Well, I don't want to talk to you about that now. We'll wait until you get home. You need to schedule an appointment with the surgeons."

I told my husband I needed to make an appointment with the surgeon as quickly as possible. We did not even entertain the implications but kept our eyes on Jesus. As soon as we returned to Washington State, I went to see the surgeon. He said that the gallbladder needed to come out. They ordered a stress test to see if my heart was strong enough to endure the surgery. They described what the problem was with my heart. According to them, I was having a problem with my left ventricle and that blood was backing up into the inferior vena cava, and the heart was not resting enough between beats. It had become enlarged and stiff.

When they were finished beating around the bush, I looked at the man point-blank and asked, "Are we talking about congestive heart failure?" He looked surprised that I had that much knowledge and nodded. I told him my friend in Tampa died from congestive heart failure about three months after knowing she had a problem. I studied and knew what it was. He told me that there were four stages before death. He explained that it was a chronic condition that was irreversible. He said that I needed further testing.

I complied with the stress test, which in and of itself causes stress. Perhaps that is the reason for the name. It was a grueling four to five hours, after which I decided they were secretly testing me for the Olympics and that I would probably not make the first team. As I was huffing and puffing, much like the wolf out to blow down the three pigs' homes, I must have looked at the assisting tech person with desperate eyes. He told me, "I'm not really supposed to tell you this, but I know what they are testing you for. It's not as bad as they think. I see you have a lot of output when put to the test."

Those were wonderful words to hear, but not as wonderful as the ones I was already studying, like Isaiah 53:3-5, *"He is despised and rejected of men; a man of sorrows, and acquainted with grief: and we hid as it were our faces from him; he was despised, and we esteemed him not. Surely he hath borne our griefs and carried our sorrows: yet we did esteem him stricken, smitten of God, and afflicted. But he was wounded for our transgressions, he was bruised for our iniquities: the chastisement of our peace was upon him, and with his stripes, we are healed."* Also, Matthew 8:17, *"That it might be fulfilled which was spoken by Esaias the prophet, saying, Himself took our infirmities, and bare our sicknesses."* 1 Peter 2:24 says, *"Whom his own self bare our sins in His own body on the tree, that we, being dead to sins, should live unto righteousness: by whose stripes ye were healed."*

Whatever they had to say were their facts, but my Bible is the truth. This was only confirmation that my God was at work. I knew He was again preparing me for another testimony that would cause the doctors and everyone else to know He is still The Healer. I was told to visit my internal doctor. She told me that congestive heart failure was the reason that I had been so exhausted for so long. (I felt guilty and made myself press through every time I worked out.) She said the heart failure was the reason I was so out of breath while trying to work out or walk up a slight incline, like the jet-way of a plane. She explained that it caused my metabolism to be almost non-existent and was responsible for why I couldn't lose weight. It didn't matter how much I dieted or exercised. There was not enough oxygen going to my organs or muscles.

I finally had an explanation of what I had been feeling for quite some time. I told my doctor that I was believing for healing and had experienced many of them before, in my own life and the lives of the people I prayed for. I also told my husband I would look into some natural remedies and supplements for the heart while believing for my healing.

The doctors began a regimen of blood pressure medicines to relax the heart, and I knew they would plan to increase medications. I did not want that. I wanted a doctor who would support me in trying some natural medications and help me come off the ones recently prescribed.

My oldest son, Joshua, called me from Florida. He is an optometrist and commander in the United States Navy. When he heard of my recent medical battles, he asked me a question. "Mom, have you ever considered some kind of bariatric surgery? It cannot be good for your heart to carry so much weight."

I replied, "No, Josh, I would never consider such a thing. I have always considered that to be a cop-out or shortcut. It would be like having your hands cut off so that you no longer can take drugs or smoke. Besides, I used to be a trainer. I know what to do to lose weight."

He replied, "I understand that Mom, but in your case, it is now life or death. They told you it would be impossible to lose weight because of congestive heart failure. You need to get it off in a hurry, so the heart is no longer beating for two people. I hope that you will consider it. Please promise me that you will think about it."

"All right, Josh, I will look into it. Thanks for your concern."

I disdained the idea of people looking for shortcuts. I wouldn't consider having my intestines bypassed, organs cut out, a band cutting off my stomach, or staples so that I can't eat so much. I felt that people should discipline themselves. They just need to get over their addiction.

However, I was in a different place, but I still didn't believe I could ever seriously consider such a thing. I was surprised that I could not get Josh's words out of my head over the next few days. I even mentioned it to my husband. "I don't understand why, but I cannot forget what Josh said. I wonder if I should look into this." He didn't seem as convinced that it was something worth considering. I put it on the back burner.

My surgeon called and said that they were prepared to do the gallbladder surgery right away. I agreed to proceed. While concentrating my faith on the bigger issue at stake, I didn't need the distraction of excruciating pain from gallbladder attacks. I knew I needed to repent for not caring for my body, weight gain, and love of junk food. I asked God to help me cope without a gallbladder. The laparoscopic surgery took place without a hitch. The Lord guided the physician's hands, and I was discharged the same day.

My Norwegian friends, Edit and Eirik Gussias, were due to arrive that very day. We didn't even have time to call them and tell them I was having surgery. Everything happened too quickly. After I was released from the hospital, I asked my husband to stop at a Scandinavian grocery store in Seattle to buy some things for them. I planned to have a surprise welcome party for them at church the following day. He could not believe that I was shopping only hours after having surgery. There was no time to waste. I stood on my feet for an hour while shopping for their Norwegian delicacies. Then, we went to the airport to pick them up. Needless to say, they were surprised to hear of the past 24 hours. I was without a body part, but feeling pretty chipper, all things considered.

I preached the next day, hosted a Norwegian welcome party, and felt everything was going great. I did not hurt inside, but I noticed that my small incisions (five in total) began to itch and burn. I felt that maybe it was because I was wearing tight clothing around the waist. I could not wait to change when the church service was over. By late Sunday night, after arriving home, the incisions were more than uncomfortable. They did not hurt like that in the beginning. I removed the bandages to take a peek. When I did, I was alarmed. I called my husband to come to have a look. I could see the alarm on his face. He said, "Oh my goodness, Debbie. These have become infected. I don't believe we should wait until morning. You need to go to the emergency room." We asked our houseguests to accompany us to the emergency room at night. I'm sure they didn't plan on spending time in the emergency room.

The military hospital in Tacoma, Washington, was an hour from our home. When we arrived, we saw many sick people waiting for their turn. They were ahead of us. One patient told us that she had been there for two hours and had not been attended to. That was not what any of us hoped to hear. I decided that I should prepare for a long wait with my itching and burning symptoms. We checked in and immediately heard my name being called to see a doctor. About 50 other patients stared at me. Their faces said it all. They wore looks of shock, disbelief, and jealousy. They might just as well have said out loud, "Who do you think you are? You just arrived. Why are you being given this favor?" If they would have asked, I would have had to say, "I do not have the slightest idea. I'm just as shocked as you are." I knew that my God was behind this, in spite of every evil intention of the enemy.

As soon as my husband and I were brought into an examination room, we were greeted by the most unusual doctor. He immediately hugged both of us. He was a total stranger. It was a warm hug as if he had known us all our lives. He began asking preliminary questions. "What's the problem? What drugs are you currently taking? What was your surgery? Can I take a look?" Upon his initial examination, he said, "Oh yes, you are having an allergic reaction to your staples. I am going to take these staples out and squeeze the infection out. I will put an antibiotic and fresh dressing on these incisions.

Before I knew it, I gave him my testimony of the healing from the blood clot.

I told him I traveled internationally for the Lord and had a recent negative diagnosis but was expecting another healing. He put his paperwork down, and I saw him crying. He said something that I will never forget. "Now I know what is going on and why I am here tonight. I never work in the emergency room. I am a surgeon upstairs. My wife is having surgery tonight for a serious spinal problem. I have not left her side and felt I should get something out of the car for her and return to her side. When I came downstairs, I heard on the inside, "Volunteer your services in the emergency room tonight." "I, too, am a Spirit-filled Christian. I go to an Assembly of God church here in Tacoma. I am a part-time missionary and want to be a full-time medical missionary someday. I know how to hear the voice of God. So, I came down to the emergency room and told them I would give them only 30 minutes of my time. They gave me a list of about 50 people tonight, and I picked your name off the list. I am here, sent by God, to get you thin and off your medicines. Do you know what I do here? I am one of the chief surgeons in bariatric surgery. Do you know what that is?" I could not believe what I was hearing. "Yes, sir, I have read about bariatric surgery, and my son called only days ago to ask me if I would consider it. I told him I was believing for a doctor who would get me off my meds instead of adding more to the list." Now, I heard these exact words come out of a physician's mouth, who was not even supposed to be anywhere near the emergency room tonight.

By now, I was crying, the doctor was crying, and my husband (who is not a crier) was smiling, knowing we had a divine appointment. I told the doctor that we had Norwegian friends in the waiting room, and he was even more excited and asked to meet them. He introduced himself to our friends, hugged their necks, listened to Edit's testimony of being healed from terminal liver disease, cried some more, and offered to take them to dinner. The other patients were staring and listening to all the testimonies. We had church in the emergency room.

Before leaving, the doctor told me to call his office in the morning. He told me there was a current waiting list of over a year but that he would have me in the program tomorrow. Sure enough, when I got home, I read about the program and saw that people were being told there was a long waiting period. I received a call before I could make my own call, welcoming me into the program. That was just the beginning of miracle after miracle.

Dr. Blair told me that the surgery he wanted to do was called a sleeve gastrectomy. It is one of the newer bariatric surgeries. It was invented because the morbidly obese had so many risks associated with gastric bypass surgery that they needed to find a way to do the surgery in two stages. Patients would no longer be on the operating table for such a long period of time, thus reducing the risk associated with surgery. In the first operation, they would simply remove two-thirds of the stomach. This enabled the patients to lose some weight before the bypass part of the surgery. The part of the stomach that is removed restricts how much a person can eat and removes the hunger hormones, which greatly curbs appetite. They discovered that many patients lose so much weight on the first part of the procedure that a second part was no longer necessary. This surgery became popular, especially for those who don't have hundreds of pounds to lose. It has replaced having bypass surgery for many people.

The Lord led me on this journey, and I believe He will direct people differently according to their faith level. When I went to the initial meeting, I was told that this would be a six-month journey before the surgery could take place. They want people to know what they are doing, what to expect, and be prepared emotionally, nutritionally, and psychologically. I would meet with a nutritionist three times, go to vocational training, have a psychological evaluation, meet with a pharmacist about how medications may change after drastic weight loss, and attend group sessions twice a week. I wondered how we could do this, pastor, and travel to the nations.

I also would have a recovery period where I would need help. I was aware of God's timing. Edit and Eirik could help me before they left. However, their visa was only good for three months, and they already had their return ticket. I was told that the hospital never makes an exception. I decided that if God had brought me this far, He would make a way when there seemed to be nothing.

After two group sessions, one visit with the nutritionist, and one with the psychologist, I had an appointment with Dr. Blair again. I asked, "Dr. Blair, is it ever possible for the six-month waiting period to be waived if someone has medical problems?" His eyes got as big as saucers, and he replied, "You won't believe this, but just this morning, before you walked in here, we received a call from headquarters. We have been fighting the six-month rule for a few years and just got an answer: if there are extenuating medical circumstances, we can waive the waiting period."

God gave me a miracle again. I mentioned this new ruling when I went back to my nutritionist for one last appointment. She looked shocked and said she had never heard of such a thing. I told her what I was told, and she said, "I believe you are mistaken. We have not received any information like that." I decided to keep the information to myself after that. I had no intention of getting Dr. Blair in trouble and realized that somehow the Lord had made way for me no one else was aware of. That is called divine favor. We can expect God to part the sea for us. Everyone else in my group who began the process at the same time was required to wait six months.

My doctor suggested that we do the surgery the very next week. I was taken aback by how quickly this was happening and was unprepared. We already purchased plane tickets to attend Pastor Rodney's fall minister's conference in Tampa, Florida. Edit and Eirik were looking forward to going with us. I did not want them to miss it, and I needed the refreshing and wisdom we would receive at the conference. I told the doctor I would have the surgery the week after returning from Tampa.

Only two months had passed from the time I had my gall bladder out to having the sleeve gastrectomy. Only my God could do that. The surgery was uneventful. I was sore but up and walking the next day. I was not allowed to eat or even sip anything for twenty-four hours. I was on a liquid diet for another week or two, then pureed foods. I graduated to soft foods and then to a fairly full diet. Edit took good care of me. I lost weight quickly, and in the first month, I lost 25 pounds. Eleven months later, I lost 90 pounds. A general rule of thumb with this surgery is that patients lose about 60% of their excess weight in the first two years. I was above that and happy. I did not have the nutritional deficits that gastric bypass patients have. I eat pretty much what I want, but in small amounts.

Am I saying that this is God's first choice? Absolutely not. His first choice is we discipline ourselves, exercise, eat properly, take care of ourselves, and trust Him for divine health and healing. However, if we have not done our part, He is still merciful and makes a way for us. He gets our attention, meets us where we are, and helps us to come out of whatever situation we find ourselves in. I am sure not everyone agreed with the path I felt led to take.

There are absolutes in the Bible. However, in areas not found in His Word, the Holy Spirit guides us according to our faith level and participation with Him. Was this a radical thing to do? Yes, and yet I have many Christian friends who have done radical things such as starvation diets, shots, health drinks, etc. If that is what has worked for them, that's wonderful. We all have to hear from the Holy Ghost for ourselves. When I was first diagnosed with congestive heart failure, God spoke to me to do all I knew to do and trust Him for a brand new heart. I was required to lose weight, change my eating and exercise habits, get enough sleep, and learn to deal better with stress. I could believe Him to do the impossible after doing my part.

Two doctors told me not to get my hopes up that this would improve my heart. They told me this was terminal and that losing weight would not help. They said my condition would continue to deteriorate. I refused that false prophecy and told them they would witness my new heart. Since that time, I have had further medical tests. The comparison between my first and second electrocardiograms is incredible. The first one showed significant enlargement of the heart. They explained how the heart muscle had become stiff. The last echo said there was no enlargement or stiffness, and I am a-symptomatic. I am off of all heart and blood pressure medicines and diuretics. My God is indeed still the healer, and my Jesus is still the same yesterday, today, and forever (Hebrews13:8). Someday, I will even ascend the Matterhorn again and give a black eye to the enemy.

NINETEEN

THE RESURRECTION OF A LOST DREAM, WORD, AND SPIRIT INSTITUTE NW

In August 2016, I hosted an event called Northwest Ablaze. I began this event in June 2013. It became my annual campmeeting. I wanted the people in the Northwest to experience old-fashioned revival. This area, specifically the state of Washington, has been known for liberal politics, witchcraft, and the New Age movement. It is where the Twilight series was created and where the tree-huggers are numerous. It was one of the first states (along with Colorado) to legalize the possession and recreational use of marijuana. However, there was now a revivalist in the state that refused to go with the status quo. I decided to swing the bat every way to see revival come to the state.

The last two Northwest Ablaze events were awesome, but I planned a very special one in 2016. It was the year of my 60th birthday, and I would celebrate 26 years of ministry. I had absent-mindedly let the 25th year go by unnoticed and felt that it was time to celebrate in a big way. After my recent diagnosis and victory, I wanted to put the enemy on notice that I was not finished. I invited four other ministers to speak, brought a young man from Florida to lead our worship, and invited people to come from all over the world. We had representation from Switzerland, Norway, Alaska, Florida, South Carolina, California, Texas, and of course, many from all over Washington State.

My keynote speaker was Pastor Mark Spitsbergen from San Diego, California. He and his wife, Anne, have been long-time friends. Pastor Mark served on Dr. Rodney Howard- Browne's board for many years, and I held revivals in his church several times. He has pastored for over 35 years and authored several books, one of which was recently released. The subject is about the last days and is called "The Last Two Kingdoms." God has also launched Pastors Mark and Anne into the nations of the world.

I believe that Pastor Mark is called to confront the present-day apostasy, call people to repentance and a holy lifestyle, and help us identify who we are in Christ until we become the true church. We are to win the lost and preach the Gospel with signs and wonders following. Pastor Mark's message is very challenging. As he spoke one night, the gift of faith came upon me. It continued to remain with me for several weeks. I suddenly knew it was time to launch a Bible school in the Northwest. I heard myself announce it with no premeditation and almost felt like I was hearing it with the people for the first time.

The school is called Word and Spirit Bible Institute Northwest; it began in August 2017. We are accredited by Transworld Accrediting Commission International. They have certified schools all over the United States. I have known Dr. Steve Anderson, the president of the Transworld Accrediting Commission, for many years. I believe in his vision and calling.

Dean Debbie with Dr. Steve Anderson and Dr. Monroe.

Establishing a Bible school has been a dream of mine for many years. One of my greatest joys has been teaching in Bible schools in many nations. I have always been a studious pupil. I was in the teacher's group at Rhema, not the fiery evangelist's class. My instructor in the teacher's lab class at Rhema wrote on my teaching lab paper, "That was excellent. I believe you will be one of the finest teachers this school has ever put out." It was only later, in revival, that God put a fire in my bones that turned me into a fiery preacher, evangelist, and teacher.

For many years, I enjoyed having two meetings a day in revival. I taught in the morning services on the anointing and healing and had Holy Ghost services in the evening. I was able to do both, teach and preach. Some are only called to teach, while some are only called to preach; I am blessed to be called to do both.

I still love to learn anything that I can. I feel that academics are important. We have ministers who cannot spell, punctuate, use English grammar, write a newsletter, and do not know good Bible doctrine. They do not know Biblical hermeneutics or exegesis. I realize that academics are not as important as the anointing, but they are important. We are to *"study to show ourselves approved unto God, a workman who needeth not to be ashamed"* (2 Timothy 2:15).

We have other schools and ministers that may know academics but are spiritually dull, and some completely dead. They know nothing of sensitivity to the Spirit of God, how to flow with Him, operate in His gifts, or even recognize when the Holy Spirit is in the room or talking to them. God is not after people with big heads and little hearts. However, He does not want flakiness either. He is not into spiritual granola; fruit, flakes, and nuts.

We began a school that is a school of the Word of God, with good, balanced, Pentecostal theology and doctrine, and yet is a school of the Holy Spirit. We teach others how to sense Him and cooperate with Him. It is a school that teaches students how to bring in the harvest of the nations, win souls, and believe for big things. We emphasize faith and how to believe in a big God who makes the impossible possible. We are training revivalists to take the nations and to preach the Word of God with signs and wonders following.

The Bible says in Psalm 2:8, *"Ask of me, and I shall give thee the heathen for thine inheritance, and the uttermost parts of the earth for thy possession."* Jesus said in Luke 10:2, *"Therefore said he unto them, The harvest truly is great, but the laborers are few: pray ye therefore the Lord of the harvest, that he would send forth laborers into his harvest."*

One or two people can only do so much. However, if we can put that same revival spirit, coupled with good Bible doctrine, into hundreds and thousands of others, look out, world! Many in the Pacific Northwest have told me that they cannot, for various reasons, uproot their families, quit their jobs, and move. So, I decided to bring the Bible school to them. I have sent many students to the River Bible Institute (now River University), Pastor Rodney Howard-Browne's Bible school in Tampa, Florida. I believe this is the best Bible school in the world, but why not have more like it?

My three sons came for Northwest Ablaze in August of 2016. They knew that I was celebrating 26 years of full-time ministry. Two of them live in Alaska, and one in Florida. They promised to be there for the last two days. That was the highlight of the event for me. The boys had sacrificed so much to enable me to travel in ministry. We have been through a lot together. They know first-hand what the journey has been. It would not have been right to celebrate without them.

Friday night arrived after an incredible week. Every speaker was dynamic, worship was outstanding, people were hungry and thirsty, and God showed up in a big way. I played videos every morning and evening, some of the Alaskan ministry (including the prison ministry), some of the nations, and the one where I was giving my testimony.

My stepdaughter and secretary at the time, Charlotte Standridge, decided to receive a special personal offering for me to honor my 26 years of ministry. Before the offering was received, she hand-picked several people to testify about how my ministry impacted them. It was beyond wonderful for me. I was so pleased that my sons were there to hear it. It was a night of tears, laughter, and celebration. It is etched in my heart and mind forever. I looked around the room and witnessed much fruit from my years of labor. We heard of marriages that had been restored, bodies healed, and more that took place through this ministry. I was reminded of how blessed I am to be called to do this. What a night! What precious memories! What love flowed in that room!

After that last meeting, we celebrated in the church's fellowship hall with pizza for all and a large anniversary cake. Our own church building was not large enough for all of the out-of-town guests and people from other churches. We knew that we needed to rent a building for this event. We decided to reach out and ask if we could rent the church my husband built and pastored for 23 years. We felt that enough restoration had occurred to make that possible. We asked, and they said, "Yes."

When my husband built the last addition to Central Park Neighborhood Church, he felt he was building it to house revival. No Pentecostal or charismatic church was large enough in Gray's Harbor County to host a large revival. My husband had a revivalist's heart and wanted to see this entire area shaken by the power of God. He finished the addition (that could seat 600 people) just before he resigned from pastoring. We were puzzled about all of the turns of events after he finished it. The irony of life, it seemed, was that he built a building large enough for revival, and when it was completely paid off, he resigned. We found ourselves pioneering another one that we had to borrow money for. It was too small, and now we were renting the one he built to hold the revivals. It was fulfilling its purpose.

God has a way of providing, answering prayer, and fulfilling every dream in its time. Pastor Joe (as we will call him) attended most of the meetings. Some of the congregation came for a couple of nights. We hoped to see more but were very happy to see a few. One lady thanked me for the week of meetings and told me that she and her husband had been set free. There were healings, baptisms in the Holy Spirit, rededications, consecrations, and people filled with the Holy Ghost. The meetings were attended by people from other churches, as well. The people will never be the same. I trust they will become soul-winners, and the harvest will come in.

We are very grateful to Pastor Joe and the church. We blessed them for the use of the building; it was a real moment of healing in the relationship. We also realized the need for a larger building, as never before. We needed it to host all of the events God wanted us to do in that area. I wanted to bring in the world's greatest revivalists and see the Northwest awakened to the glory of God.

As I started the accreditation application process for the Bible school, I realized our immediate need for a larger building. Our present building could only host the first group of Bible school students, but if we were to grow, it would not. I decided to believe God for a building large enough to allow us to grow.

You may think that if something is birthed of God, it will happen, regardless of us. Not so. Jesus asked us to pray that God's will be done on earth as it is in Heaven. If it were just going to happen automatically, we would not be asked to pray. Also, we have been given the keys to the kingdom to bind and loose (Matthew 16:19). Whatever we allow, God allows. Whatever we stop, He stops. We are to operate through His authority. He has given us a blank check, so to speak, with whosoever and whatsoever. He has promised to meet our every need according to His riches in the glory of Christ Jesus (Philippians 4:19). He said in Deuteronomy 8:18, *"But thou shalt remember the Lord thy God: for it is he that giveth thee power to get wealth, that he may establish his covenant which he sware unto thy fathers, as it is this day."* My Bible also says that our Father owns the cattle on a thousand hills (Psalm 50:10). The earth is His and the fullness thereof (Psalm 24:1). He is Jehovah-Jireh, the Lord, our provider. He tells us in Psalm 23 that we shall not want. He told us to be wise stewards, subdue the earth, and multiply. He is a rewarder for those who diligently seek Him. He is not a subtractor. We have the parable of the talents. We see that our God is a God of increase and has promised us a surplus of blessings. He has promised that we will be blessed coming in and blessed going out (Deuteronomy 28:6).

We are to establish God's covenant and get the job done. We are told to go into the world and preach the Gospel. There will be no excuses on that day for why we could not get the job done. This is why the church of the Lord Jesus Christ has to continue to stretch our faith with our giving and believing for big things. That is also why people like myself, who have been called to teach along these lines, must continue until we can be in a position for the big things.

I recently went to Pastors Mark and Anne Spitsbergen's ministry training ranch in southern Oregon. He is an inventor, scientist, pastor, evangelist, rancher, mechanic, builder, entrepreneur, author, and more. They showed us their vision of bringing pastors and orphans from the unreached people's groups and showing them how to grow crops, raise fish, cattle, and more. I watched them work from dawn until sunset, tirelessly, believing for more while putting their faith out further each time. We must have more people like this, who will work while it is yet day, for the night is coming when no man can work.

While believing God for this building, I looked at commercial real estate online and saw nothing. The Holy Spirit told me it was time to drive in my car, and He would show me. I drove to a small town east of us for about 20 minutes, then I saw it! It was an aesthetically beautiful and relatively new building on a corner lot in Elma, Washington. I was immediately drawn to it. The building had a for-sale sign on the property. I checked again and found out that it was not listed anywhere. I hurriedly scribbled the number on a piece of paper and made a phone call. I was told that the bank was asking $450,000 for the property. Yet, it was assessed by the county at almost $700,000. It was a former mortuary that went bankrupt. The building had been vacant for about two years. The mortuary left pews, an organ, a piano, speakers, tables and chairs, desks, and file cabinets. It had a chapel that seated over 200 people. The bank said that all equipment was included in the deal. I instantly knew that this was our building. There was excitement in my spirit. I realized that the first thing we needed to do was sell our present building.

I had some congregation members go with us to pray at the building. We did that several times before we were actually in it. My husband suggested we sell the previous building in Aberdeen without a realtor. However, I was somewhat concerned but submitted to what he thought, and I am so glad I did.

We had our graphic arts designer, who was Bob's son-in-law, design and print some flyers. One of the men in our church owned a barbershop. He took flyers to his barber shop that very day. A few minutes later, a businessman came into his shop for a haircut, saw the flyer, called me, and gave us cash for the building. We closed in one week. That was miracle number one.

Several of us felt to offer only $389,000, which was far lower than they were asking. Our offer was accepted on the same day that the previous building sold. We knew that we couldn't sell ours until we had a place to move into and couldn't buy one until we sold ours. I asked the Lord for wisdom and supernatural favor in these matters, and He granted it.

We made a trip to our small-town local bank. The bank's advertisement on the local billboards says, "We want to know you, have a relationship with you. This is the advantage of a small-town bank." This is the same bank with whom my husband previously paid off two large church loans and our home. They never hesitated about loaning us the money for the building we had purchased three years prior and just sold. We made double payments every month for three years. I thought that this would be a piece of cake. However, the enemy was at work. We should know that we will always have some opposition when we attempt to do big things for God. We cannot give up. We've read the end of "the book."

Our loan officer was a Christian and seemed sure we would have no problems. In just days, we were given a "good faith letter" to take to the other bank that held the title. We were on our way. We asked to borrow 80% of the purchase price with a 20% down payment. Again, the loan officer told us that sounded good. Within days, we got a call that they would only do it if we came up with 25%, and they would loan us 75%. We knew that would be a stretch for us, but we also knew that our God would do it. We were leaving in two days to head to Tampa, Florida, for Pastor Rodney's fall ministers conference. We told our church to believe and stand with us for the miracle. We realized that we needed $35,000 more. We boarded our jet with the entire matter being placed in the hands of the Great Provider.

This happened to be one of the meetings that Pastor Rodney did not use me at all for teaching on giving. We were not seated in the front row, even though we usually were. The new people did not even know who we were. I was not in a position where anyone could know what we were doing in Washington State or know anything about our financial need for this building.

After the first morning service, several people stood in line, waiting to talk with me. When the line dwindled, I saw a face I knew from somewhere but could not place. We both spoke our hello's, and she asked, "Do you remember me?" I replied that she looked familiar, but I could not recall her name. Then she told me the story.

She reminded me of a revival I had in Roswell, Georgia, in 1994 at World Harvest Church with Pastors Mirek and Linda Hufton. She, her husband, and their young daughter had just moved to Atlanta and were struggling financially. She began to give offerings out of her poverty. God kept blessing and increasing them each day over the week. Then, she told me that I received an offering for her and her family. They left that night with $1,500. As she was relating the story, the memories came flooding back. She said she had been looking for me all these years to say, "Thank you." Someone told her that I might be at these meetings. We rejoiced together. She then told me that God spoke to her that she was to give us $50,000. I literally staggered and fell back against the foyer wall. I cried.

Earlier that day, as we were getting ready for church, my husband talked to me about the financial miracle we were believing for. He said, "I've been thinking, Debbie. We don't have $35,000, and we need God to give us that miracle." I agreed. He went on, "If we have to believe Him for $35,000, why don't we believe for $50,000? That is no harder for our God, and we need some extra finances to be able to purchase furniture and equipment." I agreed.

I was usually the one to believe for great financial miracles. We need each other; husbands and wives, congregation members, friends, and family members. One time, I will lead in faith, and the next, someone else will. The Bible says that one will put a thousand to flight, and two will put ten thousand to flight (Deuteronomy 32:30).

I could not wait to give my congregation the wonderful, miraculous news. They had been praying, confessing God's Word, and believing with their pastors. Now, God had come through. What a day of rejoicing this would be. I will announce it this Sunday morning. I was also looking forward to walking into my local bank and watching their expressions. I knew that the banking players did not believe we could come up with it. Little did I know that the enemy was not through with his chess game and would make the next move.

A couple of days after our Sunday service of rejoicing, I received a call from our loan officer, saying, "Debbie, I hate to tell you this, but the officers feel that your church is too much of a risk and will not loan you the money after all."

We were already given a "good faith statement" to take to the other bank. I'm glad the faith God tells us to have isn't like the bank's faith, which means absolutely nothing. I reminded them of our history, our impeccable credit, the fact that we had never missed a double payment to them before, all the previous loans that we had paid off with them, and how they advertise that they are a friendly, local bank. I reminded them that Gray's Harbor County has the highest drug addiction, alcoholism, unemployment, and dysfunctional family record in the state. Yet, they keep loaning to marijuana stores and bars and deny a church the opportunity to make a difference. It was all to no avail. I could not believe it!

How could my God have given us this many miracles to lose it in the end? He led us supernaturally to a building that was not even listed for sale.

As I reflected on the number of miracles so far, I remembered the very next day after I saw the building, our other building sold without a realtor. That was the same day our lowball offer was accepted for the new building. Most importantly, God spoke to someone about our exact financial need when she could not have known anything about it. There were too many miracles and I knew that my God was not schizophrenic. I held onto the fact that if He had led us this far, He would give us another miracle. I just didn't know how.

My loan officer called back, told me how badly she felt and said she went to bat for us. She told us that the powers that be said that they would reconsider the loan if we could come up with half of the entire amount. That seemed so impossible again, considering the size of our congregation. However, the Bible says that Abraham considered not his age or the deadness of Sarah's womb (Rom. 4:19). We must learn to "consider not" a little better.

Miraculously, a lady in our church stepped up with an insurance policy that she cashed out early for us. We have since given that back to her. It was a loan, but it gave us just enough. I went back to the bank with the good news, expecting them to rejoice with us. I waited about two weeks for a reply. The bank officer called and said that they still decided not to take "the risk." I was with family and friends expecting to celebrate at any moment. I was so shocked that I couldn't speak for a few seconds. I wondered, "Now, God, what are you up to?"

Meanwhile, our bank ordered an appraisal that cost us $5,000. We also paid for an inspection, which amounted to several hundred dollars, and then they demanded an environmental report that cost another $500. We were now out of our pocket about $6,000. We also sent a tithe to The River of $5,000 for the check the lady gave to us while we were attending the minister's conference. What kind of bank goes back on its word that many times with no plausible reason?

Meanwhile, I was doing my homework for other loan institutions. I also called a few different minister friends. I know that they have fought the good fight of faith in these areas many times. Some felt that I was not to force it. They mentioned that maybe it was not this building or the right timing." I was disappointed. I was hoping for prayer and to hear a word of encouragement. The Devil began to whisper. "Your days are numbered. Nobody believes in you anymore. Look at all the people you have helped; they seem to have short memories. You're all alone. You're losing your mind to think you can buy this or any other building. Hang it up, woman, and just go back to being a grandma. You've blown it too much in your life."

Have you ever heard a voice like that? I had to do what you must learn to do. I realized the source, rebuked it, and talked about what God says. *"I can do all things through Christ Jesus who strengthens me* (Philippians 4:13). *Greater is He who is in me than he who is in the world* (1 John 4:4). *I am more than a conqueror through Him who loves me* (Romans 8:37). *I overcome by the blood of the Lamb and by the word of my testimony* (Revelation 12:11). *If God is for me, who can be against me"* (Romans 8:31).

Sometimes, we have to come to an end without help from anyone or anything. God is a jealous God and will have no other gods before him, including ministers, friends, business people, or others we trust. Later, God would use someone to encourage me, but not yet. He wanted my total reliance on Him.

We continued to have prayer meetings that I felt should be victorious praise meetings. I knew the battle was the Lord's, and we should praise Him ahead of time. That requires faith. Each time we received a flicker of hope, it seemed that the rug was pulled out from under us again. People gave me advice and referrals for Christian credit unions, secular credit unions, and more. I did more paperwork in six months than I have done in my entire life. We did financials, profit and loss statements, hired accountants, called to explain financials, and were given great hope each time. I thought we would be in the building by early December. That was our scheduled closing date. Now, we were forced to get extension after extension until the bank that owned the building said, "We will not give you another extension without proof of financing." I made one more call to a businessman, who is also a minister from another church. He was a personal friend and a trusted advisor. I was told he would get back to me in a few days, but I never heard from him.

In the middle of all of this, God was trying my heart. I refused to take offense or put my trust in anyone other than Him. I went down every road until there were none left to go down. However, I couldn't let go of the fact that I had a Word from the Lord. All of these institutions told me it looked hopeful, and then weeks into it, called back to say we were too small, we were borrowing too much, and others said we were not borrowing enough. Some said that we had too much income from Debbie Rich Ministries (the evangelistic branch of the ministry) and not enough from the church itself. The list of reasons went on and on. Some suggested we sell church bonds. Finally, I was told that we should call back in a couple of years after our congregation has increased.

Interestingly, some of these financial institutions admitted to me that they received orders to get out of the "church lending business." That should alarm all of us; it is all part of the plan of the enemy to shut us down. We had better wake up quickly while we can. This is another reason we need our own banks and should believe God for great prosperity. Pastor Rodney Howard-Browne says he believes we only have about an hour of daylight left (spiritually).

I felt myself wavering. A cloud of doubt and unbelief was trying to overtake me. I remembered that David had to talk to his soul when he was tempted to become discouraged at Ziklag (1 Samuel 30:6). This was after the enemy stole his wives and children, and his men wanted to stone him. I knew that I needed reinforcements that day. I decided to call my friend, Pastor Mark Spitsbergen. Pastor Mark was making trips to our church to encourage us. He teaches a lot about covenant relationships. I made the call, and I am so glad that I did. He prayed with me in other tongues for a while. He told me about some things they have done temporarily when up against tough situations for loans. I felt to put some of the suggestions on the shelf and pray about it.

A few days later, I made some inquiries online about hard cash loans. I almost got involved with some hard cash lenders on the northeast coast but had a check in my spirit about them. I should have checked in with the Holy Spirit sooner because it cost us over $3,000 before I backed out. It could have been worse, though. I called the whole thing off the day they said they would loan it to us. I was holding meetings in Ireland and was very busy. I knew I was listening to the Holy Spirit when I told the man that the deal was off. We would have had a disaster if I had continued. The Devil told me I had thrown away my last chance and was a fool, but I knew I was learning to be much more discerning in the hard places.

We returned home to hear that the bank that owned the building was putting the building back on the market and would not extend our contract any further. I asked them to loan us the money. They had refused to take the loan themselves. They could have made it much easier for all of us. However, they said it would not be a clean deal to repossess a building and then turn around and loan the money to someone else to purchase it. We were now at the end of the road.

I told the Lord that I was dependent upon Him for a miracle. That's where He wants us to be; desperate, waiting, listening closely, trusting, obeying, and dependent on His marvelous grace. Suddenly, I remembered that two weeks prior, a realtor from the bank had given me the name of a local man who does hard cash loans. At that time, I was already involved with the people from the Northeast. I almost forgot about the card. I was emotionally and physically exhausted when I suddenly remembered that I had been given this name.

Could I start over with a new packet of financials and explain our story for the umpteenth time? Should I ask the bank to extend the grace once more while we try again? Could we handle the emotion of promises that are retracted each time? I talked to an advisor and dear friend, Gayle Wasik, who was staying in our home. She came to help me start the credentialing process for the Bible school and lay out the classes. She said, "Boy, I don't know. Are you up to that? Do you have a word from the Lord, or are you just trying something else that will wear you out?" My husband said basically the same thing.

I didn't think those were powerful confirmations to go forward. I almost let it go but decided to go into my office and shut the door on everyone and everything except the Lord. "Lord, should I try one more thing? I'm beyond worn out and feel like I must have done all these things in the flesh. We have nothing to show for it. Yet, I believe you said this building is ours, and I am at the end by myself. Should I call this stranger or not?" I heard only one thing and heard it strongly. "Are you ready to give up? It's up to you." I still did not know if that meant I should call the man, if the man would grant our request for a loan, or even if we would have the building. However, I knew that I was being challenged not to quit. So I would not!

I will never forget the moment when a friendly voice answered the phone. That was my first surprise. Everyone I dealt with up to this time sounded like the mafia, complete with accents. None of them were friendly.

The first thing this man said was, "Lady, this is a miracle that you got through to me" (the word miracle got my attention). He went on to say, "I just changed phone companies, and something is messed up. I have not received any calls all day and was just leaving my office to go to the phone company and raise h*##. I have no idea how this phone call came through to me."

I was encouraged at this point. I gave a brief explanation as to why I was calling. I was so worn out from the process that I wasn't going into detail until I knew there was hope. He said, "I am interested in taking your case, but there is a problem. I am a snowbird and promised my fiancee that we would be on a plane for Arizona in twenty-four hours. I don't do business with anyone I haven't met personally or loan money on a building I haven't seen. Is there any possibility of being able to see that building and meeting you in an hour?" I was flabbergasted. I said that we would make it work. His office was 40 minutes away in the capital (Olympia).

Just over an hour later, we sat across a conference table in the building in Elma that we knew was ours. I was shaking hands with Mr. Jay Barrett of Jay Barrett and Associates. We felt he was an honest man as far as the world was concerned. He asked about our vision and seemed genuinely interested in our mission. He even offered to loan us an extra $50,000 to help with other projects. The entire deal was finished within two hours from the time of the call. He promised that he would close the deal in five business days and did. We were in the building the following Sunday.

I wanted to announce this on Facebook Live. Before going live, I asked Gayle, who was acting as my assistant, what the date would be that coming Sunday. She told me, "March 26th," and I began to cry. I had to postpone my Facebook Live announcement for a few minutes while I pulled myself together. She asked what was wrong. I said this was the date when I almost died from that massive pulmonary saddle embolism. I was told at the hospital that I couldn't live through the night. So, March 26 was supposed to be on my tombstone as my obituary date. Instead, it would be the date of the opening of our church and the building that would become Word and Spirit Institute NW. The building that previously housed death, funerals, and grieving people, would now be the host for new birth, healing, joy unspeakable, and life more abundantly. This day would be the resurrection day of this ministry eleven years after the Devil tried to kill me. Only God could have put this all together the way that He did. God did what I was not able to do in six months. He did it in two hours, enabling us to acquire a wonderful building in a nearby town.

I was led to invite Gayle Wasik to help me do all the groundwork for the new Bible school, Word and Spirit Institute, or (WSI). Gayle graduated from the River Bible Institute in Tampa, FL. She has taught there as well. She was the assistant to Pastor Adonica Howard-Browne and currently travels the world as a missionary/evangelist. Gayle is a great administrator, teacher, and preacher.

Not everyone has all of those giftings. She agreed to help me lay out the school catalog, help with the accreditation process, talk to my lawyer, and work with the state of Washington on our legalities. She helped us change our by-laws to incorporate the school. She calculated the credit hours, ordered books, and more. WSI wouldn't have launched if not for her. She helped us physically move

Me with Vince Pito, my associate Pastor.

Me in the Pulpit

from our previous building to the new one. Gayle also helped establish new bank accounts, trained my leadership team, and was invaluable in every way. She taught in the Bible school and preached in the church. If I had my way, she would have stayed with us full-time, but I knew she had her own calling, and I could not hold her back.

We officially started Bible school on August 9, 2017. This involved another huge spiritual and natural battle. The enemy feels he owns the Northwest, which he has done for so long. The New Age movement, witchcraft, liberal politics, education, and more, have gone unchallenged by the church of the Lord Jesus Christ. However, we are commanded to "take the territory." It's time to act like we are the army of the Lord. We must be diligent, submitted to God, and ready for anything, even if it costs us our very lives.

At salvation, we were asked to count the cost and to lay down our lives. It may require that. It may cost our reputation. We may be ridiculed for our faith. It will require commitments involving finances, time, and everything we are. However, we are prepared to stand our ground and take the land for this generation and the ones to come. It's time for the church to stand up and become the church, not the slumbering, patty-caking, protecting-ourselves church. We are to fight the good fight of faith. We are to stand, and having done all to stand, continue to stand (Ephesians 6:13). We must be prepared to go all the way.

I had no idea that the legalities with the state of Washington would become so involved. It was a battle that lasted over a year. We needed the help of our

What a moment when we gave Mary this van, for her & her children; she is a single mom.

Ev. Tim Hall & I filming in my studio.

lawyer, the advice of the Transworld Accreditation Committee, Dr. Steve Anderson, and especially the favor of God.

We applied to opt out of the Washington Educational Council system for religious reasons. It was quite a process. We met with the council in Olympia, answered questions, and submitted extensive documents to the state, our by-laws and other corporate papers, our Florida incorporation documents, and the school catalog, with lists of every subject and the description of those subjects. We were asked to give the length of the classes, how often we would meet, our rules, and more.

Whenever we thought we had given them everything they required, we received letters and emails asking for more or telling us we had to present it differently. We were told we could not advertise that we were a school until they approved it. We started classes the following August as planned but announced them as extensive Bible study classes out of our church. We finally received our approval letter. We had jumped a big hurdle, and everyone rejoiced.

However, we discovered that the letter only meant we were exempt from their credentialing. It did not mean that we could have our own, even though we met every criterion that Transworld Accreditation requires. That was another process; we acquired a library, prepared credit hours, invited teachers, and prepared courses and tests.

Dr. Anderson believed that because I already had a Florida incorporation, we would not have a problem. Florida is a Bible school-friendly, conservative state and still believes that the church, not the government, should decide Christian education. Many people who live in the nineteen states, which are not so friendly to the cause, obtain a Florida office to operate. I already have a Florida incorporation because it was where my base originated. We are allowed to do business in Washington under the Florida incorporation.

Dr. Anderson thought it was the perfect solution, which would be relatively easy for us. However, my first mistake was believing the Devil would allow it to be that easy. My second was in being too open. I opened accounts and filed the name of the school with the government. Then, we advertised, hoping to have students by August. Once the state noticed what we were doing, they quickly stopped everything. They told me that it did not matter to them if I had incorporated in Florida or not. I was doing business in the state of Washington, and our property is in Washington; the students and classes are in Washington, and I would have to comply with Washington laws. There was no debating or discussing this issue, even though others have done it by having an office in another state.

We persevered and finally received another letter from the state that gave us another victory. We were allowed to award our students an associate's degree in Ministry after two years and a bachelor's degree after three years.

Accreditation is only recognized by schools of like curriculum and standards. It's more about having something that says you paid the price for that piece of paper. You put in the time, studied, passed the tests, and know your material, in this case, the Bible.

On the other hand, accreditation or not, it is vitally important to me that people realize that we have a reputable school. I somewhat understand the state's concern about not allowing anyone to call anything a school. I know of people who were never good students, some who cannot even read or spell but have opened Bible schools. They do not understand sound doctrine. They do not even have much education themselves. Yet, they feel they have the right to call whatever it is that they are doing a real school. The potential students, who should do their investigative research before choosing a Bible school, are deceived into thinking it is a school like others that they claim to be associated with. It is necessary for there to be some sort of scholastic standard to identify a Bible school that is operating within some form of academic standards. That is why there are Christian accreditation institutions. That is also why I searched to find the best. We did. It is the Transworld Accreditation Association.

I feel the years ticking away. I remember that young girl sitting on Grandpa's knee, saying, "Grandpa, I see myself preaching to all colors of people throughout the world." I have already seen much of that come to pass. Now, I want to train others and pass the revival baton before I leave this earth. I believe the anointing is tangible and transmittable. I see people who taught years ago, running with the same fire, doctrine, and integrity, and still have giving hearts. They are not flaky and can be trusted. I believe many of you reading this book are called to come to a good Bible school. You want to be trained to be a revivalist to reap the harvest of the nations. You will not bend, bow, or compromise. You do not want to end up with religion or flakiness. You are called to be a revivalist!

We were privileged to have some of the most knowledgeable and anointed men and women of the Gospel teaching at Word and Spirit Institute NW. I have already mentioned one of them, Pastor Mark Spitsbergen, of Abiding Place Ministries in San Diego, California. Pastor Mark founded his church over 35 years ago. He is also a traveling minister, taking the Gospel to many unreached people groups in predominantly Muslim and Hindu nations. He is a scientist with degrees from many colleges, including St. Andrews of Scotland. He raises Wagyu beef and registered painted horses. He is skilled at aquaponics and growing thousands of acres of crops from test tubes. He has a ranch in southern Oregon where he brings in indigenous pastors and teaches them how to grow crops and raise cattle to feed their people. His degrees give him open doors in many nations where others could never get a foot in the door. He tells the country leaders that he will help them feed their people but asks in exchange for the ability to have crusades for their "throw-away people" (the orphans and the widows), which they grant him. He is raising an underground army from that. God has given him unusual methods to reach the lost.

Dr. Mark is a Hebrew and Greek scholar who wrote *The Sequential Events in the Life of Jesus Christ (A Chronological Description of the Four Gospels)*. He is also a man who moves mightily in the gifts of the Holy Spirit and knows how to flow with the Holy Spirit. There is nothing dry or religious about him. He is a true revivalist in our time. WSI was blessed that he took time out of his busy schedule to teach one class each quarter for all three years.

Dr. Stuart Graham was another excellent teacher in our school. He comes from Pastor Mark's church, Abiding Place, located in San Diego, California. Dr. Graham is a pediatrician and a very busy man. Yet, he, too, takes time from his busy schedule to teach one course each quarter. He is a history buff and a Bible scholar.

We have been blessed to have other pastors and evangelists give of their time and giftings. They all have different areas of expertise. We had missionaries take time off their itineraries to teach missions for us. We even had an extremely gifted administrator who administrated at Dr. Rodney Howard-Browne's church for many years and traveled to the nations teach our administration class. Others teach soul-winning because their churches are excellent at engaging people to win the lost. They have multitudes of outreaches.

The highlight of pastoring was being honored to have my pastor, Pastor Rodney Howard-Browne, and his team do a one-night city tour in our church in Elma. While teaching at his Fall Minister's Conference in October 2017, during my preaching, he announced that the Lord told him to go to several cities to stir the people to a Great Awakening. He said that my church would be the first. I was beyond ecstatic. We had about two weeks to prepare, with a small staff and congregation, but everything was wonderful. In spite of a storm that knocked out the electricity, and my husband scrambled to get generators going, we had a full crowd, with some in the overflow room. We put about 300 people in that auditorium and saw many mobilized for the harvest. I taught about stewardship to receive Pastor Rodney's offering. I was also moved to pay for his team's hotel bill. He and I argued about it, but it was the only time I won an argument with him. What an honor to host the man whose ministry changed my life. People came from all over Washington, and the region will never be the same.

An overflow crowd even with a big storm.

RESURRECTED

I had the privilege of receiving an offering for RMI & introducing my pastor.

Pastor Rodney in my office with my husband & I—a dream come true.

A group of revivalists: L-R Pastor Lew Wootan, Pastor Sam Dalin, Pastor Rodney Howard-Browne, myself and my husband, Kyle Brady, Pastors Hannah & Jason Gillick.

We graduated our first three-year charter class in May 2020. They received bachelor's degrees in ministry. One entire family graduated together, three generations of Clevengers.

Me giving the key-note address at our graduation.

Our Charter 3rd Year Graduates

Allyn and Tamron Clevenger, along with Allyn's mother, Marianna, and their son and daughter-in-law, Stephen and Michaela, were led to pastor in Olympia (Washington State's capital). It seemed good to us and the Holy Ghost.

We merged my church with this one in 2021. It is only about 35 miles from where mine was located. We had the grand opening of the church in October of 2021. I will continue to oversee the work for as long as they want me to. They are doing an excellent job of pastoring and have a great vision. I was led to sell my church building in Elma and use much of the proceeds for the new work in Olympia. It is important to take ground, and it is time to move to a larger population where we can reap a much larger harvest. We moved Word and Spirit Institute there as well. Other graduates are getting ready to launch other works. I am so proud of them and will continue to tell each of them to "go farther than I have gone, preach better, run faster, and continue to populate Heaven and plunder hell."

The Clevenger family went through Bible school together & are now pastoring. This is the first Sunday in their new church building.

TWENTY

TAKING A STAND IN WASHINGTON

I am quite sure that most people are aware that my pastor, Dr. Rodney Howard-Browne, was arrested on March 30, 2020, on bogus charges of unlawful assembly and violating quarantine orders during a public health emergency. He was arrested by Sheriff Chad Chronister, who caved under political pressure. Thank God that Florida's Governor Ron DeSantis overturned Pastor Rodney's arrest, and all charges were eventually dropped. The church was deemed an essential service because of the brave stand that Pastor Rodney took.

Pastor Rodney was arrested because he stood up for the Word of God, His Church, and the Constitution of the United States. He paid the price for all of us. He and his wife, Adonica, are originally from South Africa. To become United States citizens, they both had to read the Constitution of the United States and promise to support and defend the Constitution and laws of the United States against all enemies, foreign and domestic. He is more of a patriot than most naturally born citizens.

I, too, was presented with the choice of obeying my government or God. Washington State has a democratic-driven, socialistic, liberal government. The directives are more stringent than those of Florida. Pastor Rodney advised me and many others not to go to jail just because he did. He told us to be careful and that he was trying to pay the price for all of us. I sought the Lord. I had a lot at stake. I had fought this liberal government for a long time to be allowed to have a Bible school finally. I could lose both the church and the Bible school permanently. Also, I did not want to put my congregation in jeopardy. It is one thing to make decisions that affect me; it is another if it affects people I love and for whom I am somewhat responsible. Far more pressing, though, was my responsibility to my husband. Bob's health was challenged at that moment. He was considerably older than me. If I went to jail, who would take care of him?

I continued having church. I received telephone calls from the chief of police and the city attorney. They explained that I would be fined and possibly arrested if we continued. Then, just a week or so later, my secretary called and said we had a note taped to the church door. It was April 2, 2020. The humor of this story is that April 2nd is my birthday. I told my secretary, "I doubt this is a birthday card. I think you better take it down and read it to me." Sure enough, it was a cease and desist order to not have another service

Things were now getting serious. I sought the Lord again. I needed to make sure that I was hearing God, that my motives were pure, and that I was not trying to play the hero. As soon as I began to pray, I heard this on the inside. It is a verse of Scripture found in Hebrews 10:25, *"Not forsaking the assembling of ourselves together, as the manner of some is; but exhorting one another: and so much the more, as ye see the day approaching."* It was followed by this statement in my spirit, 'You can't ever do wrong by doing what is right. It is just that simple.' It was settled in my heart that day. I must obey God's word, not man's directives. Acts 5:29 says, *"We ought to obey God rather than men."*

Those directives are also contrary to the founding principles of the country. I continued to have church. Furthermore, we were very vocal about it. I did Facebook Live several times a week and was bold in my statements about why every church needed to remain open. The police station was located only one block from our church and could watch everything we were doing. We saw patrol cars regularly circling our building. We continued to have Bible school four nights a week, as well as Sunday morning and evening services. One morning, someone saw a photographer in the church's front yard, taking pictures and filming. A couple of our men ran outside, but the photographer ran off.

Eventually, King 5 News out of Seattle, Washington, called and wanted to interview us on why we were continuing to do church. We were advised about the pros and cons of doing an interview. We eventually decided to do it, but the governor had a press conference the day it was scheduled and the reporter canceled. I decided that was God.

We eventually were told that several disgruntled Christians (and I use the word loosely) and jealous pastors were among many who turned us into the city and asked the city to close us down. The mayor later told me that he didn't want to but received so many complaints that they forced his hand. Interestingly, it was jealous preachers who stood on a platform on national television to denounce Pastor Rodney on the day he was arrested. The Bible talks about that. Matthew 24:10 says, *"And then shall many be offended, and shall betray one another, and shall hate one another."*

After his arrest, mug shot, and death threats against him, his family, and his congregation, Pastor Rodney decided to begin something called "The Stand" in Tampa, Florida. He is doing The Stand not only for the church in America but for those all over the world who do not have a constitution to stand on. The first day of The Stand was May 31, 2020. He has been holding meetings nightly for over two years now. He televises them around the world. He built a state-of-the-art pavilion on the grounds of his church. The River at Tampa Bay (as his church is called) has also started growing food to feed hungry people. It is called "The Eden Project." God warned him that a food shortage was coming. Those who are sensitive to the Holy Spirit are always a step ahead of the enemy. I am so thankful for my pastors. They have forewarned us about everything that is taking place at this hour. Thank God for a true prophet in the land.

Pastor Rodney has been standing for our liberties since he arrived as a missionary to America. He has written wonderful books, such as *The Killing of Uncle Sam, The Killing of The Planet, Socialism Under a Microscope,* and *The Phantom Virus.* These books were written to warn us of a one-world agenda threatening to take away our liberties, including freedom of religion. I suggest that you read Pastor Rodney's Stand Manifesto on revival.com.

The first week of The Stand, I knew it was important for me to fly from Washington State to participate. I was privileged to be asked to preach there one evening.

I distinctly heard the still, small voice of the Holy Spirit asking me to return to Washington State and do the same thing. I began to make plans immediately. I knew that the Lord was directing me to do it up big, so to speak. He is a big God, and if you are going to make a stand, people must hear about it and know that we are serious. I knew we needed to have renowned worship leaders and speakers who would attract a crowd yet speak forth as the oracles of God. We must have the power of the Holy Spirit demonstrated. I was taking a stand for the Lord Jesus Christ, His Word, His Church, the Constitution and flag of The United States of America, our freedom, and the right to worship our God.

When I began this endeavor, we had a little over $700 in the ministry

What a privilege to preach to thousands of people and many more thousands around the world.

account. I have operated in faith with everything God has asked me to do. Once again, I would be stepping out on the water with nothing below me but His Word. You never do big things in God by waiting for them to fall on you like ripe cherries off a tree. We have been given the promised land, but we still have to take it. Matthew 11:12 says, *"And from the days of John the Baptist until now the kingdom of heaven suffereth violence, and the violent take it by force."*

I invited some of the best worship teams. We secured Eddie James to come and lead worship, as well as Joe and Becky Cruise. I invited 14 other speakers: Evangelist Frank Shelton, constitutional lawyer Kris-Anne Hall and her husband, J. C. Hall, Pastors Todd and Katie Holmes, Pastor Jason Gillick, Pastor Lew Wootan, Pastor Mirek Hufton, Pastor Greg Locke, Pastor Ken Peters, Pastor Allyn Clevenger, Pastor Mark Spitsbergen, myself, and the Republican gubernatorial candidate, Lauren Culp.

The Congregation at The Stand

As I met with my team members, I was told we needed a field, advertisement, a flat-bottom truck, platforms, port-a-potties, chairs, lights, computers, and sound systems.

We needed to bring the internet to the field. We would have to purchase televisions, screens, generators, microphones, security, and campers for helpers to stay. We needed to take care of our speakers and singers with hotels and plane tickets. I also fed our guests most of those days. We didn't have the finances, so I put it all on ministry credit cards. I finally dared to ask what our balance was and discovered it was a staggering amount of just over $72,000. Guess how much came in to pay for the event? My God miraculously provided over $96,000. I can only say one thing once again, big God!

We had two services a day; the crowds numbered about 350 to 400 some nights. There was one night that we may have had 600. Many received Christ as their personal Savior and were born again. Many were baptized in the Holy Spirit, healed in their bodies, and delivered from bondage and addictions. We had witches and warlocks come to disrupt and stop what God was doing, but they could not.

It was a time when the body of Christ came together to say, enough is enough. We are the blood-bought church of the Lord Jesus and a force to be reckoned with. We worshipped, sang, shouted, danced, prayed, preached, cast out devils, laid hands on the sick, and made a big stand in Washington State. Months later, a politician called our house soliciting our vote. In the course of the conversation, she found out who I was and said, "Oh, you're the woman who put on that Stand thing in Tumwater (a suburb of Olympia), aren't you? All of the politicians are talking about it. You were brave and made quite a splash."

I had no idea that the event made that big of a mark in our state. I am so thankful once again for a pastor who stood up and showed us the way. Romans 1:16 says, *"For I am not ashamed of the gospel of Christ: for it is the power of God unto salvation to every one that believeth; to the Jew first, and also to the Greek."*

It was from The Stand that the new church in Olympia was launched. Some of the people who attended The Stand in Washington needed a good, noncompromising church to attend. They are now a part of Faithlife Olympia (FLO). I like that acronym. God is not finished with Washington State or the Northwest in general.

We have to remember that this war is not over yet. Our government is trying to see how much they can get us to comply with small, ridiculous things. Unfortunately, they saw that it doesn't take much for most churches to comply with ungodly directives. I feel this is just the beginning of the many types of stands we will be asked to host and support.

We know of two other churches in the Northwest that I call sister churches. One is in Bremerton, Washington, pastored by Jason and Hannah Gillick. It is called The River Northwest. They also had a Stand, and I was one of the guest speakers. They are doing an awesome job of taking territory.

Another sister church is located in Salem, Oregon, called The River Salem. It is pastored by Lew and Lorri Wootan and is growing rapidly.

They, too, have taken a strong stand against governmental tyranny. Antifa tried to break up their meetings, witches cursed them, and the government threatened them. However, we won't bend, bow, or compromise. God has put Holy Ghost backbones in His people this hour. We are alive for the most exciting hour of the Church of the Lord Jesus yet. You and I were born into the kingdom for such a time as this.

TWENTY-ONE

THE HOMEWARD STRETCH

Something significant and life-changing occurred while I was in the middle of writing this book. My knight-in-shining-armor graduated to Heaven. He breathed his last breath on November 3, 2020. That just happened to be the election day. I think he wanted to check out on that day.

He is with his beloved Savior, at last, worshipping and singing with a full voice again. He has reunited with Mary, his first wife, and his baby daughter, Kathy. I am so happy for him, but I must admit I am selfishly sorry for myself. He said to me when he proposed, "I am considerably older than you. I hope to have at least five years with you (We had twelve and a half). But you will know, Debbie, for the first time in your life what it means to be loved as Christ loves the church. Then when I am gone someday, you will have your life back as it is, right now." The first part of that happened. I know what it's like to be loved as Christ loves the Church; it is so wonderful and indescribable. I want every woman to know what I have been privileged to know. However, as much as Bob meant well, he was wrong about the last part. I can never have my life back as I knew before that wonderful man of God showed me what a husband's love can and should be. A big part of my life is now missing. I was so loved and adored, and he always put me first. I was just plain spoiled. There is not a moment of any day that goes by that I do not miss him. Thank God for the comfort of the Holy Ghost! Because of my relationship with Christ, I do not mourn as those who do not know Him. I still have a river that comes from the throne room of Heaven bubbling up on the inside of me.

I can almost hear Bob's voice in that great cloud of witnesses overlooking the banister of Heaven. "Don't you lay down now, girl. God has brought you too far, rescued you too many times, and resurrected your life and ministry countless times. You have a job to do. I didn't marry you to have you quit because you miss me and are feeling sorry for yourself. Get up and get going. There is a high call on your life, and you are anointed and appointed for such a time." He's right; I am going to do just that. These latter years shall be more fulfilling and fruitful than the former. The Lord saves the best wine for last.

I thought the house that Bob had brought me to would be my last home. It brought a certain degree of security with it. I wanted to grow old with him and planned never to move again. After Bob went to Heaven, I sold our home, moved in with my secretary and her husband, and they sold their home. The three of us moved to Olympia, where the new church was launched. I thought that the Elma church building would be my last ministry building. After selling it, the Lord used me to finance the refurbishing of the Olympia building.

My plans have taken a new turn. After talking with Pastors Rodney and Adonica Howard-Browne, we agreed that it was time for me to base out of Tampa, Florida, and the River Church again. It has been thirteen years since I left, and deep down, I knew I would return someday. I have come full circle.

The Howard-Browne's ministry changed my life forever. I was torn because I have come to love people in the Northwest so very much. However, Pastors Allyn and Tamron Clevenger and others are continuing to carry out my vision in the state of Washington. I have fought hard to establish a work and want to see it continue and thrive. I believe God will make sure it does. He wants to work there more than I do.

I am learning not to hold onto anything too tightly. There is a truth that my pastor says often. "He will get it to you if He can get it through you."

I am always up for a new adventure. I can't wait to see what the Lord will have me do next. Will it include building churches, Bible schools, hosting more "Stands," traveling the globe and holding crusades? Since moving back to Tampa, I have taught at River University and have sown seeds into thousands of lives that will impact this world for Christ. My God always takes us from faith to faith and glory to glory. The question is, "Will we cooperate with His plan or be afraid to walk on the water?"

I don't want to trade this Holy Ghost adventure for an average life of someone who will never know what God wanted to do through them because of fear. Every time I moved, I was sad to let go of all the wonderful memories, dreams, and people associated with that location. I am a sentimental person by nature, but I have trained myself not to dwell in the past. Instead, I must look to the next Holy Ghost adventure with great anticipation. God has met me there every time. He turned my mourning into joy. Holy Ghost people must be adaptable. We are people who flow with the plan and purpose of God. We cannot allow ourselves to get rigid and stubborn. We cannot be dependent upon things or people. We must stay completely dependent on our Lord and fulfill our heavenly assignment.

In just over one year that I have been in Florida, God has given me huge financial miracles to finish the restoration of anything the Devil tried to steal from me.

Pastor Rodney Howard-Browne did a series on New Year's weekend, 2022. He declared 2023 to be the year of El-Shaddai, the God of More than Enough, The All-Sufficient One. He talked about making vows of consecration.

It was the most powerful preaching that I have ever heard. I was more affected than at any other time in my life. I prayed prayers of consecration many times in my life, but never with the brokenness and consecration that came from my heart that weekend. I realized, as never before, that everything that I have or ever will have, is by God's grace and power. I also saw how big our God is and how much He wants to bless me. He wants to know that He can trust me. A gift of faith fell on me. I felt that I could believe God for anything. I knew this would be a year of great increase for the ministry as well as for me personally. My dreams would become reality.

The only part of the restoration that had not come back was the Corvette that you read about earlier. After Pastor Rodney sent it home with me, I made a terrible decision that cost me greatly, including financially. I sold my dream car to pay off Dennis' debt in 2006. I learned many lessons. I have received God's grace and restoration. However, for some time, I wrestled with guilt and condemnation for making such a stupid decision. Because of that, I felt that I could never have a car like that again. Also, I was older now and felt that I would look ridiculous with a sports car. Also, I knew that I didn't want a car to detour my giving.

After I sold my home in Washington state, following the death of my husband in 2020, I could have paid cash for three corvettes. Instead, I gave over half of the money. I moved from Washington State to the Tampa area to be a part of the River at Tampa Bay Church with Pastors Rodney and Adonica Howard-Browne. I put a down payment on my home in Riverview (a suburb of Tampa, FL) and bought furniture for the home. That took care of almost all of the rest of the money. If I bought a new car, I could no longer pay cash for it.

However, after the New Year's messages, I knew that it was time to expect God to bless me with a vehicle like the one I gave to Pastor Rodney years before. The condemnation was gone, and I knew that God wanted to bless me.

At first, I wanted to believe that some wealthy person would buy one for me. These are the kinds of testimonies we hear every week at The River at Tampa Bay. People are often given cars. Because I have sown five vehicles to others, I felt that it was time for me to be given one, or at least the down payment for one. We seem to think that when God moves, He will do it the same way every time. However, He doesn't want us to get too comfortable. He wants us to stay dependent upon Him. He has many ways that He can give us a miracle.

Sometime in February, I heard Pastor Rodney say, "Some of you just need to go out and buy your car." That hit me like a sledgehammer. I knew that word was for me. I told my assistant, "I'm going to buy a Corvette today." She was shocked. She never even heard me mention that I desired one.

When I arrived at the dealership, a salesman told me that a man just brought back a 2022 Z51, performance package Corvette convertible. It only had 350 miles on it. The outside was red with a black racing stripe. It was a beautiful car that surpassed what I was looking for. I knew that it was the one God was directing me to.

I had just enough money from the sale of my Washington home to put a twenty-thousand-dollar down payment on it. I financed the rest with a seven-year loan. The payments were higher than any I ever made in my life. However, I knew that God would enable me to make those payments. This was Feb. 22, 2023. I did not realize the date until the next day. Just one year earlier, Feb. 22, 2022, I closed on my new home. Now, one year later, God enabled me to purchase my dream car. I felt that The Lord was showing me that in one year, He replaced everything that the enemy ever stole from me. What a gracious and big God! My pastor told me that he believed that I would pay it off within the year. I told him that I would agree with him in faith for that miracle.

A series of financial miracles took place over the next four months. Many times, when I have taught on the subject of stewardship, congregations gave to individuals spontaneously. However, it had never happened to me until July of 2023. My church, The River at Tampa Bay, and my pastors, Rodney and Adonica Howard-Browne, host two campmeetings and two minister's conferences a year. July is the summer "Fire Conference." I had the privilege of teaching in several of the services. In one of the evening services, Pastor Rodney spoke my name and prophesied to me about going to Alaska again for ministry. He said that God was going to honor all of my years of pioneering in that cold state, and the ministry would be blessed, and planes would be given. I fell out under the power of God, and people immediately and spontaneously gave an offering to me. Several thousand dollars were given to me personally.

Me being blessed at the Fire Conference.

The next day, I received a notice from my bank that several thousand dollars had been deposited into my account from the government. I had no idea why and knew that I better check it out. It turned out to be something related to my late husband, a retired war veteran. I never opened his veteran's case or even inquired about it. Yet, God prompted the U.S. government to remember me.

I knew that God was supernaturally bringing funds in. Every time that I saved extra money or was blessed with a gift, I applied it to the loan. The seven-year loan was supernaturally paid off in seven months.

The Corvette has been a soul-winning tool. Everywhere I go, someone asks about the car and many want to take a picture standing beside it. I tell them my testimony of being a single mother, living with other people, driving a totaled car in Alaska, and how God has blessed me. I have found that no one but religious people have a problem with God's blessing. A homeless man walked up to me, congratulated me on the car, and mentioned that he could see how God had blessed me. However, it should surprise no one that a religious woman posted a picture and price tag on Facebook of a similar Corvette. She had plenty to say about how shameful it was for me to buy such a car. It was humorous that my car is nicer, and yet, I paid less for it. I told her that she verified that I got a very good deal on the car. I also told her that I did not use offerings or ministry funds to pay for it. (Not that it is anyone's business.) No one has a problem with anyone from any other profession buying a nice car. Yet, religious people seem to think that Christians, especially ministers, should live in poverty and drive junk cars.

My new 2022 Z51 Corvette Convertible.

I flew to Alaska earlier in July to visit family. While there, I had the opportunity to minister in two churches. I discovered that a pastor friend, previously from Barrow, Alaska, had moved to the same area where my sons live. He attended the meetings and asked to take me to dinner with him and his wife. During the dinner conversation, Pastor McKenzie mentioned that he had recently been given an Alaskan bush plane. He is getting older and wants to make sure that when he goes to Heaven, the plane will be used for revival purposes. I told him that God spoke to me about ministering in Alaska again. He and Pastor Rodney agreed that the plane should come to me. It is a Cessna 1970, single-engine plane that seats six people. This is the first plane that has been given to me. I have flown in many two-seater planes through snowstorms and heavy turbulence. I felt like this was God rewarding me. Pastor Rodney prophesied a few weeks later that this would be the first of many planes and that hangars and pilots would be coming with them. I believe it.

The bush plane that was given to me.

I am willing to preach to thirty as I would to thirty thousand. I go to churches of many sizes in many different locations. It is always a step of faith to go to a small church when you have employees and commitments all over the world. However, God has always been faithful, and many of our largest offerings have come from the smallest of churches. It amazes me. It has been that way from the beginning. Some think that I can no longer afford to go to the smaller churches because the budget has increased. I am so thankful that we still can. Many of those churches are churches that feel that they do not dare invite proven ministers who carry the anointing of The Holy Spirit. I thank God that I am able to go to those churches and make a difference in people's lives.

I am in the middle of two large transactions that are taking place as a result of ministry growth. I hired an assistant this year, as well as a media person. I already have a secretary in Washington State.

I gave my assistant, Heather Mosely, one of my vehicles. It is a Chevrolet Impala with low mileage. I love that car. It was the last thing my husband purchased for me when he saw how much I liked it. So, it also has sentimental value. However, even sentiment must bow to God's voice, when He speaks.

A week before Heather started to work for me, she was hit by a driver who had no insurance. Her van was totaled. She came to me with no vehicle and I let her use my car. The Lord spoke to my heart a few weeks ago to give her the impala, even though I knew that I was about to purchase a vehicle for the ministry. The Impala would have made a nice trade-in, but I wanted to bless her. God still allowed me to purchase a new mini-van that would hold our luggage and drive us to nearby states. This will be so much better than dealing with TSA. It is a beautiful vehicle and God has blessed us again.

The Ministry Van

I invited Heather and Emma (the media person) to live in my home. However, recently, I realized that we all need more space. I probably should have bought a larger home when I moved back to the Tampa area. At the time, I felt that it was more than adequate for a lady who is living alone. However, I host many guests for campmeetings and minister's conferences. I need a filming studio, a workout room, and space for my children when they visit.

So, I leased another home in my neighborhood for my studio and for my employees to live in. I signed on both the vehicle and the home just weeks before Christmas.

My ministry team of Emma, myself and Heather.

It is time to go to another level again. That always involves expense. It would be easier at my age to begin to coast through life, but I continue to push myself. It is not time to retire. It is time to refire. These shall be the best days of Debbie Rich Ministries. I will continue to plunder hell and populate Heaven. I will continue to shake nations. I want to encourage you to do the same. The body of Christ cannot afford to pull back now. We are the restraining force against the spirit of antichrist in the world today. It is time to take territory. To do so, we must continue to exercise our faith.

Pictures of God's Great Restoration

Me before the River Car Show with my new Corvette.

I have had the privilege of taking entire weeks of The Stand being aired around the world every night.

Many times through the years, I found my physical life, the life of the ministry, and the call of God looking dead. It also appeared that way to the family of the dead young lady in the Bible. Matthew 9:23-26 tells us, *"And when Jesus came into the ruler's house and saw the minstrels and the people making a noise, He said unto them, Give place: for the maid is not dead, but sleepeth. And they laughed him to scorn. But when the people were put forth, he went in, and took her by the hand, and the maid arose. And the fame hereof went abroad into all that land."* Jesus told her family that she was not dead, but sleeping. Then He took her by the hand and raised her up. He has done that for me. I am sure many bystanders thought it was all over for me more than once. Some were already mourning. But Jesus took me by the hand and raised me to show forth His great grace and glory. I am living to hear only one sentence, "Well done thou good and faithful servant. Enter into the joy of the Lord." I want to finish my race strong.

Thank God for the total mercy, forgiveness, restoration, healing, and resurrection that has come to my life and ministry. My God has been so big, no matter how gullible, ignorant, and undiscerning I have been. All I had to do was say, "Help, Lord," and He was right there. Only a big and merciful God could come upon the scene and, with one blow of His nostrils, move Heaven and earth to rescue me. He does not love me more than He does you or anyone else. That is who He is; the Great Restorer, the Lover of my Soul, and my Mighty Deliverer. How can I say thank You? One way is to write this book and give thanksgiving and glory to my Redeemer.

I have great expectations for the years to come. I believe they will be my best years. I believe He will satisfy me with long life, as His Word says. I believe He quickens this body, and I will be able to continue to run with holy fire into my eighties if Jesus tarries His coming. I am alive to bless others in the greatest hour the Church has ever known. I was born into the kingdom for such a time as this. I have set my face like flint to finish this race and to do His perfect will. I have learned some hard lessons by His grace and keeping power, and I am determined to have no more detours. I will not continue to beat myself up for those. Let people say what they will and judge things they know nothing about. They weren't there the night my Lord touched me, and they certainly don't know the cost of the oil in my alabaster box.

I have one purpose in writing this book. I don't care if you remember my name. However, I want you to read this and see Jesus on every page. He is the one who has forgiven, restored, and even promoted and favored me. You must know that He longs to do the same thing for you. On every page is this central message: If He has done this for me, what can He do for you? Get hungry, thirsty, and desperate for Him. Ask Him to forgive you for any place and time you have missed His perfect will for your life. Call upon Him, and He will rescue you. Then, turn around, and surrender your entire life to Him. He will use you to help set others free.

I hope you can glean from my victories and mistakes so that you will not repeat the latter. Don't get so lonesome, tired, or vulnerable that you somehow miss the obvious. What is the obvious? The Devil is trying to take you out, no matter who you are. He is especially after those set apart for God's divine purpose. If you have made some of those same mistakes, learn from them. Get everything under the blood of Jesus Christ. Run to God, not away from Him. Truly repent with sorrow. Quit feeling sorry for yourself, and get up and run with holy fire. Give up your spiritual hospital bed for someone else. Quit being a victim and live victoriously. His blood is more than enough for that.

We started this book by asking the question, why do bad things happen to good people? Let's look at the Word of God. The Bible tells us in Genesis that man sold out to Satan, the enemy of our souls. Man committed high treason. Mankind was supposed to reign and rule on earth, free from sin and its results. We were supposed to enjoy all the blessings of God without any curses. The problem occurred when the Devil (another name for Lucifer, or Satan) declared war on God in Heaven. Lucifer was thrown out of Heaven to the earth and became the god of this world and its systems. He is out for revenge and looking for a way to upset God's plans. He still actually believes that he can defeat God.

After God made the heavens and earth, the seas, sun, moon, stars, galaxies, plants, and animals, He looked and saw what He had made and declared, *"It was good."* However, He could not find anything or anyone with whom He could have a relationship. He so wanted to commune with someone like Himself that He decided to make man in His very own likeness and image. He wanted a family, someone to love, and someone to love Him. After creating Adam and Eve, He was so very pleased with His creation that He threw a big coronation ceremony. The angels were watching, along with the Devil and the fallen angels that had rebelled with Lucifer. God wanted to crown his man with something very significant and precious. He looked through Heaven and realized that even the gold streets of Heaven were not worthy of being used for this purpose. The giant gates of pearls, sapphires, and diamonds would not be enough to decorate God's creation, called man. What could He crown His most prized possession with? He realized that it could be nothing less than one precious substance, His very own glory.

God's glory involves so much that this subject should be explored at another time, in another book. For now, suffice it to say that His glory radiates from Him and is the substance, weight, light, power, and integrity of all He is. God decided that nothing less would do for man's crown.

Let's watch as this story unfolds. It is time for the coronation, and God looks lovingly at His creation. He smiles with the love, concern, and pride of a father looking at His newborn child for the first time. He then moves His mighty hand to place His very own nature and power upon His creation. The angels are awestruck and stop their singing. The Devil and his demons are confused. The Bible says that one of the angels asked a question. *"What is this man, that you are mindful of him and that you would crown him with your very own glory, give him such authority and place him only under God?"* (Psalm 8:3-8). They realize this man is very important to God. The Devil began to plot. He decided if he could cause a man to sin, God's whole plan and purpose would be thwarted throughout eternity. He began to laugh with evil glee. He has nothing but contempt for the Living God. The diabolical plan was hatched.

Many of you know the rest of the story. The Devil came to Eve, as he has done to the rest of mankind ever since. He appealed to her senses. He came through the pride of life. She saw that the fruit was pleasant to her eyes and would be good for eating. The Devil questioned God's Word, as he still does today. "Did God mean what He said? God doesn't want you to be like Him. He knows that if you eat this, you will become like God." That's the same issue of pride that caused Satan to rebel in the first place. He wanted to be like God. Man still wants to be his own god and desires to rule his life the way he chooses. Like Satan, he always messes it up and then blames God for the results. Satan still comes to question God and accuse Him of not being for us and not having our best interests in mind. He causes us to believe that God has short-changed us in this life and wants to punish or tease us.

The moment Adam and Eve sinned, they knew they were naked. Why is that? They had always been without clothes. They had walked and talked with God in that beautiful paradise every day. The Bible tells us that God came down in the cool of the day and fellowshipped with them. What a life! They talked to Him face to face and enjoyed complete ecstasy in the garden. They never had a problem being without clothes before. The moment they gave into temptation and sinned, the glory departed. Sin and glory cannot cohabitate. One excludes the other. God is holy and righteous; if He hugged Adam and Eve in their sinful state, they would have died.

One of the definitions of glory is the heavy weight of Almighty God. How heavy is He? I'm not sure, but I know we don't have a scale that can measure Him. The Bible tells us He is infinite, from everlasting to everlasting. He is omniscient (all-knowing). He is omnipresent, meaning He is everywhere at one time, and He is omnipotent (all-powerful). The Bible tells us that if you climb the highest mountain or descend to the lowest hell, He is there. This is the weight that they were clothed with. The moment it was lifted, they knew something was very different immediately. "Where is the weight? Where is our crown? Where is God's presence?" Everything changed.

The Devil began to celebrate. He thought he confounded God and ruined His plan, at last. He knew that man could never live with God throughout eternity now. There would be no hope. The Devil brought the man down to his eternal damnation. He thought he crucified the Lord of glory, and God's plan to save and rescue man was demolished once and for all. However, God was not about to be out-smarted and already had a plan.

No matter how much it looks like the Devil has ruined your life, remember that it is not over, and God still has a restoration plan for your life. Once again, we must look to the Word of God, the final authority of truth for all ages. It tells us that even before the foundation of the earth, God had a plan. In His great foreknowledge, He knew that man would sin, and He (God) would redeem fallen man. The Bible says, *"all have sinned and fallen short of the glory of God"* (Romans 3:23). It tells us, *"the wages of sin is death, but the gift of God is eternal life through Jesus Christ, God's Son"* (Romans 6:23). We also read, *"God so loved the world that He gave us His only Son, Jesus Christ, that whosoever believes on Him, shall not die, but have eternal life"* (John 3:16).

The eternal Trinity—Father, Son, and Holy Spirit—met in Heaven at some point. The Father God asked the Son if He would be willing to be the supreme sacrifice for man, for *"without blood, there could be no remission for sin."* (Hebrews 9:22). The Bible tells us, *"The life is in the blood"* (Leviticus 17:11). Spiritually, the blood of Jesus Christ gives us life. The only thing that will cure sin is blood. However, not just any blood would work. It had to be sinless, spotless, pure blood. That posed a problem; no human or animal has pure blood. It would take the sacrifice of none other than the spotless Lamb of God, Jesus Christ, and the Messiah.

So, before Adam and Eve ever sinned, God had a wonderful backup plan in operation. Nothing takes Him by surprise. He knows the end from the beginning. He is Alpha and Omega, the Beginning and the End. The blood of His very own precious Son would be the answer. The Devil couldn't begin to understand it then and still doesn't understand it to this day. The blood of Jesus Christ is a complete mystery to him. The Bible tells us that if he had understood this, he would never have crucified the Lord of glory (1 Cor. 2:8). Satan thought he was doing away with his problem when he saw Jesus hanging on the cross of Calvary, but instead, his real problems were just beginning.

So, as Adam and Eve sinned, lost their crown of glory, and realized they were naked, guilt and fear set in. They found themselves dreading what they used to love. They didn't want God to find them. Consequently, they hid. Many today still hide from God in a cave of alcohol, drugs, illicit relationships, work, career, parties, and many other avenues.

Another thing we see Adam and Eve do is make for themselves clothing of fig leaves. They tried the great cover-up. Man has been good at that ever since. We run, hide, make excuses, and try to cover ourselves with our good works. Those fig leaves could not hide their sin. God came looking for them, even though He already knew where they were and to what state they had fallen. He showed them that their fig leaves were futile and could not cover their sin. Instead, God Himself killed some innocent animals and brought them animal skins still dripping with blood. The blood-soaked skins were to clothe the guilty parties. He began to teach them about the importance of blood in covering sin.

Unfortunately, the blood of animals could never declare Adam and Eve guiltless. The blood of animals did not have the power and ability to do so. Their blood could only temporarily cover the sin and point symbolically to the Son of God, who would come and do more than cover the sin. His blood would wipe out the sin and abolish it as though it never happened. God would buy man back, literally, from the Devil who legally owned us. God would become our Father twice, by right of creation and because He bought us back. Because of that blood, we could now become born again with the ability to start life over. We must only accept what that blood has done. When we become born again, we receive the blessing of Jesus Christ. He took our curse, and we get His blessing. He took our punishment, and we get His eternal life. He took our sins, and we get His righteousness. He took our depression, and we get His joy. He took our sickness, and we get His healing. No one ever made a better deal. Who wouldn't want to say yes to such a Savior?

After Adam and Eve sinned, it brought a curse upon the whole earth. The Bible tells us that the whole earth groans in travail, waiting for its redemption. Once the curse had come upon the earth, it brought sickness and disease, weeds, mosquitoes, wars and rumors of wars, drought, devastation, and every misery known to mankind. That was never the will of God, but God didn't make robots that were forced to serve Him. He created man with free will because He desires us to love and worship Him from our hearts. Even then, He so loves mankind that He was willing to give us His only begotten Son to pay the supreme sacrifice. Would you give your only child to someone who never loved you first or asked for your help?

In the future, this entire earth will be remade. There will be no more sorrow or crying, no more curse, only blessing. However, that is someday. You and I are living here now. Even those who have accepted Christ as their Savior and are truly born again still live on sin-cursed earth. We are free from the curse personally but live on an earth that is still under the curse. The Devil is still the god of this world's system and lives in this earth's atmosphere. Born-again Christians are not subject to him, but we live on an earth where many other people are subject to him and cause us grief from time to time. There are germs, bacteria, and viruses in the atmosphere. There are sins of greed, lust, temper, and bad attitudes. We encounter some of these attributes and attitudes just because we live here.

Then again, even born-again people make decisions to yield to fleshly impulses instead of living in the Spirit much of the time. When we step out of the will of God, it is costly and allows the hedge of protection to come down. That doesn't mean it was God's will, but He must allow us to make wrong decisions because we are not robots. We are His children.

The Bible tells us that there is some suffering that we can expect if we truly belong to God. The suffering it speaks of is not sickness, disease, or poverty. Jesus bore the stripes in His body for us so that we could have His healing. He became our poverty on the cross so that we could be blessed and have our needs met. Even then, the enemy of our souls will do his best to make us sick and put us into poverty. He will try to convince us that those things are the will of God. We will be challenged in our beliefs and have to stand our ground. There will constantly be a fight to apprehend the promises of God. We must be alert, take up our weapons, crucify the flesh, and not grow weary in well-doing. Every time we endeavor to obey the Spirit of God instead of our flesh, it will mean suffering to the flesh that does not get its way. We must remember that we are crucified with Christ, and no longer live our own lives.

There are many things that we may and probably will suffer. We are told that we will face persecution. We will be misunderstood, falsely accused, and lied about. We will have many occasions to forgive again and again. We may be used and abused. Those who live for Jesus are made conformable to His image by and through our suffering. We are not above our master. If He suffered, why do we think we shall escape? It's part of the growing process. The Bible tells us to rejoice when faced with trials and tribulations, knowing that it produces patience, and patience will produce her perfect work in us. We are to count it all joy when we suffer for His name (James 1:2-4).

To sum it up, we live on an earth that is cursed because of sin. Because of that, stuff happens! Also, we suffer things done by the hands and decisions of others. We also suffer sometimes because of our sins and disobedience. There is a remedy for that one, though, and it is to repent and receive the blessings of God. We suffer because of ignorance and lack of good teaching. We sometimes make wrong decisions that cost us greatly. We do not have to lie down and die or dwell in self-pity and depression. We can live again!

Let's look at the scene in hell as it must have been unfolding. The devils were preparing to celebrate as Jesus Christ was descending into hell. They thought He was dead, but the right arm of God, the Father, raised Him from the dead. He became the firstborn among many brethren. Before He ascended to the right hand of the Father in Heaven, He first descended into hell and demanded the keys of death, hell, and the grave. Can you imagine the shock waves in hell? The demons thought that God and man had been defeated, but instead, they found out that Satan and his demons were the ones who were defeated. The Bible says that God made a show of them openly, triumphing over them in it (Col. 2:15). It tells us that Jesus took His blood into the Holy of Holies of Heaven and poured it on the mercy seat for us. There would be no more need for sacrifice. Jesus was the supreme sacrifice once and for all. He won! The Bible says that He seated us with Him in heavenly places and put the Devil under our feet (Ephesians 2:6). We were brought back into that place of exaltation over the evil one. It is indeed finished for the person who accepts Christ's sacrifice.

Today is the day if you have never received Jesus Christ as your Lord and Savior. That's where it all begins. The Bible says in Romans 10:9-10, *"That if thou shalt confess with thy mouth the Lord Jesus, and shalt believe in thine heart that God hath raised him from the dead, thou shalt be saved. For with the heart man believeth unto righteousness, and with the mouth, confession is made unto salvation."* Also, 1 John 1:9 says, *"If we confess our sins, he is faithful and just to forgive us our sins, and to cleanse us from all unrighteousness."* So, if you believe in your heart that Christ Jesus came in the flesh and was crucified on Calvary's hill for you and that He shed His precious blood for you and was raised from the dead for you, and will confess that with your mouth, you will be saved, or born again.

If you desire eternal life, I ask you to say this prayer with me, "Lord Jesus, I believe You came to this earth and took on a flesh and blood body. You took my sin on the cross and shed Your blood for me. I believe the Father raised You from the dead, where You live forever as King of kings and Lord of lords. I ask You to forgive me of my sins, come into my heart, and give me a brand new life, the God-kind of life. Wash me in Your blood. Fill me with Your precious Holy Spirit. I will live for You all the days of my life as a Christian, which means Christ-like. I turn away from the world and all it offers me to live Your life. I want You to be not only my Savior but the Lord of my life. I surrender all to You. Give me a hunger for Your Word, the Holy Bible, and a hunger for Your presence. Use me to tell others of Your love. Thank You for coming into my heart right now. I pray in Jesus' name, Amen."

If you have already done that, but your heart is pricked as you read this because you have been growing lukewarm or backsliding, He's calling you home. You cannot be lukewarm, or He will spew you out of His mouth. The Bible makes that clear in Revelation 3:15-16, *"I know thy works, that thou art neither cold nor hot: I would thou were cold or hot. So then because thou art lukewarm, and neither cold nor hot, I will spue thee out of my mouth."*

Perhaps because of things that happened, you became bitter or began to think it was too late for you. I assure you that it's not. You only need to ask Him to forgive and restore you. Have you thought that too much has happened? There is never too much happening for His grace to move upon the scene. As I did in the helicopter and at the hospital, "I shall live and not die. I have a big God."

I ask you to pray, "Father God, I come to You in the name of Jesus Christ and ask You to forgive me of my lukewarmness by backsliding, bitterness, and sin. I walked away from You. You never walked away from me. I am coming home like the prodigal son in the Bible. Forgive me for feeling sorry for myself. Forgive me for holding a grudge against others and You, Lord. You are always good. Cleanse me, wash me in your blood, and give me new life. Come and fill me with Your Holy Spirit. Use me. Change me, and grace me to tell others about Your love and that what You have done for me, You will do for them."

Please let us know if you have prayed either of these prayers. We want to be able to keep in touch, help you in your Christian growth, send you some materials, and continue to pray for you. You may go to our web page at debbierichministries.org. You may also email us at office@debbierichministries.org or call us at 360-999-7672. We want to hear what the Lord has done for you. He loves you and has a great plan for your life. As you completely surrender to Him, He will use you greatly.

TWENTY-TWO

LOOKING BACK

While editing this book, I am in Key West, Florida. My son, Joshua, his wife, Stacie, and my three wonderful granddaughters are now living here. This is his current assignment and station in the United States Navy. It is a fitting place to be doing the review of this book. The weather is perfect; the breeze is blowing my hair while I am lying on a hammock with a view of the Caribbean. We just returned from a boat ride where I snorkeled on the largest coral reef ecosystem in the continental United States. My son, whom the Devil tried to kill when he was born, was just promoted to Commander in a ceremony. I was blessed to be here for the ceremony.

Upon reflection of my life, I find it interesting that I have walked on the Arctic Ocean in Point Barrow, Alaska, at the top of the United States, and now I have snorkeled in Key West, Florida, at the bottom of the United States. This trip and editing my book have brought about a deep reflection of my life.

How did I get picked to see so much, visit so many unique places, meet so many people, and impact countless lives? I stayed in a vice-presidential palace and preached at Royal Albert's Hall in London, England, and Madison Square Garden in New York City. I stayed and ate with the Vice President of Burundi, Africa.

I preached with some of the most well-known ministers in the world. I was honored to have lunch with Smith Wigglesworth's granddaughter and her husband, who were missionaries to the Congo for many years.

I flew in countless jets across the oceans and ministered on six continents. I was honored to be on television on many of those continents. I conducted crusades where thousands of people were in attendance, and I have been given standing ovations. I achieved a doctorate in theology. I watched rockets being launched at the Kennedy Space Center and have paraglided over tropical oceans. I witnessed whales breeching in Alaska and South Africa, rode an elephant in Nepal, held a Koala bear in Australia, and caught King Salmon in Alaska. I rode on horseback over mountains and valleys in Colorado and Alaska. I saw the fjords of Norway and rode a camel through the Sahara desert in Egypt. I ran roadblocks in Uganda and was interrogated by the Vietnamese communists. Magazines wrote articles about my ministry in several nations. I toured pyramids in Egypt, castles in Ireland, and several fourteenth-century churches in Europe. I gazed at the picture-perfect blue and white painted houses of Greece against the landscape of the sunset on the Mediterranean Sea.

Josh at his commander ceremony with his family and myself.

I was privileged to walk where the Apostle Paul walked and stood at his judgment seat in Corinth. I observed polar bears, Kodiak brown bears, and powerful grizzlies gorging themselves on Alaskan salmon. I stood and listened to the roar of Niagara Falls. One of my most memorable adventures was to be on a South African safari.

I walked upon ancient footbridges, took steam trains through mountains, stood at the Eiffel Tower in Paris, and rode a boat up the Nile River in Africa.

Even as I write this, I am tempted to ask, who is the person who has done all of this? Was she born with a silver spoon in her mouth? Did she come from an important city or region? Were her parents famous? If not, did all these grand things happen to her because she did everything perfectly and never made mistakes? Did she earn this?

You already know the answers to these questions because you have read the book. Yet it seems impossible that it could be me. My maiden name is Rich, but I have come from many generations of poverty. I grew up in Dakota City, Nebraska, a town with a population of one thousand.

Did I do everything right? Far from it! When I think of my mistakes in marriage, I feel like we must be talking about someone else because it is the one area I never thought I would fail in. Yet, I failed miserably in front of the church and the world.

Bob & I with the Vice-President and his wife in Burundi, Africa.

Did it all look hopeless and impossible to resurrect? Emphatically, yes! Was there shame and embarrassment? Of course! Did people come out of the woodwork to remind me of that? Was I ever tempted to get bitter at people who did me wrong? I don't think I even have to answer that. It is not a sin to be tempted. It is only a sin to give in to temptation.

So, why should I write this book instead of someone more qualified? Why are you not reading from someone who has done it perfectly? The answer is quite simple. My God is the great restorer for those who love Him, will humble themselves, will call upon Him, and hunger for more of Him. He shows up big for the person who knows they are nothing without Him and can do nothing without Him. He loves for our total dependency to be on Him alone. He delights in mercy and grace. He is so good, loving, and trustworthy. He is also no respecter of people. What He has done for one, He will do for another.

However, He is a respecter of principles. You must humble yourself the same way, repent for where you have missed the mark, and have faith that He will come through for you. You must apply yourself to His Word and yield to His presence. You must take responsibility for your actions, decisions, and the seed you have sown over the years. It is so very important to keep your heart pure through it all. It took most of us a while to get into our messes, and it may take a while for God to bring us out. We cannot become impatient. He is a God of miracles but has limited Himself to work with people. Seeds don't grow overnight, and many times, crops that have resulted from our bad decisions cannot be plucked up overnight. Yet, He is faithful to turn the ashes of our lives into something beautiful.

Thirty years ago, in Alaska, the man who would later become my pastor, Dr.

Rodney Howard-Browne, prophesied to me, "You don't have any contacts, reputation, money, or human help to do what God has called you to do. God will raise you up so that people will know that what He has done for you, He will do for others. It will give them hope. He will show Himself big on your behalf. It shall be an international ministry that will astound people." I am quite sure that Dr. Rodney nor I had a clue as to the mistakes I would make in the middle of this. However, the same God who called me, and was using Dr. Rodney to speak through at that moment, is also the same God who knew what was ahead. Yet, He called, sustained, used, forgave, and saw me through it all. He will do the same for you.

I do not want to leave anyone with the impression that we can presume upon God's grace. We must not. I have taken responsibility and have asked God to show me anything that contributed to my lack of discernment. I have continued to seek Him and be quick to repent, grow and change. I am not the same woman who made those mistakes. I pray that some of you reading this will learn from my mistakes and avoid them. I pray that those of you who have made similar mistakes will find forgiveness, hope, and restoration.

Has my God used me because I am somebody? No, I believe He has used me because I am a nobody with a capital N. 1 Corinthians 1:26-29 says, *"For ye see your calling, brethren, how that not many wise men after the flesh, not many mighty, not many noble, are called: But God hath chosen the foolish things of the world to confound the wise, and God hath chosen the weak things of the world to confound the mighty things; And base things of the world, and things which are despised, hath God chosen, yea, and things which are not, to bring to naught things that are: That no flesh should glory in his presence."*

Now you know the secret to my calling. I am a nobody with a big God. He likes to show off His mercy, grace, power, and love through me. I believe God gave me the assignment to write this book to give you hope and inspiration. It is time to surrender your life entirely to God and get on with the plan and purpose of God in your life. For others, it is time to quit feeling sorry for yourself, give up your hospital bed to someone else who needs it, and let God powerfully use you.

This will be the year of double favor, double anointing, and harvest. I have just purchased a home and moved to a suburb of Tampa. I am a part of the greatest church on the face of the earth. After some turns, twists, and detours, God has brought me home, full circle. I am overcome with gratitude. The fact that I am here, in my thirtieth year since first being touched with revival fire through this ministry, demonstrates the faithfulness and mercy of the Lord. It is also the result of the hunger and thirst of a revivalist. There is nothing to go back to. I want no part of the world and certainly no part of religion and tradition. I have always remembered that what it takes to get, it takes to keep. That is the real key to continuing in the fire of God. Once you make that determination, you will be unshakable.

Let's make history in these last of the last days. Let it be said that we never gave up. We are revivalists, fire-starters, water-walkers, and nation-shakers. Will you be the one that we can pass the baton? Are you desperate, hungry, thirsty, and in love with Christ Jesus? Do you have a holy passion and a burning fire that cannot be quenched? Do you long to see hell plundered and Heaven populated?

Will you be willing to be quick to repent and quick to forgive? Will you lay down your life, dreams, and desires for His? Will you study, humble yourself, be diligent, and refuse to give up in the hard places? Will you refuse to take no for an answer and never give in to the enemy? Will you remember that you are bought with the most precious price in the universe, the blood of Jesus Christ, our redeemer?

Many are called, but few are chosen. That means few really will pay the price and choose. Will you be that one? Let God forgive you, heal you, restore you, and use you beyond your wildest imagination. I and many others are waiting to read your book.

Pastor Adonica & me on the Nile in Cairo.

My son, Caleb at the Great Sphinx of Giza.

Myself, LaShawn, & Caleb on camels in the Sahara Desert, against the Great Pyramids of Egypt.

RESURRECTED

Pictures of the Harvest of the Nations

Burundi, Africa Church Revival

Burundi Outdoor Crusade

Medellin, Columbia, South America

Hyderabad, India

Visakhapatnam, India

Me at Visakhapatnam, India

Shillong, India

Ozamiz, Philippines

Preaching in the Philippines

Paris Christian Center—the largest charismatic church in the nation.

The River Church Paris, France

Guyana, South America

RESURRECTED

Royal Albert Hall, London, England

Bergen, Norway

The River Paris, France

Sumy, Ukraine

RECOMMENDED READING

- "The 5 Love Languages" by Gary Chapman
- "Marriage, Divorce and Remarriage" by Kenneth E. Hagin
- "Total Forgiveness" by R.T. Kendall
- "Giving, Your Key to Breakthrough" by Dr. Debbie Rich
- "The Killing of Uncle Sam" by Dr. Rodney Howard-Browne and Paul L. Williams
- "Killing the Planet" by Dr. Rodney Howard-Browne and Paul L. Williams
- "Socialism Under the Microscope" by Dr. Rodney Howard-Browne
- "The Phantom Virus" by Dr. Rodney Howard-Browne and Paul L. Williams
- "How to Increase and Release the Anointing" by Dr. Rodney Howard-Browne

DESPERATE HUNGER GETS GOD'S ATTENTION

If you're holding this book, it means you're ready to begin a journey that will challenge, inspire, and transform your spiritual life. This book will ignite a holy hunger and thirst within you that only God can satisfy.

Matthew 5:6 says, *"Blessed are those who hunger and thirst for righteousness, for they shall be filled."* This powerful promise is the core message of this book. If you're comfortable where you are spiritually, this book isn't for you. But if you're desperate for more of God, if you're willing to cry out and press in until you're overflowing with His presence, then you're in the right place.

I wrote this book because I believe with all my heart that God responds to our desperation. Just as a starving person will do anything to find food, you must approach your spiritual life with the same urgency. Think of a baby crying relentlessly until it's fed; that's the kind of desperation that gets God's attention. He hears the cries of the hungry and the thirsty, and He promises to fill them.

In today's world, many of us have lost touch with what it means to be truly hungry or thirsty. We've become so accustomed to instant gratification that we've forgotten how to yearn deeply for something. But spiritual hunger and thirst are not just casual metaphors; they are the driving forces that propel us into the depths of God's heart. This book is a call to awaken that longing within you, to stir up a passion that cannot be quenched by anything less than His presence.

Throughout these pages, I will share stories and testimonies of how God has moved mightily in my life and the lives of others who have dared to seek Him with all their hearts. You will read about miraculous healings, divine encounters, and the unmistakable power of the Holy Spirit. These stories are not just meant to inspire you but to challenge you to believe that what God has done for others, He can do for you.

We will explore together the biblical foundations of spiritual hunger and thirst. You'll learn why Jesus used these physical sensations to describe our need for Him and how they relate to our spiritual well-being. You'll also find practical steps to cultivate this holy desire, such as immersing yourself in the Word, spending time in prayer, and fasting.

As you read, I encourage you to open your heart and let the Holy Spirit take your spiritual temperature. Are you hot, cold, or lukewarm? Wherever you find yourself, know that there is always more of God to experience. Hunger is the only thing that determines how much of God you'll receive. As Smith Wigglesworth said, "The only thing I'm satisfied with is my dissatisfaction." Let that dissatisfaction drive you deeper into God's presence.

"For They Shall Be Filled" isn't just about your spiritual growth, it's also about becoming a vessel through which God's Spirit can flow to others. We are called to be carriers of revival, to let our hunger for God create an atmosphere where His presence can move powerfully. By the end of this book, I pray you will be filled to overflowing and equipped to carry His fire wherever you go.

Join me on this journey with an expectant heart. Let these words ignite a holy hunger and thirst within you. I want you to whole-heartedly seek God's righteousness and experience the ultimate fulfillment that comes from being filled with His Spirit. This is your moment. Don't let it pass by. Get ready to be filled!

Available in Paperback and eBook from Your Favorite Bookstore or Online Retailer

ABOUT DEBBIE RICH

Known as a fiery preacher who flows in the Holy Spirit while ministering the Word of God, Dr. Debbie Rich is an international teacher, evangelist, and revivalist who has carried the fire of revival to over fifty nations.

Dr. Debbie received her Ph.D. in Theology from Life Christian University following her graduation from Rhema Bible Training Center in Broken Arrow, Oklahoma. She also attended Open Bible College in Des Moines, Iowa.

As a pioneer missionary in the remote "Alaskan Bush," she traveled where few dared to go. Ministering in prisons, she saw inmates filled with the Holy Spirit after receiving Jesus as their Lord and Savior. Her ministry ignited a fire of revival across the state of Alaska as she boldly ventured into remote villages, towns, and cities where she felt called to go but had not been invited. While some local pastors initially opposed her efforts, many have since become long-time friends.

Dr. Debbie pioneered Faith Life Church and Word & Spirit Institute Northwest in the state of Washington. She teaches in Bible schools around the world.

Currently, she ministers out of Revival Ministries International in Tampa, Florida, with Pastors Rodney and Adonica Howard-Browne.

For Ministry Information Contact:

Dr. Debbie Rich Ministries
13194 US HWY 301 S,
Suite 107, Riverview, FL. 33578
Web Info: debbierichministries.org
E-mail: office@debbierichministries.org

facebook.com/debbierichministries
instagram.com/debbierichministries
youtube.com/debbierichministries

www.ingramcontent.com/pod-product-compliance
Lightning Source LLC
Chambersburg PA
CBHW050925240426
43668CB00021B/2431